GOETHE
AND WORLD LITERATURE

GOETHE
AND WORLD LITERATURE

by

FRITZ STRICH

Translated by C. A. M. Sym

KENNIKAT PRESS
Port Washington, N. Y./London

GOETHE AND WORLD LITERATURE

First published in 1949
Reissued in 1972 by Kennikat Press
Library of Congress Catalog Card No: 75-159710
ISBN 0-8046-1648-5

Manufactured by Taylor Publishing Company   Dallas, Texas

PREFACE

Preliminary studies for this book began long ago. After the First World War I was invited to give a series of lectures at London University, and it was there that I spoke for the first time on the subject of Goethe and World Literature. That seemed to me the most suitable subject for a scholar who wished to remain strictly within the bounds of pure scholarship, while using his special knowledge in the cause of better international understanding. From that time on the subject has never ceased to occupy me. I developed it in my lectures, and on being called to Switzerland in 1929 I found here, in my second home, a favourable atmosphere and soil in which the work could grow and ripen. It seemed to me that my work on world literature had been the best preparation for my coming to this country. By world literature Goethe understood the sphere of the intellect in which through their literatures the world's peoples learn to know and respect each other, and in a common effort seek to rise to higher levels of culture. In the same way I soon found here, in Nature's broad vistas of scenery of every type, from heroic to idyllic, from southern to northern, a natural sphere in which the peoples could meet. The great creations of world literature, while rooted in the soil of a single people, reach upwards into the sphere common to all men ; and I could now see that this was no less true of the creations of nature. On his second journey to Switzerland, when Goethe began the ascent of the Jura, he was told many things about the countries he would descry from those heights, and it was with thoughts of them in his mind that he reached the summit. But quite a different spectacle awaited him :

The lofty mountain-ranges alone were visible under a clear, bright sky ; all the lower regions were covered in a white, cloudy sea of mist, stretching from Geneva to the northern horizon and gleaming in the sun. Out of this rose to the east the unbroken expanse of snow and ice-covered mountain ranges owning no allegiance to the peoples and princes who claimed to possess them, subject only to one great Lord and to the rays of the sun which tinged them with colour.

Moreover, I found this natural scene steeped in that intellectual atmosphere peculiar to Switzerland, which has always

acted as a connecting link in Europe between the literatures of
Italy, France, Germany and England. As her passes form the
geographical route, so she had formed the intellectual highway
from people to people ; and thus I found that my endeavours in
the realm of world literature fitted easily into this ancient tradition. But it was by no means a tradition only, it was also a
living actuality. Here I could see three peoples with three
languages living peaceably together under one roof, with equal
rights and laws—a Microcosm, we might call it, showing that
peoples of the most diverse races and languages can exist and
thrive together in a peaceful community. It was on Swiss soil,
too, that the representatives of all the nations assembled to
discuss how war could be eliminated and foundations laid for
lasting peace. Never had the league-concept (which for me
stood out from the world of Goethe's ideas) so actual and bodily
a form before my eyes as here, and never had I known a national
temper which found it so natural to combine fidelity to its native
land with the outlook and attitude of world citizenship. I could
therefore hope that in this atmosphere my humble work would
reach maturity. Being invited in 1932 to the Goethe centenary
celebrations at Weimar, I naturally spoke there on the subject
of Goethe and world literature.

But even then, even in Weimar, ominous signs were to be
seen. One could not help feeling that these were funeral rites
doing honour to a dead Goethe. Shortly afterwards catastrophe
broke upon the world. Everything that Goethe had proclaimed
as the aim of world literature fell in ruins ; and it was his own
people that had brought this upon the human ace ! It is
understandable that thereafter I had no longer any thought of
publishing my book. It seemed to me pointless to attempt to
drown the discords and the thunder of the cannon with Goethe's
voice. Its tones would have faded, leaving no echo behind.

Now peace is here again ; but what kind of peace ? Today
we have reached a moment in world history when everything
can be lost or everything won, a moment of limitless possibilities.
Therefore this seems to me to be the moment for Goethe, that
greatest of Europeans, greatest of world citizens, to rise in all his
symbolic might and fill with his spirit of peace the house that the
peoples must build anew from its foundations. For without such
a spirit the house must collapse again.

In this spirit I hope I may be understood when I say that
this book deals exclusively with matters of scholarship and

history, and yet is not intended to be a work of scholarship for
its own sake.

From the very beginning it was manifestly impossible, and
moreover was not my intention, to achieve anything even approximately complete. I have accepted the limitations suggested by
nature and have dealt only with what came within Goethe's
own horizons, what was important to the growth of his idea of
world literature and essentially concerned it. Many literatures
were therefore eliminated as a matter of course. The great
literatures of England, France, Italy and Russia naturally took
up a central position ; those of the Scandinavian countries,
Spain and Portugal joined them, for with them relationships of
importance to Goethe were established even during his lifetime.
For the same reason I also had to look beyond Europe towards
Asia and America. I should like what concerns the period after
Goethe's death to be regarded just as an occasional excursus ;
and only in the last chapter, " Prospect ", is the exposition of
the influence of Goethe in world literature up to 1932 continued
in general outline. I did not want to make it longer, and had
therefore to forgo consideration of such an interesting work as
Paul Valéry's *Mon Faust* and the no less interesting controversy
which has arisen at the present time in England between T. S.
Eliot, in his attacks on Goethe, and the latter's champions.

There is already a wide literature of special studies on the
subject. It has been impossible, for reasons of space alone, to
give a bibliography. So I should like here to express, in general
terms, my gratitude for the use of everything that has been
helpful in the preparation of my book. I would ask the reader,
however, to look for the meaning of my work in the picture as a
whole, and in the fact that everything has been presented from
the point of view of Goethe's own conception of world literature.
In this way every detail will appear in a fresh light.

I have sought to show how this idea was formed, what were
its meaning and its aim, and how it was suggested to Goethe in
part by his experience of the cultural influences of foreign literatures, and of what he had himself awakened in them. I have
tried also to display the range of his activities in working for
the realisation of his idea. I have scrutinised the whole world
with Goethe's eyes, and followed his tracks in every direction,
and in this way I hope at least to have achieved new results.
It should be clear that Goethe cannot be claimed as the property
of any one nation, but that he fulfils the mission dictated to him

by his own nature only when he is recognised as the property of all the world, and as a spiritual bond between the peoples. This at one time he was, and may again become.

Finally, may I express my most grateful thanks for all her kind co-operation to my ever faithful and willing assistant, Dr. Gertrud Sattler.

BERNE,
   Autumn 1945.

PART I

GOETHE'S IDEA OF WORLD LITERATURE

CHAPTER 1

THE IDEA

The term " world literature ", coined by Goethe, immediately brings to the mind a feeling of liberation, of such gain in space and scope as one feels on entering a larger and more airy room. However vague the expression is, it at least suggests the removal of intellectual barriers between peoples ; and it is one of the objects of this book that this feeling should gradually develop into clear understanding, and thereby exert a doubly liberating influence.

Some sadness must be ours too, when we read of Goethe's confident proclamation of the idea, and realise that his hope was never fulfilled. But that should not shake our belief in Goethe's idea ; for it is one of the demands that the human spirit must make in spite of all difficulties, and for the realisation of which it must strive, whatever the resistance of an unresponsive world. Today, Goethe's idea is more alive than ever. For what is, in the spiritual sense, alive ? Not merely that which at any given moment actually exists, but also that which is striving to be born.

First let us ask what is the meaning of this magical term. It is all too familiar in the countless histories of world literature. But there it is in fact completely without significance, indicating merely the aggregate of all national literatures, French, English, German, Italian, Russian and Chinese, which are simply dealt with in succession. The only justification for calling these treatises world literature is that they are bound and published together.

That is not how Goethe thought of world literature, and in this sense, or rather in this lack of sense, the word cannot be put to any serious use.

We know it, however, in other connections. We hear that some work, such as Homer, Dante's *Divine Comedy*, *Hamlet*, *Don Quixote*, *Faust*, belongs to world literature, and some other work does not. What is meant by this ? Why, that such a work of art has passed the frontiers of the nation within which it originated, and the limits of the language in which it was written ; that it has been translated into the languages of at least the most important civilised nations and belongs to the common treasury of human culture ; that it has therefore gained for itself international significance. But there is more to it than this. Many books have crossed the boundaries of nationality and been translated, and yet do not in our sense form part of world literature. It is often the poorest specimens of light or sensational literature that captivate the world, mere fashions of the moment, which vanish from the ranks of international literature as rapidly as they appeared there. What German writer had the greatest international reputation in Goethe's day ? The answer must be not Goethe, but Kotzebue ; yet no one today would say that Kotzebue belongs to world literature. Again, even a writer of such infinite charm as Salomon Gessner, who has been translated into every language, read everywhere, imitated and admired, does not belong to world literature. For something is lacking : the power to last. When in ordinary speech we talk of world literature we mean not a product of fashion, however widely acclaimed, but literature which has gained a significance transcending not only nationality but also time. The world is both space *and* time, and only what belongs to world space and world time, belongs to world literature. But time is the regulating principle in history, which sifts the chaff from the wheat, a vogue from the intrinsically valuable. World literature would therefore mean the choice literature which has gained for itself a significance transcending nationality and time. And this is a perfectly sound conception. But, like most words in human speech, this word is highly ambiguous, and Goethe meant by it something quite different from our colloquial use of it. This fatal ambiguity of language, this Babylonian confusion of tongues, is largely to blame for the fact that men find it so hard to understand each other and that they so often speak to deaf ears. By the same word each understands something different. At this point, therefore, it is necessary to differentiate Goethe's conception of world literature as clearly as possible from all others.

There is yet another conception of world literature, one particularly current among historians of literature, for whom it has a special meaning. What it expresses is the fact that comparison of the various national literatures shows the diversity of language to be insufficient to justify any division into national literatures. Rather do the various literatures show such similarity in the course of their history, the sequence of the styles of different periods, their ideas, themes and characters, also so much mutual influence and overlapping, that one cannot fully understand any literature by itself, but must regard all as an indissoluble unity, in this sense a world literature. This in itself gives our ambiguous word comprehensible sense as a basis for discussion, even if not dealing with its significance beyond space and time. But Goethe's idea is not this either. When we remember that, after all, Goethe was the originator of the term, we may well wonder if it would not be wise to adopt his use of it, and to find other words to express other ideas ; thus ambiguity would be avoided. What the intellectual world lacks is precisely agreement, and here confusion of language plays an important part. How many useless and superfluous arguments could be avoided by clarity of language ! In our case, however, agreement should not be so difficult, as it is, after all, agreement with Goethe.

It must be admitted that such agreement would immediately come upon an obstacle, for at no point did Goethe himself un-equivocally state what he wished to be understood by world literature. Indeed, he avoided any short definition of it. It falls to us therefore to build one up from the many allusions in Goethe's writings and conversations. We must place these in relation to his whole thought-stream and compare them with the literary activity of the last ten years of his life (which he dedicated to the service of world literature). Thus we shall obtain a clear picture. The material for this is to be found at the end of this book. Let us begin with the result.

World literature is, then, according to Goethe, the literature which serves as a link between national literatures and thus between the nations themselves, for the exchange of ideal values. Such literature includes all writings by means of which the peoples learn to understand and make allowances for each other, and which bring them more closely together. It is a literary bridge over dividing rivers, a spiritual highway over dividing mountains. It is an intellectual barter, a traffic in ideas between peoples, a literary market to which the nations bring their intellectual treasures for exchange. To illustrate his idea Goethe himself uses such images taken from the world of trade and commerce.

World literature is thus the intellectual sphere in which, through the voices of their writers, the peoples speak no longer to and of themselves but to each other. It is an international conversation, an intellectual interest in each other, a mutual helping and supplementing of each other in the things of the mind.

But what ways and means are at the disposal of a literature which is to open up communications between the peoples ?

The most important means, and therefore the most essential element in a universal world literature, is the literature of translation, which is the first step in intellectual barter between peoples. As Goethe says, every translator should be regarded as an active agent in this universal, intellectual commerce. For, whatever one may say of the inadequacy of translation, it remains one of the most valuable activities in the general traffic of nations. The Koran says : God has given to every people a prophet in their own language. Every translator is then a prophet among his own people.[1]

One might be inclined to regard it as a weak point in Goethe's idea, that world literature lives on translations. For naturally no genuine literature can be so translated that the translation can replace the original. The differences in forms of language, and disparities in ways of thinking, make this impossible. A tune can be transposed into any key and yet remain identical. But no literary work can be translated, however brilliantly, without undergoing some change. Creative stimulation by a foreign work can of course produce a translation equal to or even surpassing the original. But this will then be rated not as a translation but as a separate original creation. It does not aim at being a medium of world literature.

Various motives may stimulate translation. One may be a kind of creative rivalry. Another may be the urge of the writer to expand and express himself by means of translation. Schiller, for instance, seeking a way out of his " Storm and Stress " period and aspiring to Classicism, translated Euripides and Virgil. A third motive may be the wish to promote the education, the language, the art of one's own people.

German Baroque made translations from every European language in order so to shape the German tongue that it might reach the level which other literatures had already attained at the Renaissance. Goethe and Schiller translated Shakespeare, Racine and Voltaire, in order, with their help, to guide the German theatre out of the swamps of naturalism. The French Romantic writers translated German dramas to free themselves from what had become the too restrictive bonds of Classicism. This can be a motive for creating world literature. But there is a fourth : by means of translation to establish intercourse between peoples, to make them known to each other and effect an exchange of ideas. The possibilities of the translator's art are, however, restricted, and Goethe was of course aware of this. He writes to Chancellor von Müller in 1828 : " In translating, one must above all avoid coming into direct conflict with the foreign language. One must advance as far as the untranslatable, and respect it ; for precisely there lies the worth and the character of any language." We find the same sort of thing in Goethe's *Maxims and Reflections*. So when he still demanded and worked for a world literature, he must obviously have placed a high value on the blessings it can convey even through translations with all their limitations. Showing his usual wisdom and sense of proportion, he recommended a quite gradual approximation to the ideally accurate rendering, and found this exemplified in the history of the art of translation. His essential ideas on this subject are contained in the speech to the Freemasons' Lodge " In memory of our brother Wieland " (1813) in the eleventh book of *Dichtung und Wahrheit* (1814), and in the *Notes and Discussions on the West-Eastern Divan* (1819). He saw a lively impetus to the development of world literature in the fact that the art of translation arrives at the ideal by three stages, corresponding to the three possible principles of translation. The first is that, abandoning the artistic form, one can convey in simple prose the bare sense and content of a foreign work. For prose, by dispensing with all that is distinctive in poetic art, and retaining only the gist of the passage, renders it in this first stage a great service. Its sphere of influence is extended, and it is made intelligible to all readers whatever their national idiom. Luther's Bible and Wieland's Shakespeare are examples of this first stage. The second is that at which one assimilates the sense of the foreign work and tries to reproduce it in one's own manner. The French show a preference for this method, and Wieland's translations of Greek and Roman classics belong to this second group. At the third stage however, the highest and the last, the translator's national characteristics are surrendered and he tries to make a translation identical with the original in form and content. The greatest exponent of this supreme art of translation is Johann Heinrich Voss. Thanks to him, the German language has acquired such adaptability and flexibility that now Ariosto and Tasso, Shakespeare and Calderon can, in very truth, be accepted as "foreigners completely Germanised ". At this stage, if we may supplement Goethe's ideas, the translator can safely disregard the former limitations of his language, mould it into new forms, and infuse it with fresh powers of expression, even should he at first shock his own countrymen thereby. No language is for ever static. Indeed, it is by means of translation that one language can be enriched by others, can create un-imagined new possibilities of linguistic expression, can extend its bounds and broaden the minds of a whole people.

In these three stages, then, Goethe saw translation, the most important instrument of world literature, approaching its ideal. But of course he did not mean by this a chronological sequence of the three stages. This gradual approximation will necessarily be constantly repeated. Though with Voss and the Romantic writers the last and highest stage has been reached, it will again and again be necessary to guide through these three stages a work of art just entering the nations' field of vision—for example the *Sakuntala* of Kalidasa—in such a way that all three principles of translation retain their value.

But world literature is not limited to translation alone. In fact, the translations themselves set a task for world literature. In connection with an English translation of his *Tasso* by Des Voeux, begun in Weimar with Ottilie's help and encouragement, Goethe wrote in 1828 to Carlyle :

I should like to have your opinion on how far this translation can be considered English. You would greatly oblige me by enlightening me on this matter ; for it is just this connection between original and translation that expresses most clearly the relationship of nation to nation and that one must above all understand if one wishes to encourage a common world literature "transcending national boundaries ". [2]

Thus, anything that expresses the relationships of nation to nation belongs to world literature, and literature which makes foreign work accessible is a means of intellectual intercourse between peoples. This is a necessity if the nations are to visualise and learn to know one another, and can be done by periodicals which publicise and criticise foreign literatures. But the pictures thus drawn of a foreign people and its literature must next be made known to that people, so that it may realise how other nations stand in relation to it, and how it is mirrored in another's mind. That is why Goethe, in his own organ devoted to world literature, the periodical *Kunst und Altertum*, not only reports on foreign literatures but also constantly informs the general public how he himself, Schiller, Herder and the German Romantic writers, are dealt with in the periodicals of France, England and Italy. He states which of their works are being translated, how they are received, what influence they exert on foreign literatures, and what proofs of interest he himself has received from foreign writers and authors. All this was done not merely with the desire to draw attention to himself and his work, but in an attempt to promote the growth of a general world literature. " Not merely what such men [as Carlyle] write of us," Goethe wrote once, " must be of first importance to us ; we have also to consider their own relationships, for instance with the French and the Italians. For that, after all, is the only way towards a general world literature—for all nations to learn their relationships each to the other." [3] Letters between authors of different nations can also form part of world literature. Goethe made the German public conversant with his letters from Manzoni, Scott, Byron and Carlyle ; and one of Goethe's letters to a Russian author was published in a Russian periodical and had an enthusiastic reception.

Travel in foreign countries also belongs to world literature, when it finds literary expression. Even when it does not, it may still be so considered and, for this reason, was urgently recommended by Goethe. For he had learnt from experience that no letter, no appraisal of literary works, can take the place of actual contact between the minds of men of different nationalities. Moreover, to understand a foreign writer or a foreign literature, one must get to know something about the soil, the climate, the mode of life, the manners, the people and the society, in fact the whole environment in which the writer lives and produces his work. " To understand a writer, you must be at home in his country."

If I were younger [wrote Goethe in 1800 to Bitaubé, the French translator of *Hermann und Dorothea*] I would plan to visit you, to learn more of the manners and customs in France, the characteristics of its inhabitants, and their moral and spiritual needs after this great crisis. It may be that I should then be able to write a poem which, as a pendant to *Hermann und Dorothea*, and with you as translator, would not be without influence—limited enough, perhaps, but still sufficing for both translator and author.[4]

Goethe, who had been in Italy but never in England, was quick to note with what different insight he read an Italian and an English writer. The former appealed to his whole mind at once, and gave him a more or less complete picture ; the latter remained largely dependent on his power of imagination, and he was never quite certain if he was thinking and feeling aright. Goethe had, however, no need to travel to see foreign writers. They came to him, and his house in Weimar was the actual headquarters, the visible centre, of world literature, where French, English, Italian, Scandinavian, Russian and Polish authors met, spoke of their homes and their native literatures, and discussed the differences and the common factors of their nations.

Lastly, we must mention as an essential part of world literature in Goethe's sense, the subject of this book—world literature as a branch of scholarship. It is usually called the comparative study of literature, but this is not a good name for it. For all study of literature uses the comparative method. It compares, for instance, the German Renaissance with the German Baroque, the German Classical with the German Romantic movement, in order to show the historical change in outlook. It compares Goethe with Schiller, in order (while maintaining the distinctive traits of these great contemporaries) to show also their common effort to reach a Classical style. No study of literature can dispense with the comparative method. When we speak of the comparative study of literature, we mean the study which compares the different national literatures with each other in order to bring out, not only the national character of each, but also their unifying, human or contemporaneous character. Its most fruitful method is that of comparing translations with their originals, or contemporary translations in various languages of a single work, or comparing the interpretation and treatment of similar subjects and themes by the various literatures, or comparing indigenous literary forms with borrowed ones. But, as comparison is by no means confined to the study of literature, it would be better to use the term " study of world literature ". And this is not restricted to comparison alone. Its work is to investigate the historical connections between different literatures, to find out when, at what points, and why, they influence each other, what they give and take. It has to deduce the reasons for this reciprocal giving and taking from the national characteristics which give each literature a special service to perform for another. It has to indicate which works have been translated and how these translations were received, what further effect they had, what writers appeared to establish intercourse between the literatures, and what form their attempted intercourse took. It has to show with what eyes the different litera-

tures saw and judged one another. It has to examine the
personal relations between the writers of the different nations.
It has to trace the historical course of themes, ideas, images,
from one literature to another.   At the same time it belongs, in
all that it does, to world literature in Goethe's sense.   It establishes
intellectual relations between nations, whether by systematic
comparison or by historical exposition.   Indeed, no study of
literature can dispense with the outlook of world literature.   It
is quite impossible to treat any literature in isolation.   There has
never been a national literature in the sense of a purely autoch-
thonous one, independent, creating its own material, self-in-
spired.   Literatures are so interwoven, to such a degree indebted
to each other, that any study of literature is forced to look beyond
the national boundaries and to place each unit in its setting in
world literature.   Books, too, which bring together the literatures
of different peoples under uniform aspects would certainly be
included by Goethe under world literature.   He praised one such
attempt, Ludwig Wachler's *Handbook of the History of Literature*,
in his *Kunst und Altertum* (1825).   The work afforded him " most
pleasant entertainment.   One who throughout a long life has
occupied himself with literature in all its aspects, seems as he
reads this work to be living a second time, and in much greater
comfort."   In the same passage Goethe also speaks of literature
as a " common world-council " to which he too was called ; and
we may regard this word as a preliminary stage in the creation
of the expression world literature.

All this Goethe meant by world literature, and perhaps it
will now be clear that, in Goethe's sense, it can be developed
among contemporaneous persons and nations.   This may be the
new and most stimulating element in Goethe's idea.   Goethe
writes of it thus :

> In venturing to announce a European, indeed a world literature,
> we do not mean merely to say that the different nations should inform
> themselves about one another and about each other's work, for in this
> sense it has long since been in existence and is still growing.   No
> indeed ; rather is it a matter of living men of letters getting to know
> each other and, through their own inclination and similarity of tastes,
> finding a motive for corporate action.[5]

And this is no mere isolated aperçu, but belongs essentially to
Goethe's idea of world literature, one might even say to Goethe's
idea of life itself.   For Goethe felt life to be where one creature
reacts on another, an impregnating, engendering force.   One

lives with those who are alive.   Hence Goethe's delight when he saw that his contemporaries absorbed, understood and worked for the realisation of his hopes.   For only then did he feel that he and they were parts of one living entity.   Goethe was perhaps the first who ever realised the power of co-existence to make men comrades, or the fateful significance of the time-link between men.   He sought to give a deeper meaning to this contemporaneousness, that of true intellectual fellowship, unity in striving towards one goal, participation in influence and production.   The period of time in which men live together forms a bond so strong that it cannot be completely broken by differences of national character.   Contemporaneousness triumphs over frontiers, and contemporaries ought therefore to join hands across them.   And so they do, in what Goethe calls world literature.   For that is the intellectual sphere in which contemporaries, whatever their nationality, may meet and co-operate.   This constitutes the great difference between Goethe's idea of world literature and all earlier conceptions of it.   Admittedly the German Romantic writers translated from all literatures, but what did they translate ? Dante, Petrarch, Cervantes, Shakespeare, Calderon, the old Indian writers.   Their contemporaries in other nations were practically ignored.   For the German Romantic movement thought of time only as a sequence, essentially only as a past not as something co-existent and uniting men who live together as contemporaries. " If we go back in history," Goethe once wrote, " we find at every point personalities with whom we would agree and others with whom we could certainly be at variance.   But the most important element is after all co-existence, because it is reflected most clearly in us and we in it."

But is there not a stronger bond between peoples than contemporaneouness ?   Something that triumphs over all time, eternal and capable of fusing the nations in a higher unity ? The answer to this question leads us to an understanding of all that Goethe meant by world literature, and why he strove for it so untiringly.   For Goethe such a bond exists : the Universal, the eternally human, of which the nations are but variants and species.   Just as there is for plants an archetype of which all plants are but variants and aspects, so there is an archetype in the world of art and intellect, of which all men and nations are but variations.   For Goethe it is man's task to make this archetype even clearer and more effective in human life.   This is the highest task that Goethe assigned to world literature :   to foster the growth of a common humanity in its most perfect and universal form : to advance human civilisation. This does not mean that national differences should be effaced in favour of uniformity and unanimity of all thought and feeling. Goethe was too much of a realist to think such a thing possible, nor did he desire it. The function of world literature is to make the national characteristics of peoples intelligible to each other, thereby encouraging tolerance and mutual respect.

These periodicals [Goethe once wrote of the Scottish-English Reviews] as they gradually reach a wider public, will contribute most effectively to the universal world literature for which we hope. We must repeat, however, that the point is not that nations should think alike, but that they should become aware of each other, and that even where there can be no mutual affection there should be tolerance.[6]

The recognition of the need for toleration of national differences was founded, in Goethe's case, on the realisation that these differences are natural (as is the variety in the plant world and in all species in nature), and that uniformity would rob the intellectual world of its richness and beauty. On the other hand, the diversity in natural phenomena is but the visible manifestation of a higher unity—" it is the Eternal One-ness, displayed in many forms ". It should be thus also in the realm of man's mind. The national pattern of his works and thoughts should be but a characteristic manifestation of one eternal spirit, the archetype of man. That is why it is the second, and in Goethe's view equally important, mission of world literature to develop in the literatures of all peoples the core common to mankind.

It is obvious that for a considerable time the efforts of the best writers and authors of aesthetic worth in all nations have been directed to what is common to all mankind. In every field, whether the historical, the mythological, the fabulous, or the consciously imagined, one can see, behind what is national and personal, this universal quality becoming more and more apparent. In our daily lives, too, some similar principle exists, breaking through the world's harshness, deceit, and selfishness, everywhere seeking to foster a more humane spirit, and although it can hardly be hoped that universal peace will be achieved by this means we may trust that conflict will decrease, war become less cruel and victory less arrogant. Any such tendency in the literature of any nation should be assimilated by other nations. One must learn to note the special characteristics of every nation and take them for granted, in order to meet each nation on its own ground. For the characteristics of a nation are like its language or its coinage, they facilitate intercourse and even make it possible. The sure way to achieve universal tolerance is to leave untouched what is peculiar to each man or group, remembering that all that is best in the world is the property of all mankind.[7]

Goethe traced back the tremendous influence everywhere exerted by Werther to this universal human content, and explained the success of his Faust by saying that Faust fixed for all time a stage in the development of a human spirit, visited by all the torments of mankind, shaken by all its doubts, vexed by all its hates, and blessed with all its aspirations. " To creative writers nowadays such conditions seem remote ; the world has other battles to fight ; yet the state of man in joy and sorrow remains for the most part the same, and even the latest comer will find occasion to look back to bygone pains and pleasures, in order to prepare himself for what is in store for him." [8]

If, however, we wish to preserve Goethe's idea of world literature in its true sense, we must realise that it is not identical with literature of universal and changeless human content. Goethe's *Faust* belongs to world literature, not for itself but because, translated into so many languages, it has made other peoples familiar with the German mind. But it must always be remembered that every real literature does include an unchanging human element and must be brought within the reach of, and become the property of, all. Great works of this kind were, however, reckoned by Goethe as belonging not to world literature but to world poetry, and the two should never be confused. It was Herder who first awoke in Goethe the realisation that poetry is a gift to the world, part of mankind's common property ; and this was surely the most precious gift that Goethe received from Herder. This " common world poetry " belongs so much as a matter of course to the essential nature of man, that Goethe thought its development as certain as the sunrise, needing no man to dictate its content or form. Being completely independent of culture and social status, it is the property of the most primitive and the most highly cultured nations alike. It appears in every age and among every people. It was folk-songs that first confirmed Goethe in this belief, and the marked interest he took in them is understandable from this point of view. He found irrefutable proof of the reality of a common world poetry in the fact that, for instance, Serbian folk-songs show such a striking similarity to those of the " sociable French ", of Béranger in particular, although the two belong to such widely distant ages and to peoples of such differing stages of culture. He found it again in the fact that the folk-songs of the most diverse nations,

German, Serbian, Old Bohemian, Modern Greek and Lettish, reveal a fundamental similarity. Of course Goethe also stressed the no less striking differences in local conditions, manners and character between the songs of different peoples. When thinking of them in their sociological aspect, and contrasting them with the songs of cultured society, he called them simply folksong or folk-poetry. When considering them as examples of national diversity, however, he would call them (as Herder did) " Songs of the people, that is to say songs which denote a particular people, and give happy expression to some of its distinguishing features." [9] He also called these characteristic folk-songs national songs, national poetry, provincial poetry and on one occasion in his periodical, *Kunst und Altertum*, composed a number of articles on Serbian, Greek, Lithuanian, Old Bohemian and other poems under the title " The Poetry of the Nations ".[10] But he never failed to see the universal, eternally human, core, encased in the varied outer layers of national individuality. In an account of some Serbian, Lettish and Norse songs he writes :

More and more we find ourselves in a position to realise what folk-poetry and national poetry might be ; for there is really only one kind of poetry, genuine poetry, which belongs neither to the common people nor to the aristocracy, neither to king nor to peasant ; anyone who truly feels himself to be a man can produce it ; it appears with irresistible force amongst a simple, even barbarous, people, but it is also not denied to cultured nations. We must therefore make a great effort to get the widest perspective, so that we can recognise talent wherever it appears and trace it as an integral strand running through the history of mankind.[11]

This, then, is what Goethe meant by world poetry, which must not be confused with world literature. The title which, after his death, was given to one of Goethe's poems in the Cotta edition (1840) of his works, rests on this confusion, for there it is named " World Literature ". Even today it is found in many editions under this false title. In *Kunst und Altertum*, where it first appeared, it had no heading. In the last edition during Goethe's lifetime it stood as preface to the section " Folk-poetry " :

Wie David königlich zur Harfe sang,
Der Winzerin Lied am Throne lieblich klang,
Des Persers Bulbul Rosenbusch umbangt,
Und Schlangenhaut als Wildengürtel prangt,
Von Pol zu Pol Gesänge sich erneun,
Ein Sphärentanz harmonisch im Getümmel ;
Lasst alle Völker unter gleichem Himmel
Sich gleicher Gabe wohlgemut erfreun.

This poem ought of course to be entitled " World Poetry " and not "World Literature ", just as the poems named " World Poetry " by Rückert and Hebbel should be called " World Literature ". But although the two are far from being identical, there is an essential connection between them. World poetry is, as it were, the essence of world literature. Comparative world literature recognises that there is a common world poetry, and (as Goethe did untiringly) will make the peoples, or one particular people, familiar with it. This it will do in order to bring to the level of consciousness that element in the universal human gift of world poetry, which is always present but is not always consciously recognised, namely, the element of common humanity. In this way it will form a spiritual bond between the peoples. Through such intercourse Goethe sought to give warning of the dangerous presumption that any single nation is exclusively called to true poetry. He certainly wished to point out the national differences in world poetry, but only so that the peoples should learn greater understanding and tolerance, and so have a stronger bond of union.

One last explanatory note to Goethe's idea. In present-day speech practically no distinction is made between world literature and European literature—and this is a serious error. For Europe is not the world. There are two passages in Goethe's observations on his idea of world literature which indicate that this question occupied his attention. The first draws this distinction : " If we have ventured to proclaim a European, or what is more a world literature." [12] The second says simply : " European, that is to say, world literature." [13] (In the first draft of the passage it is simply " world literature ".) The contradiction can be resolved in this way : For Goethe, world literature is, to start with, European literature. It is in process of realising itself in Europe. A European literature, that is a literature of exchange and intercourse between the literatures of Europe and between the peoples of Europe, is the first stage of a world literature which from these beginnings will spread in ever-widening circles to a system which in the end will embrace the world. World literature is a living, growing organism, which can develop from the germ of European literature, and in his *West-Eastern Divan*, which was to throw a bridge from east to west, Goethe himself began the task of incorporating in it the Asiatic world.

CHAPTER 2

BENEFITS AND DANGERS

It must be clearly understood that the writers who are to carry out the noble task indicated by Goethe must first cultivate themselves and their own people. Goethe often and quite openly admitted that he regarded his interest in foreign literatures from the point of view of world literature as the surest means towards his own education, just as he studied nature and art with a similar motive. This self-culture had as its object so to complete his own necessarily restricted personality that he could develop from a limited, narrow individual into a whole man and poet, of universal significance for humanity. This was not mere egoism, as is so often falsely imagined. Goethe knew that only a man who has chiselled the marble of his own character to true human form dare apply his tool to the marble of his people. Whenever he studied or visited other countries, it was always in order to identify the universal human factor, and to rediscover and encourage it in his native land. " For it is the destiny of the German to become the representative of all the citizens of the world." This education and advancement of his people, through the enrichment of his personality from the spiritual wealth of every nation, appeared to Goethe to be the best thing he had done for Germany. That he had no thought of influencing other countries he admits himself. Goethe once gave the following reply to the reproach, so often repeated, that he lacked patriotism : the writer as a man and a citizen will love his native land, but the native land of his poetic powers and his poetic work is the Good, the Noble, the Beautiful, limited to no particular province and to no particular land ; and these he seizes and develops wherever he finds them. In this he is like the eagle whose gaze ranged freely over all lands. What *is* then love of one's native land, and what *is* a patriotic influence ? If a writer seeks all his life long to fight prejudice and narrow-mindedness, to bring enlightenment to the minds of his people, to refine their taste, to ennoble their judgments, is that not the best service he can render his country ?

Goethe saw a fundamental difference between the German and the Frenchman in the fact that the Frenchman seeks to exert his influence in an outward, the German in an inward, direction. He himself, as he once wrote towards the end of his life, had always had only his own Germany in view, and it was only very recently that it had occurred to him to look westwards to see what our neighbours across the Rhine might think of him. And he was gladdened and moved when in his old age he saw how all that he had undertaken for his own development and that of his people was reacting in the happiest and most fruitful way on nations throughout the world. Not only was it received with interest and admiration, but it also wrought a fundamental change in the European mind. It surprised him that his work, carried on in such seclusion, serving so exclusively his own ends, should have found in the world such an echo as now in his old age came to the poet's ear. And in its turn this world echo reacted so happily, so beneficially, on him that it became his strongest motive for calling for world literature, so that he might bring to everyone the blessing which he had himself experienced.

The benefit, then, to be derived from world literature should not consist merely in common tolerance between the nations, and in development of a universal human culture ; the individual and the nation should also derive some benefit. This consists, in the first place, in what Goethe has often called " reflection ". It is of great advantage to a man, as to a people, to see his reflection in the mirror of the world and so to learn what others think of him. The distant standpoint of the stranger gives him an objectivity, an impartiality and clearness of vision which fellow-countrymen cannot have. Goethe felt that he was more truly understood by an Ampère, or a Carlyle, than by his own people. And Carlyle in his book on Schiller had evaluated him throughout as it would have been difficult for a German to do. Similarly we can judge Shakespeare and Byron perhaps better than the English themselves.[14]   Goethe lived to see the Italian Romantic writer, Alessandro Manzoni, who had been little regarded in Italy, gain credit in Italy, England, France and Germany, and in fact rise to world fame. This was after Goethe had championed him against criticism in Italy and England, and had supplied an introduction, " Goethe's interest in Manzoni " for an edition of his works. Goethe even found that the French journal *Le Globe* took his part against the violent attacks made on him by the German author Wolfgang Menzel, while in Germany hardly a voice was raised in his defence. " It is charming to notice ", he wrote on this occasion, " how the Kingdom of Literature is gradually extending its bounds. We need no

longer defend ourselves against opponents among our own
countrymen ; our neighbours will protect us." And to Eckermann, summing up, he said it was a very good thing that now,
with this close intercourse between France, England and Germany, we had the chance of correcting each other. " This is
the great advantage that world literature affords, one which
will in time become more and more obvious." [15] He did not
live to see his champion in the *Globe* joined by further critics of
other nations ; in Russia there appeared Belinsky, in America
Margaret Fuller. Goethe found it particularly stimulating not
only to see himself reflected in foreign opinion, but also to gain
a clear picture of himself through the kind of reaction which he
set up in the world. He even thought it would be worth while
to live long and to endure the manifold sorrows of life, if in the
end through others we learned to see ourselves clearly and if our
struggles and mistakes resolved themselves in the reactions which
we evoked. For him this was equally true of one's own personality and of the whole nation. For a nation it must be salutary
to recognise itself in foreign literatures, and in the reactions it
has on other literatures, and to make this a basis for self-examin-
ation. Goethe hoped for this beneficial kind of " reflection "
from, for example, Mme de Staël's *De l'Allemagne* ; and in this
sense everything that a writer reports to his own people about
foreign literatures may profit not only his own but also that
other nation.

And yet it is not merely a matter of increased self-knowledge
by " reflection " in a foreign mind. The benefits of world
literature can penetrate more deeply and more widely than that.
They can consist in what Goethe often called "Revival" or
" Renewal ", and this may happen to the individual writer or
to the literature of a whole nation. We do well to recollect at
what stage in his life Goethe himself became sensible of the
world's interest, and proclaimed the idea of world literature.
The word " world literature " occurs for the first time in January
1827. Goethe was then 78, and he was about 70 when the idea
began to take definite shape in his mind. It was then that the
echo began to come back to him from all corners of the world ;
and what an echo ! The rising generation of every land in
Europe owned him as their head, their master—one may say their
spiritual father. And when Goethe considered the literatures
round him in France, England and Italy, the almost magical
feeling might well have come over him that in the youth of Europe

he was witnessing the resurrection of his own youth. For what was now bearing fruit among the young in Europe was the out-put of his own youth : *Werther, Götz von Berlichingen, Egmont, Faust,* his lyrics in the folk-song manner ; admittedly also *Tasso* and *Wilhelm Meister,* but these, from the standpoint of the seventy-year-old poet, were also monuments of his youth.

The situation had something of pathos in it. Although Goethe himself had travelled so far beyond the wild surging and seeking and wanderings of youth, he was now surrounded not by the clear, calm light of old age but by the fires of his youth which were catching the world and setting it ablaze.

But even this too meant a blessing for him, the blessing of " renewal ". " The happiest transmigration ", he once wrote, " is that in which we see ourselves reappearing in another." At that time he saw himself thus coming to life again in Byron, his spiritual son, in Manzoni, in the French Romantic writers. " Foreign nations ", he notes at this time, " learn only after a lapse of time to know the works of our youth. Their sons, their adults, ambitious and full of energy, see themselves in our mirror ; they realise that they want what we wanted, they draw us into their company and delude us with the mirage of returning youth." [16]

This gratitude and respect paid by the youth of Europe to Goethe in his old age, and especially when it came from Byron, meant for him strength and refreshment, as though from a rejuvenating draught ; and in the works produced by Goethe, thus rejuvenated, new notes are heard. The most splendid poem of his old age, the *Marienbad Elegy,* seems to glow with subdued yet Byronic fire. And Goethe admitted this in conversa-tion with Eckermann. In the case of Carlyle, Goethe openly stated that he counted him among those who latterly had been active comrades, and by their constant interest had inspired him to effective action ; who also, themselves refreshed by noble endeavour, had drawn him along with them. What he had so richly experienced himself he hoped that world literature would achieve for the entire literary production of his people. " Flag-ging national literature," he notes in one place, " revived by foreigners." " In the end every literature grows stale if it is not refreshed by foreign interest. What scientist does not delight in the wonders wrought by ' reflection ' ? In the moral sphere everyone has experienced it, perhaps unconsciously ; and, if he stops to consider, will realise how much of his own develop-ment throughout life he owes to it." Here, too, Goethe meant that a people gradually ceases to concern itself with its literature unless that literature is continually refreshed by the experience of foreign interest in it. When he saw men in France, England and Italy taking an interest in German literature, he informed the German public of it in his journal *Kunst und Altertum*, hoping that, as a result, they would turn again to their own neglected literature and study it afresh. When the German people realise how Carlyle's book on Schiller has made the works of the poet an inspiration to the English nation, it must surely awaken a new interest in Schiller among his own countrymen, who owe him so much. Moreover, even a work that has almost fallen into oblivion may once more begin to exert a powerful influence, if it should prove to be playing an active part in foreign literatures which are at an earlier stage of development. Herder's work, *Ideas for a Philosophy of the History of Mankind*, had become so much a part of the nation's knowledge that only few who read it learned directly from it in the first place ; most readers had already become familiar with it through other channels. But this work was now translated into French by Edgar Quinet, simply because he felt that thousands of cultivated Frenchmen could learn from it. " This work, written fifty years ago in Germany, had an incredible influence on the development of the nation, served its purpose, and is as good as forgotten ; now it is considered worthy to do the same for another nation of equal culture, and to exert its influence over all who are striving towards the truth." [17]

Thus Goethe's idea, as new as it was stimulating, was that translations confer benefits in both directions ; on the people into whose language the works are translated, and on those from whose language they come ; and once more it was Goethe's own experience to which he owed the realisation of this truth. One of his poems, called " A Parable ", runs :

> Jüngst pflückt' ich einen Wiesenstrauss,
> Trug ihn gedankenvoll nach Haus,
> Da hatten von der warmen Hand
> Die Kronen sich alle zur Erde gewandt.
> Ich setzte sie in frisches Glas
> Und welch ein Wunder war mir das !
> Die Köpfchen hoben sich empor,
> Die Blätterstengel im grünen Flor,
> Und allzusammen so gesund
> Als stünden sie noch auf Muttergrund.
> So war mir's als ich wundersam
> Mein Lied in fremder Sprache vernahm.

Goethe ceased to enjoy reading his *Faust* in German ; but in Gérard de Nerval's French translation it produced on him the effect of something fresh, new, brilliant.   When, after a lapse of years, he once more read in an English translation (by John Bowring) his favourite Serbian folk-songs, he felt " as we feel with attractive people whom we love, who surprise us each time with a new charm whenever we see them unexpectedly in a new dress ".[18]   Such was his mood when we read once more, in English, the well-known Serbian poems.   They seemed to him to have acquired a new value ; they were the same figures, but in new attire.   An English translation of Schiller's *Wallenstein* made a particularly strong impression on him.   The work had become commonplace to him, from being too well known ; then for twenty years he had neither seen nor read it.   Now in 1828, when he unexpectedly met it in Shakespeare's native language, he suddenly saw it, a picture restored, and delighted in it as he had done long ago, and in a new way also.

Here we note something new, perhaps scarcely felt and never expressed before : that the translator is working not for his own nation alone but also for the nation from whose language he takes the work. For it happens more often than we think, that a nation draws vigour and strength from a work and absorbs it so fully into its own inner life, that it can take no further pleasure in it and obtain no further nourishment from it.   This is particularly the case with the Germans. They are prone to excessive enthusiasm and, by too frequent repetitions of something they like, destroy some of its qualities.   It is therefore good for them to see one of their own literary works reborn in translation.[19]

But the most essential " revival " or " renewal "—and the most fruitful in its results—which any literature can experience through world literature is, in Goethe's view, the supply of new themes and ideas and the loosening of forms which have grown rigid by adopting a receptive attitude to foreign literatures.   Goethe noticed this particularly about French literature ; and it certainly made an important contribution to his idea of world literature. For in the twenties, and even before, he saw French literature, which had for so long kept German literature at a distance, reaching out towards it.   It was obviously hoping, with German help, to free itself from the old Classicism, now grown rigid. And it did succeed, with the help of the " Storm and Stress " writers, and in particular of young Goethe, in loosening up its antiquated poetic forms, and introducing into them new ideas and themes. In the realm of philosophy and religion also, with the help of German idealism it overcame its traditional sensualism and empiricism. In the natural sciences it developed the more active and organic conceptions that Goethe had introduced into German science. These were proofs of the possibility of resuscitating one literature through another, and Goethe realised this in connection with the French Romantic school. He once wrote that, as a citizen of the world, he could rejoice to see a people, refined by a period of suffering, turning now for new sources of refreshment and strength to a neighbouring people who had not yet reached maturity, but were still engaged in struggle and effort—the German people. The French are very wise, Goethe mentions elsewhere, in beginning to study and translate our authors. For, limited as the French are in form and in themes, they have no other means of reaching out beyond themselves. And as French literature was enabled, with the help of German " lawlessness ", to loosen its hampering fetters, so, on the other hand, Goethe could see how beneficially the strict conventions of French literature could influence, æsthetically as well as sociologically, the too individualistic spirit of German literature.

But there is still another benefit to be mentioned which made Goethe hope and work for world literature : namely, that it should be in a position to settle the domestic quarrels within any one literature. In this connection, Goethe noted once that the growth of world literature would be much stimulated if the differences existing within one nation could be settled through the insight and judgment of other nations. In *Kunst und Altertum* Goethe spoke thus of Carlyle, who wrote the life of Schiller and in a collection of translations from the German Romantic writers ably assessed the merits of each writer represented. Carlyle shows, writes Goethe,

a calm, reasoned, sincere sympathy with German efforts in literature and poetry. He follows sympathetically the nation's endeavour, he concedes to each his proper place and in doing so lessens the conflict inevitable within the literature of any people. For to be alive and active means to join groups and to take sides. No one can be blamed for struggling for breathing space and for a position which will ensure his existence and a chance of success in the future. And while this conflict often clouds a literary horizon for many years, the foreigner lets the dust settle, and can quietly look ahead into the distance, seeing its lights and shadows as clearly as we do the moon on a cloudless night.[20]

In this spirit Goethe himself interposed to mediate in the quarrel between Classical and Romantic writers in Italy. For, when Goethe framed the idea of world literature and began to advocate it, every literature in Europe was rent by an inner conflict. The Classical-Romantic quarrel, which flared up first in German literature, had spread to all the European literatures and split them into two camps. This was the typical situation in every literature of Europe in the twenties. And it was at this moment that Goethe formulated the idea that it was German literature that must settle this quarrel, not only because German literature had first fanned it, but because it had already survived the first impact of opposition, and both sides had begun to understand each other. Goethe, then, from his point of vantage, sought to mediate in this European conflict. " Classical and Romantic writers in Italy, in violent opposition " is the title of an article by Goethe ; and another is called " Modern Guelfs and Ghibellines ". Why, he asks, are the two parties quarrelling so passionately in Italy ? The Romantics want to write in the spirit of the times. They apply the word romantic to what lies in the present and exerts an immediate influence ; and they reproach the Classical writers, whose productions are in the form and spirit of the Græco-Romans, with being as dead as mummies. But a closer view reveals that there is no real contradiction here. For every writer, owing his youthful development to the Greeks and Romans, will gratefully admit his debt to them, even while devoting his mature talent to the living present. Without his realising it, his end is modern though his beginning was classical. Similarly there is no contradiction in the fact that the Classical writers borrow from the Græco-Romans but the Romantics from the Bible because it lies nearer to our own times. But the Bible is just as near and as far off as the Greeks. Both are equally the eternal sources of our civilization, the Greeks for our æsthetic, the Bible for our moral culture. In the same spirit Goethe tried to settle, by a calm discussion of the pros and cons, the dispute about whether the poet should take his material from Greek mythology or from northern tales of devils and witches. When Goethe completed the Second Part of *Faust* and married Faust to Helen, he said that this episode was meant to suggest a reconciliation between the Classical and Romantic antagonists. The important thing is to acquire culture—by what means is immaterial, so long as we need not fear that our models are false. Goethe created Euphorion, son of Faust and Helen, in Byron's likeness, giving this reason : " Byron is neither Classical nor Romantic ; he is like the present day itself. And I needed such a one." It was the theme of world literature, the appeasement of the conflict in European literature, that had guided Goethe in the Second Part of *Faust*. During the last years of his life he tried to mediate in the scientific dispute which broke out in France between Cuvier and Saint-Hilaire, between an analytic and a synthetic, a mechanistic and a dynamic, an empirical and an intuitive explanation of Nature. He tried to bring the two parties closer together, by clarifying their ideas about themselves. But complete reconciliation between such divergent ways of thinking seemed to him out of the question.[21]

We must note, after weighing the beneficial effects of world literature, that Goethe did not overlook its limitations. He gave warning against exaggerated hopes and expectations, and even pointed out the possibility of harmful results. About the limitations, Goethe writes :

If such a world literature should shortly be developed—as is inevitable, from the ever-quickening speed of intercourse—we must not expect more from it than it can do. The whole world, however wide, is after all but an extended homeland and, when we examine it, will not yield us more than did our native soil. What suits the masses will spread and will, as we can already see, give pleasure far and wide. But what is really worth-while will not be so popular. Those, however, who have dedicated themselves to higher aims will learn to know each other more quickly and more intimately. Everywhere in the world there are men who concern themselves with fundamentals and the progress of humanity. But the path they tread, the pace they make, is not for everyone. The pleasure-seeker wants to hurry, and thus obstructs the progress of that which could actually help him. So the serious-minded will form a quiet, I might almost say an oppressed community. It is vain to try to stem the tide ; one must simply try to keep one's foothold until the flood has swept past. The chief consolation, in fact the greatest encouragement, for such men must be that Truth has its function and performs it. If they discover this for themselves and can point it out to others, they will have a profound effect on their generation.[22]

Goethe had only too often been forced to remark how literature in its transit from one people to another runs the risk of distortion. He realised, for instance, that the old rigid so-called Classical form of the French theatre must be disrupted. Here our example was of use, and the French began to look more favourably upon our productions. Yet they could take over nothing from our theatre or that of England, without distorting it. Goethe pointed to the French experiments with *Hamlet*, *Macbeth*, *Wallenstein*, *Faust*. In the case of *Faust* in particular, he heard from Paris how *Faust* was there being made ridiculous, materialistic, theatrical, how " the sauce was laced with strong spices and piquant ingredients ", to render the work tasty to the French palate.

And yet such adaptations are harmless compared with the situation created when a literature is indiscriminate in welcoming foreign idiosyncracies not adapted to its own nature. For then an influence, which might in itself be stimulating and helpful, becomes what Goethe calls an " influenza ". And an " Influenza " of this sort, which transfers one nation's peculiarities to another, is always dangerous and often harmful. For it is doubtful how these acquired symptoms will agree with the native ones, and their blending may lead to a diseased condition. It is for future men of letters to place on record, writes Goethe, into what errors Shakespeare and particularly Calderon have led us, to what extent these two great stars in the poetic firmament have become for us will-o'-the-wisps. Goethe himself noticed something similar in connection with the Romantic movement in Europe, especially in the extravagances and exaggerations which appeared in France, making the originally healthy influence of the German Romantic movement seem a harmful " Influenza ". This is what Goethe calls the ultra-Romantic tendency, and its chief representative was for him Victor Hugo. In France they wanted at first to take over from the German Romantic movement nothing but a freer form, and they ended in complete lawlessness and licence. They began by wanting only to enrich the content of their literature, and to replace the figures of Greek mythology by some witches and demons from Northern Europe. But they ended by filling their poetry with atrocities and revolting ugliness, swindlers and galley-slaves, vampires and monstrosities as their heroes. Goethe called Victor Hugo's *Notre Dame de Paris* the most odious book ever written, and he compared the French Romantic movement to a state of high fever and a spreading epidemic. It was at this time, when Goethe was tormented by the extravagances of the European ultra-Romantic period, that he made his famous but often misapplied statement that the " Classical is the healthy, the Romantic the diseased ", and also used the words " pathological, in other words Romantic ". He would certainly not have written thus at the beginning of the movement. But while this French Romantic movement was reacting on Goethe, he wrote to Zelter : " The exaggerations forced upon the theatre of your great, vast Paris do harm to us who need nothing of the sort. Yet these are the consequences of advancing world literature." [23] So Goethe was by no means blind to the fact that his great idea of world literature, when realised, may bring not only blessing, but also danger and harm, particularly so when one nation adopts the mannerisms of another. If these are unsuited to its own nature they become foreign bodies in its organism, and causes of disease. One remembers, too, Goethe's idea that world literature should leave undisturbed national characteristics, should tolerate and even welcome them, and that peoples ought to take over from one another only what is common to all and contributes to the steady progress of human civilisation.

Goethe also asked himself the grave question : which peoples have most to gain or lose in this development of literature ? Here we come upon a rather obscure statement : " Now, at the beginnings of world literature, if we look closely we can see that the German stands to lose most ; he would do well to consider this warning." About the French, on the other hand, he writes : " The various branches of world literature react sharply and strangely against each other ; if I am not mistaken, taking a broad, general view, the French gain most from it ; they have too a kind of premonition that their literature will have, in the highest sense, the same influence on Europe as it had in the first half of the 18th century." [24]

Why did Goethe address that warning to the German ? He certainly assigned to German literature an honourable part in world literature and was thinking first and foremost of the activities of German translators. Goethe once said to a young Englishman : " It is part of the nature of the German to respect everything foreign for its own sake and to adapt himself to foreign idiosyncracies. This and the great suppleness of our language make German translations particularly accurate and satisfying" (Eckermann, 10th January 1825). He considered the German language particularly suitable for purposes of translation because it easily conforms to any idiom, puts aside its own mannerisms and is not afraid of being accused of using unusual or objectional expressions. This faculty makes it possible for the German translators' art to contribute substantially to world literature. "Anyone understanding and studying the German language finds himself in a market where all nations are offering their wares ; he acts as interpreter while enriching himself." Goethe says this in his discussion of Carlyle's *German Romance* (1827) and again in his article about the *Serbian Songs*, translated by Talvy (1825) ; and he said the same thing in conversation with Prince Pückler-Muskau (1826). So in Goethe's view the honourable part played by German literature in world literature amounts to this, that foreign peoples have only to learn the German language and then, through its accurate translations, they will be able to master the literatures of all other countries. And not only the Germans but all the other nations too will reap the benefit. This is the most considerable contribution which German literature has to make to world literature. On the other hand, it has most to lose in this developing world literature. To understand this striking idea, we must remember what Goethe regarded as the main characteristic of German literature. For he could only mean that German literature ran the risk of losing its characteristic quality. This quality he believed to be a kind of isolationism. Each German writer works and creates for himself alone. In his works he feels impelled to express only his individual self, without regard to any influence he may exert on a public, or on other countries, and with no wish to collaborate with others. In every German there lives the ideal of personal freedom. Just as in Germany there is no political capital such as France possesses in Paris, so in German literature there is no centralising tendency in things of the mind. German poetry is as it were a monologue, a conversation with oneself. Every poet speaks his own native language and is not concerned with whether he is understood or not. In fact, if widely understood, he is apt to doubt the validity of his work. And German literature as a whole, in its relation to other countries, is just like the isolated individual. The Germans, Goethe says, work for their own benefit, without regard to other countries. They direct their influence inwards, not outwards. "If we look back on our literature during the last half-century, we find that nothing has been done for the sake of the foreigner." [25] In this self-centred aloofness Goethe recognised the weak point of German literature, but also the source of its virtues, and its most characteristic quality. But world literature requires something different, and for this reason German literature stands to lose the most by it. World literature

requires above all the intellectual, moral and æsthetic agreement
of a people, because only such an intensified and united power
has sufficient driving force to penetrate the outer world, just as
the military power of a nation develops out of its inner unity.
Also, world literature cannot be a monologue addressed to
oneself, but must be a conversation between the nations, an
exchange of thoughts. Any writing which, like that of the
Germans, is a characteristic expression of individuality, is bound
to arouse opposition in other nations. Even Goethe found this
to be the case when he read in the French journal *Le Globe* :

> The reason why Goethe's reputation spreads so slowly among us
> is largely to be found in his most striking quality, originality. What-
> ever is in a high degree original, that is to say deeply impregnated
> with the character of a particular man or nation, is rarely appreciated
> at once ; and originality is the most prominent virtue of this writer.
> Indeed, one might say that in his independence he carries this quality,
> without which genius does not exist, to excess.[26]

For these reasons, then, German literature stands to lose the
most when it comes to the development of a common world
literature, because German literature must of necessity find it
most difficult to adapt and accommodate itself to world literature. France, on the other hand, the country of the social
graces, which neither knows nor suffers such segregation of the
separate personality, which centralises its intellectual as it does
its political power, which, as Goethe once wrote, has ever been
accustomed to direct its influence outwards—France prides
itself on its influence on the rest of the world, and has in fact
disseminated over Europe [27] what goes by the name of good
manners. Such a nation seems positively predestined for world
literature. For this reason Goethe could promise the greatest
gain and the strongest influence in the world literature of the
future to French literature. Besides, German literature had
always opened wide its doors to foreign literatures and therefore could expect no further gain from world literature, whereas
French literature had up to now rather shut itself off from any
foreign influences and could therefore hope for great enrichment from world literature. And Goethe pointed out a further
reason. An essential part of world literature consists in reciprocal
criticism, and Goethe believed he recognised in the French
journals which at that time were beginning to concern themselves with foreign literatures, an outstanding gift for literary
criticism.[28] Goethe himself found that in the journal *Le Globe*

he was more truly understood than he usually was in Germany. We see now why Goethe uttered that warning to German literature, stating that now at the beginning of world literature, it stood to lose most, while the French would be the greatest beneficiaries. But that is not to say that he issued a warning against his own idea of world literature. His whole endeavour was to promote and hasten its growth to the full extent of his power, for he realised the blessing it would be to every people, the Germans included. He realised, too, that it was inevitably bound to come, because the hour demanded it. It was with that in mind that he wrote to the Russian statesman and author Uvarov that the Germans imagine strength to lie in limitation, which may in the strictest sense be true, but that the march of time requires other and wider views.

CHAPTER 3

SOURCES

What do we mean by saying that the march of time demands world literature ? We must bear in mind how often Goethe compared the exchange of intellectual assets between the nations with the international market to which the peoples bring their wares for exchange. And this was not merely a simile, for Goethe did follow with the greatest interest the improvement in commercial intercourse between peoples after the Napoleonic wars. This was aided by the ever-quickening tempo of means of communication, such as postal and steamship services. He spoke of the " age of speed ", of " Rotation " achieved by such speed of intercourse, the march of time in this sense. And in a developing world literature he saw an inevitable consequence of this march of time, drawing the peoples nearer to each other and bringing about an intermingling of their interests. And not only did he see that intellectual traffic between the nations must develop out of this and could not be stopped, because the march of time demanded it ; he saw also that it was the duty of every thinking man to help and hasten it, so that the enrichment of the peoples might be not only material but also intellectual, that mind and matter must help each other to lead mankind to a truly humane culture. It is therefore just as much a duty to exert a moderating influence in intellectual relations between peoples as it is to facilitate navigation or to open up passes through the mountains. Free traffic in ideas, not less than trade in produce, increases the wealth and general welfare of mankind. This led Goethe to hope that world literature would make an active contribution to expanding trade and commerce, and that on the other hand the ever-increasing speed and ease of intercourse would facilitate the formation of a world literature. He saw how speedy communications and periodicals were drawing the nations nearer to each other, and he wanted to devote the remainder of his life to assisting this process. The work of translation seemed to him one of the most important items in this general international traffic as he understood it. At a time when the paths of express messengers from all the ends of the earth were constantly crossing, he judged it a necessity for every progressive citizen to determine his position relative to his own and other nations. " For this reason an intelligent man of letters ought to abandon provincial trivialities and cast his eye round the great world of commerce." Goethe by no means ignored the dangers that modern civilisation held for the intellectual life, but he found it profoundly gratifying that the organisation of our civilised world should concern itself with gradually lessening the distance between honest thinkers of similar outlook ; and he was ready to forgive it a good deal for that.

The march of time, then, demands and promotes world literature, and there is a second time-factor, the universal need of peace which moved the nations after the Napoleonic wars. Even during the Napoleonic era, Goethe was able to note the beginning of this need. For him there was not the slightest doubt that through Napoleon the nations were indeed being torn asunder but were nevertheless growing to know each other better, and that Napoleon's attempt to found a politically united Europe must involve the idea of an intellectual union also. The occupation of Germany resulted in French officers and officials learning to know the German language and literature. Even the opposition to Napoleon bore fruit for world literature. Without it, Mme de Staël's book would not have been written. In 1830 Goethe writes :

There has for some time been talk of a universal world literature ; and rightly so, for the nations, flung together by dreadful warfare, then thrown apart again, have all realised that they had absorbed many foreign elements, and become conscious of new intellectual needs. This led to more neighbourly relations, and a desire for a freer system of intellectual give-and-take. This movement has been in existence only a short time, it is true, but long enough for one to form an opinion on it and to acquire from it, with business-like promptitude, both profit and pleasure.

Goethe found considerable comfort in the certainty that although a singularly tumultuous age had divided men, even alienated them, yet a human bond still stretched across the ages, and that fate, which had wrought so much confusion, would yet restore order among men.[29]

This European need for understanding among the peoples, which appeared strongest in post-Napoleonic France, met with opposition, particularly in Germany. Goethe's idea of world literature, although developed and encouraged by the march of time, was at first opposed by his own people. He contrasted it with that nationalism which he hoped, by its means, to over-come, and which had developed in Germany as a result of Napoleon's oppression and the liberation from the Napoleonic yoke. In fact one can trace Goethe's idea back to its sources in the time when German literary men, particularly the younger Romantic writers, began to rely on themselves, and to accept no foreign influences. This was the time when the idea and the expression " National literature " came into being, and when Goethe saw it as his mission to remind his own people of what it had always owed, and did still owe, to foreign nations. No doubt he founded his journal *Kunst und Altertum* in 1816 with this as his principal aim. From the very beginning it was devoted to the cause of world literature, although that word had not then been coined. In this journal Goethe continued the struggle which he had begun as early as 1813 against " purism ", i.e. the purification of the German language from all foreign elements. This, oddly enough, was known by the foreign term " purism ". More than once, he wrote in a letter in 1813, it had been brought home to him that it was the unintelligent who insisted with such eagerness on the purification of the language. " For, as they cannot appreciate the value of an expression, they can easily find a substitute which seems to them just as good." In his journal, *Kunst und Altertum*, he inveighed against " purism ", referring to an article by a Swiss, Karl Ruckstuhl, " On the per-fecting of the German language, with reference to endeavours recently undertaken with this intent ". This article gave warning of the irreparable harm which can be done to a nation if—even in all sincerity and with the best intentions—it is given a wrong turn, as was at that time happening to the German language. Following up this idea, Goethe now developed his own : that for the German there could be no more mistaken policy than to circumscribe himself and imagine that he could live on his own resources, regardless of all he owed to foreign peoples. The time would surely come when he would once more ask how his forebears had managed to raise the German language to the height of independence which it now enjoys. Nothing is easier than to ignore the content and concentrate on the expression. The man of intelligence utilises his linguistic material without concerning himself about its origin. It is easy for the brainless man to speak with flawless correctness, for he has nothing to say. He cannot realise what a paltry substitute he uses in place of a significant word, for to him such a word

never lived and never conveyed anything. Think how the
German language was enriched at the time when Latin was still
the universal language, and what beneficial influences flowed
from France and Italy into the German language and literature.
" The power of a language ", Goethe writes elsewhere, " lies
not in its resistance to what is foreign, but in its assimilation of
it." One of his poems, " The Purists ", runs :

> Gott Dank ! dass uns so wohl geschah,
> Der Tyrann sitzt auf Helena !
> Doch liess sich nur der eine bannen,
> Wir haben jetzo hundert Tyrannen.
> Die schmieden, uns gar unbequem,
> Ein neues Kontinental-System.
> Teutschland soll rein sich isolieren,
> Einen Pest-Cordon um die Grenze führen,
> Dass nicht einschleiche fort und fort
> Kopf, Körper und Schwanz von fremdem Wort.
> Wir sollen auf unsern Lorbeern ruhn,
> Nichts weiter denken als wir tun (1815).

At the same time, Goethe protested against the false
nationalism which contended that the learning of foreign languages was unnecessary and sought to forbid it. He maintained
that it was the duty of every true friend of the Fatherland to
discard the petty restrictions of a linguistic patriotism and to
foster the spread of foreign languages. Without them no higher
civilisation, science or poetry could thrive, no cultured social
life be possible. All this seems to symbolise Goethe's idea of
world literature in contrast to the exaggerated nationalism of
post-Napoleonic Germany.

Goethe was approached in 1808 (while Napoleon was still
dominant in Europe) with a project for a popular treasury of
lyrics which would give the German people a collection of the
best poems in their language. When he was asked for advice
and editorial help, his sole recommendation was that German
translations from foreign literatures ought to be included. If we
remember that no nation, and above all none of the younger
nations, can lay claim to absolute originality, no German need
be ashamed of owing much of his culture, and particularly his
poetic technique, to foreign influences. What was foreign has
become our own. What we have acquired by translation or
by taking to our hearts should be reckoned with, in fact special
mention ought to be made of such acquisitions. Translations
are an essential part of our literature. Every branch of it is
incomplete without them. But which foreign items ought we

to select ? For everything of importance has been or will be translated. The answer is : everything, of all times and places, that has appealed to men of all times and types ; what appeals to the unlettered as something new, and to the man of culture as something ever new. Here is the meeting-point of all the roads to culture.

These were Goethe's thoughts at the time of Napoleon's foreign domination and after the Wars of Liberation, when he was seeking to banish the menace of spiritual autarchy. In fact, Goethe found all Europe at that time so unbearable, with its battles of the nations, its struggles for power, its isolationism, its nationalism, its bringing of politics into everything, that he felt he could no longer breathe in that cramped and airless place. He needed space, and room to expand, and fled in spirit from Europe eastwards to the land of the Persian poet Háfiz. The fruit of this spiritual journey across the world was the *West-Eastern Divan*. And it also assisted the growth of world literature. For this contact with the spirit of another nation, and the joy of surrender to a way of living so different from his own, renewed his own powers. Both as man and as poet he recorded his gratitude for the experience.

Penetrated by the oriental consciousness of Universality and Unity, in the *West-Eastern Divan* he realised the higher unity of the peoples as of the continents of the world.

> Gottes ist der Orient !
> Gottes ist der Okzident !
> Nord- und südliches Gelände
> Ruht im Frieden seiner Hände.

But before this, about the turn of the century, Goethe had opposed the German Romantic writers. They were demanding in place of the Weimar school of thought (Classical and universal) a patriotic national art. In his journal *Propyläen*, when setting a prize-subject for the year 1801, he wrote : The universally human is being ousted by the patriotic. " It is to be hoped that people will soon be convinced that there is no such thing as patriotic art or patriotic science. Both belong, like all good things, to the whole world, and can be fostered only by untrammelled intercourse among all contemporaries, continually bearing in mind what we have inherited from the past." This is actually the whole idea of world literature as Goethe had been proclaiming it since 1827. So in both the Napoleonic era and the German Romantic period we trace, as it were, the negative origin of the idea : namely, his opposition to the European chaos, to national separatism and to Romantic nationalism.

But we must retrace our steps still further to reach the original source. For Napoleon was only the outcome of the French Revolution, which had already torn asunder the peoples of Europe, shattered individual nations, and even threatened to disrupt all human relationships. To visualise social conditions in the 1790's even in Weimar, one has only to read the announcement of a new journal, the *Horen* (1794), which Schiller edited with the laudable intention of putting an end to these unhappy conditions :

> At a time when the loud din of war alarms the country, when the conflict of political opinions and interests causes this war to spread far and wide, too often banishing the Muses and Graces, when there is no escape either in the conversations or in the writings of the day from this relentless fury of political criticism, it is perhaps as rash as it is praiseworthy to invite the sorely tried reader to consider something quite different. Indeed, present conditions seem to offer poor prospects to a journal which is pledged to strict silence on the most topical subject of all, and which will pride itself on striking out quite a new line. But the more we are distracted and depressed by present conditions, the more urgent it becomes to turn our thoughts to things which lie beyond the individual and the temporal, and which concern humanity. So may we hope to unite the politically divided world under the standard of truth and beauty.

Schiller's invitation to Goethe to help him with this journal laid the foundations of the friendship between them, for Goethe recognised in him a kindred spirit and could hope to co-operate with him successfully. Goethe contributed to the *Horen* the " Conversations of German Emigrants " entirely in the spirit of Schiller's and his own idea of bridging the gulf which politics had opened up between men. In these conversations a company of emigrants, forced to flee from the French Revolution, is so split up by political partisanship for or against the Revolution, that ties of long-standing friendship are broken, social intercourse becomes impossible, until they resolve to banish politics from their conversations and to discuss only matters of general artistic and scientific interest. When after a few years the *Horen* was discontinued, Goethe himself founded a journal, the *Propyläen* (1799) ; this was an attempt to save something in those days of general dissolution at the close of the century, when the evil spirit that was rampant was working its destructive will particularly on art and all that pertained to it. In this journal there appeared articles on Nature and Art contributed by a company of like-minded friends (i.e. by Goethe, Schiller and the Swiss Heinrich Meyer), also letters from Wilhelm von Humboldt in which the German and French theatres, the German and the French national character, were compared and a plea was made for understanding through reciprocal education. There were also translations by Goethe from Diderot's *Essay on Painting* and Voltaire's *Mahomet*; unfortunately, Goethe never carried out his project of comparing " the views of German, English, French and Italian artists and connoisseurs on Art ".

It is in the idea of universal humanity that one finds the true source of world literature, in the idea of universally human art and science, which leads mankind, distracted by war and politics, back to common ground, and so heals and reconciles it. That is why in Goethe's *Propyläen* we read : " Many will perhaps be of the opinion that the pressure of outward circumstances, the collapse of states and peoples, call for attention to more serious matters than critical reflections on works of art. But the more unsettled outward circumstances are, the more beneficial it may be to enjoy awhile the ageless peace of the arts."

But where are the sources of Goethe's idea of peace and reconciliation ? When Goethe was trying to mediate in the Italian controversy between Classical and Romantic enthusiasts, he wrote (1820) : " Although men disagree over many temporal things, yet Religion and Poetry, which are fundamentals, unite the whole world." Religion and Poetry ! With this reference to religion we reach the original source of Goethe's idea of reconciliation. At a time when Goethe's thoughts were occupied with the idea of world literature, when from England there came news of the interest taken in him and in German literature, he wrote to Carlyle :

In the next number of *Kunst und Altertum* I intend to make friendly mention of this contact from outside, and warmly to recommend this kind of reciprocity to my friends at home and abroad, using St. John's message, and stressing it as the substance of all wisdom : Little children, love one another. I hope that these words will not strike my contemporaries as they did the followers of the Evangelist, who expected a quite different and profounder revelation.

This is from a letter written in 1828, when Goethe was 79. But we shall show that this sentence from *St. John's Last Testament,**

* Discussed by Lessing in 1777, the *Testament Johannes* summed up St. John's message in these words.

on which he now based his idea of world literature, had been his creed his whole life long, and that for him Christianity was comprehended in this one sentence. To take one instance, as early as 1816 he wrote to his friend, the musician Zelter : " I will not deny that I know my influence during these few summers on the Rhine and the Main has been for good, for I have only preached the message of St. John : Little children, love one another, and, if you cannot manage that, at least bear with each other." And again when he was quite young, as early as 1786, Goethe had written to Herder in connection with a tribute to Spinoza : " This all goes to show that I repeatedly endorse St. John's message, which comprehends Moses and the Prophets, Evangelists and Apostles : Little children, love one another." In the statement that Christianity is summed up in ·this one sentence from St. John, Goethe is seen as a true son of the 18th century. Lessing had proclaimed this creed, and it formed the ground-work of Herder's *Ideas towards a Philosophy of the History of Mankind*. We can see how near Goethe's idea of world litera-ture is to Herder's idea of humanity, for Herder's work traces through the centuries the gradual development of the " universal spirit of Europe", a "Europe acting as a corporate whole" and the irresistible progress of the " strengthened corporate activity of the nations ". Goethe's epic fragment *The Secrets* (1784) was written as a tribute to Herder, the prophet of humanity, and dealt with the rise of mankind through corporate activity to ideal perfection. In later years Goethe gave this explanation of *The Secrets* : The reader is led through a kind of imaginary Monserrat ; each time after he has passed through the different regions of mountain peaks, crags and dizzy heights, he safely reaches a wide plateau. Each of the hermit knights is visited in his dwelling ; only the noblest from all the ends of the earth are gathered here, each of them silently serving God in his own way. The reader or listener who is guided by Brother Mark will realise that the most diverse ways of thinking or feeling are intended to be represented here by selected individuals. All these differing points of view express the desire for the highest pitch of culture, which appears imperfectly in the individual but worthily in a corporate existence. To make this possible, they have gathered round one man who is called Humanus, because they felt an affinity with him. The history of his life shows that each religion reaches a moment of richest fruition, at which it draws nearer to this supreme leader and is eventually identified with him.

These epochs appear embodied and fixed in the twelve representatives. In this way every recognition of God and Virtue,
in however strange a form, would be found worthy of respect
and love. Now if we substitute, by way of experiment, the
development of humanity through world literature for these
representatives of the different religions bound together by the
mediator Humanus, we find it makes sense, fits in quite naturally.
This shows how early the fundamental ideas of world literature
were formed, and how they developed out of the religion of
humanity.

It is obvious that the form and idea of Freemasonry influenced
this " imaginary Montserrat ". We must remember that as
early as 1780 Goethe was initiated into a Lodge, and after the
movement revived in 1808 he became an active member. What
Goethe saw to be the task of the Order (into which he and Herder
thus first breathed a quickening spirit) is clear from his Lodge-
songs and his memorial addresses on former members. To him
it was a brotherhood which called all men to work together and
to influence each other in the service of the highest cause, the
development of humanity. It is a chain of living links, encircling
everything, in which every man finds his place as an actively
useful unit, and his happiness not in his individuality but in
submission to the whole. At the celebration of the fiftieth anniversary of Goethe's admittance into the Order, Friedrich von
Müller bore witness that no one had more successfully promoted
the aims of the Order : the spread of humane feeling, the harmonious development of spiritual powers, in a word, Humanity.
Within this community he constantly endeavoured to lead the
several powers to harmonious co-operation. As Müller said in
his memorial address in the Lodge, the whole direction of Goethe's
mind and nature made him a Freemason. The conception that
great and noble aims were reached only by faithful co-operation
among many kindred spirits was characteristic of him, and was
the result of his absolute conviction, his profound study of history
and nature. To use his own words, he knew that fundamentally
man is all mankind, that·the individual can be happy and contented only when he has the courage to be conscious of himself
as part of the whole.

It is quite obvious how, from the standpoint of this international Order, the way lies open to world literature which
seeks to promote the development of humanity through co-
operation between living writers of all nations.

The sources of Goethe's idea of world literature stand revealed. They were the idea of the rolling stream of time, the ease and rapidity of modern intercourse between the peoples, their need for understanding and peace after the Napoleonic wars, the exaggerated nationalism of the Romantic movement, the European chaos and, not least, Christianity as the religion of humanity from the 18th-century standpoint. But all the sources which are seen in time and nation and tradition can be traced back to the one original source, without which all these others would have sprung up in vain : the very core of Goethe's personality. The idea of world literature was the fruition of Goethe's whole being. Schiller once declared that Goethe was the most " communicable " of men, and this estimate of his character is borne out by everything that we know of him. No one ever felt such an inner necessity as he to communicate, sympathise and share. The word " sympathy " (*Teilnahme*) is found conspicuously often in Goethe's use of the language. He owed his own education to this profound need, and the world owes its education, as far as it received it from Goethe, to this passion of his for communion with others. " It is not good for anyone to be alone, especially to work alone ; he must have interest and stimulus if his work is to prosper." This utterance of Goethe's remained one of his watchwords all his life. In it he formulated his deepest personal experience. This need was so rooted in his own nature that he was even obliged to turn monologue into dialogue, to transform lone thoughts into sociable conversation, as he relates in *Dichtung und Wahrheit*. He did this, when he was alone, by calling up in his mind someone of his acquaintance, however far away he might be. Then he developed his thought in imaginary conversations with him. Goethe's vast correspondence is only an obvious symbol of this deep-seated need. Even his writings, as he often admits, were the outcome of an urge to reveal himself, to make confession to his friends. Goethe has said, however, that man is called to influence only the present. Writing is a misuse of language, reading in silence and alone a sorry substitute for speech. Man exerts what influence he can on others by his personality. Again and again in private and in public Goethe acknowledged how much he owed to actual conversation, how, particularly in his scientific work, he could not have got on without exchanging thoughts and observations. When, for instance, he was occupied with his theory of colour, he talked about it to people who had never before heard of such things, but also, once their interest was aroused, noticed phenomena which he had overlooked. This often enabled him to correct some too hasty assumption, or to progress more quickly and with less laborious investigation. This is one case out of many in which co-operation makes for success. While Herder was writing his *Ideas towards a Philosophy of the History of Mankind*, Goethe held daily conversations with him which were useful to both. By this interchange of thought their intellectual resources increased daily. " Often a word, a warning, encouragement or contradiction at the right moment marks a definite stage in our development." But it was in his friendship with Schiller that Goethe first experienced in full measure the blessings of conversation and mutual communication of ideas : this friendship which helped the education of both through successive stages. Goethe in particular realised through this friendship that it is interaction between the most diverse, even the most diametrically opposed, characters which achieves the greatest results. He quotes from his own experience in the introduction to the *Propyläen*.

Our culture does not advance by our merely setting in motion what lies within us and taking no trouble about it. Every artist, like every man, is only a single creature and will grasp only a single aspect. That is why everyone must try, in theory and in practice, to absorb as much as he can of what is opposite to his own nature. The frivolous should seek out what is serious and earnest, the serious concentrate on something light ; the strong should cultivate gentleness and the gentle strength ; each will develop his own nature in proportion as he seems to depart from it. Every art demands the whole of man, and the highest stage of art requires the whole of mankind.

It is completion, then, that Goethe felt to be the issue of a relationship like this, and his relationship with Schiller rounded off his character.

But there is another result which follows from this kind of co-operation, namely, education towards objectivity, i.e. towards judgments of ideas of objective validity. For man as an individual is inevitably bound up in his own subjectivity, and objective truth can be reached only as his ideas gain in clarity and integrity. This can come about through exchange of ideas, even through disagreement with others. For even disagreement postulates company, not solitude. And the sciences, like everything that has a basis of truth, gain as much by disagreement as by agreement, perhaps more. Who will not readily admit, Goethe writes

in the introduction to the *Propyläen*, that unbiased observations
are rare ? We are so prone to mix our feelings and opinions
with the facts we have learned that we do not long remain
impartial observers. We are soon making observations whose
validity is affected by the nature and acquired habits of our own
minds. Co-operation with others can give us greater confidence
—the knowledge that we think and act not as single units but as
members of a team. The fear that our mode of thought may be
peculiar to us alone, which so often assails us when others express
an opinion contrary to our own, is removed if we find ourselves
one of a number. It is only then that we feel confidence in these
principles which we have gained from experience. When
several people are associated with each other in this way and
can all call each other friend, working for progressive self-
education and pursuing like aims, they can be certain that however devious their ways they will eventually meet. This is what
Goethe found so happily true when working for the *Propyläen*
with his Swiss friend Heinrich Meyer and Schiller. They had
the liveliest exchange of thoughts on nature and art. The three
friends reached such a point of mental intimacy that, although
their ideas might diverse widely, no real discrepancy was possible,
and their work showed only the more variety. In the form of
conversations, displaying this harmonious collaboration, Goethe
publicly developed in the *Propyläen* his ideas on nature and art.
These ideas had matured as the result of the Weimar friends'
collective work. Conversation was always a favourite literary
form with Goethe, showing him to be a disciple of Plato. Even
when conversation developed into controversy and sparks were
struck—indeed particularly then—Goethe found it stimulating.
A one-sided exposition always seemed to him a stiff and lifeless
thing. " Man is not born to instruct, but to live, to do, to
influence. Joy comes only from action and reaction." These
words are taken from Goethe's " Confession of the Translator ",
which prefaced his verson of Diderot's *Essay on Painting* ; and this
translation is the best evidence of how his love of conversation
is linked up with his idea of world literature. For in this case
he is not content with a mere translation ; he changes it into a
discussion between Diderot and himself. And world literature
is a conversation between the nations. But even where actual
conversation and personal contact are impossible, letters can be
exchanged and it is well known what a vast correspondence
Goethe kept up not only with friends but also with scientists of

all nationalities. If ordinary observant people can be of such
assistance to us (we read in Goethe's scientific writings), how
much more should we benefit if specialists would work together.
Any branch of knowledge is in itself too vast for any single man
to deal with it. It requires a combined effort. Knowledge,
like enclosed but running water, gradually rises to a certain
level, and some of the greatest discoveries have been made not
so much by individuals as by the process of time, conclusions of
great importance being reached simultaneously by a number of
experts. We owe much to society and to our friends, and still
more to the wide world and the age we live in. In both cases
we cannot exaggerate our debt to all the instruction, help,
reminders and even opposition which have set us on the right
road and led us on. That is why Goethe held it necessary in
the scientific field to publish every finding, even every hypothesis,
and to erect the scientific edifice only when the plan for it, and
its materials, were agreed on by all. With art it is naturally
rather different, and in scientific matters one has to do the
opposite of what the artist finds necessary. For it is as well he
should not let his work of art be seen in public until it is complete.
No one can easily advise or help him. It was quite contrary to
Goethe's nature to discuss his poetical projects with anyone.
He turned them over in his own mind and as a rule no one heard
anything of them until the whole was complete. In the realm
of art, the stimulating co-operation of the outside world begins
only when the work of art has been made public. The echo that
it sets up is of great importance to the artist. He has to consider
and take to heart the blame or the praise, to incorporate it in
his experience and utilise it in his future work.

In a deeper sense, Goethe differentiated little between the
arts and the sciences. Neither can dispense with society. It
may seem as though the poet needed no one else, and heard
the promptings of the Muse most clearly when by himself.
People have often persuaded themselves that the finest works of
this kind have been produced by poets in solitude. But this is
self-deception. What would poets and artists be like if they
had not access to the literature of all the world and did not try,
in this exclusive company, to be worthy of their surroundings?
What works are produced when the artist is not in touch with the
best kind of public? In Ancient Greece, inspiration was found
in noble rivalry, the competitive impulse that obliged each one
to exert himself to the utmost to produce the maximum of which

he was capable.   The desire for approbation felt by the writer is an instinct which nature has implanted in him to call him to higher things.   However small may be his aptitude for instructing others, he longs to address himself to those who feel as he does but who are scattered all over the world.   He desires to renew his contacts with his old friends and to continue them with new ones, and in the younger generation to gain others whom he will have for the rest of his life.   He wishes to spare the rising generation the bypaths among which he himself lost his way.   And, while profiting by the criticisms of his contemporaries, he wishes to keep the memory of past endeavours.

At this point we must call to mind one of Goethe's characteristics without which we cannot understand his personality and activity, especially on the scientific side ; this is his capacity for gratitude.   He himself openly admitted that he was by nature no more grateful than anyone else, but said that it was possible by self-discipline and practice to develop one's sense of gratitude and to make it an active force.   He had done this, and now every one of his possessions reminded him of how, and from whom, he had acquired it.   He knew in each case exactly to whom he was indebted, and it was a delight to him to pay his debt of gratitude. When we read his autobiographical and still more his scientific works, we constantly meet this grateful reference to spirits of the past and to living contemporaries, whatever their ages, by whom he felt he had in some way been helped.   This gratitude had its origin in Goethe's invariable frankness and flexibility of mind, which he retained even in old age.   It crystallised in him the conviction that every man, even the greatest and most highly creative, is to be seen as a collective being.   From his birth onwards the world begins to influence him, and so it goes on till the end.   We bring faculties with us, but we owe our development to countless influences of nature, art, science and society, from which we absorb what we can and what suits our own nature. We must all learn something from those who went before us, and from those among whom we live.   Even the greatest genius would not go far if he aimed at being indebted to no one but himself.   Originality is only an illusion.   Goethe once said that any artist who thought himself original had only to look at the sketches of the great masters on the walls of Goethe's room, and, if he had any real genius, he would go away a changed and wiser man.   He himself was infinitely indebted to the Greeks, the

French and the English, as well as to others. The vital thing, and what a man could really call his own, was the energy and the will, the soul that loved and absorbed truth wherever it found it ; the power and inclination to attract to ourselves all the cultural aids the world affords, and to make them serve our highest aims ; to see, to hear, to choose ; to quicken what is chosen with one's own spirit and to give it a unified form. No accretions can harm one's native individuality, or in the slightest degree impair one's own essential nature, what is called one's character ; in fact, they rather bring it out. For what constitutes our real selves is not only what is ours from birth but what we are capable of acquiring. We see now why Schiller called Goethe the most " communicable " of men.

Goethe had an immense capacity for giving and for taking, a great need for intellectual companionship. If remembering this, we remember also the circumstances in which he was obliged to live, the tragedy of his existence becomes obvious. How few were his opportunities to satisfy this most profound longing ! True, he had friends and like-minded acquaintances with whom he could have stimulating interchange of thought, Herder and Schiller, Graf Reinhard, Wilhelm von Humboldt, Heinrich Meyer and Zelter and others. He could talk and exchange letters with them. But those were only isolated bright patches in his life. He was painfully aware how slow and lonely was the course of his self-culture, and how many possibilities for collaboration with his German contemporaries were closed to him. It horrifies one to read of the " dreadful loneliness in which his *Wilhelm Meister* was written, in spite of its continual striving towards the Universal". His *Werther*, and indeed his whole work, is understood only when one realises that the complete absence of social life in Germany forced him back upon himself and drove him to find his material in himself alone. From youth to old age we find these painful references to the loneliness of his path, and he often analysed the causes of the loneliness in which not he alone but every German poet had to live. He explained it by the absence of any stable, unifying tradition whose natural growth he could have fostered, of any spiritual unity in the nation. There was no centre of social life and culture (such as France possessed in Paris), where writers could habitually meet and help each other to achieve the way of life on which their hearts were set. Everything was decentralised and in a state of anarchy. The *Horen* for 1795 contains an essay by

Goethe, " Literary Sansculottism ", in which he describes the depressing circumstances in which the best German writers were obliged to work. A Classical author of nation-wide reputation can arise, Goethe writes, only if he finds among his countrymen a compelling tradition, a spiritual agreement, and a high level of culture which enables him to develop his own powers. But this culture did not exist, so he had no opportunity to test his own particular genius against it. German writers, born one here one there, were left very much to themselves and to the effects of widely differing backgrounds. Each had to tread his lonely way, trying to advance his own culture as best he could without help or interest from outside. But Goethe's perception went deeper than this. He realised not only that the reason lay in the politically and socially divided state of Germany, but that this division itself was a consequence of the German national character, and that no German writer or scientist really wished it to be otherwise. Each one of them longs to be an Original, independent of what his predecessors or contemporaries have done. He desires to follow no well-trodden path but to make his own. Each wishes to express himself alone, to speak his own language, to begin anew as if there had been nothing before him and there were nothing beside him. He calls that personal freedom, and he likes to exercise it in religion, art and science and every other sphere. No one wants to co-operate or even to admit foreign merit. Each hinders the other. And, as the German writer has no corporate society behind him, he has no desire to address himself to any public, being content if he has reached the standard he set for himself. German poetry is the poetry of a scattered nation or, in milder terms, " the poetry of individuals for individuals ".

Goethe saw that there was one circumstance of which the nation might be justly proud, namely, that no other had produced at any one time so many outstanding individuals. He agreed with the French writer Guizot that it was the Germanic people that had introduced to others the idea of personal freedom. But the Babylonian confusion that arose from the exaggeration of German individualism, the solitude and isolation of German writers which precluded the growth of any general German culture, appeared to him to be the most serious defect in the spiritual life of Germany. And it betokened a grievous fate for one who sought spiritual companionship. Goethe repeatedly contrasted this picture of conditions in Germany with its opposite in France. That was an example of a naturally sociable nation which had created a centre for its spiritual life in its capital. Writers, authors, artists and men of learning, imbued with one spirit, had a common meeting-ground on which they could exchange their ideas and, with friendly rivalry, spur each other on to greater achievements. He traced back the high level of general culture in France, which did not possess so many outstanding individuals, to this sociable co-operation and adherence to a common tradition. But to Goethe the loftiest exemplar was always Ancient Greece, in which the highest pitch of general national culture was combined with an abundance of great men. The constant and unified character of their literature and art was no handicap to genius. We can see now why Goethe's rôle among his own people and in his own age can without exaggeration be called tragic, and why he sought to remind his people so constantly of the advantages of collaboration, and drew their attention to the difficulties of his own lonely path. He believed he was doing his people the greatest service in showing, as he did in his autobiographical work, *Dichtung und Wahrheit*, how each successive age in Germany had tried to suppress and supplant its predecessor, instead of being thankful to it for what it had taught them.

But Goethe's mission was not limited to warnings or the statement of a creed. He went on to actual example, by seeking to create in the Weimar circle a model of German social life centering in himself. In the history of German literature there had of course been previous attempts to form such circles, and Goethe pays tribute to them in his diaries and year books. He admitted that the better part of the nation had realised by the 18th century that this state of things could not be continued. Many people were then moved by the same impulse. They acknowledged each other's merits, and felt the need to join forces. They sought each other out and enjoyed each other's company ; but they achieved no unity because their common interests were too vague, and lacked direction. So the large group split up into smaller, mostly local, ones which did achieve something, but the intellectuals tended to become still more isolated. Literary circles were formed, without actual personal contacts, merely on the strength of a common object of veneration, such as Klopstock or Wieland, for example. On the other hand in Strassburg, Darmstadt, Wetzlar and Frankfurt, real communities of persons sprang up round Herder or Gleim or young

Goethe himself. Goethe called them " little world systems ". But they lacked, as we said, any real unity, and they rather exaggerated than cured the state of isolation. Now Weimar was to be the nucleus of a German spiritual community, a centre whose circumference, limited at first, was to extend farther and farther. We have a false picture of Weimar if we do not see that here a fully conscious organising spirit was at work, creating a pattern for German social life. In 1791 Goethe founded in Weimar a " Friday Club " whose sole aim was that each member should report for discussion and criticism what was occupying him at the time, so that there might be a useful exchange of ideas whether art or science were concerned. The subject of Goethe's inaugural address to the society was the necessity and the benefit of friendly collaboration in science and art. After Schiller had settled in Weimar a new society was formed, for whose regular meetings Goethe and Schiller, after the example of the " Scholia " of the Ancients, composed " sociable songs ", which were sung in honour of all the powers which can bind men together. But the Weimar writers soon went beyond their own small group and tried to form a wider circle, in fact to draw all German artists and the whole German public into their community. The association of the Weimar Friends of Art, formed by Goethe, Schiller and the Swiss Heinrich Meyer, offered annual prizes to the sculptors and painters of Germany. It was stipulated that they should all deal with the same subject, probably from Greek Mythology, so that the scattered artists should unite in friendly rivalry, and lose the feeling of isolation. A prize was also offered for the best comedy. Schiller sought out the best brains in Germany to contribute to the successive numbers of the *Horen*, describing himself as merely the mouthpiece of the group which had come together to publish the journal. " But ", he proceeded, " as the society here mentioned in no way regards itself as a closed community, any German writer who agrees to the conditions which the institute has found it necessary to impose may at any time contribute to it." The *Propyläen* is Goethe's monument to the value of intellectual collaboration. The articles in it, which often took the form of conversations, were reflections on nature, art and science, contributed as the result of an exchange of ideas between kindred spirits. " In the arts and sciences," Goethe writes in his introduction to the *Propyläen*, " as well as this kind of fellowship, a link with the public is as beneficial as it is necessary. The fundamental quality in any creative thinking belongs to the world, and the world will bring to fruition whatever it can utilise from among the individual's efforts." So the *Propyläen* aimed at linking up the Weimar circle with the German reading public. Its object was to attract the interest of the public to the work that was being done by the Weimar writers. In later years, whenever Goethe saw similar circles being formed with scientific or artistic aims, such as the Friends of Art in Frankfurt (or other groups anywhere) he got into touch with them and began an exchange of ideas. He wrote on one occasion to a society in Batavia : " To a friend of the sciences there can be nothing more gratifying than to see societies being formed all over the world which study nature's infinite variety and associate themselves with other groups devoted to similar ends." In this way he hoped that the various circles would gradually blend into one ever-widening one, as ripples on the water merge into a single ring. Goethe in his later years made contact not only with German but also with European and even extra-European societies interested in art and science. He hoped gradually to affiliate German literature, creative as well as scientific, with the other literatures of Europe and of the world. In this way his efforts at unification, begun in and for Weimar, merge in his idea of world literature. In the last decade of his life, in 1823, Goethe was able to tell a foreign guest that he belonged to a society equal to the best in any great city. " Its roads lead to the ends of the earth." From these words we can gather that the Weimar circle, this little world-system, had grown into one with wide ramifications. First a group owing its origin to Goethe's characteristic quality of " communicableness ", then a great expansion, and what began as the literature of Weimar became German literature, and finally world literature. Not long before his death, in 1831, Goethe drew up a memorandum for the inauguration of the circulating library in Weimar. It was called " Epochs of Social Development ", and was to be the basis for a ceremonial poem or a speech by Chancellor von Müller. This is how it runs :

I

From amongst a more or less crude mass, narrow circles of cultured people are formed ; they are on the most intimate terms ; a man entrusts his thoughts only to a friend, sings his song only to the loved ones ; an atmosphere of domesticity prevails. The circles are closed to outsiders as a protection from the harsher aspects of life. They tend therefore to keep to the mother tongue, and this stage may be called

The Idyllic.

II

The small groups multiply and expand, their inner circulation quickens, the influence of foreign languages is no longer banned, the circles remain separate but draw closer in mutual respect. I would call this stage

The Social or Civic.

III

The circles multiply and continue to expand till at last they touch and prepare to merge. They realise that their aims are the same, but they are unable to break down the barriers that divide them. This may provisionally be called

The More-or-less General.

IV

To reach the universal stage requires goodwill and good fortune, and today we may pride ourselves on enjoying both. For, though for many years we have faithfully fostered these successive stages, something more was needed to accomplish what we see now. This is no less than the uniting of all cultured circles which up to now had merely touched, the recognition of one single aim, the realisation of how needful it is to become aware of contemporary affairs, and familiar with the trend of thought in the world we live in. Foreign literatures are all on an equal footing with our ow, nd we play our part in the world circulation of ideas.

Goethe here sketches and represents as an organic growth the whole progress which he had himself initiated and led. The Weimar circle of a few like-minded men with a common aim had developed into a partnership embracing the whole of Europe. The literary collaboration of the men of Weimar had become a collective European literature. The harmony which such diametrically opposed thinkers as Goethe and Schiller had reached by reciprocal assistance had become the harmonious completion of France by Germany, of Germany by France. The personal contact between the chosen spirits of Weimar had become an exchange of thoughts and a traffic in ideas between the nations. For that is what the world literature which developed during Goethe's later years really was, the world-wide expansion of the little circle round Goethe. Goethe remained the central point round which the literatures of Europe revolved, and Weimar became the intellectual capital of Europe. Writers of every nation acknowledged their debt to Goethe, honoured him as their intellectual father, the leader of the intellectual life of Europe, and Weimar was the spot to which not only the writings of European authors came, but to which they themselves made pilgrimage. The Goethe-house in Weimar was the focal point at which converged writers from France, England, America, Italy, Scandinavia, Russia and Poland. The little world-system, the microcosmos Weimar, had grown to a great world-system, a macrocosmos, in which the planets of the intellectual universe revolved round the fixed star, Goethe.

CHAPTER 4

HISTORY

Goethe's idea of world literature took the form neither of a command on his part that it should develop nor of a seer's vision that it was bound to do so. The idea evolved from his realisation that a world literature was in actual fact taking shape in his own time. It was only a new name for an actual historical process which Goethe was witnessing, and which presaged the dawning of a new literary age. For Goethe nothing had real existence unless he had himself experienced it. Therefore his idea of world literature developed out of his own feeling of indebtedness to foreign literatures. The culture he had imbibed from them had helped to make him what he was, a power in the literary world of Europe. The rising generation in Europe hailed him as its leader and spiritual head. This experience indicated to Goethe that German literature was now no longer merely receptive, modelling itself on others which despised and neglected it. It now had something to contribute ; it played an active part in the development of European literatures, and in particular had a rejuvenating effect on the jaded spiritual life of Europe.

So, when Goethe speaks of world literature as something that is taking shape, we must ask the question whether it was really only beginning to develop in his time. In the Middle Ages and the Age of Humanism there existed a universal language, Latin, in which not only could the learned men of every nation exchange their thoughts but in which also an extra-national poetry grew up. Although Goethe himself refers expressly (when opposing linguistic " Purism ") to the beneficial influence which this had on the intellectual coherence of Europe, Latin literature cannot be claimed as world literature in Goethe's sense. For, in the first place, the circle which knew and used it was limited to scholars, and in the second place world literature ought to be not a colourless unity but a lively conversation. The nations ought not thereby to lose their special characteristics, but with one another's help should develop their common human qualities and learn tolerance for each other. Goethe saw in Ancient Greece a universal model for all literatures. When he developed his idea of world literature in conversation with Eckermann, and spoke of the need for acquainting oneself (as he did) with foreign literatures, he added that, however much one admired them, none could serve as a pattern. If we look for a model we must turn to the ancient Greeks, in whose works the perfection of human endeavour was represented. We must look at everything else from the historical point of view, appropriating, as far as we can, what is good in it. But Goethe certainly did not recognise as world literature merely any literature written in one universal language. On the other hand there had been, from classical times onwards, contacts between the peoples suggesting world literature in Goethe's sense. If we take German literature in particular, it has always been open to literary influences from abroad, has modelled itself on them, interested itself critically in them, and developed a vast activity in the work of translation. Through every age, German literature shows a tendency to look to the Romance literatures for guidance in form and proportion, purity and beauty. Middle High German literature took its formal and social education from France. Through the influence of Chancellor Johannes von Neumarkt (whose enthusiasm for Italy had almost the same origins as Goethe's) at the court of the Emperor Charles IV, famous writers of the Italian Renaissance, Petrarch and Rienzi, became models for a Latin and also a German literary style. Translations from Boccaccio, Poggio and Æneas Silvius affected the incipient German Renaissance. French literature was used in the 16th century to help to overcome German crudity in art and society. Even the Baroque movement, consciously national in its ambition to raise German literature to the level of other European literatures, employed translation and imitation to show that what was possible in other languages was possible also in German. German classicism, superseding the Baroque style, copied the example of the French from whom it learned to endow German poetry with symmetry, clarity, good taste and reasonableness. And the German Rococo, the Anacreontic poetry of which Wieland's is the finest example, learned from French poetry charm, grace, and lightness, until finally both classicism and rococo were superseded by the foreign—though this time Germanic—help of England. Foreign literary influence on German literature assumed such proportions that German writers of the 16th, 17th and 18th centuries had repeatedly to oppose it. There was no cause to complain of spiritual autarchy; the danger was rather that German literature, from sheer excessive open-heartedness, would lose its individual character. We have only to recall Klopstock's famous lines addressed to his Fatherland : " No country has ever been so appreciative of others as you. Do not be over-appreciative." In the great age of German literature which began with Lessing, Klopstock and Herder, and meant an awakening to self-awareness, Herder interpreted the demand for preserving the national character of literature by concluding that one must hear the voices of all the peoples in their songs. A universal human harmony would be achieved only by uniting the voices of the nations in one great choral song. The German Romantic movement largely realised this idea through translations taken from all the literatures of the world. Goethe himself repeatedly drew attention to the vast amount of translation in German literature which had been of mutual benefit.

Why then did Goethe identify the beginning of world literature with his own age, and characterise it as something only now taking shape and drawing near ? He did so from the point of view of German literature. For Goethe's idea of world literature is that of reciprocal relations between peoples, an exchange of thoughts and ideals. No world literature is possible without exchange. But what had been the case up to now ? German literature had undoubtedly preserved an open attitude to foreign influence and had always shown an interest in other literatures. But was the opposite true ? Had the literatures of Europe concerned themselves likewise with German literature ? Had they translated from it, learned from it, and judged it fairly ? They had indeed judged it, but without real knowledge and care, and above all without goodwill, and their judgment was therefore merely condemnation and contempt. German literature was called barbaric, uncouth, harsh, ugly, Hyperborean. You can almost count on your fingers the translations from German literature up to the 18th century. The German works which did penetrate to other countries were, for the most part, not strictly speaking works of literature but religious, mystical and philosophical writings. The great philosopher Nicolas of Cusa certainly had an important influence on the Italian Renaissance, partly because he lived and worked in Italy. On March the 8th, 1588, Giordano Bruno delivered a farewell speech in Wittenberg where, after banishment, persecution and fear of death, he had found a welcome and freedom to continue his studies. In this speech, Bruno expressed his gratitude for the kindness shown to him, by proclaiming what he and all the

world owed to the German spirit. It is a hymn in prose honour-
ing Nicolas of Cusa, Copernicus, Paracelsus and Luther, the first
acknowledgment of Germany's world-standing, a defence of
Germany against the charges of barbarism and boorishness.
The temple of Wisdom, formerly in India, Egypt, Greece and
Rome, he writes, now stands in Germany and welcomes seekers
after wisdom from all the ends of the earth. This was certainly
a rhetorical flight of fancy, but it is true that the eyes of every
land were directed to Luther, and the writings of Paracelsus and
of Agrippa of Nettesheim were read everywhere. Some few
works of imaginative literature, too, crossed the borders of
Germany. Sebastian Brant's *Ship of Fools* (at the close of the
15th century) was translated into every language and was the first
work in German literature to attain world-wide significance.
The German chapbook of Doctor Faust travelled to England,
France and the Netherlands, and towards the end of the
16th century inspired Christopher Marlowe's work of genius,
his Faust tragedy. Till Eulenspiegel, too, and other German
popular figures, became naturalised in the literatures of Europe.
At the beginning of the period of modern German, it really
seemed as though its literature had a part to play in the world, and
it is of great interest to reconstruct the concept that the world
then had of the German spirit and to note the influence which
it exerted. For it is practically the same concept and the same
influence as we find in the 19th-century phase of Romanticism in
Europe. There are, in other words, some constant factors in
world literature. Even then Germany stood for mysticism, the
home of exorcists, magicians and alchemists, of seekers after the
Philosophers' Stone, the supernatural beings, the home of Faust
and Paracelsus. Even then it was German popular poetry in
the form of chapbooks and popular ballads that the other countries
absorbed. It was the Faustian spirit of Nicolas of Cusa that
made the idea of the infinity of space and time and the human
spirit a European idea. It was the message of individual freedom
that Luther brought. But it all halted at the first stage. It was
a prelude to the world-wide significance of German literature,
which was to take centuries to reach fulfilment.

At the time when German literature began its struggle to rise
to the artistic level of the Renaissance literatures of Europe, it
had ceased to play its part in the world. There was a reason
for this. At that period, German writing had actually lost its
own characteristics to such an extent (from modelling itself too

much on foreign literatures) that it had nothing fresh to offer.
It was a real tragedy. The more German literature struggled
by means of imitation to achieve significance, the farther it went
astray. Even its efforts passed unnoticed or were regarded as barbarous eccentricities. This came to an end in the 18th century,
when the nations, filled with the idea of one universal humanity,
began to look beyond their frontiers and to attempt just criticism.
But although Gottsched, Wieland, Gellert and other German
writers now found acknowledgment and acceptance in French
literature, we must remember that this happened only because
these writers were themselves the product of the French school,
and France was merely getting back what she had given. German literature had as yet nothing of its own to bestow. Even
Lessing could hardly give anything to France which Diderot had
not already expressed.

But there were signs which can be regarded as a beginning
of world literature in Goethe's sense. In the first place there
were the new journals which appeared in the course of the 18th
century. The second half of the 17th century had of course its
journals, such as the *Journal des Savants* (from 1665), the *Nouvelles
de la République des Lettres* (from 1684), the *Bibliothèque Universelle*
(from 1685). They adopted a universal European tone and
dealt with the German point of view, but their main concern
was with scientific literature. Imaginative literature came only
exceptionally within their purview. These journals were supra-
national in their desire to found a republic of the sciences. The
18th century, on the other hand, witnessed the founding of the
Bibliothèque Anglaise (1717), the *Bibliothèque Germanique* (1720), the
Bibliothèque Italique (1729), and these were conscious attempts to
familiarise the nations of Europe, whose interests so far had
been restricted to French literature, with English, German and
Italian literature. While each of these journals had its specialised
sphere of activity, the *Bulletins littéraires* of Fr. Melchior Grimm,
the *Journal étranger* and the *Journal littéraire* (from 1754) and many
other journals in France had real influence in the direction of
world literature. This was especially the case with the *Journal
étranger*, in the preface to which the hope was expressed that this
journal would be popular in France, would find a wide circulation
throughout Europe and would help to unite the individual literary
republics in one single intellectual confederation, in a "république des lettres". Every nation, the *Journal* goes on to say,
will be enriched by the treasures of its rivals without losing any of

its own, and so the whole of Europe will become better educated, more philosophical ; and the *Journal étranger* hopes to have the good fortune to help in this task. Many voices were saying much the same thing. The most influential was of course Voltaire's. In a dedicatory letter for a French translation (by Antelmy) of Lessing's *Fables* he writes : French literature is very widely known in Germany, and journals publish reports of all our doings. There is also much just criticism. The example that Germany gives ought to incite France to emulation, " que votre langue devînt plus commune parmi nous ; que nous puissions nous intéresser à vos travaux littéraires, comme vous vous intéressez aux nôtres ; qu'après avoir contribué avec deux de nos nations voisines à épurer votre goût, nous profitassions à notre tour de vos lumières " (1764). These journals did justice to German literature by pointing out how far it was from being barbarous and rough. Soon, too, contributors began to mention their hopes for the wholesome and rejuvenating influence which German literature might have on French. This is particularly noticeable after France had become aware of Albrecht von Haller, Salomon Gessner and certain German writers who carried on their traditions. Huber's *Choix de Poésies Allemandes*, which appeared in 1766, was so successful that one can almost say there was a germanophil fashion in France in the sixties, and can trace Swiss and German influences in the works of the greatest French writers. Tacitus, in his *Germania*, had contrasted the simple moral and religious life among the German peoples with an over-civilised and decadent Rome. In the same way the idyllic poetry of a Haller or Gessner is contrasted as the ideal image of return to nature, to simplicity, to morality and religion. The Swiss and German writers make their entry into French literature with Rousseau. In the seventies and eighties the works of the younger German dramatists became known in France through the *Théâtre Allemand*, edited in 1772 by Junker and Liebault, and the *Nouveau Théâtre Allemand* by Friedel and Bonneville (1782–85). Even the early dramas of Goethe and Schiller are included among them. There is no doubt that this paved the way for the tremendous influence of *Werther*, which swept across France.

In Goethe's early years, then, world literature in his sense had made a beginning. But this was all a prelude compared with what happened in Europe after the publication of *Werther* ; the traffic in ideas between the peoples gained not only in scope

and speed but in depth and productiveness. There were, however, important obstacles to be overcome.

The opposition which German literature found in other
countries was far greater than that found by any other literature
among the civilised nations of Europe. There is a reason for
this, and it lies in the very nature of the German spirit. It is
indeed a staggering thought that even today writers like Hölder-
lin and Kleist have not yet succeeded in gaining a worthy place
in world literature, while French writers of infinitely lower
rank are quite well known in Europe. Has the German language
ever become a universal language, as the French did ? The
universal language of Germany, known and loved everywhere,
has been up to the present day not its poetry but its music.

What then delayed the acceptance of German literature as
work of world importance ?

The first difficulty was one that Goethe was constantly
lamenting, German literature's lack of uniformity and unity, of
concentration of forces and so of driving power.

How can we expect the nations to agree [in their judgment on
Germany] when even its own citizens cannot arrive at any agreement ?
We have in the literary sense many advantages over other nations ;
they will learn more and more to appreciate us, even if their appreciation should take the form of borrowing from us without thanks, and
making use of us without acknowledgment. Just as, however, the
military strength of a nation grows out of its inner unity, so æsthetic
strength is the gradual outcome of a similar unanimity. But this is
possible only with the passage of time. I can look back over so many
years as one of the collaborators, and I can see how German literature
has been composed of heterogeneous, not to say warring, elements.
It is really one literature only in the sense that it is written in one
language. But the widely differing elements of which it is composed
are gradually revealing the nature of the people.

How much more fortunate was France in this respect.

Men of the type who contribute to the *Globe* [the organ of the
French Romantic movement], men growing greater and more important from day to day and all filled with one spirit—[Goethe said
on one occasion to Eckermann] are quite unimaginable in Germany,
where such a periodical would be a sheer impossibility. We are all
mere individuals ; agreement between us is unthinkable ; each of us
holds the views of his province, his town, even his own personality,
and we have a long way to go to reach any common level of culture.

So Germany was accepted by the world only slowly and gradually.
And yet, is this defect not merely the consequence of the German
idea of the individual and his personal freedom ? Mme de Staël

in her *De l'Allemagne*, which introduced German literature to
the world, contrasts the German with the French writer, saying
that the German is forced to live and work for himself, without
social ties, without national agreement, tradition or code of
manners ; each has to start from the beginning and create his
own language.   In noting this, she points not only to a tragic fate
but also to a high ideal, and to the most fundamental quality
in German poetry.   But how can this idea of a free, creative,
detached individual form any union between the peoples ?   It
was this very idea that hindered Goethe's progress in Europe,
though he came nearer than any other German has done to
representing universal humanity.   Other peoples found it hard
to understand Goethe's way of putting his whole personal experience into poetic form, writing " occasional " poems to express
the mood of the moment.   In the French journal *Le Globe* there
appeared this explanation for the fact that so little was known in
France of what Goethe had written after *Werther* :

The reason why Goethe's reputation spreads so slowly among us
is largely to be found in his most striking quality, originality.   What
is in a high degree original, that is to say deeply impressed with the
character of a particular man or nation, is rarely appreciated at once ;
and originality is the most prominent virtue of this writer.   Indeed,
one might go so far as to say that in his independence he carries this
quality, without which genius does not exist, to excess.   Every other
writer follows a consistent and easily recognisable course ; but he is so
different from the others and often from himself, one can so seldom
guess his drift, he so diverts the usual course of criticism, even of
admiration, that to enjoy his works one must have as few literary
prejudices as he has ; and no doubt it would be as hard to find a
reader quite devoid of these as to find a writer who rises above them
all as he does.   So it is not suprising that he is not popular in France.
The Frenchman is inclined to shirk unnecessary trouble, and is quick
to mock at what he does not understand for fear that someone else
should begin to mock at it before he does, in a community which
admires only as a last resource. [30]

This idea of originality and individuality, this inner freedom,
which is an essential contribution of the German spirit to
humanity, the monologue-character, as it were, of German literature, is an obstacle to its progress in the world.   One could
hardly characterise German literature more aptly than by saying
that it has never created any form, such as for instance the
classical ode, the romantic sonnet, or the eastern ghazal.   These
are by their very nature so formally defined that, even when
dissociated from their former content and their creator, they

outlive the ages and are constantly filled with new life by new poets. When German poetry requires forms like these, binding and detached from personality, it must borrow them from other literatures.

German poetry, when left to itself without imitation of foreign literatures, has never subscribed to the ideal of perfect beauty, so common elsewhere. For German po y has always been essentially expressive, aiming at truth rather than at beauty, however hard and painful and intolerable that truth might be. A writer of Kleist's relentless forthrightness could scarcely find it easy to touch the hearts of other nations. It would be hard to find in any other literature anything comparable to Kleist's " Letter from one Poet to Another ", where the poet protests against praise of his poetic form, and expresses his concern that his poems may contain rhythmic and musical qualities which might distract attention from what he considered essentials. " If as I write I could turn inward, to my heart, seize my thoughts and lay them as they are in your hands, then, believe me, my soul's whole sincere desire would be fulfilled. And you too, my friend, would have all you could wish for ; the thirsty man sees not the proffered bowl but the fruits it contains."

As for the content of German poetry, it too is governed by the spirit of isolation. The German God is no common deity shared by all, and accepted as a traditional possession. The German is a seeker after God. One has only to compare Wolfram von Eschenbach's *Parzival* with Dante's *Divine Comedy* which belong to approximately the same period. Dante leads one through a world-system of hell, purgatory and paradise. But Parzival seeks his god along lonely untrodden ways. The spirit of the Greeks, Virgil's sure hand, led Dante in safety through all the horrors of the world ; Parzival's only guide was his faithful heart and unswerving will. Think of Goethe's Faust, too, who like Parzival sought his particular god along dark and lonely ways, with no guide, only the tempter Mephistopheles by his side. He reached his goal only because a sort of instinct guided him and he kept faith with himself. When we remember that it was with the Faust-spirit in the widest sense of the word that German poetry was destined to inspire other literatures, we shall better understand the prolonged opposition which that spirit had to overcome. It is a spirit of longing, never satisfied even in the moment of delight, never content at any stage, unappeased by any happiness, seeking and striving beyond any passing moment, always suffering in contact with the world, always unsatisfied because always fired by the vision of a distant and barely divined goal. The way matters more than the aim, the search more than the finding. Every form is irksome and must be broken ; every limitation intolerable and must be ignored. Forever wandering, forever seeking, never knowing either security or contentment, this spirit sets itself obstacles to prove itself capable of overcoming them. Where else than in German literature would Lessing's statement in his *Duplik* have been possible during the Age of Reason in Europe :

A man's worth lies not in the truth, which any man may possess, or think he possesses, but in his honest endeavour to arrive at truth. For it is not by possessing, but by enquiring after, truth that he develops the qualities in which alone his growing perfection consists. Possession makes a man content, lazy, proud.—If God held clasped in His right hand all truth, and in His left only the ever-active urge towards truth, together with the certainty that I should repeatedly stray from it, and if He said to me Choose ! I would humbly grasp His left hand and say, Father, give me this ! Pure truth belongs to Thee alone.

Voltaire, for instance, though a contemporary of Lessing, would never have said that, for he believed that he possessed the truth. But the spirit fired by a spark from Faust's is stricken with a sorrow that will never be healed, a longing that will never be stilled. This was Goethe's tragic mission : to instil Werther's melancholy and Faust's eternal restlessness into European literature, startling it out of its complacency and leading it forth along an endless path towards an unseen goal. But more than one man has already chosen this way, and is ready to be Faust's companion. The French Romantic writer, Alfred de Musset, in his *Confessions d'un Enfant du Siècle*, curses Goethe, the creator of Werther and Faust, for having so darkened his whole outlook on life without vouchsafing one comforting ray of light.

Other nations find German poetry uncomfortable and disturbing, with its absolute demands, its continual admonitory references to an idea which has apparently no counterpart in reality.

And yet all these obstacles seem slight compared with the fact that world literature is inextricably bound up with the progress of civilisation, the adjustment of differences, a common culture, and the establishment of a rational order. The idea of world literature is a product of modern European civilisation, and the two develop together. The aim of the German spirit was to rescue and preserve the values which seemed threatened with extinction by the progress of that civilisation. To the ever-spreading mechanisation of life, it opposed the organic growth of nature ; to the domination of reason, the irrational, obscure, creative energies of the soul, to the process of levelling, the aristocracy of genius. The German Romantic movement, which sponsored the European Romantic movement, was really a bold attempt to hold up a Europe devoted to progress. It was Germany's fate that its spirit should have conquered the world at a time when it was forced to try to stem the progressive movement ; that the first contribution of the German spirit to world literature threatened to shatter its outward form, which was after all founded on civilisation. It was not Goethe the citizen of Europe, the representative of reason and proportion, that dawned on the world of the Romance tongues ; it was the young Goethe of Storm and Stress ; not the German Classical but the German Romantic movement. This was natural, for herein lay the distinctive characteristic of German literature which the Romance literatures did not possess and could acquire only from this source, to free them from their over-rigid forms. The German Classical movement also had taken foreign models, Greece, Italy, France. The prolonged opposition of the world, which German literature had to overcome, was just as understandable.

How then did it come about that in spite of all opposition Goethe conquered the world ? Was it the power of his genius alone that swept all before it ? It is true that in Germany more than anywhere else it would take a genius of this immense stature to make his voice heard throughout the world. But even the greatest genius is not always heard by his own age. The times must be favourable. But when do they become favourable for any particular nation ? History makes it clear that Europe is so much one entity that every style either in art or poetry, whether Gothic or Renaissance or Baroque, becomes the common property of Europe. But we find also that every style originates with one particular people who bring it to perfection before it spreads to the others. Which shows that this style answers the universal, supra-national demands of the moment, but that these demands must first be realised by one people whose nature corresponds to them. So the times are favourable to a particular people when their need coincides with the universal demand of the moment, and they are able to meet it. Then it is that a nation's hour strikes, as it did for German literature towards the close of the 18th century. At that time Europe had grown tired of the

French Classicism and western culture which had dominated it throughout the century. Western civilisation with its narrow foundations of reason and uniformity had grown so effete, so old and hide-bound, that it was impossible for humanity's other deeper-lying powers to stir and force their way to the surface. Now the universal demand of history coincided with the true capacity and bent of German poetry. German poetry was able to renew and refresh a tired and ageing world, because its nature was so different from the French, and also because it was itself still young and still developing. The renewal of the European world, Goethe has noted, could come only from a nation such as the German which was not fully developed and static but was still vigorously struggling towards maturity. Only a people of this sort could become a fresh fountainhead for Europe. At that moment all Goethe needed to do was to express his own personal sufferings in Werther and in Faust, and he spoke for and to Europe. The world listened, and a world literature began to develop. Interaction and exchange began. It had been impossible to speak of a world literature as long as the literature of a great and civilised nation like the German was ignored.

It must be clear from all this that the influences which the literatures of different peoples exert on each other differ widely. They have the power to bind or to loose, to apportion systems or freedom, to mould or distort. The rhythm of any organic life in the individual, as in the life of peoples, swings between loosing and binding. In youth a man needs freedom, expansion, room for the development and blossoming of his life. In his prime he needs order, proportion, system, so that the fruit may grow to maturity, shapely and complete. There is the same rhythm in the life of peoples. But these two powers of binding and loosing are not given to every people. If we look at the history of human civilisation we see that some peoples can regulate themselves by their own sense of proportion, yet need the help of others when the moment comes for freedom. Other peoples must turn to foreign civilisations when the time comes for restrictions. Here we have the interaction between peoples. Their influence on each other differs according as they bind or loose, regulate or liberate. This is precisely the difference between the influence which German literature had on the Romance literatures, and vice versa. The Romance literatures, particularly French and Italian, received from German literature the benefit of release from rules and restraints. German literature received from Romance literatures the benefit of order, form, proportion. This may explain why, among the Romance peoples who in race and speech are a blend of the Germanic with the Classical, the Classical inheritance has never quite been lost, and why the educative influence of the Classics in Germanic literature almost always goes hand in hand with the Classicism of the Renaissance and of France. On every emergence of the Classical spirit the Germanic literatures have sought the help of France ; and in the hour of Romanticism, the Romance literatures call in the assistance of England and Germany.

It may seem strange that this word " romantic " comes from " romance " and was at one time identical with it. This is because the term " romance " was given to the languages and literatures resulting from a fusion of Roman and Germanic elements, to distinguish them from the old Roman language and literature. The new element which had been added to the Classical inheritance was the Germanic one. This explains why the name Romantic came to have a sense of contrast with Classical works and the Classical spirit, and was finally used for the literatures of the Germanic nations of England, Germany and Scandinavia. We can at least see clearly how the Romance literatures came to find the most essential quality of German poetry in its " romantic " aspect, and how it was this aspect which had a refreshing effect on the Romance literatures. The German Classical movement (i.e. the Classical element in German literature, even Goethe's and Schiller's works of the Weimar period) was considered romantic by other countries, and as such influenced the literatures of France and Italy. So even in this German poetry, which owes so much in inspiration and form to the Greeks and Romans, the Italian Renaissance and French Classicism, it was always the Germanic-Romantic element which was fixed upon as the essential feature. But, far more than the Classical Weimar period, it was the works of Goethe's and of Schiller's youth, the German " Storm-and-Stress " period, that influenced the Romance literatures. It was the literature of " Storm and Stress " that precipitated the Romantic movement in Europe by freeing it from the traditions and rules of Classicism. These traditions, radiating from France, had hitherto governed literature in Europe, even in Germany.

But Goethe, whose influence on the Romance literatures was so liberating, achieved quite another effect on the Germanic literatures, on English as well as German. Later we shall see more clearly how Goethe had quite different missions to fulfil in the Germanic world and in that of the Romance peoples. In the Germanic literatures he was the great advocate of form and proportion, the representative of morality and reason. For France he was a liberator from a rigid set of laws. For Germany, England and Switzerland he was a law-giver. That became possible only when Germany had learned proportion and form from the civilisations of the Græco-Romans and the Romance peoples. But this self-education on the part of Goethe, and the difference in his influence on Germanic and Romance literatures, reveal what is specifically German, namely the profound inner tension, which takes the form indeed of a tragic polarity, between the German nature and the German spirit. There is no doubt that by nature the German tends to Romanticism and is as far as can be from the Ancients. But the spirit of the German is one of absolute idealism, not content simply to take what nature has given him, but conscious of a mission, anxious to reach beyond his own propensities and to win for himself what nature has not endowed him with. The German nature finds its most complete expression in music, but the German spirit demands a concrete form. The German nature feels at home in a world of obscure, irrational forces, but the German spirit seeks the light of reason. The German nature claims the inner freedom of the personality, but the German spirit wants limitation by society, or the state, or art, in conformity with law and proportion. The German nature is content to seek pure truth, but the German spirit must have beauty. This is what makes German Classicism, of whatever origin, different from any other. Being a subjugation of its own nature, it developed in response to an ethical demand of the spirit, while the Italian Renaissance grew naturally out of Italy's innate feeling for form, and French Classicism out of France's innate love of reason. In short : it is natural for Faust to overstep his own personality and seek to unite himself with Helen. It is their union that first gives complete expression to what is specifically German, and this explains why the longing to forge a link with the Græco-Romans has always been a motive in the life of the German spirit. This longing was realised in Goethe, who in himself and in his art achieved the union of Faust and Helen ; and this makes it clear why his messages for the Germanic and the Romance literatures differed so greatly.

Why did Goethe's idea of world literature and its realisation, although a beginning had been made, never reach full expression, though we shall see how nearly this happened ?   The background of ideas was there.   Goethe's experience of the influence which foreign literatures had on him and he on them, confirmed his conviction of the desirableness of world literature.   In his youth, England had roused him to self-awareness, as France and Italy moulded him to Classicism.   His acknowledgment to England was his youthful speech on Shakespeare's Birthday, and the translation of *Ossian* in *Werther*.   His acknowledgment to Italy was the translation of Benvenuto Cellini (1796–7), and later his *Italian Journey*.   His acknowledgment to France was his translation of Diderot's *Essay on Painting* (1799) and *Rameau's Nephew*, which he translated from the original and first made known to the world in this way.   In the Weimar theatre he produced versions of Voltaire's dramas, in order that the whole German theatre might benefit by his own education through French art.   As for his own influence in the world, it began in his early years with his *Werther*.   He disliked speaking of this, and had good reason to do so.   He disclaimed responsibility for the Werther-fever.   It was not his work that had caused it ; his work had merely exposed the malady that lay hidden in the youth of Europe.   He was little inclined to speak openly of the influence which his works exerted abroad, as long as it was merely a question of isolated cases, of voices crying in the wilderness. There is proof enough that he was pleased to hear of translated versions of his maturer work.   For instance, he got his publisher Unger to issue a special *de luxe* edition of William Taylor's English translation of his *Iphigenia*.   He thanked his translators in letters full of cordial feeling.   In 1799 he devised a plan for publishing a comparison of the four translations of his epic *Hermann und Dorothea*, the Danish one by Jens Smith (1799), the French by Bitaubé (1800), the English by Holcroft (1801) and by Mellish (1798).[31]   But the project was never carried out.   Goethe made no public mention of any translation or of any influence of his works until the world-wide reactions to Mme de Staël's book *De l'Allemagne* made it clear that he had helped to arouse the Romantic spirit in Europe.

The second period in the development of his idea of world literature, and of his efforts to achieve it, then began.

In 1816 he became acquainted with Byron's *Manfred* and at once realised how his Faust had stood godfather to this poet who had charmed the world. They exchanged gifts and were soon on terms of intimacy. After Byron's death he made contact with Sir Walter Scott, who had once translated his *Götz von Berlichingen*. In 1818 he learned that the quarrel between the Classicists and the Romanticists, which had first flamed up in German literature, was now beginning to smoulder beyond the Alps in Italy. He established cordial relations with Manzoni. In France, since the appearance of Mme de Staël's book, signs were multiplying that even French literature, which had for so long been closed to German literary influence, was beginning to be conscious of it. There, too, the quarrel between Classicists and Romanticists broke out. The *Globe*, the organ of the French Romanticists, which Goethe began to read in 1824, marked a real epoch in his labours for world literature. For, from now on, Goethe in his journal *Kunst und Altertum* drew the attention of his fellow-countrymen to everything in the literatures of Europe that in any way reflected the German spirit. This was not done in an attempt to exalt German self-confidence but rather to increase German self-awareness, toleration and recognition of foreign nations.

By the 1820's, there were so many inter-connections between Goethe and foreign literatures that he thought of devoting a whole volume to them in the definitive edition of his works. Vol. XXXVIII was to be *Rameau's Nephew, by Diderot, and other excerpts from French, English and Italian literature, with reference to the author's relations with writers and men of letters belonging to these countries* (1826). A scheme he drew up tells us Goethe's intention more clearly. " French literature. Diderot and relevant matter. English literature. Lord Byron, Walter Scott. Italian literature. Monti, Bondi and Manzoni. All with special reference to my own point of view."

In his diary for 8th May 1826 he notes : " Dictated matter concerning my relations with foreign literatures and men of letters." This is in three sections and is only in the form of notes. It shows that Goethe planned one single comprehensive treatment of the attitude adopted to him in other literatures and by men of letters in France, England and Italy ; also of his reactions to them, from *Werther* onwards. Obviously the chief stress was to be laid on his relations with the French Romantic movement taking shape in the *Globe* and with Byron and Manzoni. What interested him was not establishing the fact of his influence, but something deeper : What was the cause of this influence ? Why was *Werther*'s influence greater than that of his other works ? How did it come about that his works had such a powerful influence on the French Romantic movement, as the *Globe* showed to be the case ?   On 15th January 1827 he dictated to Schuchardt matter " concerning French and world literature ".   The phrase shows that a step has been taken, and that there is a certain change in his attitude to world literature.   It was his own personal relations with foreign literatures and men of letters, that had crystallised his idea in the first place.   But it is clear from the Scheme " Towards a History of French Literature " (January 1827) that Goethe wished to show also the influence of German literature on the French, who had first been familiarised with it by Villers, Constant and Mme de Staël.   Three connected Schemes belong to the year 1828 : " French Interest in German Literature ", " English and Scottish Interest in German Literature ", " Italian Interest in German Literature ".   The titles themselves show an important difference between this plan and that of 1826, in which Goethe had wanted to point only to his own personal connections with other countries.   Now he wanted to treat all the relationships from the points of view of the countries concerned.   There was the philosophical influence of German idealism which helped the French to overcome their bias towards sensationalism and empiricism.   There was also the æsthetic influence, through which their modern spirit (already " far along the Romantic road " although not admittedly so) was breaking down the rigidity of the classical form.   When dealing with the interest of the English and the Scottish in German literature, Goethe wished to mention the thorough nature of their studies to which they had given wide publicity.   They valued public opinion, and were ready to meet any intelligent opposition, however strong.   German literature was being read in England and Scotland, but could not yet be said to have an effective influence there ; that might be expected to develop later.   In the case of Italian influence, Goethe sought to trace Manzoni's sympathetic attitude to the fact that he had been justly appreciated in Germany.   The virile character of the journal *L'Eco* and of the Italian public, were to be referred to.   We can see that Goethe's endeavours in the cause of world literature have taken on a largely objective character.   While they originated in the realisation of his own personal influence, he was later able to view the relations of literatures to one another on their own merits.   The next Scheme belongs to the year 1829 and to it Eckermann has given the title : " German attitude to other countries, in particular to the French ".[33] This Scheme aims at making Germany realise the advantages of being increasingly known and recognised by foreign nations. It must distinguish clearly how and what other nations choose to take from it, and how they deal with what they have selected. In this connection the following questions arise :

1. Whether other nations admit the ideas which we hold with regard to our morals and our art.
2. How far they can appreciate and utilise the results of our learning.
3. To what extent they make use of our æsthetic forms.
4. To what extent they handle, in ways of their own, material which we have already treated.

Goethe gave the following answers with regard to the French :

(1) The French now profess the German philosophy which admits what is due to man's inner nature, as distinct from what he receives from outside. They have also reflected on the union of the two elements. (Goethe was thinking here of Victor Cousin.)

(2) They now admire those of our works of learning which we also esteem, especially Savigny and Niebuhr.

(3) They are obviously making an attempt to adapt themselves to our æsthetic forms, for the dramatised histories of the more recent school, for example *The Barricades* (by Vitet), are paving the way for real theatrical works of this type. We could also show, in our literature, parallels to the *Theatre of Clara Gazul* (by Mérimée).

(4) It often happens that they handle material which we have already treated. But the French writer is constantly obliged to make alterations, for he has his own particular attitude to his public whom he must humour in the old traditional way. But what chiefly hinders him from producing a serious work is the fact that he has to cater for an *impatient* public that demands to be stimulated and shaken up all the time. So it is rare that any of our works can reach them in their original form. It is noticeable too that a morbid element has grown up among them along with the Romantic one, and that recovery is more likely to come from our side.

The next Scheme belonging to the year 1832 " For *Kunst und Altertum*, Volume VI, Number 36 ", shows that Goethe was on the point of carrying out his plan, and was going to publish it in

Kunst und Altertum. Its title is " European, that is to say, world literature ".[34] It is more coherent than the earlier Schemes, is supported by more instances, and also differentiates more clearly between the nations in their relation to German literature. Obviously the interaction between the nations, not merely German influence, was to be treated, and this meant a new and higher level of objectivity. The Germans, it is said here, work for themselves without reference to other countries, and have reached a high point of learning and culture. But the French have always been accustomed to exert an influence on others. They rate this influence highly, and have in fact dispensed from their superior level what one may call social culture. But in the deeper aspects of culture they have not been able to avoid foreign influence. They have to enlist the help of English and Scottish philosophy to free them from sensationalism. They will gradually become aware of German philosophy and find it will open up for them a world of ideas. It will help them to utilise their knowledge in a manner which from the empiricist's narrow point of view might appear romantic. Some acquaintance with the work of isolated German authors is found here and there among Englishmen ; among the Scots the German influence was apparently deeper and more general.

All the Schemes prove that Goethe planned a comprehensive exposition of the relations between the German, French, English and Italian literatures of his day in connection with world literature. There are also contemporary proofs that he planned a systematic exposition of his idea of it, including what he understood by it, what aims and limits were assigned to it, what benefits and dangers it involved, what were the tasks of the different nations within it. There are notes [35] intended as material for Goethe's preface to the German translation of Carlyle's Schiller-biography. This preface is one of the most important statements of Goethe's idea of world literature, and much of the material in the above-mentioned Schemes is incorporated in it. No doubt Goethe's intention was to develop this preface and to make it a comprehensive and systematic statement of his idea.

Why did Goethe not carry out any of these plans although he had this idea so much at heart during the last ten years of his life, and his thoughts were so constantly focused on it ? We can only suggest that Goethe always showed a certain disinclination for any systematic exposition of philosophical subjects. Even those on scientific topics are somewhat in the nature of facile aphorisms. As he advanced in years, all his expositions, even those in his creative works such as the *Wanderjahre* and the Second Part of *Faust*, became slighter and less detailed. Indeed, his ideas had always sprung not so much from any strict system of thought as from an intuitive quality. This was certainly fed by his experience, but was most naturally and easily expressed in the form of suggestions and aphorisms. Goethe called the whole body of his poetical work occasional poetry, a poetic confession. One might equally call his scientific work occasional science, a scientific confession, for it too was the outcome of his preoccupation of the moment. But there was also a special reason why no full and systematic exposition of his work for world literature was possible. In 1827, he wrote to Streckfuss, the translator of Dante : " If there is any foreign literary work on which you would like to make a brief pronouncement, do so and let me know of it. The productions of the different nations tumble over each other so fast that we must find some new way of getting to know them and discussing them." This gathering speed of material and intellectual traffic between the nations was characteristic of the time and had always been one reason for Goethe's confidence in the advent of world literature. And the short review was an excellent means of keeping up with its rapid progress.

All this combined to prevent Goethe from realising his plans for a comprehensive systematic exposition of his idea of world literature based on an empirical view of history. It is remarkable how Goethe in his writings, letters and conversations, when he does speak of it, repeatedly makes evasive observations such as : that further detail would lead one on too far, that he must refrain from it, leave it to others, that for the present he wishes merely to hint at it, that he has no space to deal further with the matter. One is obliged therefore to build up the structure from hundreds of scattered fragments.

Such fragments are to be found in letters, conversations, diaries, schemes and the interest he showed in Byron, Manzoni and Carlyle ; also in his journal *Kunst und Altertum*. This journal was begun in 1816 as the result of his travels in the Rhine and Main valleys. Its original aim was to deal with whatever national antiquities he found in his own district, and to discuss how he could preserve and breathe new life into them. Soon, however, German was joined by Greek antiquity, and pictorial by poetical art. By the second volume (1820), we have articles dealing with world literature, the Classical and Romantic writers in Italy, Byron, Manzoni. The third volume (1823) contains a great deal about world poetry. In 1824 Goethe began to read the *Globe*, and through it realised that the longing for international friendship and intellectual intercourse was no longer confined to isolated individuals but was a universal characteristic of the youth of Europe. He had further proof of this soon after, in 1827, in the English and Scottish periodicals and the Italian *Eco*. This brought him to realise to what an extent foreign literatures were growing aware of German literature. Following the example of the *Globe*, Goethe urged German literature to look round to see itself reflected in the judgments of other nations, to collect its own impressions of other literatures, and to encourage reciprocal interest. " These journals," he wrote, " as they gradually reach a wider public, will contribute most effectively to the universal world literature for which we hope." ³⁶ After 1826, when his translations from the *Globe* began to appear, in the last period of his efforts for world literature, Goethe used his journal to show his own nation how it was reflected in foreign literatures. He was tireless in urging it to reciprocate the efforts of other nations to do justice to the German point of view. Goethe began to pass on those " reflections " of German literature by displaying the picture of himself as he had seen it in the *Globe*. This was by no means a sign of pride or vanity. In all his works, creative as well as theoretical, Goethe needed to make use of his own personal experiences, and he had to experience the benefit of " reflection " in his own case before he could make others share it with him. He found his own example of German influence in the world the surest, because he had experienced it himself. So, in 1827, when he heard of Alexandre Duval's adaptation of his *Tasso*, and the comparisons between the original and the adaptation which were made in the *Journal de Commerce* and the *Globe*, he wrote the following words : The reports which he gave from foreign journals were not merely intended to remind people of him and his own works ; they had a higher aim at which he would for the present merely hint. One heard and read on all sides of the progress of the human race, of the widened prospects in world conditions and the state of mankind. Whatever might be the truth of this in general, he would like to draw the attention of his friends to his personal conviction that a universal world literature was developing, in which Germans had an honourable part to play. The eyes of every nation were upon them ; they praised, blamed, imitated or misrepresented them ; they were for or against the German influence.

It is still more important to establish the fact that, in the third period of his activity in the cause of world literature, from 1827 onwards, there is a marked increase in Goethe's objectivity. The reports on the reception abroad of his own works continue. He notes Stapfer's translation of *Faust* with Delacroix' illustrations, " Helen in Edinburgh, Paris and Moscow " and the reception in France of his ideas of world literature. In his introduction to Carlyle's *Life of Schiller* he speaks of his own contacts with the Scottish author, as he had spoken of those with Byron and Manzoni. In his poem " A Parable " he expressed the feeling of refreshment that came over him when he heard his poems in a foreign language ; and he published the poem he wrote for the fifteen English friends who had sent him a gift in token of their admiration. During the same period, he reported how the editors of the *Globe* had praised Schiller's works when writing about Alexandre Soumet's *Elisabeth de France*, a drama modelled on his dead friend's *Don Carlos* ; and how they had made honourable mention of Schiller's *Warbeck* and *Demetrius* when writing of Fontan's *Warbeck*. They had stressed Schiller's great superiority and, in urging further work on the lines of *Wilhelm Tell*, they mentioned the refreshing influence that George Moir's English translation of *Wallenstein* might have, and with what respect, love and insight Carlyle had written his *Life of Schiller*. Goethe also recommended Quinet's translation of Herder's *Ideas for a Philosophy of the History of Mankind*, with Quinet's introduction. (When he later heard of Goethe's death, Quinet dedicated to Goethe the new edition of his work.) Goethe drew attention also to Carlyle's *German Romance*, versions of masterpieces of the German Romantic writers ; and he recommended the German papers to translate Carlyle's prefatory notes on the individual authors. He also informed his readers of the critical discussions of the works of German Romantic writers in the English and Scottish periodicals. It is obvious that his activities went far beyond his own writings and dealt with the whole of German literature as it was seen in other countries. Indeed it is noticeable that, although deeply gratified by it, he made no public mention of what was perhaps the greatest tribute ever paid to him. That was the presentation, at the close of his life (1830), by the French Romantic writers of their works along with medallions bearing the portraits of the authors.

Deschamps did much to broaden the content of French poetry by his use and adaptations of foreign forms in the *Études Françaises et Étrangères*, which he sent to Goethe. His preface to these studies is one of the most important manifestations of the French Romantic movement, in spite of his including among them a translation of the *Bride of Corinth*, which Mme de Staël had declared to be untranslatable. Deschamps had to be content with a verbal message of thanks (brought by the sculptor David) which did not even mention the translation, although in conversation with Eckermann Goethe had praised it as accurate and successful. This " approbation of the distinguished Goethe, an ample recompense for so much criticism " was enough to make Deschamps feel it his sacred duty from now on to spread abroad, by every means, the principles and methods of application laid down in the preface. We read this in the preface to Deschamps' later collection of poems *Poésie*, which also contains translations of the Mignon- and Gretchen-songs, the " Erlking", the " Fisher " and the " King in Thule ". Goethe made no public mention even of Gérard de Nerval's translation of *Faust*, the third and most important after those by St. Aubain and Stapfer, and the one which really gave *Faust* to France and determined its influence in French literature ; yet Goethe in conversation with Eckermann expressed great appreciation of it. And the public were not informed of the tribute Berlioz paid in 1829 by sending the score of his *Faust* with an accompanying letter.

But the growing objectivity in Goethe's labours for world literature is seen not only in acts of renunciation like these, nor in the fact that he called attention to the influence of German literature (not merely his own influence) abroad. It is seen also in his recommendation of foreign works which had nothing at all to do with German literature, and with whose authors Goethe had had no previous communication. Examples of these are Lemercier's historical comedy *Richelieu*, and the memoirs of Robert Guillemard which appeared in 1827 in a German translation introduced and prefaced by Goethe, and Taschereau's " *Histoire de la Vie et des Ouvrages de Molière* ". Of course these recommendations are unimportant compared with articles which actually portray German literature. But Goethe prompted other authors, Streckfuss the translator of Dante, for instance, to send him reports on foreign works for his *Kunst und Altertum*. (At Goethe's instigation Streckfuss wrote critiques of Manzoni's novel *I Promessi Sposi* and Niccolini's tragedy *Antonio Foscarini*, which Goethe had sent him. At Goethe's suggestion Streckfuss also translated Manzoni's tragedy *Adelchi*.) When writing about the Comédie Française and describing the transformation of the French stage from the " pure, regulated, so-called classical type " to the romantic dramatisation of history, it is noticeable that Goethe does not mention the remarkable influence of his *Götz von Berlichingen*, although many references prove that he was aware of it. But he reached the highest pitch of objectivity in his comparisons between the different literatures of Europe. These displayed his sovereign standpoint overlooking every nation, and his judgment which nothing could disturb. Goethe had often deprecated comparisons, as he did in the " Warnung " among the notes to the *West-Eastern Divan*. Here he bids us compare the oriental poets with each other, honour them by their own standards and forget all about the Greeks and Romans. We ought not to compare Firdusi with Homer, for he would certainly be the loser in every way—in material, form and treatment. Goethe claims that we have done untold harm to our glorious *Nibelungen* by this kind of comparison, measuring it by the yard-stick of Homer, which was absurd. We ought to praise, choose and reject without comparison. In a letter written in 1826, he writes : " Not to confine all our praise and honour to the English, I must inform you that the coronation poem by M. De Lavigne is really excellent. It strengthens my conviction that comparisons are unnecessary ; one ought to treat and judge nations, poets, authors and persons individually." These remarks mean, of course, that a sense of justice ought to prevent us from estimating one production by comparison with another. Differences in the nature of the works, and the intentions underlying them, would make the application of the same standard of judgment to all impossible. But Goethe's scientific studies had so thoroughly accustomed him to comparing phenomena as to their similarity and characteristic differences that he did the same in the world of thought. " All natural history is based on comparison," he writes in his *Morphology*. As a disciple of Herder he had always been accustomed to comparison, and he appreciated the valuable results of the comparative method in Wilhelm von Humboldt's treatment of language, and in Humboldt's letters on the German and the French theatre. In fact, we can fairly consider Goethe as one of the most important precursors of the study of comparative literature, and how indeed could the creator of the idea of world literature have dispensed with

comparison ?   It is one of the most important methods by which
world literature establishes intercourse between the nations and
makes them known to each other.   As early as 1801, Goethe
had thought of publishing a comparison of four translations of
Hermann und Dorothea.   When he was writing the *West-Eastern
Divan* he was amazed to see how the different nationalities—
French, English and German—treated the vast amount of oriental
literary material, each in its own way, as indeed one must if one
is to gain anything from them.   *Kunst und Altertum* for 1817
contains an item, " Verdicts of French Critics ".   For Goethe
had observed that the intellect and character of a man, as of a
nation, are seen most clearly in his judgments.   He found in
French criticism more blame than praise.   When, however, the
Brussels *Vrai Libéral* protested against his findings in support of
the French spirit, he admitted readily in his journal (1820) that
he had taken all his extracts from Grimm's literary Bulletin.
At the same time he announced his intention " to speak in the
near future on this extremely important subject".   But he never
did so.   The notes that Goethe added as early as 1817 to the
" Verdicts " collection contain suggestions of comparisons with
English, German and Russian criticism, and this subject
demanded further development.   In the latter period of his
activity in the cause of world literature, when he had reached
the highest level of objectivity, comparison between the nations
is found in an open and methodical form.   We find it several
times, also, in connection with his own works, which he saw
being treated in different ways by different nations.   Here too
we can observe an increasing objectivity.   In the essay, " The
Three Pariahs " (1824), he compares his own pariah legend with
a German and a French pariah tragedy.   In this case, however,
it is not what is specifically national that he stresses.   He contrasts the " tragic, cruel motive " of those dramas " for entertainment and edification " with his own treatment, which represents
the supreme deity as reconciling the contrasting elements.   If
we compare this essay with the later one (1828), " Helen in
Edinburgh, Paris and Moscow ", the higher degree of objectivity
in this later period is obvious.   For now Goethe is comparing
an English essay on his Helen by Carlyle, a French one by
Ampère, and a Russian one by Shevirev, and he remarks with
laconic simplicity : " The Scot tries to penetrate the work, the
Frenchman to understand it, the Russian to assimilate it.   In
so doing Messrs. Carlyle, Ampère and Shevirev have, without

knowing each other's intention, exemplified every one of the possible categories of interest that may be taken in any product of art or nature." But comparisons of this sort belonging to the last period by no means invariably deal with Goethe's own works ; and they are not limited to a comparative treatment of lands and peoples, and their ways of expressing themselves in world poetry. In the essay, "English Drama in Paris", he compares the German and French treatments of Shakespeare. The Germans seek with characteristic thoroughness to penetrate to his essential nature and pay willing tribute to the value of his material and the subjects of his works ; they try to trace the course of his method, to analyse his characters, and in spite of all their efforts they do not seem to reach their aim. The French, on the other hand, with their active practical sense, go to work in quite a different way. They first savour the delight of seeing the most outstanding English actors in the most famous and popular works, and seeing them as it were at home ; this gives them, in dealing with what is foreign to them, the great advantage of retaining their own standards. So, when they throw aside worthless prejudices and apply these standards with an open mind to what is foreign, they do so with the best chance of forming an impartial judgment. They do not concern themselves with the essential nature of the poet or his works, which would in any case be quite unfathomable. They note the effect, on which after all everything depends. And, as they are favourably disposed to it, they put into words what every spectator feels or ought to feel, whether he is aware of it or not. Goethe compares the "French Drama in Berlin" with the English drama in Paris. Also the virile qualities of the Italian and French journals *Eco* and *Globe* are compared, and both are then compared with the German journals, which for the most part are written by, and almost exclusively for, women.[37]

We see that Goethe sought by all means to draw attention to the beginnings of world literature and to foster its growth ; and for this work his most important medium was his journal *Kunst und Altertum*.

In carrying out its lofty intentions this journal met with considerable obstacles from the start, as indeed did the whole literature of Germany. The *Globe*'s greatest source of strength was that a whole generation met and worked together for it in one spirit and with one aim. Unanimity like this gives a spiritual movement driving power, and it was just this that Goethe so sadly missed in German literature, where each writer worked as an isolated individual. The concentration in one capital, Paris, was not merely a political symbol but an embodiment of the communal spirit of French life. Germany had no capital resembling Paris, and its literature had no intellectual fraternity such as would have made possible a journal like the *Globe*. When Schiller tried with his *Horen* to create a literary group to be the editors of the journal, and so to unite the German public round an intellectual centre, the enterprise soon failed, although some of the greatest minds in Germany were among the members of the groups. That is one of the greatest differences between the journals in Germany which then served the cause of world literature and those of France, between the *Globe* and *Kunst und Altertum*. The *Globe* was the rallying-ground of the " Globists ", among them the best French writers of the day : whereas Goethe had to carry the burden of his journal almost alone. The collaboration of other authors in the field of world literature was negligible. The journal *Kunst und Altertum* was Goethe's mouthpiece only, through which he tried to speak to his people and to the world. This was not due to any Olympian aloofness in Goethe—he simply found no helper available. The Romantic writers were quite out of the question. The older Romantic writers' idea of world literature differed widely from Goethe's. His chief aim, the bringing of contemporaries from different nations to work together, was completely foreign to that movement, which concentrated on the past. And the younger Romantic writers extolled a nationalism to which Goethe's idea of world literature was directly opposed. Goethe himself did not consider even Germany's best writers capable of the refined and polished social tone which struck him so agreeably in the *Globe*. Their isolation, as he put it, was always obvious, whereas one felt the Globists to belong to " good society ". So that, in contrast to German critics, they were polite and courtly even where they blamed, and this was a very necessary attitude in an international exchange of ideas. The writers of " Young Germany " had hardly yet emerged. True, they took up Goethe's idea ; for example, Gutzkow in his essay " Goethe at the Turn of the Century " (1835) and Wienberg in his article " Goethe and World Literature ". But in his lifetime Goethe stood completely alone, and his work for world literature failed to unite the German public (except with reference to himself). Nor did it convince other countries that German literature had become or was in process of becoming world literature, however much that literature and its influence rose in the estimation of other countries. Goethe's isolation was then the first obstacle in his success as a medium in the cause of world literature.

The second was the language. What an immeasurable advantage both the French and English journals had in speaking a world-wide literary language, and how little Goethe was read even in those days in England and France! And journals do not lend themselves to translation.

The third obstacle was Goethe's age. We must bear in mind that the *Globe* represented the literary youth of France, and this gave it energy. Goethe had imagined Ampère, perhaps the *Globe*'s most outstanding critic, to be a middle-aged man, on account of his ripe judgment, his understanding of the inter-actions of life and poetry, and his wide range of interests. So he was astounded when in 1827 Ampère appeared in Weimar, and turned out to be a cheerful youth of about twenty, and when he found that the entire staff of the *Globe* was composed of young men. Goethe decided that the reason for this pheno-menon (unthinkable in Germany) lay in the atmosphere of Paris. There the best brains of a great empire were gathered together, helping and stimulating each other in daily intercourse and rivalry. There the world's treasures of every realm of nature and art were assembled for all to see. There one was surrounded by reminders of a glorious past. And there, during three generations, men like Molière, Voltaire and Diderot had gradu-ally created an intellectual atmosphere such as might never again be found anywhere. This was the reason, Goethe affirmed, why in France talent could develop so quickly and so happily. In Germany there was no such fertile soil for growth. How hard and slow Goethe's own self-won education had been, although he might seem to be Germany's most fortunate poet. German youth was for the most part too self-absorbed to be capable (as the Globists were) of a frank and ready approach to others. To German eyes it was the ageing Goethe who surpassed the youth of any foreign literature in range, wisdom and intellect. But to the world at large the ageing Goethe meant almost nothing. It was his youth that lived again in the youth of Europe, in the Romantic movements. It was this that brought about such a strange relationship between Goethe and his contemporaries. He felt gratified, it is true, when he saw that the results of the solitary questing of his youth had become the common property of Europe. But the Romantic movement in Europe, which honoured him as ancestor and as head, did not correspond in any fundamental way to his last stage of development. He could enrich Europe by the achievements of his youth. But his maturer years inevitably suffered from a certain disparity with the youth of Europe, and, in spite of all Goethe's elasticity, this disparity began to be apparent. The mere title *Kunst und Altertum* reveals much. In his journal, Goethe was trying to rescue an old tradition from which the youth of Europe wanted to shake itself free.

There was, of course, one great compensation to set against all these handicaps : Goethe's international reputation, the stupendous power of his name, which gave to his every pronouncement incomparable weight. This is made clear, for instance, by what he was able to do for Byron, for Manzoni, for the Serbian folk-songs. But his work for world literature was limited to a certain extent by the form its evolution took during his maturer years. The European Romantic movement, which unlike the German Romantic movement was a foretaste of modern literature, showed its modernity in its political, even revolutionary, character. Even in the *Globe*, in its literary criticism, in the collapse of the rules dear to the classicists, one could feel the revolutionary spirit which did not escape Goethe's notice, and which he could not approve. The fusion of literature and politics was against his principles, and, as Soret once said, he was against " anything that has a revolutionary look ". When the *Globe* became a daily paper and began to carry political as well as literary articles, Goethe's interest in it lessened considerably. In this, too, the difference between him and the European Romantic movement is clear. But the course of modern history has decided against Goethe. The turning aside of the mind of Europe to politics has had the effect of heightening the tension between nations. It has thwarted the realisation of Goethe's dream of an international community of the spirit ; and the eyes of hope must still be fixed on the future.

PART II
BENEFITS RECEIVED

CHAPTER 5

THE STIMULUS OF ENGLISH LITERATURE

Goethe knew from his own experience that a receptive attitude to the intellectual influences of other nations was beneficial and had helped him to formulate his idea of world literature. Apropos of this, influence must not be confused with imitation to which it bears the same relationship as does the natural growth of organic life to mechanical production. Influence becomes effective only when the moment is propitious and where there exists a predisposition in the recipient, called " Influenz " or Influenza. A foreign element provokes a diseased state, and may irritate or even quite destroy the living organism. Owing to Goethe's immensely healthy condition, he knew with the certainty of instinct at every stage of his development what suited his own nature, what stimulus he needed from outside, what spiritual nourishment he must take and what avoid as a potential danger. He would suffer no foreign element in his nature, and kept his distance from even the greatest and most influential minds when these were not suited to his development at that particular juncture. On the other hand, he always welcomed any influence which he could expect to help and stimulate his own nature at the appropriate time. In his youth, when he stood in need of an awakening and liberating influence, he had been profoundly affected by Shakespeare. Later, at a stage when Shakespeare might have endangered the Classical maturity which he had reached, Goethe turned elsewhere. One has only to compare young Goethe's enthusiastic Shakespeare-day speech with the frigid tone of the older Goethe's essay " Shakespeare Without End ". Similarly, in his youth he resisted Voltaire, but later singled him out as a master. He gave himself up to the Persian poet Háfiz at a time when he felt himself in danger of stiffening in the Classical mould ; he was ready to suffer extinction in order to live anew, to emerge from his surrender refreshed and transformed. The meaning of " Stirb und Werde " is that surrender may lead to a rebirth.

But influence from a foreign mind may be one of two kinds. It can take the form of one creative spirit being roused to self-knowledge, and stimulated to further creation, by a kindred one ; this reinforces his own nature and gives him the courage to be himself, as Shakespeare did in Goethe's case. We recognise an active influence when we find a writer following Herder's injunction and imitating a foreign writer by whom he feels deeply moved. He can do this simply by being as primitive and original as the other, relying, as that other did, purely on his own nature and that of his nation. But the influence may be of a totally different kind when it proceeds not from a kindred spirit but from one which is different or even opposite, at least at the time when the influence is felt. This influence need not necessarily confirm and arouse, it may transform. But even then it is helpfully stimulating (as opposed to " Influenz "), only when it coincides with a moment at which a man of creative mind is himself urgently desirous of transformation. This influence must not change his actual being, must not draw him aside from his path, but must help his transformation and raise him to a higher stage of organic development. This is what happened to Goethe in his contact with French Classicism, and later with the East. No one can hope to understand the relationships between the literatures of the different peoples who has not grasped this difference in the types of influence, or who does not realise that effect and influence, at least with creative minds, means only the advancement of a man's own natural organic development, the fertilisation of his own creative power. This can be achieved either by arousing or by transforming him. And what is true of the individual is true also of the whole people.

But there is another point. Goethe himself declares in his autobiography *Dichtung und Wahrheit* that from his youth up he had been firmly convinced (whether as a result of his own or another's thought, he did not know), that in every work handed down to posterity the important thing is the basis, the meaning of the work. In these lies what is original and active, what can neither be disparaged nor destroyed, whose real essence time cannot touch ; whereas the framework, that is to say the language, the characteristics, the style, may not be completely understood by other men at other times and in other places. It is therefore the duty of each one of us to examine what is essential and intrinsic in any writing to which we feel particularly drawn, and above all to consider what relation it bears to our own essential nature and how far its vital power may stimulate and enrich ours. But everything extrinsic that leaves us cold, or raises a doubt in us, should be subjected to criticism. For criticism, though it should be capable of analysing the work in question, can never go so far as to rob us of the essentials to which we cling, or to confuse even for an instant our adherence once established. On this conviction, the result of belief and experience alike, the structure of Goethe's moral and literary life is built. Through it the Bible, for example, first came to have a meaning for him. It is essential to grasp this if we wish to understand the influences exerted on Goethe by literary works : they proceeded from the spirit, the real essence of the work, and not from its perishable framework.

Goethe's autobiography, from which these words are taken, is our chief source of information about his education through foreign literatures—for the period of his youth only, of course ; he carried the autobiography only up to his arrival in Weimar. It was his absorption in it that first made Goethe decide to identify all the sources which had contributed to his education and development. In his endeavour to describe the impulses from within, the influences from without, the theoretical and practical stages which he reached, he was gradually drawn out from his narrow private existence into the world of others. The figures of many men of mark, who in a greater or lesser degree had influenced him, can be seen ; and the vast movement of political evolution, which had exerted such a profound influence on him, as on his whole generation, must be particularly noted. In Goethe's view, the chief task of a biography is to place a man in relation to his age, and to show how far it hindered or helped him, how he derived from it a philosophy of life, and how as artist, poet or author he reflected it in his own work. But for this there are certain requirements ; the individual must know himself—the self which in all circumstances remains identical— and he must know the age he lives in. The age in which a man lives bears him along with it, willing or unwilling, conditioning him so irresistibly that a man born a mere ten years earlier or later might, in his own development and his influence on others, be a completely different being. Thus, when Goethe speaks of effect and influences, he does not merely mean those that have their origin in literature, but the whole political, social, moral, religious and æsthetic circumstances of the age. In *Dichtung und Wahrheit* we learn that he derived his education from all these factors. It may be dangerous to isolate literature and deal only with its influences, for it is but one item in a complex whole. Yet this item, if understood aright, can be taken to represent the whole. For literature is the most essential precipitate of the spirit of any age.

The age in which Goethe was born displayed the supremacy of the French spirit at its zenith, and up to his arrival in Strassburg young Goethe's education was exclusively modelled on French literary standards. The works of his earlier youth testify to this. The easy grace of the Rococo, the conventional, aristocratic dignity of Classicist tragedy, the materialistic view of nature taken by the Encyclopædists, and particularly the rationalistic religion of Voltaire : these were the forces which first shaped him. Even in his old age, Goethe confessed to Eckermann what enormous importance Voltaire and his great contemporaries had had in his youth, and how they had dominated the whole civilised world. He added that his autobiography had not sufficiently stressed what an influence these men had had on his youth, and what it had cost him to resist them and to win for himself the right relationship to nature.

Thus the age into which Goethe was born was not merely under the spiritual domination of France, but the zenith of that domination had already been reached and was gradually being passed. Goethe's youth coincided with the liberation of the German spirit from a foreign mould, and in opposition to it a new German literature was beginning to develop. Frederick the Great's struggle with France had awakened national consciousness in Germany, and Lessing with his *Hamburg Dramaturgy* went still further. He protested against imitation of French Classicism as being unsuited to the German mind, and asserted that Shakespeare, the Germanic writer, was the appointed leader of the German drama. Rousseau, too, had appeared as the great counterpart to Voltaire, and contrasted the doctrine of return to nature with the social conventionalism and over-refinement of French culture. Even before Rousseau, Albrecht von Haller's poetry of the Alps had in the same way applauded the national life of the Swiss in contrast to the perversion of French civilisation. Salomon Gessner's idylls sang the glories of primitive man's natural morality. Bodmer and Breitinger, natives of Zürich, voiced the adverse criticism of the exclusive preoccupation of Gottsched and his followers with France, and drew attention to Milton, the English writer of *Paradise Lost*. This explains how it was that Swiss literature became, for young Goethe and for his age, an awakening force of considerable importance. Even in France the literary revolution against Classicism had begun, for Diderot had revolted against its disregard for truth and nature, and was urging realism in artistic presentation. This was a proof of the way in which transformation in literature and art corresponds to a universal demand of the particular moment in history, and that the demand which can be realised fully only by those peoples whose nature and conscious trend are most suited for it. Diderot, like Lessing, remained under the influence of England. Thus the literary epoch into which Goethe was born developed by opposition to the preceding one. And the literatures which raised this opposition to the world of French art and French society were the Germanic ones, the literatures of Switzerland and Germany, and still more that of England, which had roused the others to self-awareness. It was in Strassburg, on the fringe of France, that Goethe suddenly freed himself from everything French. French literature no longer attracted the eager youth, because (to use his own words in *Dichtung und Wahrheit*) it had grown too " correct ", too " old ", and because the influence of conventional society had gradually so gained the mastery over the writers that they had nothing to offer a young man in need of freedom. The French language had been a favourite of Goethe's from his youth. Through contact and practice it had become like a second mother-tongue to him. But, when he wished to acquire greater fluency in it and for that reason went to Strassburg, he was repelled rather than attracted by this very language, and those very manners. His watchwords were now nature, truth, sincerity of feeling and expression ; and his aversion to Voltaire grew daily stronger.

There is no doubt, as we have already said, that Swiss literature, Rousseau and Haller and Gessner, played a very important part in awakening Goethe to a consciousness of himself and his own nature. But Switzerland was turning its gaze away from France to England, and thus it was English literature which exercised the deepest and most decisive influence on young Goethe. It was English literature which directed the teutonisation of German literature in the 18th century.

When we consider really great men in their relation to the intellectual world, we can always see how they regard the possessions of all times and peoples as their own, and how they laugh at the carping minds that seek to cast up an account, and reproach them for appropriating what belongs to others. They absorb these possessions as they do air and food. These are the air and food of the spirit, and in the presence of the best works of any age and people great men do not scruple to ask whether those works are calculated to arouse and promote their own productivity. They express their gratitude in their own work, which reaps the benefit and passes it on to the rest of the intellectual world. Goethe himself vigorously repelled any reproach levelled against him for borrowing from this or that writer. He wished that Byron had done it also.

What is there is mine ! he ought to have said, no matter whether it is taken from life or from a book ; all that matters is that I should use it rightly. Sir Walter Scott used a scene from my *Egmont*, and he had a right to do so ; and because he did it with understanding, he should be commended for it. He also modelled a character in one of his novels on my Mignon ; whether he was wise in doing so is another question. Lord Byron's transformed devil is a continuation of my Mephistopheles, and that is quite in order. If in straining after originality he had tried to introduce some variation he would certainly have done worse. My Mephistopheles sings a Shakespeare song, and why should he not ? Why should I trouble to devise one of my own when Shakespeare's fitted in and said just what was wanted ? If the exposition in my *Faust* has some similarity to that in the book of Job, that is again perfectly in order, and I ought to be praised for it rather than blamed " (To Eckermann, 1825).

But we need not think in this connection merely of such details as one literature takes over from another, nor of all the themes and subjects which are no one man's possession but belong to all peoples and all ages. We must think rather of those most vital and profound influences which one spirit can exert over another by the power to bind or to loose. For the rhythm of binding and loosing is the rhythm of the spiritual life of peoples and men. One can distinguish the influence of peoples on each other within world literature by their power to bind or to loose, to form or deform, to dispense laws or freedom. This is the great difference between the Germanic and Romance peoples. The rhythm of binding and loosing coincides with the rhythm of organic life ; in his youth a man requires to loose and free himself, to make room for the urgent, budding life within him. A grown man needs control, order, proportion, law and form. And old age once more breaks down the rigid forms, relaxes the strict control, because at that stage a new and higher life is pressing for room. In this sense youth and age meet.

This, then, was the kind of influence which the English spirit had on Goethe, and Goethe's development and growth were supremely natural and organic. The liberating power of English literature stimulated him in youth and in old age, but particularly in youth. To a young Englishman who in 1825 visited him in

Weimar, he said : " For fifty years I have been interesting myself in English literature, so I know your writers and the life and ways of your country very well. If I were to come over to England I would be no stranger there " (Eckermann, 10th January 1825).

In his old age, remembering his youth with gratitude, Goethe urgently recommended to young Eckermann the study of the English language, and pointed out that German literature had to a great extent developed out of English literature. " Our novels, our tragedies, where did we take them from if not from Goldsmith, Fielding and Shakespeare? " He might have named others, as he did elsewhere : Percy, Ossian, Young and Sterne.

We must now make an attempt as clearly and consistently as possible to trace the powerful influence of English literature on young Goethe. We might indeed sum it all up in the one word " nature ", to which the youth of Germany was then beginning to pray as to a god. Nature was to them everlasting and yet ever new, a creative force endowed with genius, and the opposite of convention and rule in art and society. Rule must not be confused with law. Nature works according to laws, not rules. A rule, one might say, is a law grown lifeless, rigid and mechanical. It is autocratically imposed by convention on men, art and society. It is a dominating principle which distorts nature. But law is inherent, a creation of nature, or man, or art, of which, or of whom, it is an essential part. It is not imposed forcibly from without. It follows naturally and inevitably from within and, far from hampering the freedom of an individual, rather preserves it. You have only to contrast an English garden with a French park : the English garden seeks to preserve faithfully the essentials of the natural landscape, while the French park trims, encloses, measures, rationalises and forces itself into symmetrical patterns and geometrical figures. You can see the same difference between Shakespeare's and Corneille's tragedies (though the two men were contemporaries)—works of art produced according to laws and according to rules, examples of freedom and of restriction. It was as a force of nature, then, that Shakespeare exerted his immense influence on young Goethe. It was Shakespeare who freed him from the formal regimentation of French Classicism, and showed him for the first time in a work of art men who acted in accordance not with conventional rules but with the laws of their own nature, their own individual fate, or in other words their own inner freedom. " Nature, Nature, nothing like

Shakespeare's men for Nature," exclaimed young Goethe in his Shakespeare-speech.

Friedrich Gundolf has rightly traced the tremendous influence which Shakespeare had on young Goethe to the fact that, for the first time in the history of the German spirit in its relation to Shakespeare, one creative artist met another. The Shakespeare speech after all contributes no new ideas. Herder had really said it all already. But Herder's approach to Shakespeare was that of a historian and critic ; and Goethe's was that of a poet. Herder contributed new knowledge of Shakespeare ; but Goethe paid a personal tribute to him, and we can even say, as Gundolf did, that no one has ever written about the influence of a genius as Goethe did in this speech. Young Goethe's eyes, which had been blind, were opened by Shakespeare, and everything seemed to him new and fresh ; he felt his whole outlook infinitely extended. He had no longer a moment's hesitation in renouncing the regular theatre of French Classicism, for he found the unities and the rules altogether intolerable. Shakespeare reacted then on young Goethe as a creative writer, breaking his bonds, opening his eyes. It cannot be denied that Goethe read a good deal of himself into Shakespeare. The conception of Shakespeare as showing free will brought into conflict with the inevitable course of events is certainly largely Goethe's Titanism, his Storm and Stress. In his *Götz von Berlichingen* Goethe neither imitated nor counterfeited Shakespeare ; he tossed off his work with the new power that Shakespeare had released in him. It was his own creative urge that fashioned new worlds which, like the creations of nature or of Shakespeare, are real and living. From Shakespeare young Goethe derived confidence in his own power to create, courage to be his real self and to reveal himself in his work. It is of course true that Shakespeare caused him at that time to see everything in dramatic form, and this was unsuited to Goethe's nature ; *Götz* was essentially epic rather than dramatic. It may be that this is why the vast projects for the tragedies of Prometheus, Mahomet and Cæsar were never realised. Certainly *Götz* shows the influence of Shakespeare's historical dramas, in so far as Goethe transplanted his own experience far back into the nation's past, gave it historical colour, and altogether made of the tragedy a piece of dramatic history ; for at that time he saw the world as history. But the character and the fate of the hero are authentic Goethe ; the work is his own creation. Perhaps Goethe adopted a mistaken idea of Shakespeare's dramatic form, exaggerated its freedom and was too little conscious of the law in it ; reckoned insufficiently with its underlying law, and was to that extent misled by it. Certainly the construction of a Shakespearian drama is very different from the formlessness of *Götz*. We must add that this incomparably freer form was Goethe's own method of expression at the time. In any case, when Goethe repeatedly acknowledged that it was to Shakespeare that he owed all that he had become, he had in mind this awakening to self-awareness, this release of his creative powers, this opening of his eyes to the truth about the world, men, nature and history.

Yet it may be that Goethe would not have been so profoundly influenced by Shakespeare, if his English contemporaries had not thought of Shakespeare as a classic example of a genius, theorised widely on the nature of genius, and proved their case by numerous examples. It certainly did not come about by chance that a Germanic literature was the first to do this, contributing with its idea of genius to the German Storm and Stress that was to follow. Edward Young in his " Essay on Original Composition " saw the nature of genius in the primitiveness and originality with which a creative spirit sets to work. It disregards restrictive rules and accepted models ; it fashions new and unknown worlds as nature does, simply out of its own urge to do so, and follows its own law. Bishop Lowth, in his work on the sacred poetry of the Jews, interpreted the writers of the Old Testament as geniuses in that sense, and Blackwell and Wood revealed the original genius of Homer. All these English thinkers first influenced young Goethe through the medium of Herder who, with their help, had arrived at his own theory. This was that true imitation of the Bible or the Græco-Romans lay in producing poetry as they did, freely, originally and spontaneously, inspired by their own nature and their own world. It was in England that this idea of such liberating power originated.

Folk-poetry, also called nature-poetry, now came to be interpreted as a particular instance of inspiration in this sense, and was contrasted in England with the poetry of society. For it originates in the nature and traditions of a people, not in its civilisation or in knowledge of artistic models of rules, or any social convention or attitude. Folk-poetry is a primitive, original, inspired creation, and in this sense all genuine great poetry, even the Bible, even Homer and Shakespeare, is considered folk-poetry. Bishop Percy, who collected the Reliques of Old English and Old Scottish popular ballads, prompted young Goethe to abandon the Anacreontic style and write in the strain of folk-poetry.

Nature, however, was extolled in English poetry as the changeless pattern not only of life but also of art. Oliver Goldsmith did this in his novel, *The Vicar of Wakefield*, which Goethe describes as one of the best novels ever written. It was obviously the poetry of rural life in it which so impressed young Goethe. A country parson, we read in *Dichtung und Wahrheit*, is perhaps the best subject for a modern idyll. Goethe regarded as typically English the way in which the small circle round this central figure is related to the outside world, how this little boat floats on the full tide of English life. But that was not all that delighted young Goethe, when Herder first read this novel aloud to him. Everything seemed to him to be so living, so actual, that he did not merely enjoy it as a " work of art " whose outward form was there to be admired, he felt its influence as a " natural growth ". At this point a strange thing happened. From this fictitious world of the novel, Goethe was transported into a similar real world. At Sesenheim, the family of the country parson, Brion, reminded him so vividly of Goldsmith's novel, its setting and its characters, that the worlds of imagination and reality merged as in a dream. He thought himself actually among the Wakefield family, and used their names. Goethe would not have appreciated this Sesenheim idyll as he did, had it not seemed to him the materialisation of Goldsmith's novel, a writer's dream come true. The work of art had anticipated reality. Once more we realise how English poetry had opened young Goethe's eyes to life and nature, and not only to the forms and laws of art. Goldsmith's influence touches that of Shakespeare at this point. The work of art proved to be the road to a natural life free of conventions, and, in its turn, the natural life was shaped in its changeless human form into a work of art. In *Werther*, and again in *Hermann und Dorothea*, we hear the echo of this English novel. Werther's Lotte reads it and finds in it a reflection of her own domestic circle.

In his youth Goethe also translated Goldsmith's poem, " The Deserted Village ", because it affected him profoundly. In this poem, Goldsmith no longer extols a natural way of living which, although driven into the country, still belongs to the actual present. Instead, he utters a sentimental plaint, an elegy on a lost paradise shattered by the advance of civilisation. In Goethe, the effect of this poem combined with that of Gessner's etchings to increase his sympathy for things rural.

We come now to another influence which English literature exerted on young Goethe, one without which there would have been no *Werther*. Goethe has told in the thirteenth volume of *Dichtung und Wahrheit* how Werther's mood of gloom culminated in suicide. This was the mood of the youth of his day, and had been induced by English literature, with its keynote—to Goethe's ear—of melancholy. In *Dichtung und Wahrheit* Goethe tries to explain this phenomenon in terms of the Englishman's reaction to environment. The Englishman, he says, is surrounded from his youth up by a world full of significance, takes part either actively or as an onlooker in the political affairs of a mighty Empire, and thus, in his early years, becomes aware of the variable and transitory nature of all earthly things. This is seen in the rise and fall of forms of government, and in the ephemeral nature of public taste and popular favour which determine the fate of a politician. He learns that there is a universal law of transience and frailty governing all things, and sees it in the constantly changing cycle of the seasons, as in the decay and death of all that has lived. We leave undecided the question whether this is a satisfying explanation. But it is certain that the cloudy skies and perpetually hazy atmosphere of England contribute to this striking note of melancholy in English literature. Goethe could have cited early examples of this, such as Timothy Bright's remarkable work, *Treatise of Melancholy* (1586), Robert Burton's *Anatomy of Melancholy* (1621), and *Tasso's Melancholy*, a drama by an unknown author and unfortunely now lost, which was acted in London towards the end of the sixteenth century. Goethe heard this same note in Shakespeare's *Hamlet*, in Milton, and still more in contemporary literature in England where to the above reasons there was added a puritan version of Christianity continually directing man's thoughts to decay and death. He heard it also in Young's " Night Thoughts ", in Gray's " Elegy ", in Goldsmith's " Deserted Village ", in Richardson's novels (where the immorality and un-Christian spirit of society are lamented in a sentimental vein) and most markedly in the Ossianic poems, where the spirits of dead heroes sing laments for past ages and dead loves. It was Macpherson's *Ossian* more than any other work that created such a fitting background for the disillusioned mood of the age. As Goethe wrote in *Dichtung und Wahrheit* : " We wander over a grey, endless expanse of heath, mossy gravestones jutting up here and there, and gaze at the surrounding grass stirred by an eerie wind and at the darkly overcast sky above us." Goethe heard this English note again in Byron's poetry, at a time when he had become proof against it and demanded of true poetry that it should be a gospel of this life, freeing men from the world's burdens and able to temper both joy and sorrow. But at that time this English disillusionment found an echo in the youth of Germany and in Goethe, because, as he says, the serious tendency of the German mind, and still more the spirit of the times, were in tune with it. Of course in Germany, Goethe's explanation involving political activities in the public sphere of state or world did not apply : for there was no such sphere. But just because that was so completely lacking, the youth of Germany was driven back upon itself into inner isolation. It had no external sphere of activity in which to exercise and develop its powers. And when a man is driven back upon himself in this way, there arise unsatisfied enthusiasms, unfulfilled longings, disappointed expectations, exaggerated claims to which no reality can correspond. But the most profound reason lies in the fact that at that period, for the first time in German history, a rising generation refused to endure restrictions imposed by a culture grown conventional, old and pompous. This rising generation was young, and was thrusting at every turn against the limitations and restrictions of a social order governed by French customs, regulations and conventions. The longing for freedom and nature, characteristic of genuine youth, had been roused in Germany by Germanic literatures, but could not find fulfilment. All that was needful was for Goethe to experience an unhappy love-affair, one that was thwarted by conventionality. With that came the moment for England's poetry of disillusionment to loose young Goethe's tongue and help his grief to find expression in *Werther*. When Goethe read an English translation of *Werther*, he was moved at the thought of reading it in the language of his " teachers ". It is quite obvious from the novel itself that *Werther* belongs to the moment in the history of the German mind at which it awoke to self-awareness, and sought to throw off the bonds of French civilisation. For *Werther* is not merely a love-story ; it is the story of a young artist whose mind rebelled against the stifling tendencies of French Classicism, just as his heart, charged with emotion, revolted against French social conventions. *Werther* is an impassioned attack on an antiquated culture within which a new type of young man of the middle classes could no longer breathe or work. The unhappiness of love thwarted by conventions serves to release the general suffering of youth in an artificial world dominated by an ageing culture, a suffering that culminated in general disillusionment.

This, then, was the influence of English literature, rousing and rejuvenating even through suffering and grief.

But the same literature also brought to young Goethe and to all youth a draught to heal their suffering and grief, a means of reconciliation with the world ; and we ought not to forget this if we wish to have a clear idea of what Goethe owed to English literature. We mean English Humour, England's great humorists of the 18th century, whose greatest glory was Laurence Sterne. It certainly did not come about by chance that " mal du siècle " and humour together and from England exerted an influence on young Goethe : For this English brand of humour comes from the same source as the universal " mal du siècle " and is really only a sublimation of it. It is the standpoint of a mind viewing the world from such a height that it no longer bewails or denounces the futility, frivolity, and frailty of humanity. It smiles, albeit through tears, and, smiling, is able to endure it. Such a mind finds more folly than vice in the world of men ; in its general disillusionment it measures everything by the standard of absolute significance, and finds that the differences between great and small, good and evil, high and low are blurred. By this standard everything must seem small and insignificant ; so the humorist feels pity for the world rather than anger, and can love even man's weaknesses. This sublime type of humour is perhaps attainable by the Germanic mind, which more than any other is prone to disillusionment, because it is accustomed to applying the standard of absolute significance. Such is the spirit of Faust. On the other hand, it has a natural sympathy with everything that is characteristic and individual. Humour is woven of these two threads, and that may explain how English literature produced the two great humorists Fielding and Sterne and how, particularly in German literature—in Jean Paul, for instance—their influence was so fruitful.

In his old age, when Goethe was gratefully recalling the forces which had moulded his youth, he wrote these words in *Kunst und Altertum* about Sterne (whom he much admired), author of *Yorick's Sentimental Journey* and *Life and Opinions of Tristram Shandy* :

In the rapid strides which our literature as well as our general development is making, it often happens that we forget to whom we owe first impulses and initial influences. We imagine that what exists and occurs must so be and so happen. But this leads us astray, for we lose sight of those who have guided us along the right path. In this connection I wish to draw attention to a man who first prompted and helped the dissemination of truer knowledge of man, of high-minded toleration, of tender affection, in the second half of the last century. I am often reminded of this man, to whom I owe so much and think of him too when I hear of the fluctuation of error and truth in men's minds. One might also refer in a kindly way to his eccentricities. For there are some human phenomena that are best expressed by this term. Seen from without they are mistaken, from within they are right, and judged aright they are psychologically important. It is they that make up the individual, that point to what is universal ; and even in what is strangest there is some measure of sense, reason and goodwill, which attracts us.

In his old age Goethe wrote on another occasion to Zelter :

It would be impossible to estimate the influence that Goldsmith and Sterne had upon me at this crucial moment in my development. This sublime, benevolent irony, this fairness in breadth of outlook, this meekness in adversity, this constancy in change, with all the other virtues of like nature, gave me the most valuable education, and indeed these are the principles that guide us back after all our false steps in life.

" Yorick-Sterne ", he writes in another passage, " was the noblest spirit whose influence was ever felt ; reading him, you feel yourself free and noble ; his humour is inimitable, and not every kind of humour liberates the soul." If we had to use one term to describe Sterne's influence on Goethe as a young man, we could say that he educated Goethe to a conception of humanity, in the particular sense in which the English-Germanic idea of humanity differs from that which Voltaire preached. The French idea of humanity is based on the perception of reason, which, though it appears in different guises, remains the same for all peoples and ages and men, a common human core. But the English idea of humanity is based on kindly tolerance and consideration for human peculiarities and foibles. In this way English humour helped, along with Shakespeare and other English writers and thinkers, to free young Goethe from the domination of rules, to show him that men cannot all be reduced to one pattern, and that one must respect their idiosyncrasies. English humour contributed largely to Goethe's tolerant attitude and blended well with a theory emanating from England and popularised by Herder. This maintained that there can be no universally applicable canon of art that will cover every development arising out of the varying conditions laid down by period, nation, environment and our Creator. The humorist's view of life, together with the historical one, became a basic part of Goethe's idea of world literature. For he held that world literature should draw attention to the individual characteristics of peoples and so lead to mutual consideration and tolerance.

The Christian basis of Goethe's idea of world literature also gained fresh support from England. After Howard's researches into cloud-formations had proved of decisive importance to Goethe's scientific work, Goethe was at pains to trace the outlines of Howard's life. He wanted to discover how his mind had been formed, what had led him to observe nature in such a natural way, to subordinate himself to her, to learn her laws and lay down others for her. He received a personal letter from Howard in reply, giving a detailed account of his family life, education and views, which was at his disposal for publication (21st February 1822). In this letter, which Goethe published both in English and in translation, we read :

The sincere practice of Christianity will spread to every nation and will become the common faith of man. This has already taken place to some extent in the moral and in the practical sense ; wars will cease, together with other degrading superstitions and noxious practices ; society will be reformed ; the present self-seeking and dissension will give place to general agreement and kindliness between nations and individuals.[1]

" Indeed," added Goethe, " nothing could have given me more pleasure than to find the sensitive religious nature of such an outstanding man so much in sympathy with me that he feels drawn to disclose so candidly the facts and cultural influences of his life, as well as his personal views."[2] It confirmed his experience, that sensitive, moral natures are best fitted to observe nature, for the best results are obtained by a sensitive nature at peace with itself and with the world.[3] And the reference to Christianity in the letter obviously made a deep impression on Goethe, for, in a conversation with Chancellor von Müller (11th June 1822), he says of Howard : " As a Christian he lives and moves entirely in this faith, and on it bases all his hopes for the future and for the world ; he does this so logically, so calmly, so reasonably, that while reading him one would fain hold the same belief; and there is much truth in what he says. He wants the nations to consider each other as members of one corporate body, and to recognise each other." In this desire Goethe recognised his own, which he felt so urgently : to promote knowledge of each other among the nations. So the Christian message of this man whom he esteemed so highly no doubt gave him new strength and confidence. This is apparent in his proclamation of world literature which reminds one so clearly, almost word for word, of Howard's letter.

The scientific discoveries of this English investigator were, however, of still greater importance to Goethe. Although his disagreement with Newton brought him into violent conflict with English science, yet he could in one respect acknowledge himself its adherent, for Howard's doctrine of the formation of clouds became an integral and effective part of his scientific approach. Goethe's opposition to Newton's theory of colour revealed a fundamental contrast between the English and the German mind which was obvious also in the philosophy of these peoples—that between empiricism and idealism. Newton had made optics into a mathematical science. Light, he affirmed, can be analysed, measured, calculated and expressed arithmetically, for the essence of nature consists in number and relation. But for Goethe nature is an effective, active force, not rigid and fixed : a living and developing manifestation not to be measured and numbered, but rather observed and interpreted. Newton's method was calculation, Goethe's observation. Newton's mathematical method isolated, divided and analysed what the senses called a unity : it was an " atomic conception ". But Goethe's method of observation comprehended the whole and also the unity, for he held its unity to be intrinsic and not the result of experience. Newton examined the objects independently of the subject which apprehends them. Goethe could not understand an effect apart from the person affected, who is himself a force making itself felt upon the outside world. For him there was no object without an actively receptive subject, no action without counteraction, no colour without the eye which sees it. For Goethe, then, the aim of optics was to represent this interaction of object and subject, the conditions and manifestations of colour in the seeing eye. That is how Goethe came to believe that light is not, as Newton taught, composed of darker beams, nor is it analysed by being passed through a prism : colours are not parts of light : light is an indivisible unity which cannot be analysed. Colours are the result of interaction between light and the eye, they represent the " deeds and sufferings " of light. Goethe's theory of optics might almost be called a Holy War waged by a light-worshipper for the unity and purity of light ; it is a scientific counterpart to his work, *Old Persian Testament*. It was the struggle of a writer and artist, but at the same time the struggle of a mind inspired by German idealism against English empiricism.

Howard's theory, on the other hand, appealed to Goethe's artistic sense. It was that, however evanescent the cloud-formations in lower or high regions may be, certain forms and types can be distinguished. Goethe learned of these researches in 1815, and " over his whole scientific work there hung Howard's doctrine of the clouds ". Goethe's great essay on a meteorological subject, " Cloud-formations according to Howard " (written in 1817, published in 1820), is a testimony to Howard's powerful influence, and so in a still greater degree is his poem, " Homage to Howard's Memory ". In it Goethe uses the principal words employed by Howard because " keeping this terminology ", besides other advantages, facilitates " intercourse with foreign nations ". He pays tribute to the four types of cloud, Stratus, Cumulus, Cirrus and Nimbus, as visible signs of the metamorphosis which despite apparent evanescence and formlessness reveals nature striving, in accordance with its own laws, towards form and system. The first few verses, intended to complete and illustrate the meaning, are as follows :

> Wenn Gottheit Camarupa, hoch und hehr,
> Durch Lüfte schwankend wandelt leicht und schwer,
> Des Schleiers Falten sammelt, sie zerstreut,
> Am Wechsel der Gestalten sich erfreut,
> Jetzt starr sich hält, dann schwindet wie ein Traum,
> Da staunen wir und traun dem Auge kaum.

> Nun regt sich kühn des eignen Bildens Kraft,
> Die Unbestimmtes zu Bestimmtem schafft ;
> Da Droht ein Leu, dort wogt ein Elefant,
> Kameles Hals, zum Drachen umgewandt ;
> Ein Heer zieht an, doch triumphiert es nicht,
> Da es die Macht am steilen Felsen bricht ;
> Der treuste Wolkenbote selbst zerstiebt,
> Eh' er die Fern' erreicht, wohin man liebt,

> Er aber, Howard, gibt mit reinem Sinn
> Uns neuer Lehre herrlichsten Gewinn,
> Was sich nicht halten, nicht erreichen lässt,
> Er fasst es an, er hält zuerst es fest ;
> Bestimmt das Unbestimmte, schränkt es ein,
> Benennt es treffend !—Sei die Ehre Dein !—
> Wie Streife steigt, sich ballt, zerflattert, fällt,
> Erinnre dankbar deiner sich die Welt.

The English translation of the poem (by Hüttner and Bowring) showed Goethe that he " had caught the point of view of the English and had pleased them by his appreciation of their

fellow-countryman ''.   The inclusion of both his poem and the
translation in his scientific writings points to a '' reciprocal
relationship with England, which has recently been proved once
again ; it is always a matter of time before nations appreciate
each other, and when it happens, it is usually due to talents on
both sides making themselves felt in advance of the bulk of the
nation ''.[4]

This connection between Howard and Goethe is of particular
importance because it shows how England came to influence
Goethe once more in quite a different sense from what happened
in his youth.   Then it was an influence which broke down forms
and freed from the domination of laws : now it revealed to him
the power of form and law in a new manifestation.   It was no
longer the Goethe of the Storm and Stress, but Goethe the
Classical writer, who here received from England a new expansion of his Classical knowledge and view of art.   When publishing Howard's letter to him, Goethe used the following words :
'' How greatly I was attracted by Howard's definition of clouds ;
and how much I welcomed the giving of form to the formless, the
metamorphosis of the indefinite according to laws, is made clear
in all my scientific and artistic work ''.   Here the contrast between the influences of Germanic and Romance civilisations
loses its sharpness, and we can pass to what Goethe owed to
France and Italy.   Whereas Howard's definition of clouds
brought only confirmation and expansion of views and knowledge already acquired, the Romance civilisations were cultural
forces which transformed him, and led him from the Storm and
Stress towards Classical perfection.   When this transformation
took place, the influence of English literature was less apparent,
as it was also in his strictly Classical period.   It regained importance only when, in his old age, Goethe became aware of his own
influence on it : on Scott and still more on Byron.   In short, on
the English Romantic writers.   Transformation and education
through English literature were now no longer possible.   It
could only refresh and renew.   He had become the donor.   His
changed attitude to Shakespeare indicates this.   We must once
more call to mind his essay '' Shakespeare Without End ''.   In
connection with his classical reform of the Weimar theatre,
Goethe planned an adaptation of *Romeo and Juliet*.   But it was
a transposition from baroque into classical style.   The comic
figures (Mercutio and the Nurse) were discarded, because they
now appeared to him to be merely '' farcical intermezzo figures ''

which must be intolerable to our " logical, harmony-loving way of thought ". He speaks of extraneous matter and dissonances. All prose is sacrificed to a rhythmic form throughout, and parts are even written in Alexandrines. The Classical reform of the Weimar theatre demanded similar adaptation of Shakespeare to the new style which kept closer to French Classicism than to English dramatic style. Schiller's *Macbeth*, too, exhibits a transmutation of Shakespeare's style in favour of a new Classicism. Here, too, we have the discarding of the comic element and of prose. Goethe's translations of Voltaire's tragedies, on the other hand, were able to keep closer to the original, as was Schiller's *Phaedra*.

CHAPTER 6

THE CULTURAL TRADITIONS OF ITALY

The term " Classical art " in modern times suggests the Italian Renaissance, during which modern man evolved from mediævalism, and the art of the Græco-Romans were reborn. In other words, the Græco-Roman world was the cradle of modern man. This is why, wherever in Europe an example of true Classicism is produced, it is felt to be not a reversion to an atavistic past but something alive, modern and European. But a resuscitation of mediævalism, such as took place in the Romantic period, does appear to be a reversion to the past, an interlude, often repeated in the course of European history, but one against which the conscience of Europe protests. For Europe was born endowed with the conception, of which Greek culture was the realisation, that man is the measure of all things ; man, who within himself has harmonised all Nature's gifts and possibilities, who has a sense of beauty, and creates a world of beauty in his own image. This is what was done by the Italian Renaissance, whose art may be called truly Classical.

But one cannot apply this epithet to the French Classicism which reached perfection in the 17th and 18th centuries. That is called not Classical, but Classicistic ; and this difference is not one of mere terminology ; it is fundamental. Undoubtedly the heritage of the Græco-Romans is still apparent in the Classieistic. But what in the case of Græco-Romans and the Italian Renaissance was an embodied idea became for the Classicistic an exemplified theory. Innate law became a rule, living customs became traditional conventions, an intuitive form became a conscious one. The Classicistic is what can be taught by, and learned from, the Classical, what has become academic in it. In the Italian Renaissance the measure of all things was man, the whole man, the man of beauty, with bodily senses as well as soul and reason. But in Classicistic art intelligence became the primary criterion. The universal humanity of the Græco-Romans takes on in Classicistic art the stamp of a society conditioned by the times, in this case a courtly and aristocratic society, which seems to have no significance for other ages. Indeed French Classicism appears to have been the pattern only for certain definite times and styles, while the Italian Renaissance, like the Græco-Roman age, became because of its integrity a model for dissimilar and even opposite ages and styles ; for each is able to concentrate on one of its aspects. The Italian Renaissance appeared to the Storm and Stress group as the ideal picture of a life free from restrictions, an emancipation of life, of the senses, of nature. The German Romantic period hailed the writers of the Italian Renaissance as the true originators of Romantic poetry, because of the expansion of fantasy (almost to the point of being fantastic), and because of all the qualities which showed them to be nearer to the Middle Ages than to the Græco-Romans. For Nietzsche, a Cesare Borgia was a personification of the superman, beyond good and evil. But for Goethe this same Renaissance signified something quite different. Of course he had not overlooked the difference between its conformity with natural laws and the superimposed rule of French Classicism, between its harmonious beauty and the latter's wit, between its changeless humanity and the other's conventional attitude. ·He made a clear distinction between the Classical and the Classicistic. French writing came to mean for him a useful discipline in strict form and tone. But to Goethe the Renaissance represented something richer, more deeply felt, less restrictive and more liberating. It helped him to overcome both his Storm and Stress period and also the Faustian tendencies in his own nature.

With Goethe it was not primarily Italian literature which gave him this new conception of culture. Dante, Ariosto and Tasso were much more important to the Romantic movement than to him. This was due to its composite character, made up of mingled Roman, Germanic and Catholic-Christian elements. Goethe never established a really intimate relationship with Dante. When he was in Italy he once said he had never been able to understand how anyone could wish to study Dante. He found the *Inferno* odious, the *Purgatorio* ambiguous and the *Paradiso* tedious. Only against his will he let himself be transported into Dante's dark, gloomy world. He speaks of Dante's " repulsive and often odious greatness ". He calls him repellent, and warns artists not to seek inspiration at this troubled source. One can of course make interesting comparisons between the *Divine Comedy* and *Faust,* and this has frequently been done. But, apart from the common universality of the two poems, particularly from the end of the Second Part of *Faust,* there are more differences than similarities between them. As for Tasso and

Ariosto, when Goethe was in Rome he was asked which he considered to be the greater writer. He answered that it was by the bounty of God and nature that a single nation had been granted two such outstanding men, each of whom, though living in such different periods and circumstances, and, differing so much in temperament, could afford us moments of the highest pleasure. But these moments lay chiefly in Goethe's early youth, and we gather from the clearly autobiographical story of Wilhelm Meister's youth that Tasso's *Jerusalem Delivered* had a romantically sentimental influence on young Goethe rather than a formative force. The *chevaleresque* love-story of Clorinda incited him at that period to a dramatic improvisation. Altogether, Tasso obviously represents one of the first counterpoises to French Classicism ; for in his letters of 1766 and 1767 Goethe defends Tasso against Boileau's attacks, siding with Marmontel, just at the time when he was defending Shakespeare against Voltaire. The first sketch of his *Tasso* drama was written before his Italian journey and is not now extant, but we have Goethe's later reference to give us some idea of it. This sketch certainly made of the Italian poet a self-portrait, a picture of Goethe still caught up in Storm and Stress, and revolting against society. It is this Tasso-picture that has remained in Italian drama, despite the transformation which it underwent. But now Goethe had himself undergone a change, and applied a new standard to Tasso. He now becomes the symbol of that stage in Goethe's own development as man and poet, which he overcame in Italy by renunciation. This makes it finally clear that Tasso is not to be counted among the formative influences which affected Goethe. Goethe found it most apt when the French writer Ampère called his *Tasso* an intensified *Werther*. Little weight can be attached to the fact that Goethe took the material for his cantata " Rinaldo " from Tasso's epic.

In his old age, when Goethe received the first volume of the *Parnasso Italiano* (Dante, Petrarch, Ariosto, Tasso), which the editor Adolf Wagner dedicated in an Italian terza rima " to Goethe the prince of poets ", he expressed to the editor his gratitude for this magnificent gift. He said it was a complete library, sufficient to occupy a whole lifetime and to mould a complete personality. It is, however, remarkable how little Italian writing is mentioned in Goethe's *Italian Journey*. It was only popular song in Venice and Rome, the verses of Tasso and Ariosto which the people sang there, the ritornelles, vaudevilles, ballads and hymns that engaged his attention, because in this popular type of song he sought the character of the Italian people. Later, in 1815, he ascribed to Italian literature, in contrast to German, the " national advantage of a living view of life ". He attributed this to the public nature of the Italian way of life, which allows the youth of Italy to see every facet of society, its members and its institutions. This public life of the Italians gives to their literature a kind of serenity and brilliance.[5]

But the real benefit which Italian works of literature brought to Goethe lay in the musical beauty of the Italian language which he loved, and in the stability and plastic quality of its world of forms and figures. Both these things helped him to advance beyond the Storm and Stress period, with its passion for expression and its " boundless longing to be free, and to draw nearer to classical art ". They imposed salutary limitations on his imagination, and gave harmony to his language, stability to his form, without loss in depth or richness of feeling. As for the limitations on his imagination, Goethe commended Dante, with whom he was otherwise not much in sympathy, for having made his strange, abstruse world so definite and vivid to the imagination. At the end of the Second Part of *Faust*, when Goethe was faced with the task of representing spheres beyond human ken, not to be perceived but only to be divined, it was Dante's Christian-Catholic world of figures to which he turned. They helped him to define his vague intentions, to give them form and substance, so that he did not lose himself in a void. All this is treated in a conversation with Eckermann. As for the music and harmony of the Italian language, one of Goethe's most beautiful poems, " Nachtgesang ", was inspired by a Roman Canzone. The refrain of this is retained in a literal translation. The rest of the poem is not a translation but a derivative version which obviously developed out of the refrain. Thus transformed, the simple Italian popular song is given a mysterious depth, a range and richness of content which it did not possess. Nowhere has Goethe written purer music than in this nocturne, inspired by this Italian song. No other poem of his can to the same extent be called music in words. The very sound of Italian vibrates and echoes here. Goethe meticulously retained the shape of the Italian song, the third line of each verse becoming the first of the following verse. Indeed, he made the shape still more formalised, for with him the refrain is not an interruption, as it is in the Italian original, but an integral part of the composition, and the similarity of the beginning and the ending completes the formal unity of Goethe's poem.

Notturno	*Nachtgesang*
Tu sei quel dolce fuoco l'anima mia sei tu ! E degli affetti miei— Dormi, che vuoi di più—	O, gib vom weichen Pfühle, Träumend ein halb Gehör ! Bei meinem Saitenspiele Schlafe ! Was willst du mehr ?
E degli affetti miei, tién le chiavi tu ! E di sto cuore hai— Dormi, che vuoi di più—	Bei meinem Saitenspiele Segnet der Sterne Heer Die ewigen Gefühle ; Schlafe ! Was willst du mehr ?
E di sto cuore hai, tutte le parti tu ! E mi vedrai morire— Dormi, che vuoi di più.—	Die ewigen Gefühle Heben mich, hoch und heer Aus irdischem Gewühle ; Schlafe ! Was willst du mehr ?
E mi vedrai morire, Si lo comandi tu ! Dormi, bell'idol mio— Dormi, che vuoi di più ?	Vom irdischen Gewühle Trennst du mich nur zu sehr, Bannst mich in diese Kühle ; Schlafe ! Was willst du mehr ?
	Bannst mich in diese Kühle, Gibst nur in Traum Gehör ; Ach, auf dem weichen Pfühle Schlafe ! Was willst du mehr ?

Italian literary forms made a special appeal to Goethe ; they gave him something that German poetry would never have been able to develop independently. They are forms which by the strictness of their construction lend to the poet's personal experience a character beyond his personality, a universal significance, and so act as a check on excessive individualism in his poetry. The form of the Octave influenced the shape of Goethe's " Geheimnisse " and " Zueignung ". Dante's terze rhyme became the recognised form for prophetic poems such as that on Schiller's skull. In the definite structure of the sonnet, so formalised both in content and in form, Goethe's love for Minna Herzlieb found an expression that seemed to reach beyond his own personality. If we compare the wild, Nordic rhythms of the end of the First Part of *Faust* with the southern lyrics and terze rhyme at the beginning of the Second Part, we have tangible proof of the transformation which his *Faust* underwent.

But the new conception of culture that Italy gave Goethe derived much more from nature and the plastic arts in Italy than from literature. As a factor in world literature this is of the greatest importance, and undoubtedly contributed to his idea of it. Goethe's conception of world literature included not only literary productions, but also any stimulus found by writers in nature, art, or any branch of a country's civilisation.

Goethe in Italy represents a recurring phenomenon, symbolic in world-history ; an example of the almost magical power of attraction which the South has over the North, an enchantment which may bring with it the danger of extinction for the individual personality, as has been the case with so many German and nordic writers and artists. But Goethe in Italy suffered neither surrender nor extinction, any more than did Albrecht Dürer, of whom Goethe was reminded in Italy. The " influence " did not grow into " Influenza " but only assisted the development of an inevitable and organic growth. There was no breach of faith with the German spirit, no false step. To call *Iphigenie* such is to be guilty of breaking faith with the German spirit. We ought not to forget that, even in the midst of his Storm and Stress period, young Goethe wrote a poem of the type of " The Wanderer ", in which he succeeded in calling up with magical effect the image of the southern scene, and in which there is a premonition of what was to come. Nor ought we to forget that Mignon's song of longing, " Kennst du das Land ? " was written long before Goethe's Italian journey, and that in this song Goethe's longing for Italy reaches such a pitch of vividness that in imagination it seems almost to have fulfilled itself. His longing for Italy had grown so acute that he could not see a picture of the country or read a Latin book without a pang. Yet he delayed the fulfilment of this desire, the elimination of this suffering, because he felt himself not yet quite ready for the experience. His instinct always guided him to the next step in his development, and told him when his receptive powers were adequate. It has been the curse of many a northern artist and writer that he went south too soon, and returned home with nothing but meaningless forms. In Goethe's case it was only when Spinoza's *Ethics* had brought about a great change in him and prepared his mind, and when his *Iphigenie* had been completed in Weimar, that he knew the time had come for him to enjoy the blessing of the South. It was no turning aside from his path, but only the result of his own mental processes that took him at last to Italy. In his own country he could not complete the partial transformation of which he was conscious. Although he himself had grown mature and calm, there was no outward manifestation in the North to correspond to his inward state ; there was no nobility in the life or art around him. His eyes, opened wide to the sun,* could see no sun ; his spirit, athirst for beauty, could perceive no beauty. So there could be no development that would produce a Classical work. When he reached Italy, he had the feeling that he was arriving at his true home, or seeing once more the one he had lost. There are many signs that the South had the effect on his inner life that he wanted. The " Urphänomen " of nature, which he thought he saw in Italy, in Padua and later especially in Sicily, he had already anticipated in Weimar. All that *Iphigenie* needed was strict rhythmic form. This came, not from literature, but from the plastic art of the Græco-Romans and of the Renaissance, which he now saw before his eyes. It was the ideal style in art, the conception of Italian nature as an " Urphänomen ", that his art needed for its development into Classical art. In southern art he found a visible expression of Spinoza's idea which already filled his mind : the identity of the inner necessity with God. Influenced by southern art, he renounced all arbitrariness, subjectivity and illusion in his own work. He wanted nothing more than to see the world clearly and accurately and without illusion or veil. Nature now revealed to him the inwardness of art, and in the laws of art he was amazed to recognise those by which nature works. Now that he saw actually before him all that had been present in his mind, all he had been longing for, there followed the most important effect which the South had upon him : it stilled his longing. Goethe viewed what remained of the Classical age in Italy without a trace of melancholy or sentimentality, freed from the spell that ruins can cast. They wove no dream of the past around him. The presence of the " Classical ground " from which the art of the Romans sprang and on which their history was enacted, failed to produce in him the pang of longing and remembrance which, later on, was experienced by Romantics in the South. In Sicily he first realised and understood Homer. He learned to understand the Odyssey on seeing with his own eyes those coasts, capes, gulfs, bays and islands, those bush-covered hills, rich pastures, fruitful fields, gay gardens, well-tended trees, hanging vines, those fair levels, rocks and steeps, and the sea embracing all. A tragedy, *Nausikaa*, which he began, was to be saturated

* Cf. " Wär' nicht das Auge sonnenhaft,
Die Sonne könnt' es nie erblicken."
Zahme Xenien III.

in this Sicilian atmosphere. It was the same scene, the same light, the same air, the same sea and the same sky, that the art of the ancient Greeks had seen ; and this made even ruins seem to him images of completion and fulfilment. All this enabled him to embody peace, serenity and freedom of spirit in a Classical work of art. *I too in Arcady* was the original title of the *Italian Journey* surely suggested by Goethe's admission to the " Arcadian Society ". This Society had been founded towards the close of the 17th century, to bring back life to Classical antiquity, to the nobler Tuscan school as opposed to the " barbaric " Marinism which was ruining Italian literature. When it was founded, one member is said to have cried out in delight : " Here is our Arcady."

But the poetry of Goethe's that owes its existence to Italy is Arcadian poetry in a deeper sense than that of the society's pastoral verses. What the South gave to Goethe is nowhere more clearly seen than in what happened to his *Faust* during and after his visit to Italy. Goethe had taken *Faust* with him in order to finish or at least to work on it, and we have a fascinating glimpse of Goethe in Italy : his transformation is nearing its completion, and his longing its fulfilment ; he can lose himself in the present and all its beauty. Surrounded by examples of classical art under a southern sky, he seeks to forget the mist-wrapped North ; and here he is in Rome, in the garden of the Villa Borghese, working at his *Faust*. What new portions were written there ? What appeared in this first published version of *Faust* (*Faust, a Fragment*), which was printed in 1790 after Goethe's return from Italy ? In the first place the scene " The Witch's Kitchen " in which Faust recovers his youth by drinking the witch's magic potion—in other words the most abstruse, grotesque, typically " nordic " scene in the whole of *Faust*. It was just in Italy that he called up the northern phantoms, although he remarked that notions of spirits, witches and devils belong to the northern latitudes, and were little used in Italy. " Abhorrence of these things is universal." What does this mean ? Is it really an incomprehensible statement ? The words with which Faust opens this scene, are :

> Mir widersteht das tolle Zauberwesen ;
> Versprichst du mir, ich soll genesen,
> In diesem Wust von Raserei ?
> Verlang' ich Rat von einem alten Weibe ?
> Und schafft die Sudelköcherei
> Wohl dreissig Jahre mir vom Leibe ?

Weh mir, wenn du nichts Bessers weisst !
Schon ist die Hoffnung mir verschwunden.
Hat die Natur und hat ein edler Geist
Nicht irgend einen Balsam ausgefunden ?

I loathe this mad sorcery ! It is the Italian Goethe who speaks here, and Faust treats with contemptuous sarcasm and disdain all the devilry, the gibbering monkeys, the jargon of the witch's spell. Quite clearly, Goethe shows us here his southern transformation, his new attitude to the northern Faust-story, the abhorrence which he now feels to it ; and, in Faust's abhorrence, Goethe exhibits Faust (in contrast to the original figure) at a higher stage of spiritual development. In the witch's kitchen, where Faust is held in rapture by one moment and one vision —in other words, when he sees Helen's image in the magic mirror, we recognise Goethe's transport of delight at the sight of Classical art in Italy, and the hint is given that Faust's way leads southwards and that he will win Helen for himself. This is the starting point of Faust's upward journey which leads, at the end of the Second Part, to his renouncing all magic arts and sorcery ; and when he might have banished the Spirit of Care with a spell he does not do so.

Könnt ich Magie von meinem Pfad entfernen,
Die Zubersprüche ganz und gar verlernen ;
Stünd' ich, Natur ! vor dir ein Mann allein,
Da wär's der Mühe wert ein Mensch zu sein.

In Italy Goethe won for himself what was once the Greek contribution to world literature : the victory of " Logos " over all gloomy, disordered and confused thinking about the universe, the victory of beauty over all formless and chaotic barbarity, the victory of man over sorcery and charlatanism, the victory of clarity over delusion and witchcraft. Goethe could believe in the Greek gods, because they portrayed for him the æsthetic ideal of man deified ; he could not believe in the phantoms and demons of the North.

The Faustian spirit was that of eternal longing, dissatisfaction with every moment however fair, the wild pursuit of man's inclinations and endless warfare with the world. Goethe's attitude to all this appears completely transformed in Italy. Absorbed in the happy present, given up to the pleasure of contemplating art and nature in the South, Goethe had found calm and peace. And so it comes about that in Italy he wrote a scene in which this new, so un-Faustian, spirit is given shape.

It seems strange and almost out of place in the work, because it represents Faust prematurely in a completely un-Faustian condition, free from his northern restlessness, in serene contemplation of nature and art—in a word, in Goethe's own Italian mood. This scene is the monologue " Wald und Höhle " :

> Erhabner Gesit, du gabst mir, gabst mir alles,
> Warum ich bat. Du hast mir nicht umsonst
> Dein Angesicht im Feuer zugewendet.
> Gabst mir die herrliche Natur zum Königreich,
> Kraft, sie zu fühlen, zu geniessen. Nicht
> Kalt staunenden Besuch erlaubst du nur,
> Vergönnest mir in ihre tiefe Brust
> Wie in den Busen eines Freunds zu schauen.
> Du führst die Reihe der Lebendigen
> Vor mir vorbei, und lehrst mich meine Brüder
> Im stillen Busch, in Luft und Wasser kennen.
> Und wenn der Sturm im Walde braust und knarrt,
> Die Riesenfichte stürzend Nachbaräste
> Und Nachbarstämme quetschend nieder streift,
> Und ihrem Fall dumpf hohl der Hügel donnert ;
> Dann führst du mich zur sichern Höhle, zeigst
> Mich dann mir selbst, und meiner eignen Brust
> Geheime tiefe Wunder öffnen sich
> Und steigt vor meinem Blick der reine Mond
> Besänftigend herüber : schweben mir
> Von Felsenwänden, aus dem feuchten Busch,
> Der Vorwelt silberne Gestalten auf,
> Und lindern der Betrachtung strenge Lust.

At this point, Faust has attained everything for which he had longed, perfect harmony with Nature now fully felt and appreciated. Here too Faust is enraptured at the sight of Classical art, for the silvery figures of past ages are surely the Greek gods, in marble splendour. It is in this monologue that, for the first time in *Faust*, we have the five-foot iambics, the Classical metre of *Iphigenie*. When Goethe published *Faust* after his return, he published it as a Fragment ; and this plainly reveals the transformation he had undergone in the South. He published only a fragment, and it was much more fragmentary than the *Urfaust*. The *Urfaust* contains the whole Gretchen tragedy from beginning to end ; the Fragment ends with the Cathedral-scene : " Neighbour, your smelling-bottle ! " Gretchen's fate is not completely depicted in the Fragment ; it does not contain the scene " Trüber Tag, Feld ", which shows Faust in a state of absolute despair, nor the scene " Nacht, offen Feld " in which Faust and Mephistopheles sweep past the Rabenstein, where the gallows has been erected for Gretchen, nor the prison-

scene, with Gretchen dying in chains, murderess of her child.
Clearly all these scenes were too harrowing, too rigidly naturalistic
for Goethe's judgment which had matured in the South.   Goethe
had not yet found a suitable form for this rounding-off of the
Gretchen-tragedy in the First Part.   The confused scene from
the *Urfaust*, "Auerbach's Cellar", could find a place in the
Fragment, not only because the new form it took on in Italy
shows Faust as a greater and nobler man (it is not he, as in the
Urfaust, but Mephisto, who performs the wine-trick; in this
scene Faust says nothing but "And now I wish to go"), but
because in Italy this scene, which in the *Urfaust* was in prose, was
recast in poetic form, and its language purified and refined.
Thus, by a stricter artistic reshaping, the barbarity of the *Urfaust*
was so mitigated that it could find a place in the Fragment.
But for Gretchen's end he could find no form in which "the idea
shines as it were through a veil and the direct effect of the stupendous theme is subdued".   He preferred therefore to omit it
entirely and to publish his *Faust* as a Fragment.

Such was the effect of the South on Goethe.   He, as a German, knew Faust's yearnings, and found it impossible to live
and linger, as the Romantic writers did, in such a state.   He
needed fulfilment, not in the world of dreams or phantasy, but
there and then.   Longing seemed to him the most dangerous
enemy of inner peace, of serenity of spirit, and also of artistic
form.   It was a necessity for him, then, to free himself from
Faust's yearning, and he did so in Italy, where he overcame
the Faust-spirit.   Just as the Titans, vanquished and bound by
the Olympian gods, yet threaten Olympus from below, so this
spirit still lies in the depths of Goethe's nature, giving his Classical
works a profundity not found in the Classical productions of other
literatures.   It is significant that after his return from Italy, that
"land of plastic vision", to "formless Germany", after exchanging "a clear sky for an overcast one" (perhaps fearing that any
work on Faust might endanger the new stage in his development,
or more probably because of the change the South had wrought
in him), Goethe put Faust aside for some considerable time.   He
then resumed work on the Nordic Faust-drama, although with
some reluctance and amidst constant interruptions.   "*Faust*",
he wrote to Schiller in July 1897, "has been laid aside meanwhile, the Nordic phantoms have for a time been driven out by
southern memories."   Five months later he wrote: "I shall
probably start work again on *Faust*, partly to rid myself of the

burden of it, and partly to prepare myself for a nobler frame of mind, possibly for Tell." And in the same month : " For the moment I am as far as possible from pure and noble subjects like this (*Laokoon*), for I am finishing my *Faust*, and hoping at the same time to rid myself of all nordic barbarity." In April 1798, when he was busy on an epic, the *Achilles*, he wrote : " It is as if a curtain had been drawn before the beautiful Homeric world, and nordic figures—Faust and his like—had crept in." How clear it is that in working at *Faust* Goethe had to overcome a deep distaste, that he felt this work an unwelcome distraction from other, higher, tasks. He speaks of his *Faust* as a witch's progeny, a Nordic monstrosity, a phantom of the air, an excursion into misty regions, a haze of rhyme and verse. And he was insistent in openly expressing his own attitude to the Nordic matter which he himself had outgrown. He did so in a prologue " Zueignung " and in an epilogue " Abschied ". The dedication sounds almost like an apology for calling up these shadows of the past at all.

> Ihr naht euch wieder, schwankende Gestalten,
> Die früh sich einst dem trüben Blick gezeigt.
> Versuch' ich wohl euch diesmal fest zu halten ?
> Fühl' ich mein Herz noch jenem Wahn geneigt ?
> Ihr drängt euch zu ! nun geht, so mögt ihr walten,
> Wie ihr aus Dunst und Nebel um mich steigt ;
> Mein Busen fühlt sich jugendlich erschüttert
> Vom Zauberhauch, der euren Zug umwittert.

They were indeed shadows of the past which he called up as he completed *Faust*, and this whole world seemed to him now to have become a world of illusion, no longer the clear and actual present in which he lived. And the change the South had wrought on him is still more obvious in the epilogue, which is unfortunately little known, for Goethe did not publish it at the time, and it appeared only after his death. It begins :

> Am Ende bin ich nun des Traurspieles,
> Das ich zuletzt mit Bangigkeit vollführt,
> Nicht mehr vom Drange menschlichen Gewühles,
> Nicht von der Macht der Dunkelheit gerührt.
> Wer schildert gern den Wirrwarr des Gefühles,
> Wenn ihn der Weg zur Klarheit aufgeführt ?
> Und so geschlossen sei der Barbareien
> Beschränkter Kreis mit seinen Zaubereien.

It has an air of tragedy. The greatest work of literature in the German language, Goethe's *Faust*, was completed as its writer drew further and further away from it, because he had taken the road to the South, the road that Faust took to reach Helen. It seems like a curse, and yet it was a blessing. For how could Goethe ever have shaped into a work of art this tragedy of endless striving, of ever-unfulfilled longing, of restless purpose, if he had not himself been thus transformed and healed ? The casting of *Iphigenie* into iambics, begun on the journey to Italy, was completed there. It must surely have been with strange feelings that in his old age, in 1826, Goethe read in Poerio's Italian translation this memorial to the change wrought on him by the South, and declared himself pleased with it. *Tasso* was completely rewritten, for now characters, plot and atmosphere no longer bore any relation to his outlook. The first two acts remained roughly the same in plot and sequence, but even there all haziness was dispelled by the predominance of form, and the introduction of rhythm, in accordance with Goethe's new outlook.[6] Texts of light operas (Singspiele) which he had brought with him were adapted in Italy to the form of the Italian opera, for which Goethe developed a great liking. *Egmont* also, the last two acts of which begin with a strange rhythmic movement, is approximated to opera by the important part that music plays in it. In Italy, rhythm and music help Goethe to progress from a naturalistic to an idealistic style.

When Goethe was obliged to leave Italy, his reluctant departure gave the whole of *Tasso* a new background of experience in place of the old : the tender sadness of a passionate spirit inexorably driven into irrevocable banishment. Tasso's banishment from Ferrara symbolises Goethe's feeling on leaving Italy, his banishment from the happy South which had become his spiritual home, to the gloomy North. As he left Rome, he must have remembered another writer, the exiled Ovid, who had to leave Rome by moonlight. Ovid's reminiscent elegies, written far off by the Black Sea in sadness and despondency, haunted Goethe's mind.

But Goethe's own reminiscent poems, his *Roman Elegies*, written after his return from Italy, were far from being elegiac laments or sighs of longing. Italy had now become so completely his own and had so penetrated the fabric of his being, that to him it was ever-present. So the farewell elegy he had planned was never written. The *Roman Elegies* are completely saturated in the beauty of the present. They are thus another sign that Italy had cured him of the Romantic longing of *Faust*,

and shown him how to live and work in the present. An inner
calm had come to him since his longing to see Italy had been
fulfilled. To use his own words : " Longing for art itself had
taken the place of longing for the land of the arts." He had
learned to know it, and now he wished to master it.[8] After he
had come back thus refined and transformed, his aim was to
radiate in his northern home the brightness of the South which
still shone within him. The " Musenhof " in Weimar took on a
southern splendour through the festival-plays and masquerades
composed after the pattern of the Italian Renaissance. The
theatre in Weimar went in for Italian operas, and Goethe himself won a victory over naturalism in adapting their texts. And
in the Second Part of *Faust* we read :

> Denkt nicht ihr seid in deutschen Grenzen,
> Von Teufels-, Narren- und Totentänzen,
> Ein heitres Fest erwartet euch.
> Der Herr, auf seinen Römerzügen,
> Hat, sich zu Nutz, euch zum Vergnügen,
> Die hohen Alpen überstiegen,
> Gewonnen sich ein heitres Reich.

It is true that Italian literature played no further part of any
importance in Weimar up to the Italian Romantic period. The
artist Fernow, a contributor to art periodicals, who had a thorough knowledge of Italian literature on this subject, was appointed
librarian to the Dowager Duchess. But this resulted in only a
short interlude during which he fostered the love of Italian
literature and provided occasions for stimulating reading and
conversation. With Fernow's death in 1808 there dried up for
the second time a source which since the death of Jagemann
(the previous librarian) had practically ceased to flow. For
foreign writings " must be brought nearer, even urged upon us,
must be offered cheaply with little trouble, if we are to take
them up, and enjoy them in comfort ".[9] Goethe was therefore
extremely gratified to receive (in 1813) from the Empress Maria
Ludovica a *de luxe* edition of the works of the Italian Abbé
Clemente Bondi. He replied with a sonnet addressed to Bondi :

> Aus jenen Ländern echten Sonnenscheines
> Beglückten oft mich Gaben der Gefilde :
> Agrumen reizend, Feigen süss und milde,
> Der Mandeln Milch, die Feuerkraft des Weines.
> So manches Musenwerk erregte meines
> Nordländ'schen Geistes innigste Gebilde,
> Wie an Achilleus lebensreichem Schilde
> Erfreut' ich mich des günstigen Vereines.

Und dass ich mich daran begnügen könnte,
War mir sogar ein Kunstbesitz bereitet,
Erquickend mich durch Anmut wie durch Stärke.
Doch nichts erschien im grösseren Momente,
Voll innern Werts, von so viel Glück begleitet,
Als durch Louisen, Bondi, deine Werke.

This sonnet is obviously more an expression of homage to the Empress (who sent him copies of the edition she had commissioned), and a debt of loving gratitude to Italy, than the outcome of any profound impression made by these unimportant poems. The works of the Muses which stimulated his northern spirit to deeply-felt creative processes did not belong to Italian literature but to the plastic arts.

Even Goethe's great contemporary, the Italian dramatist Alfieri, cannot be reckoned as a cultural influence in Goethe's case, although his tragedies are written in the style of Classicism. Goethe had Alfieri's drama " Saul " acted in Weimar (in Knebel's translation). This was an attempt to help the German theatre to conquer naturalism by turning to foreign drama which had a nobler artistic style. But Goethe, while admiring Alfieri's fine character, admits that he took only a superficial interest in him because of his lack of imagination and the exaggerated sententiousness of his manner and expression. He found him unsympathetic, in fact antipathetic. But in 1813, when Goethe was engaged in editing his " Italian Journey ", he remembered what his artistic and general development owed to Italy, and was all the more amazed when in 1820 he found this Classical land welcoming the German Romantic movement, whose fires had begun to glow beyond the Alps.

CHAPTER 7

THE SENSE OF FORM IN FRENCH LITERATURE

English literature had given young Goethe an understanding of his own nature. The art of Italy and of the South in general had set limits to his Faustian spirit. French literature exercised an educative and formative influence upon him. Its mission for him was one that Romance culture has always had, that of imbuing the German mind with a sense of form. As soon as Goethe realised the need for this, the effect followed naturally. Of course it presupposed a change in his view of French literature. It is no accident that the first sign of this change should be in Goethe's novel dealing with education, *Wilhelm Meister*, and in the first version of it. The change is clearly seen if we compare this work with the Shakespeare speech, in which Goethe has nothing but scorn for French literature. Now Wilhelm Meister, in his impulse towards self-education and effort to comprehend the nature of dramatic art, turns to French tragedy, to Corneille ; his opinions are both shaken and enlightened. He ceases to reject the Three Unities of Action, Time and Place, and demands only that they should not be isolated but should be considered as elements in the necessary unity and integrity of every work of art. Wilhelm Meister now admires Corneille's great and noble heroes, and is filled with an irresistible desire to compose a tragedy in the style of Corneille's. But it was not Corneille who exercised a formative influence over Goethe : it was Racine, whose gentleness and humaneness were certainly more akin to Goethe's natural disposition than the heroic Corneille. The latter had more affinity with Schiller. Two influences enabled Goethe to complete his *Iphigenie*, that of the South which he experienced in Italy and which engendered simplicity, dignity, serenity of spirit and beauty of form ; and that of French tragedy. Germans are perhaps insufficiently conscious of how great was the influence of French tragedy at the outset of German Classicism. Yet that of Racine is quite unmistakable. Traces of it are visible in the noble restraint and self-control of his characters even in acute suffering, in the avoidance of confusing side-issues in favour of one single plot, its scene the souls of the characters. His influence is also obvious in the retention of the Unities, in the rigid proportion and symmetry of the dramatic structure, in the dignified style and the harmonious and rhythmical language. The difference between them is of course no less obvious, and if we compare Goethe's *Iphigenie* with Racine's, we can trace even in Goethe's Classical creation its Germanic, Faust-like, Romantic character. For *Iphigenie* has not merely avoided the conventional rhetorical character of French Classicism. It seems as if here the Titans, though vanquished and bound, still threaten from beneath this world of happy Olympian serenity. This restraint and restfulness obviously result from an immense victory over himself, and it is the Faust-spirit which has won for itself Hellenistic form. Even this classically-objective work of art is clearly a work of experience in Goethe's sense, while in Racine's *Iphigénie* one neither seeks nor finds his own ardent feelings. The subtle vibration perceptible in every line of Goethe's *Iphigenie* reveals on what foundation it is erected. That he could and did command this form, he owes to the helping hand of French Classicism.

When Goethe returned from Italy he translated Choruses from Racine's *Athalie* (1789), with a view to providing a translation of his own to supersede Cramer's ; for, in Goethe's opinion, Cramer lacked as a translator the feeling for what was " fitting ". And what was " fitting " was just what the works of German literature now sought to take over from the French. It is particularly significant that it was the choruses that Goethe translated. Since his visit to Italy, where he had developed a fondness for operatic form, Goethe had come to realise that the defeat of naturalism (which was from now on his artistic purpose) might also be accomplished by approximating drama to opera, by the introduction of music and musical forms into tragedy, as Racine had attempted to do in his *Athalie*. This is the beginning of the work which culminated in *Pandora* and *Helena*.

When Goethe had himself assimilated the Classical technique, he was able, with the help of French tragic and dramatic art, to begin the great task of raising the artistic level of the German theatre, which was the focus of the nation's culture, out of the swamps of naturalism in which it was still caught. He aimed also at strengthening the frontiers between nature and art, and at educating the German stage to formal, noble, Classical style. The Weimar stage, on which this educative campaign began, was thus to be a model for the whole German theatre. With this in mind Goethe translated Voltaire's tragedies, *Mahomet* and *Tancred*, into rhythmic form and had them produced in Weimar. He called *Mahomet* " a model of dramatic restraint in the matter of

ction, time and place ". In a masquerade belonging to the
ear 1818 Mahomet appears :

> Der Weltgeschichte wichtiges Ereignis :
> Erst Nationen angeregt,
> Dann unterjocht und mit Propheten-Zeugnis
> Ein neu Gesetz den Völkern auferlegt ;
> Die grössten Taten, die geschehen,
> Wo Leidenschaft und Klugheit streitend wirkt,
> Im kleinsten Raume dargestellt zu sehen,
> In diesem Sinn ist solch ein Bild bezirkt.—
>
> Das einzig macht die Kunst unsterblich,
> Und bleibt der Bühne Glanz und Ruhm,
> Dass sie was gross und würdig, was verderblich,
> Von je betrachtet als ihr Eigentum.
> Doch musste sie bei Füll' und Reichtum denken,
> Sich Zeit und Ort und Handlung zu beschränken.

With a view to improving the Weimar theatre Goethe also
ketched out, in 1803, his " Rules for Actors " which are still
xtant, not as drawn up by Goethe but edited and published by
ckermann from actors' notes. They are closely modelled
hroughout on the rules for French actors, and are designed to
nould the German actor into an instrument usable in the service
f German Classicism.   Goethe himself once admitted that this
xperiment would not have been successful had Wilhelm von
Humboldt not written him from Paris a long, fully-detailed letter
' on the tragic stage in present-day France ", a letter which
Goethe published in 1799 in his *Propyläen*.   In this letter Hum-
oldt, basing his views on what he had seen in Paris, interpreted
he difference between the art of acting in Germany and that
n France as a difference between the characters of the two nations
s a whole.   The German actor portrays a unique, characterised
ndividual, the French a type, a general personification of a
assion.   The German actor is concerned solely with the inner
ruth of his feeling, which he does not translate into visible form.
Here Humboldt describes the German people as a gestureless
ation.   But the French actor seeks to give to the whole inner
ife an outward, visible form in free attitude and gesture.   In this
he French actor approximates to the plastic arts and conforms,
s they do, to the demands of a noble beauty and symmetry.
imilarly, French declamation complies with the demands of
usic, expressing itself in euphony, melody and harmony.   In
peech, too, the German actor rates naturalistic truth above
eauty.   The French actor is ever faithful to the social education
haracteristic of his nation, and on the stage never offends social

decorum. He is always conscious of appearing before a social
group, a public which even in moments of intensest feeling he
bears in mind, never turning his back on them, for instance,
always speaking in their direction. But the German actor is
regardless of all this. He plays and speaks for himself, and may
even appear crude, when it is a question of portraying the truth.
In a word : the French actor's allegiance is to an æsthetically
idealistic style, the German's to a natural one.

These remarks of Humboldt's, to which he appends an
invitation to both nations to benefit by learning from and supplementing each other, were really enlightening to Goethe, as he
told Humboldt. In his early youth he must have seen troupes of
French actors in Frankfurt, Leipzig and Strassburg. But evi-
dently the difference did not strike him at that time. It was
this letter of Humboldt's that clarified his views, not only on the
art of acting in France but also on French tragedy of the period
of Classicism. In matters of style this naturally had a controlling
influence on the actor's art. All this was of great help to Goethe
in his translation of Voltaire's tragedies, and now, as Director
of the Weimar Theatre, he tried to train his actors on French
lines. For the rules for actors that he set up correspond to an
astonishing degree with the reports he. had from Humboldt. In
1800, when he published in the *Propyläen* " Some scenes from
Mahomet, adapted from Voltaire ", he added, " No friend of the
German theatre will read the article on the tragic drama in
present-day France without wishing that, without prejudice to
our own principles, the excellences of the French theatre might
be adapted to ours also." It was a question, then, of utilising
the tragic and histrionic art of the French, their highly social
manner, and their strictly regulated forms to improve upon
naturalism. That was the aim of Goethe's translations from
Voltaire, of the performances of Racine's *Mithridate* and his
Phèdre in Schiller's translation, and of the rules which Goethe
drew up for his actors. Even when Goethe produced Shakespeare's *Romeo and Juliet* he altered Shakespeare's style (as was
noted at the time) in the direction of the French theatre. He
did this by simplifying the action, eradicating as " jarring and
extraneous matter " the comic and coarse elements, because " our
mode of thought favours consistency " and so cannot endure such
elements. He also recast in rhyme the prose passages, even
translated parts of the work in Alexandrines and harmonised the
whole into one homogeneous unity. Schiller, his faithful helper

in raising the idealistic level of the German theatre, did much the same in his translations of *Macbeth* and Gozzi's *Turandot*. The last work that Schiller completed was his translation of Racine's *Phèdre*. When Goethe produced Voltaire's *Mahomet* on the Weimar stage, Schiller wrote a Prologue for it which is printed here because it clearly reveals the design behind this resuscitation of the French theatre in Weimar. Also it is one of the most characteristic efforts towards world literature, showing in what sense a foreign literature can be made to stimulate one's own without any loss of its national character.

An Goethe, als er den Mahomet *von* Voltaire *auf die Bühne brachte*

> Du selbst, der uns von falschem Regelzwange
> Zu Wahrheit und Natur zurückgeführt,
> Der, in der Wiege schon ein Held, die Schlange
> Erstickt, die unsern Genius umschnürt,
> Du, den die Kunst, die göttliche, schon lange
> Mit ihrer reinen Priesterbinde ziert—
> Du opferst auf zertrümmerten Altären
> Der Aftermuse, die wir nicht mehr ehren?

> Einheim'scher Kunst ist dieser Schauplatz eigen,
> Hier wird nicht fremden Götzen mehr gedient,
> Wir können mutig einen Lorbeer zeigen,
> Der auf dem deutschen Pindus selbst gegrünt ;
> Selbst in der Künste Heiligtum zu steigen,
> Hat sich der deutsche Genius erkühnt,
> Und auf der Spur des Griechen und des Briten
> Ist er dem bessern Ruhme nachgeschritten.

> Denn dort, wo Sklaven knien, Despoten walten,
> Wo sich die eitle Aftergrösse bläht,
> Da kann die Kunst das Edle nicht gestalten,
> Von keinem Ludwig wird es ausgesät ;
> Aus eigner Fülle muss es sich entfalten,
> Es borget nicht von ird'scher Majestät,
> Nur mit der Wahrheit wird es sich vermählen,
> Und seine Glut durchflammt nur freie Seelen.

> Drum nicht in alte Fesseln uns zu schlagen,
> Erneuerst du dies Spiel der alten Zeit,
> Nicht uns zurückzuführen zu den Tagen
> Charakterloser Minderjährigkeit ;
> Es wär' ein eitel und vergeblich Wagen,
> Zu fallen ins bewegte Rad der Zeit :
> Geflügelt fort entführen es die Stunden,
> Das Neue kommt, das Alte ist verschwunden.

> Ertweitert jetzt ist des Theaters Enge,
> In seinem Raume drängt sich eine Welt,
> Nicht mehr der Worte rednerisch Gepränge,
> Nur der Natur getreues Bild gefällt,

Verbannet ist der Sitten falsche Strenge,
Und menschlich handelt, menschlich fühlt der Held ;
Die Leidenschaft erhebt die freien Töne,
Und in der Wahrheit findet man das Schöne.

Doch leicht gezimmert nur ist Thespis' Wagen,
Und er ist gleich dem acheront'schen Kahn ;
Nur Schatten und Idole kann er tragen
Und drängt das rohe Leben sich heran,
So droht das leichte Fahrzeug umzuschlagen,
Das nur die flücht'gen Geister fassen kann.
Der Schein soll nie die Wirklichkeit erreichen,
Und siegt Natur, so muss die Kunst entweichen.

Denn auf dem bretternen Gerüst der Szene
Wird eine Idealwelt aufgetan ;
Nichts sei hier wahr und wirklich als die Träne,
Die Rührung ruht auf keinem Sinnenwahn,
Aufrichtig ist die wahre Melpomene,
Sie kündigt nichts als eine Fabel an,
Und weiss durch tiefe Wahrheit au entzücken ;
Die falsche stellt sich wahr, um zu berücken.

Es droht die Kunst, vom Schauplatz zu verschwinden,
Ihr wildes Reich behauptet Phantasie,
Die Bühne will sie wie die Welt entzünden,
Das Niedrigste und Höchste menget sie ;
Nur bei dem Franken war noch Kunst zu finden,
Erschwang er gleich ihr hohes Urbild nie,
Gebannt in unveränderlichen Schranken
Hält er sie fest und nimmer darf sie wanken.

Ein heiliger Bezirk ist ihm die Szene,
Verbannt aus ihrem festlichen Gebiet
Sind der Natur nachlässig rohe Töne,
Die Sprache selbst erhebt sich ihm zum Lied ;
Es ist ein Reich des Wohllauts und der Schöne,
In edler Ordung greifet Glied in Glied,
Zum ernsten Tempel füget sich das Ganze,
Und die Bewegung borget Reiz vom Tanze.

Nicht Muster zwar darf uns der Franke werden,
Aus seiner Kunst spricht kein lebend'ger Geist,
Des falschen Anstands prunkende Gebärden
Verschmäht der Sinn, der nur das Wahre preist ;
Ein Führer nur zum Bessern soll er werden,
Er komme wie ein abgeschiedner Geist,
Zu reinigen die oft entweihte Szene
Zum würd'gen Sitz der alten Melpomene.

These endeavours, made in Weimar in the interests of French tragic art, rectified a great injustice which Lessing had done to it. His derogatory judgment had remained for several decades a canon of German literary theory. In Lessing's day, Corneille and Racine were cold-shouldered because German drama had

in fact declined into a slavish imitation of French Classicism from
which it had to be emancipated before it could reach self-awareness and spread its wings. But Lessing's picture was a distorted
misrepresentation and, since German drama had gained its
freedom with the help of Shakespeare, there was really no ground
for supporting such a view any longer. Now French Classicism
might rather afford a wholesome training for German drama,
which had gone too far in throwing off all restrictive rules, and
in imitating nature. Unfortunately this did not take place. The
German Romantic movement returned to Lessing's standpoint,
and August Wilhelm Schlegel's comparison of Racine's *Phèdre*
with that of Euripides neutralised all the efforts that had been
made in Weimar. Goethe interpreted Schlegel's grotesque
judgment on Molière almost as a personal affront. Since the
Romantic period, French Classicism could no longer be reckoned
among the important factors in German culture, which had
thereby deprived itself of valuable assistance. There were but
a few voices crying in the wilderness, proclaiming the great value
of this art and the benefits which it could bestow on the German
theatre. Grillparzer and Hebbel did so, and to the credit of the
Swiss it must be added that not only did Conrad Ferdinand
Meyer acknowledge his allegiance to Racine (" j'adore Racine "),
but also Gottfried Keller defended him vigorously against the
German verdict. (His letter to Hermann Hettner on this subject
was incorporated in Hettner's essay on French tragedy.)

But the French spirit did more than educate Goethe in the
direction of a noble Classical style. He said on one occasion
to Soret that even in the Napoleonic era he did not hate the
French : how could he, to whom culture and barbarism were
the sole standards, have hated a nation which belonged to the
most cultured in the world, and to which he owed so great a
part of his own education ? And he was not thinking of education merely as affecting Classical form. It was not only as a
dramatist that Voltaire, who appeared to Goethe to be the epitome
of French culture, exercised a formative influence over him. He
guided Goethe's mind towards the Classical way of thinking, and
the Classical conception of humanity. Goethe and Voltaire
have often been compared in foreign literatures, and Goethe has
often been called the " German Voltaire ". The comparison is
just, if at the same time one remembers the essential difference
between them. This difference is not necessarily the one which
Heinrich Mann has made the theme of an essay on Goethe and

Voltaire, in which Goethe comes off badly. For this writer the difference is that Voltaire was a fighter who protested in the name of the spirit against force, in the name of truth against all forms of delusion and deception, in the name of freedom against all tyranny, in the name of justice—as in the Calas case—against the condemnation of an innocent man. Voltaire was Europe's great civiliser, the crusader of progress, freedom and humanity. Goethe, on the other hand, made the—admittedly dangerous—statement that he would rather endure injustice than inconsequence ; never raised a finger in the cause of justice, never helped to abolish any instance of inhumanity. Though as a poet he created Gretchen, as Minister of State he voted for the death sentence for infanticide ; he yielded to force, and contented himself with noble creations in the world of art without working for their translation into actual life. This comparison is just in saying that Goethe's nature, in contrast to Voltaire's, is that neither of a fighter nor of a revolutionary. But one must deny the validity of the comparison, because there is more than one way in which the transformation of society may be achieved : not only through a combatant and revolutionary spirit, but perhaps with even profounder and more lasting effect through a purely scientific examination of the truth and its representation in art. Is it not true that simply through his *Iphigenie*, his *Faust*, his *Wilhelm Meister*, Goethe has—without any active intervention —done at least as much for the idea of humanity as Voltaire ? The difference, which is a characteristic one between the German and the French spirit, is rather that Goethe was the Faust-type, struggling, endlessly seeking, a wandering spirit. But it seems as if Voltaire thought himself in secure possession of the truth, and from this height shed its light into the darkness below. But Goethe, and especially Goethe in the maturity of his old age, once said truly to Eckermann that he was one of those who struggle out of darkness into light ; and what is Goethe's Faust but such a spirit ?

Yet this struggling halted at a point which Voltaire did not observe. Reverence was one of Goethe's most essential characteristics. In this he differed from Voltaire who, in Goethe's judgment, in spite of his wealth of mind and wit, knew neither awe nor respect, to whom nothing was sacred. Goethe remarked to Eckermann that Mme de Genlis was perfectly right in

revolting against Voltaire's freedom and effrontery ; for, after all, however witty it all might be, the world is none the better for it ;

nothing comes of it all.   In fact, it can do the greatest harm by
bewildering men, depriving them of the stability they need.   Besides,
what do we really know, even with all our wit !   Man is not born
to solve the world's problems, but to find out where the problem begins
and to limit himself to what he is able to comprehend.   To measure
the events of creation is beyond the reach of his faculties, and to wish
to rationalise the universe is, for so puny a creature, a hopeless
endeavour.   The reason of man and the reason of God are two very
different things.

It seemed to Goethe that the greatest happiness of thinking
man was " to investigate the comprehensible, and trustfully to
revere the incomprehensible ".   It is this reverence that Voltaire
lacks, and this constitutes the essential difference between them.

But it was precisely this difference that enabled Voltaire to
help Goethe on his way out of darkness into light.   It was not
without reason that Goethe once, in his old age, described
Voltaire to Eckermann as the universal source of light, and
recommended him to young Eckermann as a guide and a master,
although at the same time he was not blind to Voltaire's weak-
ness.   But he recommended him because he was deeply conscious
of the extent of Voltaire's formative influence in his own case.

It is always dangerous to try to analyse accurately the rays
of any intellectual light ; yet we must make an attempt to show
in what directions Voltaire's mind formed and trained Goethe's.
The first was surely that Voltaire's Latin clearness, his easy
cheerfulness, and his French grace helped Goethe to emerge from
the mystical dusk, in which the German poet delights to move,
to clarity of mind ; to pass from Werther's *mal du siècle* to serenity ;
and to transform German gravity into an easy grace.   These
were the qualities which Goethe particularly admired and praised
in Voltaire : clarity, cheerfulness, lightness, ease of mind.   But
Goethe also saw that the most essential difference between the
German and the French writer lay in the aloofness and self-
absorption of the former and the social propriety of the latter.
What he hoped that France would give his own people was
social education.   Indeed he saw it as the true mission of France
to teach good social behaviour to the world.   He felt that he
owed his own social education to French literature.   This led
him to say once to Eckermann : he had known and loved Molière
since his youth, and had learnt from him all his life.   He never
failed to read some of his plays every year in order to keep in
constant touch with him.   It was not merely the finished artistic
treatment that delighted him, but more than anything else the

lovable disposition, the highly cultured personality of the writer. Molière had an ease and a feeling for what was fitting, and a tone of cultured conversation, arising out of his own native good taste but developed by daily intercourse with the most outstanding men of his age. What Goethe himself so sorely missed, namely personal contact with the great men of his time, he made up for by constant intellectual intercourse with them ; among these his older contemporary, Voltaire, had pride of place. Why had he recommended Voltaire so warmly to young Eckermann ? Because Eckermann, by his own account, lacked what is called a sense of propriety, and of this Goethe was richly possessed. For that reason Goethe recommended Voltaire to him as a master. So there we have it : his sense of propriety, or as Goethe also calls it, of fitness, his tone, his taste, his elegance—in a word, Voltaire's social demeanour, which Goethe so sorely missed in the German writers, was the reason for his formative influence on Goethe. But there is still what is perhaps the most important influence that Voltaire had upon Goethe. Voltaire was probably the most cosmopolitan spirit of the century, a citizen of the world for whom there was only one society, world society, whose irony and derision banished all national self-sufficiency and every popular prejudice, who recognised and proclaimed common humanity as the bond uniting all the nations. And as this became the fundamental *leitmotif* in Goethe's works and in his philosophy, we must not forget the cultural influence of Voltaire, that incarnation of the European intellect. Of course, with Goethe the conception of man is not conditioned so narrowly by reason as it is with Voltaire ; with Goethe it is much more universal, comprising all human powers and potentialities. This was another difference between Voltaire and Goethe. But we ought, all the same, to recognise in Voltaire in this respect one of Goethe's " sources of light ". Indeed, even Goethe's idea of world literature—in its essence a realisation of universal, unchanging humanity as a bond between the peoples—had in Voltaire a forerunner and an ancestor.

It is instructive to compare the change in Goethe's attitude to Voltaire ; how in the Storm and Stress period he turned from him, and how he later yielded to the other's formative influence, and reacted in precisely the opposite way to Diderot. It shows that in fact German and French literatures had already begun to exchange rôles.

In *Dichtung und Wahrheit*, Goethe speaks of the venerable and

stately character of French literature, which repelled the youth
of Germany, as well as of the exaggerated and ever-increasing
influence which society exerted on French authors.   Here he
mentions Diderot who was so different from Voltaire.   " Diderot
was very much akin to us ; in fact, in everything that the French
criticised in him, he is a true German." Goethe approved of
Diderot's " children of nature ".   And indeed it was Diderot who,
like Rousseau, spread a " feeling of disgust " towards social life,
a quiet prelude to those vast world changes in which everything
seemed to perish.   But what was Rousseau's and Diderot's
attitude to art ?   " Here too they referred us to nature, from art
they urged us to turn to her."   And it is true that in art Diderot
who, like Rousseau, was susceptible to English influences,
demanded nature and truth, and set up against the Classicistic
poetic tragedy, governed by strict rules, his more domestic prose
tragedy.   At the same time an actor, Aufresne, opened a campaign
against everything on the stage that was contrary to nature, and
as a tragedian tried to concentrate on portraying truth.   Diderot's
advocacy of naturalism in art exerted a profound influence on
young Goethe and drew him away from that of Voltaire.   In
Dichtung und Wahrheit, however, Goethe calls Diderot's poetics the
doctrine of " false naturalism ".   It is, he said, a mistaken
endeavour to try to absorb nature into art.   In 1799 Goethe's
translation of Diderot's *Essay on Painting* appeared.   At that time
Goethe, together with the Weimar " Friends of Art ", was investigating the rules governing the plastic arts.   The idea that
governed his researches was that art should not copy nature but
should live by its own laws, its own truth.   It ought not to conjure
up, as naturalism would have it do, an illusory reality.   About
that time Goethe, using the form of a discussion on Diderot's
Essay on Painting, gave an exposition of Diderot's revolutionary
æsthetics.   They were directed against French Classicism with
its social proprieties, empty declamation and disregard for nature,
and designed to lead French literature and art back to truth and
nature.   Goethe protested against Diderot's demand for the
removal of the dividing line between art and nature, and claimed
their strict separation on the ground that the laws of nature are
not the laws of art, and that the artist should aim at producing
not a world of nature but a finished work of art.   In his speech,
too, Goethe defended the academy and the academic study of
art against Diderot, saying that genius and the inspiration of a
passing mood are in themselves insufficient.   In doing this,

Goethe showed himself more French than Diderot, and Diderot appears more German than Goethe. Behind this change of Goethe's outlook we can surely see not only the influence of the Classical period and of Italy, but also that of French Classicism, which Goethe now champions against Diderot.

And yet Goethe's liking for Diderot survived all differences between them. Goethe continued to admire him. When in 1805 he was sent a copy of the original manuscript text of Diderot's *Rameau's Nephew* from Russia, he translated it from the manuscript, and this is the form in which the work became known first of all, even in France. Goethe's notes to this translation give a brilliant and comprehensive sketch of French literature, music and painting in the 18th century. The translation was soon forgotten in Germany, for after 1806 no one felt any desire to concern himself with an enemy nation and its literature ; and Goethe's plan for an edition of the French original text was frustrated by Napoleon's invasion and the hatred of the invader that it excited.[10] In 1818, however, plans were made in France for a complete edition of Diderot. In the advertisement of the work, this manuscript (known only in a German translation) was mentioned, the contents of the work were quoted from it, and some passages from Goethe's translation were given in French. The complete edition, published in France in 1821, was, in fact, identical with the copy from which Goethe's translation was made. With this gift to France of Diderot's work Goethe is now shown as a donor, not a recipient, and his notes, published separately in 1823 by the French translators Saur and de Saint-Geniès, enabled France to realise the depth of Goethe's sympathy with French literature and French culture, and also his knowledge of it. Thus the way was prepared for the warm reception that awaited him in France.

CHAPTER 8

THE SPANISH SENSE OF THE THEATRE

It cannot be claimed that Spain exerted on Goethe any influence comparable in degree with that of other Romance cultures, such as the Italian and the French ; but Goethe had a great admiration for Cervantes and Calderon. The descriptions of his travels which Wilhelm von Humboldt sent to Goethe in the form of letters written during his visit to Spain, giving accounts of literature and the theatre, had to be a substitute for Goethe's seeing things for himself. But at that time (1799) he was reading Cervantes's tragedy *Numantia* with great pleasure. And he certainly grew to know Cervantes well when later, under the influence of Spinoza and Italy, he felt the need to free himself from all delusion and self-deception and was trying to look at life with undistorted vision and see it as it was. Some bond must have been established between him and the writer of *Don Quixote*, that spirit shrouded in delusion and illusion, to whom reality appeared in the form of a dream conjured up by his phantasy. In 1823, when Goethe wrote in *Kunst und Altertum* on " Spanish Romances ", he stated that the fundamental characteristic of the Spanish nation was the tendency to embody the idea in the commonest and most ordinary circumstances of life. But when it is directly manifested, the idea always evokes a kind of embarrassment, even aversion, against which man somehow or other " brings up his defences ". To avoid a tragic effect, it must be clearly seen to belong to the world of imagination, and it takes its refuge there to preserve its purity. Even the vessel in which the idea manifests itself is shattered if it lays claim to such purity. And yet the idea, in crossing over to the world of imagination, loses its value. This explains why such a world, when shattered by reality, excites no pity, but is ridiculous because it gives rise to comic situations. This was Goethe's interpretation of the humorous Ballads of the Spanish writers, which hover between two elements seeking to meet and yet mutually repellent : the Sublime and the Commonplace. To be " squeezed " between them is never tragic ; in the end one has to smile and wish one had the luck to have this kind of thing happen to oneself. Goethe considered the most successful work of this kind to be *Don Quixote*. " I would be hard put to it ", he wrote, " to find anything of this kind that we Germans had done so well." German idealism, seen in Fichte's philosophy or Schiller's works, for instance, has a certain affinity with the Spanish spirit as summed up by Goethe ; for German idealism too seeks to present the idea as absolute. But it lacks the humour, the sense of the comic consequences, which follow any attempt of this kind. In Schiller's case it leads to tragedy, without renouncing its absolute demands. On the other hand, Wieland's poems have a profound resemblance to Cervantes's *Don Quixote* and bear his impress. Cervantes was one of the educative influences which led Wieland back to earth and to reality from the visionary heights of exaggerated idealism and metaphysical fanaticism. Cervantes showed him the comic nature of the contrast involved in the attempt to introduce the idea into reality. It is possible to link Wilhelm Meister and Faust too with Don Quixote. Wilhelm Meister's chimerical artistry, and his delusive ideal of the theatre-world, are dissolved by the touch of reality ; Faust, in his desire to bring the idea into direct contact with life, becomes a visionary who has a long way to go before he recognises that with all its limitations the earth is where he has to live and work. And as a visionary and a fanatic, " squeezed " between the sublime and the commonplace, he is treated by Mephistopheles with irony. Here we have a slight flavour of Cervantes. But there is no sign of any influence exerted by *Don Quixote*. It was quite different powers that Goethe " brought up as defences " against the idea when it was manifested and that delivered him from any such desire. The " slight flavour " of Cervantes was one of these coincidences, so often met with in any literature, which are founded not on the interplay of one mind on another but on a common human relationship which also governs the frequent similarity in figures of mythology. If it had been otherwise, Goethe, who always acknowledged his debt to those who contributed to his development, would have mentioned Cervantes among them. He never did so, although he expressed deep gratitude to the English humorist Sterne for the humane culture which he owed to him.

In Calderon's case, we possess one eloquent testimony of Goethe's. The important point, he once said to Eckermann (1825), is that the nature of the man from whom we are to learn should be akin to our own. For instance Calderon, great though he was and greatly though he (Goethe) admired him, could have no influence, good or bad, upon him. But Calderon constituted a danger for Schiller, who would have been led astray by him, and it was therefore fortunate that it was only after his death that Calderon became generally known in Germany. Calderon was most outstanding on the technical and theatrical sides, but Schiller was sounder, more serious, higher in his aim ; and it would have been a pity to forfeit some of these virtues without attaining Calderon's greatness in other respects.

Goethe certainly learned to know Calderon too late for the latter to exercise a formative influence over him. He first read the *Wonder-working Magician*—which he compared to his own *Faust*—long after the First Part of *Faust* was completed (1812). He then wrote : " Einsiedel has translated the *Wonder-working Magician*. It is the theme of Dr. Faust treated with incredible grandeur." [11] It was not till 1802 that Schlegel's translation caused him to take more interest in Calderon, who immediately roused his astonished admiration. In 1804 he wrote to Schiller with reference to the *Constant Prince* that, even if all poetry completely vanished from the earth, from this one work it could be restored. Goethe often and with enjoyment gave readings from this drama at the court, at Johanna Schopenhauer's and in other houses. In the notes to *Rameau's Nephew*, he ranks Shakespeare and Calderon, both judged faultless by the highest æsthetic tribunal, as equals, and even champions them (bearing in mind their nationality and their period) against the Greek standards of taste in art : We Northerners cannot be remade to the Greek pattern. We boast a different ancestry and different models. If the Romantic interest in the barbarous ages had not brought the prodigious and the absurd together, where would a *Hamlet*, a *Lear*, an *Adoration of the Cross*, a *Constant Prince* have come from ? It is our duty to keep courageously to the heights of these barbaric vantage-points, for we shall surely never rise to those of the Græco-Romans. But it is our duty also to know and to appreciate justly what others think and what they accomplish. [12] Goethe was even inclined, when he read the *Adoration of the Cross* in Schlegel's translation, to rate Calderon above Shakespeare. It is easy to see why, when we compare the two. In 1829, when he first read Calderon's drama *Absalom's Locks* in a translation by Gries, he wrote that in Calderon truth had reappeared as of old : that just as in modern times Shakespeare's works intimately combined nature and poetry, so Calderon's fused poetry with the most advanced civilisation. It goes almost without saying that the Goethe who had been moulded by the influences of Greece, Italy and France, had more affinity with the highly cultured

poetry of Calderon, which he thought bordered on excessive
culture, than with the "native woodnotes" of Shakespeare, the
idol of his youth. The Romantic writers, too, turned from
Shakespeare to Calderon. But this cannot have influenced
Goethe. For what raised Calderon above Shakespeare in the
opinion of the Romantic writers was his Catholicism, his Christian
mysticism ; and Goethe paid no homage to this even at the time
when he was in sympathy with the Romantic movement. There
does, however, exist a plan of Goethe's for a *Tragedy in the Christian
Era*, which, obviously under Calderon's influence, was to be a
martyr-play emulating Calderon's richness of style. Goethe
considered Calderon's influence on German literature, as far as
this Romantic conception of it was concerned, to be extremely
dangerous and harmful. When he expressed his admiration for
the drama *The Daughter of the Air*, he did so expressly because the
subject-matter of this drama seemed to him superior to·that of
any other of Calderon's tragedies. Its theme was a purely human
one, with no more of the demonic element than was necessary
to reveal the element of extravagance that lies in human nature.
Only the beginning and the ending were miraculous ; everything else took a natural course. Goethe also expressed his
admiration for the way in which stress was laid on religious
significance, the mysteries of Christianity, in the *Constant Prince*.
Goethe saw in this character, said to be a Christian martyr,
nothing less than a Christian Regulus. The Prince was constant,
not to his faith, but to the greatness and honour of Portugal.
Unfortunately many of Calderon's works show that noble and
independent mind at the mercy of an obscure delusion, trying to
give the irrational a rational artistic form. This puts us at odious
variance with the writer himself, for his material repels while his
treatment attracts us. Shakespeare, on the other hand, possessed
the great advantage of being born and brought up a Protestant.
Every one of his works shows him completely at home with what
is human ; he surveys delusion and superstition, and simply plays
with them ; he brings in supernatural beings to serve his purposes,
he calls up tragic ghosts and droll sprites for his own ends. But
everything undergoes a process whereby the writer escapes the
embarrassment of having to worship what is absurd—surely the
saddest state into which a consciously reasoning being can fall.[13]
The baroque conception of Catholicism always stood between
Calderon and Goethe. It stands, too, between the Wonder-
working Magician and Faust ; and even at the end of the Second

Part of *Faust*, where Goethe seems to draw nearest to Calderon, his artificial, elaborate way of handling the figures of Christianity is very obvious.

There are special reasons why, in spite of all this, Goethe turned from Shakespeare to Calderon. It was not only because Calderon, compared with classicism, must have seemed more vivid, richer, more alive, and compared with Shakespeare stricter, more uniform, more restrained ; so that Goethe was lost in admiration of the architectural element in Calderon's dramatic art, his " mastery of technique ". A much more important reason was that in Calderon Goethe found the dramatist he needed. It was part of the change in Goethe that he learned, as did the writers of classicism, to consider the limitations of the theatre. This knowledge was a necessity to the Classical writer as to the theatre director and the reformer of the German theatre. Goethe wanted to raise the German stage and German dramatic art above naturalism, and to give them a nobler artistic style. How drastically Goethe and Schiller had then to adapt Shakespeare for their theatre, to make him conform to the style of Weimar, and to be of use for their purpose ! With Calderon it was quite different. In his essay " Shakespeare Without End " Goethe aired the curious view that Shakespeare was not a writer for the stage : he spoke through living phrases to the inner sense, and addressed himself to the imagination, not the eye. He naturally belonged, therefore, to the history of poetry, and it was only by chance that he figured in the history of the theatre. For only what immediately appeals to the eye as a symbol is theatrical. His whole nature can counter to the stage. It is true to say that though Calderon could no longer be counted as a factor in Goethe's personal development, yet, through Goethe, he became one of the cultural and educative influences in the German theatre and dramatic art. The richness of his lyrical and dramatic forms alone were enough to achieve this, being especially calculated to supplant theatrical naturalism. Goethe instigated Gries to translate the lyrical portions of *Great Zenobia* for performance in Weimar, and this led to Gries's complete translation of Calderon, the best that exists.[14] It was purely from the standpoint of the theatre that Goethe concerned himself with Calderon. This is clear from a letter to Heinrich von Kleist, who had sent him his *Penthesilea* with the remark that it was designed for the theatre of the future. Goethe replied that in front of any trestle-stage he might say to the real theatrical genius : *Hic Rhodus, hic salta !*

On any fairground, even on planks resting on barrels, he could bring—*mutatis mutandis*—enormous pleasure to the masses, both cultured and uncultured, with the works of Calderon (1808).[15] He certainly appreciated the purely poetical merit of this type of drama. " These works transport us to a magnificent sea-girt land, with flowers and fruit in abundance, and lit by clear stars," he wrote in 1816 to Gries. And yet " magnificent Calderon " seemed to him too much committed to the conventions of his age and his people. It was difficult for an honest observer to see the writer's great talent behind the etiquette of the theatre. In bringing this type of work before the public, one presupposes considerable goodwill which will incline them to accept what is strange to them, to enjoy an outlook and a rhythm foreign to their own, and to forgo for a time what is most akin to their own nature. Individuality in expression is the beginning and end of all art. But one should not yield oneself so completely to another's idiosyncrasies that they come to swamp one's own individual temperament.[16] Even Shakespeare is no exception here, much less Calderon. " It is for future men of letters to record into what error Shakespeare, and still more Calderon, have led us, how these two great stars in the poetic firmament have become for us will-o'-the-wisps." Goethe had thoughts of supplanting Gries's translation of Calderon's works by introducing to the German public that strange and distant epoch in the development of the Spanish nation, of which Calderon alone is intelligible to us.[17] So in the first place, it was as a master of theatrical technique that Goethe selected Calderon to carry on the education of the German theatre, as he had selected Voltaire, Racine and all those dramatists whose works he had performed in Weimar. In 1811, after long and careful preparation, the *Constant Prince* was given on the Weimar stage, and Goethe thus gained for that stage " a whole new province ". In 1812 there followed *Life is a Dream* (adapted by Einsiedel and Riemer), and in 1815 *Great Zenobia*. In 1820, J. G. Keil, a former Weimar librarian, dedicated his edition of Calderon to Goethe, who was happy to see the name of so esteemed a writer as Calderon thus linked with his own. It was especially gratifying that this should be done by a man who had seen in Weimar the love and reverence with which he had then treated Calderon's works, and his " anxious hesitation " in not daring to produce them in public until he felt assured of really satisfactory results. He did not omit to thank the man who recalled this time to his mind.[18]

When Goethe was busy writing the *West-Eastern Divan* and was steeping himself in the poetry of the East, he was reminded once more of Calderon, as he noted the affinity of the Spanish writer's flowery, allegorical style, with that of his own favourite author Háfiz.

Herrlich ist der Orient
Uebers Mittelmeer gedrungen ;
Nur wer Hafis liebt und kennt
Weiss, was Calderon gesungen.

Goethe's spiritual sojourn in the East heightened his appreciation of " admirable " Calderon, who had made no secret of the Arabian elements in his education ; " it is a pleasure to rediscover and admire noble ancestors in their worthy descendants " ; and so Calderon formed for Goethe the first bridge from Europe to the East. The confluence of East and West had begun.

CHAPTER 9

NEW LIGHT FROM THE FAR EAST

We now have to deal with influences which extended Goethe's horizons, as did the Far East and America. These drew Goethe's gaze away from Europe to distant regions, and as a result he, his poetry, and his growing idea of world literature acquired an international significance beyond the confines of Europe. The differences in the outward influences appear to correspond to the stages of Goethe's organic development. In his youth England roused him to self-awareness, the Romance civilisation moulded him into a complete personality ; now in his maturity Goethe stood in need of expansion, in order not to grow rigid in his present form but to be transformed and to rise to a higher stage of life.

The Romantic movement was turning from Greece to the East, and in 1812 there appeared *The Divan of Muhammed Shemsed Dín Háfiz*, a translation by the orientalist Josef von Hammer of Persia's greatest lyric poet, Háfiz. In 1814 Goethe began to steep himself in this Eastern world and to write poems in the Persian poet's style. In the same year, fired by the Romantic movement, he made a journey to the Rhine, the Main and the Necker, and in Frankfurt he met Marianne von Willemer, with whom, at the age of sixty-five, he fell in love. This was the experience that gave a soul to his Eastern poems, that made them " occasional poems " in his use of the words. Stimulated by this love the Eastern poems by 1815 numbered a hundred, and they continued to multiply until in 1819 the *West-Eastern Divan* was completed.

What was it that drove him in spirit to the East? The explanation that he was at that time in sympathy with the Romantic movement is insufficient. Why did this 13th-century "Bard of Shira" delight him to the pitch of poetic rivalry? Goethe got his first impression of him from the character-sketches which Hammer appended to his translation. His reputation as the great authority on the Koran had earned him the title " Háfiz " (that is to say : Preserver of the Koran). But Hammer compared him as a poet with Anacreon and Catullus. For he was the bard of wine and love, inns and maidens, roses and nightingales, spring and youth ; he derided monastic life, orthodoxy and asceticism. Later, however, he was known in Persia as " the Voice of Mystery ", and his poems were interpreted allegorically by profound commentators. The love he sang was said to be divine love, the intoxication a holy, heavenly ecstasy. But these refinements were merely read into the poems which grew to be genuine popular songs, in order to rid them of their dangerously demoralising influence. No doubt many of his ghazals have mystical significance. But Háfiz was fundamentally the poet of the joy of living. As his poetry was the result of this kind of life, he was violently maligned by moralists and priests. Yet he continued to live, love, drink and sing all his life till he was a very old man. Surely Goethe must have felt a strange affinity with him ? He too, even in old age, was always ready to abandon himself to love and was often criticised on this account. Háfiz meant to him a kind of pledge that this would continue and, in fact, scarcely had he learnt to know the Persian poet when he renewed his youth by falling in love with Marianne.

Another and more important element in the feeling of kinship which drew him to Háfiz was the similarity of the ages in which they lived and wrote. Háfiz had lived " in one of the most stormy centuries in Oriental history ". The Persian dynasties warred fiercely with each other, until the dread conqueror Timur overrun Persia and set all Asia ablaze. Háfiz was brought before Timur, whose questions he answered with such wisdom that he was overwhelmed with marks of favour. But he paid no heed to the tyrant, continued his serene existence unmoved by the political storms, and went on writing his joyous songs. This was of capital importance for Goethe. For he too was living in an age convulsed by political storms. Napoleon was setting Europe ablaze, as Timur had done in Asia, and Goethe's country too was subjugated. He too was brought before Napoleon, in whose presence he conducted himself with such dignity that he was honoured and distinguished by him. The Emperor commissioned him to write a tragedy on the subject of Julius Cæsar, which was of course to have Napoleon as its hero. But, in spite of his great admiration for Napoleon's genius, Goethe neither wrote a " Cæsar " nor did he avail himself of Napoleon's invitation to follow him to Paris. Napoleon could make him deviate from his course as little as Timur could affect Háfiz. Háfiz and Timur in the *West-Eastern Divan* are the likenesses of Goethe and Napoleon. The only difference was that Goethe was unable to preserve the serenity that remained to Háfiz. Goethe was greatly distressed at the fate of Europe. The revolutions and wars threatened European civilisation with extinction. Goethe's own work, creative and scientific, was rendered infinitely harder by unrest and worry. It is true that in 1814, when Goethe first read the Persian poet, Napoleon had already been vanquished and the Wars of Liberation were over. But that had not brought peace to Europe, and tension within threatened to result in fresh revolution. Goethe felt that it was no longer possible to breathe freely within this Europe, that its political fate was affecting him too nearly and was to an intolerable degree retarding his personal development and that of all European countries. He needed distance, space, a new scene. This was the mood that drove him beyond Europe to the East, where he found in Háfiz a brother as regards circumstances, and also a model of how a poet can retain his peace of mind and freedom of spirit in spite of the pressure of the age he lives in. This is how the *West-Eastern Divan* came to be written, and its opening poem begins as follows :

> Nord und West und Süd zersplittern,
> Throne bersten, Reiche zittern,
> Flüchte du, im reinen Osten
> Patriarchenluft zu kosten,
> Unter Lieben, Trinken, Singen
> Soll dich Chisers Quell verjüngen.

There was also another motive. The Greek world had meant everything to him. It had moulded him. But now it had grown too narrow. The Classical restraint of the individual and of artistic form had led almost to rigidity. His drama *The Natural Daughter* was said to be as smooth and as cold as marble, and it may be that Goethe did not altogether disagree with this judgment. He always knew when the moment had come for a change in himself, and now he needed expansion of a form which had grown too rigid. This longing for change, for transformation, in order to avoid rigidity, was surely the most profound of the personal motives for his turning sympathetically at this time to the Romantic movement and the East. This was what he expressed in the poem from the *West-Eastern Divan* entitled " Selige Sehnsucht ".

But, behind every personal motive, the most important factor was Goethe's desire to extend the spiritual intercourse between nations, and to link up the continents of Europe and Asia.

It must be admitted that, in turning their attention to the East, the Romantic writers confined themselves to the India of the Vedas, which Friedrich Schlegel in his important work *On the Language and Wisdom of the Indians* (1808) contrasted with the pagan Greek world. India did not deify Nature in a spirit of pantheism but conceived reality as an emanation from the deity ; recognised the word of place and time not as truth but as the semblance and veil of the Maya, and honoured the gods, not as deified human beings as the Greek gods were, but as symbols of the deepest mystical profundities. It was Romantic spiritualism that caused the Romantic writers to turn to the East in the hope that some form of religious regeneration would travel thence to Europe. But it was precisely while his spirit was dwelling in the East that Goethe protested against Schlegel's work ; and it was in the notes and discussions on the *West-Eastern Divan* that he pronounced his curse upon these Indian gods, whom he looked upon as nothing but distorted monstrosities, contrary to nature. He called the Indian religion an " insane and monstrous religion ". Goethe could think of the deity only as clothed in a glorified human form, or as entirely amorphous and without a symbol.

Goethe had no sympathy, either, with Indian Buddhism, that later religion of India, whose revival in Europe was to be the work of Schopenhauer. This religion taught that life is a misery enduring beyond death. The soul's transmigration brings a recurrent rebirth, that is to say a recurrent entanglement in the inevitable continuity of the world, and leads to the repeated necessity of death. From this cycle of a life dying, being reborn and dying once more, there is only one deliverance. That is knowledge of the cause of misery : knowledge that this world of variety and movement is only a veil enshrouding the spirit, and that it is only the will towards life in individual form that leads to delusion and entanglement. Behind the deceptive forms of time and space, and beyond all life, variety and movement, lies Nirvana. The way of deliverance, trodden by the enlightened spirit, is the way of asceticism, destruction of the will to live, extinction of individual consciousness and absorption in Nirvana. The spirit that can attain this is delivered from life and death, from ceaseless rebirth, from the misery of the world.

This Indian teaching could not become Goethe's creed, even during his " Eastern " period. For then, and particularly then when he was experiencing a rebirth in love, he could not possibly interpret life and this rebirth as misery. This world's wealth of colours, forms and shapes delighted him still, he could not deem them a delusion or a veil ; holding fast to an existence which had brought him many blessings, enjoying all the things of beauty that graced the universe, he could not accept the idea of non-existence. He remained faithful to the earth and to life, as he had done when his full allegiance was given to the Greek world. In this respect Goethe had nothing in common with the East, even while he lived in it. Yet an Indian literary work, the *Sakuntala* of Kalidasa entranced him, and we find traces of it even in *Faust*, in the " Prologue on the Stage ". For years he was filled with admiration for it, for in it he found a changeless human content, humanity's purest and most natural conditions : woman's purity, innocent submission, man's forget-- fulness, a mother's loneliness, a father and mother united through their son.[19] What moved him so much in this work was not a specifically Oriental element, it was not any accretion of hitherto unknown beauty, neither completion nor enrichment of what Greece had given him. It was the meeting with a kindred spirit, a breaking down of Greek conventions only in the sense that he now found his ideal belonged not to Greece alone but was a universal possession. This Indian work showed him that the same human nature is to be found at any point in space and time. In fact his own poem, " God and the Bayadère ", written long before his " Eastern " period, was evidence of the same truth ; for there an Indian legend could so effortlessly convey a Classical Christian conception of humanity. But in other respects it was neither the India of the Vedas nor that of Buddhism that attracted Goethe. The East in which he steeped himself at that period was Persia and the work of the Persian poet Háfiz. He could not see the mysticism that others claimed to find in him.

> Sie haben dich, heiliger Hafis,
> Die mystische Zunge genannt,
> Und haben, die Wortgelehrten,
> Den Wert des Worts nicht erkannt.
>
> Mystisch heissest du ihnen,
> Weil sie Närrisches bei dir denken,
> Und ihren unlautern Wein
> In deinem Namen verschenken.
>
> Du aber bist mystisch rein,
> Weil sie dich nicht verstehn,
> Der du, ohne fromm zu sein, selig bist !
> Das wollen sie dir nicht zugestehn.

Goethe could acknowledge the religions of Persia ; the older one of Zarathustra and the more recent one of Islam, which was that of Háfiz.

To understand the religion of Zarathustra one must avoid thinking in terms of Nietzsche. What Nietzsche put into the mouth of Zarathustra was the most occidental of all conceptions : that of the superman and of the will to power. But Zarathustra's gospel is oriental and of the morning, and affirms nothing but the sanctity of the morning light rising in the East. This religion of light develops into a living gospel, Zend Avesta, and a guide to the path that must be trod. So Zarathustra became the founder of a religion, and a law-giver. Light is goodness and purity, the power that engenders life and fosters its growth, so the law is this : the purification of the body as of the spirit, the quickening of dead elements, the activity which, like the light, banishes all gloom, the struggle against darkness. Each in his own sphere must act in this spirit, must in this way be a servant of the sun's light. Zarathustra proclaimed enlightenment, but in a totally non-European sense. For his teaching is founded not upon the light of human reason, but upon God's light, and is real religion, a cult.

Goethe was filled with admiration on realising that the fatal nearness of the Indian idol-worship had had no power to influence this religion of Zarathustra's, that in Persia the temples of the pure fire still stood. In the great poem from the *West-Eastern Divan*, " Testament of the Old Persian Faith ", and elsewhere, he readily acknowledged this religion of the light of the sun. He worshipped it and thought that every new-born child ought to be held up to the East, facing the rising sun. For the Eastern light, he felt, is purity and brightness. But as it can take effect only where it is worthily received, where life is lived in purity and brightness like the sun, so the religion of light means for him the doctrine of the path that must be followed : purification and clarification. This process must begin in the elements themselves. Water must be kept pure and clear in canals ; trees must be planted in rows. And the spirit must develop pure and clear conceptions of all the things of this world. This was indeed Goethe's own constant endeavour : to keep his life pure and clear, to develop pure and clear conceptions and to preserve his physical as well as his spiritual eye from every illusion. He repeatedly gave warnings against delusion and darkness and in this sense was a disciple of Zarathustra. The " Testament of the Old Persian Faith ", which closely follows Zarathustra's gospel, can be claimed as his own message also. He too sought to enlighten, not in the rational, occidental sense of the

18th-century "enlightenment", but in the sense of the oriental religion of light. And his message of purity, order and brightness, because it was a religious message and the outcome of his religious experience, pointed a way for the spirit of the West that was to lead beyond the borders of Europe and beyond the West's conception of enlightenment. This message closed a gap which had opened in the tragic novel *The Elective Affinities* and which threatened Goethe's spirit in its great struggle for unity : the gap between the natural and the moral law. The Eastern religion proclaimed the natural law as that which governed man also, and thereby pointed the path and the way. Even the unity of science and revelation, whether religious or poetic, which had been shattered throughout the West, was visibly restored in Goethe's Eastern period.

And in a strange way the later religion of Mohammed, Islam, the religion of his favourite poet Háfiz, found a follower in Goethe. The word Islam means literally "surrender". This was the word to which Goethe was led through all his speculations about a supreme law. The fundamental idea of the Mohammedan religion is predestination ; there is a destiny which is the will of God, and everything that befalls a man is preordained by His changeless will. Religion means surrender to this will. This thought moved Goethe profoundly, and he was deeply touched by the idea that every thinker among the "dwellers in the East" is inevitably led to "claim surrender as the sublime law of politics, morality and religion". We must all acknowledge Islam, Goethe once said, and when Ottilie von Pogwisch's life hung in the balance he trusted to Islam alone. It is certain that when Goethe turned to the East he was no longer the Titan for whom this Oriental message of surrender could have brought a cure for *hybris* and presumption. He had been cured by Spinoza, who, in spite of his Western education, could never deny the oriental cast of his mind, and whose idea that God is identical with changeless necessity is akin to the Eastern idea. Thus Spinoza prepared Goethe for Islam, and that breath of peace which drifted to him from Spinoza and which gave his soul rest and calm, once again drifted to him from the East. And was there not also something in his Classical, European nature, as man and as poet, that craved to be released by the influence of the East?

Now we are in a position to express more clearly what was so new about Goethe's West-Eastern period in contrast to his

Greek phase, and in what way the *West-Eastern Divan* differs from his poems in the Classical manner. There is first of all the feeling of universality from which they spring and with which they are pervaded ; there is the urge towards expansion, surrender and extinction which Goethe had neither felt nor expressed in the nineties or during the early years of the century. At that time he had been intent on the rounding off of his form, the completion of his personality, the growth and shaping of his life and work. Now, after the intake, came as it were the moment for the release of breath. The lines from the *West-Eastern Divan*, " Höchstes Glück der Erdenkinder sei nur die Persönlichkeit " are often quoted as if they were meant to express Goethe's own conviction at the time. Nothing is more misleading or more erroneous. It is indeed a prodigious misconception. For the poem that contains these lines specifically denies what they state.

> Volk und Knecht und Überwinder
> Sie gestehn, zu jeder Zeit :
> Höchstes Glück der Erdenkinder
> Sei nur die Persönlichkeit.
>
> Jedes Leben sei zu führen,
> Wenn man sich nicht selbst vermisst ;
> Alles könne man verlieren,
> Wenn man bliebe was man ist.

Goethe had no intention of identifying himself with " Volk und Knecht und Überwinder ". He speaks, on the contrary, with his own voice, in Hatem's words, replying to this view taken by the vulgar or tyrannical mind :

> Kann wohl sein ! so wird gemeinet ;
> Doch ich bin auf andrer Spur :
> Alles Erdenglück vereinet
> Find' ich in Suleika nur.

The European ideal of personality content with, and complete in, itself yields here to oriental expansion, a lavishing of one's self. Love in the *West-Eastern Divan* is different from love in the *Roman Elegies*. There, as in the Classical-Greek Eros, it meant enjoyment of physical beauty ; a love which ennobled himself and his sense of beauty, a love that enjoyed, drew all into itself, a conquering and acquisitive love. In the *West-Eastern Divan* love acquires something of an oriental character, becomes surrender, expansion and sacrifice of personality, a blissful longing for extinction of the self. The poet has no wish to remain what he is, but seeks to be transformed. The poem

" Wiederfinden " extols love as a restoration to the Universal of life at its highest. A love-poem which with a kind of pantheism of love sees the loved one in every earthly form is in the spirit of the East. But where love does not attain to this universal significance, and is neither the consciousness of universality nor the rapture of transformation, even where it appears lighter, more graceful, more playful, it shows signs of an intoxication of love, a self-oblivion, which the *Roman Elegies* do not possess. Even the wine-songs and drinking-songs of the *Divan*, although restrained and contemplative in the Eastern manner, have tones not heard in Goethe's Classical period.

Goethe's idea of poetic form, too, has undergone a corresponding change. He now contrasts the Greek " creation " with the Eastern " songs ", and ranges himself with the latter :

> Mag der Grieche seinen Ton
> Zu Gestalten drücken,
> An der eignen Hände Sohn
> Steigern sein Entzücken ;
>
> Aber uns ist wonnereich
> In den Euphrat greifen,
> Und im flüss'gen Element
> Hin und wider schweifen.
>
> Löscht' ich so der Seele Brand,
> Lied es wird erschallen ;
> Schöpft des Dichters reine Hand,
> Wasser wird sich ballen

Now Goethe commands the infinite scope of Háfiz's song—Goethe, who up to now had insisted on selectiveness as the quality that raises art above the level of life.

> *Unbegrenzt*
> Dass du nicht enden kannst, das macht dich gross,
> Und dass du nie beginnst, das ist dein Los.
> Dein Lied ist drehend wie das Sterngewölbe,
> Anfang und Ende immerfort dasselbe,
> Und was die Mitte bringt ist offenbar
> Das was zu Ende bleibt und anfangs war.

Goethe was charmed with the oriental way of linking up the most distant and seemingly strangest and even contradictory objects by means of images, tropes and comparisons. This was the method chosen by the oriental mind to give poetic expression to the unity of all things, and Goethe, who had hitherto been accustomed to a strict and clear-cut separation of all heterogeneous elements, was led on to imitate it. The oriental technique of blending component parts, like a kind of internal rhyming, and the use of rhyme itself as an essential element of artistic form, was now recognised as a good medium for the expression of love. This was used in a new sense by Goethe, who had formerly favoured the Classical kind of rhythm with its feeling for quantities and pauses.

> Behramgur, sagt man, hat den Reim erfunden,
> Er sprach entzückt aus reiner Seele Drang ;
> Dilaram schnell, die Freundin seiner Stunden,
> Erwiderte mit gleichem Wort und Klang.

> Und so, Geliebte, warst du mir beschieden,
> Des Reims zu finden holden Lustgebrauch,
> Dass auch Behramgur ich, den Sassaniden,
> Nicht mehr beneiden darf : mir ward es auch.

> Hast mir dies Buch geweckt, du hast's gegeben ;
> Denn was ich froh, aus vollem Herzen sprach,
> Das klang zurück aus deinem holden Leben,
> Wie Blick dem Blick, so Reim dem Reime nach.

> Nun tön' es fort zu dir, auch aus der Ferne,
> Das Wort erreicht, und schwände Ton und Schall,
> Ist's nicht der Mantel noch gesäter Sterne ?
> Ist's nicht der Liebe hochverklärtes All ?

It is worth while to compare this poem with " Nachbildung ", which also gives to rhyme a significance that was new to Goethe. Later, in the Second Part of *Faust*, we notice Eastern influence, when Helen's awakening love for *Faust*, and her change from a Classical to a Romantic world, are expressed in the passage which changes from the measured Classical form to a rhyming one. And in the *Divan* itself there is a short poem contrasting the Classical form with that of the East, and acknowledging the new form as superior.

> Zugemess'ne Rhythmen reizen freilich,
> Das Talent erfreut sich wohl darin ;
> Doch wie schnelle widern sie abscheulich,
> Hohle Masken ohne Blut und Sinn ;
> Selbst der Geist erscheint sich nicht erfreulich,
> Wenn er nicht, auf neue Form bedacht,
> Jener toten Form ein Ende macht.

Finally, another new element is the " symbolic digression, from which, in the oriental regions, one can scarcely refrain ". Up to now Goethe, true to the Grecian ideal, had understood by the poetic symbol the complete unity of idea and embodiment,

of " Urphänomen " and outer form.   Now he was guided by
the spirit of the East and saw, in what the senses offered, a dis-
guise behind which a nobler spiritual life lay hidden to entice us
on and lead us up to higher regions.   In the announcement of
the " Buch Suleika " Goethe observes that here a spiritual
significance often obtrudes, and the veil of earthly love seems to
shroud a higher relationship.   This too leads on to the end of
the Second Part of *Faust*, where everything transient is but a
symbol.

An example from the " Buch Suleika " :

Gingo Biloba

Dieses Baums Blatt, der von Osten
Meinem Garten anvertraut,
Gibt geheimen Sinn zu kosten,
Wie's den Wissenden erbaut.

Ist es Ein lebendig Wesen,
Das sich in sich selbst getrennt ?
Sind es zwei, die sich erlesen,
Dass man sie als Eines kennt ?

Solche Fragen zu erwidern
Fand ich wohl den rechten Sinn ;
Fühlst du nicht an meinen Liedern,
Dass ich eins und doppelt bin ?

The breath of an Eastern spirit is quite unmistakable in the
Divan.

But why did Goethe call it West-Eastern ?   There seem to
be several meanings to the term.   He wanted to combine East
and West, as he always sought to unite, to reconcile, to strike a
harmony.   Secondly, the single, indivisible, universally human
" Urphänomen " was to be revealed in the West as in the East.
The third motive was the actual historical connection which
the "rolling stream of time" was in process of establishing
between East and West.

Wer sich selbst und andre kennt,
Wird auch hier erkennen ;
Orient und Okzident
Sind nicht mehr zu trennen.
Sinnig zwischen beiden Welten
Sich zu wiegen lass' ich gelten ;
Also zwischen Ost und Westen
Sich bewegen, sei's zum Besten !

It was Goethe's intention to unite East and West, past and
present, Persian and German, to let their customs and ways of
thought be mingled.   He wanted to be considered as a traveller

who is praiseworthy only in so far as he readily adapts himself
to foreign ways, tries to make the speech of others his own, and
can share their views and adopt their customs. He is excused
if he yet remains unmistakably a foreigner, with his own accent
and a certain unavoidable stiffness. The same is true of Goethe,
for even in oriental costume he never denied his European
personality, but openly maintained it. He did not hesitate to
address Greek and Christian deities in the poems of the *West-
Eastern Divan* : and in the same sense he made use of both Western
and Eastern forms. Free rhythms, Hans Sachsian Knittelverse,
and other German forms are found alongside the Eastern ones,
and it is particularly noticeable that the rejuvenation which
Goethe then experienced brought back with it these German
forms that he had prized during the Storm and Stress and
renounced in his Classical period. Even the Houris occasionally
speak in Knittelverse. And if we compare a true oriental ghazal
with Goethe's imitations it is quite evident to what an extent
he holds his own. The Persian ghazal is probably the purest
and most striking form of verse that the oriental spirit has created.
It is animated by the same spirit that grasped the conception
of metempsychosis. For here in a poetic motif the first distich
moves like a wandering soul through repeated transformations,
taking on new manifestations, and ever returning to the beginning with its principle of recurring rhyme. The course of this
poetic form is by its nature infinite, for it need never be completed. The soul of the poem can undergo constant new transformations and be for ever embodied in fresh images and
similitudes. This soul (of the poem) is an undivided unity, for
the ever-recurrent rhyme overflows and unites all sections and
divisions. It is determined by the rhyme of the opening, as if
by fate, and can never leave the river-bed of the first rhyme.
This is as it were the configuration of unity and eternity. But
in a ghazal of Goethe's, as for instance that famous poem " In
tausend Formen magst du dich verstecken ", the endless stream
falls into similar recurring verses and introduces a definite
shaping into the liquid flow of the Eastern form. With the last
verse, it leaves the bed of the single rich rhyme, and in content
also it is a whole of clearly distinguishable parts. The immense
number of images, comparisons and metaphorical expressions
in the Eastern poems have been toned down in Goethe's *Divan*,
and his images, even when taken from the Eastern world, respect
the limitations of the European's imaginative powers. The

" symbolic digression " is, in comparison with Háfiz's, not only rarer but clearer. Comparison of one of the most beautiful poems in the *Divan*, " Selige Sehnsucht ", with its source, one of Háfiz's poems, will make abundantly clear the difference between the Eastern and the Western spirit. The following is from Hammer's translation of Háfiz's poem :

Wie die Kerze brennt die Seele
Hell an Liebesflammen
Und mit reinem Sinne hab' ich
Meinen Leib geopfert.
Bis du nicht wie Schmetterlinge
Aus Begier verbrennest,
Kannst du nimmer Rettung finden
Von dem Gram der Liebe.

Du hast in des Flatterhaften
Seele Glut geworfen,
Ob sie gleich längst aus Begierde
Dich zu schauen tanzte.
Sieh', der Chymiker der Liebe,
Wird den Staub des Körpers,
Wenn er noch so bleiern wäre,
Doch in Gold verwandeln,
O Hafis ! kennt wohl der Pöbel
Grosser Perlen Zahlwert ?
Gib die köstlichen Juwelen
Nur den Eingeweihten.

Goethe's " Selige Sehnsucht " :

Sagt es niemand, nur den Weisen,
Weil die Menge gleich verhöhnet,
Das Lebend'ge will ich preisen
Das nach Flammentod sich sehnet.

In der Liebesnächte Kühlung,
Die dich zeugte, wo du zeugtest,
Ueberfällt dich fremde Fühlung
Wenn die stille Kerze leuchtet.

Nicht mehr bleibest du umfangen
In der Finsternis Beschattung,
Und dich reisset neu Verlangen
Auf zu höherer Begattung.

Keine Ferne macht dich schwierig,
Kommst geflogen und gebannt
Und zuletzt, des Lichts begierig,
Bist du Schmetterling verbrannt.

Und so lang du das nicht hast,
Dieses : Stirb und werde !
Bist du nur ein trüber Gast
Auf der dunklen Erde.

Háfiz's poem is filled with the Oriental mysticism that aims, by the sacrifice of self, at complete absorption in the One and Eternal. But Goethe's poem brings back to earth this Eastern spirit that seeks to lose itself beyond space and time, and the " self-sacrifice " " Selbstopfer " (a former title for the poem) means for him the earthly transformation that every creature must suffer in order to preserve or rather to renew its life. Here we have Goethe's idea of metamorphosis, in which the secret of life consists. In the *West-Eastern Divan* Goethe was contrasting the preservation of the personality with the prodigality of love. But the devout longing of the living for a fiery death is only the longing for an ever-repeated resurrection of the personality out of the fire, for a lasting continuance through countless transformations.

Goethe's devotion to the East is itself a kind of devout longing to be transformed through self-sacrifice, to be purified and born again out of the East to rise anew as a European. The exaggeration of an exclusively Western culture of Grecian pattern had brought with it the danger of rigidity. The European cult of personality threatened to destroy religion, its feeling of corporateness, interdependence, submissiveness. These dangers were dispelled by the East. But once the East had fulfilled its mission in extending Goethe's scope, he could return within his European confines. He had become West-Eastern. The Oriental feeling of Universality prevented the " true, sincere, inevitable self-awareness " of the European from degenerating into darkness and *hybris* ; and the Occidental feeling for personality prevented Goethe from degenerating into an amorphous vagueness. The religion of reverence towards one's own self, proclaimed in the *Wanderjahre*, was the outcome of Goethe's West-Eastern-ness, and was the highest self-apotheosis possible for Western man. For all Western culture is based on man's self-awareness, of which the European Renaissance was another rebirth. But Goethe's self-reverence contains a deeper element ; Western self-assertion has acquired unction from the East and has become a humanistic religion. Goethe's self-perfection, his work of shaping his own marble, was not self-seeking, it was selfless devotion to the great powers of which he was conscious in man, and which led him constantly to a higher level of culture. Goethe plunged deep into the Oriental experience of Universality and unity. But it was a process of purification from which he rose new-born. The spirit of the East suffered in him a Western transformation. The spirit of the West received in him the blessing of Eastern renewal. Everything about Goethe is still of the West, and yet everything is different, for its centre has shifted. He is like the original, the pattern of the spiritual quality of Europe in its purest form. And he was able to keep himself inviolate only because he remained open to the influences of the East, whether the Bible or Spinoza or Persia or Islam. He was the last Westerner so to be affected by the East and yet to remain intact. Schopenhauer's Oriental gospel was a negation of European culture. But Goethe was by nature far too noble, indeed too positive, to have betrayed the European spirit to the East. He is the best example of how one can retain one's own quality and yet remain absorptive. In 1827, when he had heard some of his *Divan* lyrics sung, he declared to Eckermann that he had noticed that evening that the lyrics of the *Divan* had ceased to bear any relation to him. What was oriental in them no longer lived on in him. It lay like a sloughed snakeskin beside his pathway.

The East had fulfilled its mission.

Later in 1827, like echoes of the *Divan*, there appeared Goethe's translations of Chinese lyrics and other poems prompted by them. And now obviously it was truer to say that Chinese poetry confirmed him in his belief that the poetry of all peoples and ages has a common, changeless human content than that any specifically Eastern spirit inspired him. In conversation with Eckermann on 31st January 1827, Goethe said, further, that Chinese novels were not as strange as was imagined. The characters think and feel almost as we do, one soon feels how much they resemble ourselves, except that everything seems clearer, simpler, more correct. Everything about them is sensible and bourgeois, so that they are very like *Hermann und Dorothea*.

The Chinese lyrics that Goethe learned to know through Thoms's English translations in his *Chinese Courtship* showed him likewise that even in this remarkable land one can live, love and write. Goethe published in *Kunst und Altertum* translations from the *Gedichte hundert schöner Frauen*, under the title " Chinesisches ". These show how, in contrast to the English translation, he transforms every foreign element in the originals so that the poems acquire a universal quality like all his work. This is still more true of the *Chinesisch-deutsche Tages- und Jahreszeiten*. This is a short series of poems inspired by themes from Chinese novels and poems, and showing by their character—unmistakably

Goethe's—how in Chinese poetry he found more affinity than strangeness. The very title reminds us of the *West-Eastern Divan* : West-Eastern : Chinese-German. But in such matters comparison is impossible. In the *Divan* Goethe was ostensibly a European travelling in the East, in oriental costume, and adapting himself to foreign ways while obviously remaining a foreigner. But in the *Chineissch-deutsche Tages- und Jahreszeiten* this, with negligible exceptions, is no longer the case. These poems have the wisdom and artistry of Goethe's maturity, and they are of the very highest order. What he saw in all Chinese poetry had always been a feature of his own lyrics : the thought that nature, as well as man, has a life of its own. So West-Eastern-ness was now no longer a synthesis of West and East in the sense of world literature. A revelation of world poetry had been granted : that all poetry is a common gift to the world, an " Urphänomen " common to all, a link between peoples and continents, achieved not by joining separate foreign elements but by stressing this " Urphänomen ", this quality that poets and men of West and East have in common.

CHAPTER 10

NEW CONCEPTIONS OF SOCIETY FROM AMERICA

America, after the Far East, was one of the most important sources of reinvigoration to Goethe in his old age. This extended beyond Europe the sphere of spiritual intercourse between the peoples, of which Goethe watched the rise and development through world literature, and made it world-wide. It was a new direction to which his eyes now turned, and a new point in time. For the East had plunged him into the distant past ; America awoke in him prophetic visions of a new world of the future. Goethe had once said of European literatures that if they wished to be refreshed and reinvigorated they should turn not to a nation whose culture was already fully developed, but to one which was still in process of growth, in other words to the literature of the German people. And now Europe was turning to what was in a much more literal sense a new and growing world. Of course Goethe was not the first to bring America within the German horizon. But before his time it had been a different America : the home of political freedom, of the assertion of man's rights, anticipating even the French Revolution. German poets who had begun by greeting the Revolution with enthusiasm, turned away from it with aversion when it degenerated into the Reign of Terror, and now looked with hope to the United States and sang their praises in Klopstock's works, among others.

But it was only by Goethe that America was presented as a contrast to a weary and ageing Europe labouring beneath the burden of its cultural traditions. An amazing thing indeed ! It is Goethe, not just somebody in search of adventure, but Goethe, the pattern of European culture, a follower in the footsteps of the Græco-Romans and an embodiment of all the great traditions of Europe who greets the New World, sees it beginning fresh, unburdened by the past, primordial, void of history but big with the future. And yet after all we need not be amazed, for it is typical of Goethe, who always sought change as a means of enriching life, whose device was " Stirb und Werde ! " and who, in virtue of this and not merely of his long life, spanned the ages and reached from the 18th century beyond the Romantic period into modern times. In the fire of his youth, he had broken through the forms that bound the old Europe, and in the maturity of his middle years, himself the product of many cultures, he had shaped their organic development. In his prophetic old age he felt it, in his own words, " worth while to look into the heart of such a growing world " and there he recognised the spirit that was to govern the future. He felt that the tradition of Classicism was gaining too much power even over him, and was threatening to paralyse him. But it was not only there that he saw danger. It lay still more in the cult of the past, the charm of ruins, the revelling in memory in which Romanticism indulged. In these Goethe's foreboding saw a germ of Europe's decline. It is clear from a memorandum dated 1819 that he saw America's safety in her lack of Classical traditions : " North America is fortunate in having no basalt. No ancestors and no Classical soil." [20] Yet his famous poem " The United States " (1827) obviously contrasts America with European Romanticism.

> Amerika, du hast es besser
> Als unser Kontinent, das alte,
> Hast keine verfallene Schlösser
> Und keine Basalte.
>
> Dich stört nicht im Innern,
> Zu lebendiger Zeit,
> Unnützes Erinnern
> Und vergeblicher Streit.
>
> Benutzt die Gegenwart mit Glück !
> Und wenn nun eure Kinder dichten,
> Bewahre sie ein gut Geschick
> Vor Ritter-, Räuber- und Gespenstergeschichten.

A continent with neither Classicism nor Romanticism and therefore without a cause of dispute ! What a wealth of meaning that could have for a European revival.

It would, however, be a mistake to imagine that Goethe in his old age suddenly, and without any period of transition, had turned his back on Europe. This was far from being the case. With him every moment of his life bore as it were the germ of the future ; and the line of his life, for all its changes, still remained a line. His great novel of education, *Wilhelm Meisters Lehrjahre* already contains this germ, which matured in the *Wanderjahre*. The *Lehrjahre* hints how the " Tower ", the secret society that guided the course of Wilhelm Meister's education, was to develop into an organisation which would spread to all parts of the world, and be accessible to all. This belongs to the period before

French Saint-Simonism, with its central theme of a world-organisation of industry, had left its traces in the *Wanderjahre*, and the transformation in Goethe's idea of personality had culminated in that of a world-wide society of the future. In the *Lehrjahre*, Jarno decides to emigrate to America and invites Wilhelm to go with him. Wilhelm is not yet ready for emigration and Lothario returns from America (where he had thought he would be useful) to his own country in Europe. Once more in his home, in his orchard, among his own family he declares : " Here or nowhere is America." And yet the note first sounded in the *Lehrjahre*, the idea of emigration to the United States and the above-mentioned transformation of the " Tower " into a world community, links the first part of the novel with the second in which Wilhelm Meister decides to emigrate. In the Old World he sees that everything follows the good old customs ; what is new is treated in the old way, what is growing is pressed into a rigid mould. The new world organisation, in which every member shall be assigned his place where he can be useful to the community, which will bring into being a new society, a new state, can only make a beginning on virgin soil such as America offers. In the *Wanderjahre*, the theme of emigration is taken up once more. The " Uncle " comes from America to Europe. Here he finds a priceless culture, which had taken thousands of years to develop and spread, and which gives him a totally different conception of what mankind is capable of. He had no wish to play the rôles of Orpheus and Lycurgus, centuries late, in America. But that did not mean that Europe needed men from the New World to work for the creation of a new order of society. His device is· " Wealth and the Common Weal ". This means that, in the world to be built up, all property, although held sacred by the community, is only entrusted to an individual as a steward and he has to use it for the common good. The theme of emigration is, however, much more important in the *Wanderjahre* (and especially in the 1827 version).

Between the *Lehrjahre* and the *Wanderjahre* lies the stupendous study that Goethe made of the New World, its geological, climatic, social, economic and political conditions. Works on America, maps and descriptions of travels, piled up round him, and the young Americans who visited him in Weimar were amazed at his precise and extensive knowledge. It cannot be said that Goethe's conception of the world underwent any radical change because of his intellectual survey of the continent of the future.

The idea of the harmonious development of personality, a European idea to which Goethe gave expression in the *Lehrjahre*, contained the demand for a humanity acting for the good of all. But this aspect was stressed under the influence of a new world founded on this conception of humanity, and the *Lehrjahre* is entirely devoted to the conception of an organised world-wide community in which man's worth is judged by his positive usefulness in its service. It is a development often noted and quite natural, which leads from the idea of a personality complete in itself to that of such a community. But even natural developments can be helped from outside. Already in the *Urfaust* the Earth-spirit, whom Goethe himself calls the Genius of Action, holds up to Faust's eyes the image of the man of action. But Faust does not understand him yet, for he does not yet resemble him. He does, however, resemble him by the end of the Second Part, and before the end of his earthly journey he is devoting himself to the service of human society. It is probable or at least possible that this last activity of Faust, who reclaims land from the sea to make a settlement for millions of men, builds canals, equips fleets, drains swamps, fertilises land, was written under the influence of American pioneering enterprises. In his old age Goethe was so fascinated by the new young world that he once told a young American, Cogswell, who visited him in 1819 : if he were twenty years younger, he would even now sail over to North America.

The young Americans who came from the University of Harvard to continue or complete their studies in Germany, were able to give Goethe an idea of how the sciences were beginning to flourish in America, and that there was no fear that culture in the intellectual sense would die out on the other side of the Ocean. Among these young Americans who visited him in Weimar or Jena were the Classical philologist Everett ; Ticknor, later the author of the well-known history of Spain ; the mineralogist Cogswell, with whom he was particularly intimate ; Bancroft, the future historian of the United States ; Calvert, who was able to acquaint Goethe with the American voting-system ; and Brisbane, with whom he held lively discussions on modern French philosophy. At that time, of course, there was not much to be said about American literature. Goethe talked of Byron with Everett and Ticknor. He spoke, too, of the future of American literature, and during the years 1826–29 he made an intensive study of Cooper's novels. He also published (in *Kunst und Altertum*,

1827) his project for an adaptation of Ludwig Gall's *Emigration to the United States*, saying that its adaptor must be prepared to vie with Cooper. Goethe himself wished to do something for science and art in the New World, and when Cogswell sent him a mineralogical collection from America he decided to present to the State Library in Boston some writings (among them some of his own) which might be of interest to those abroad. " I hope to have the pleasure and profit of gaining a more intimate knowledge of your wonderful country, whose peaceful and orderly conditions and immense possibilities of development are of interest to the whole world." [21]   And in 1819 Goethe sent thirty of his own works to Harvard University with this dedicatory letter : " I give the enclosed poetic and scientific works to the University of Cambridge in New England in token of my profound sympathy with its high scientific character and with the zeal, so richly rewarded, which it has shown throughout so many successive years for the promotion of sound and humane culture. With the respectful greetings of the author J. W. Goethe."

PART III

GOETHE'S MISSION TO EUROPE

CHAPTER 11

THE SORROWS OF YOUNG WERTHER

Up to now we have shown how the European literatures moulded Goethe into a European, how the East and America led him beyond the limits of Europe, and how this experience naturally contributed to his theory of world literature. Now we must examine how Goethe came to exert an influence on other literatures, and how this brought his idea of world literature to maturity. After the publication of the *West-Eastern Divan* Goethe became aware of the radiation of his influence throughout Europe, and this gave him considerable happiness. Seeing his own youth live again in the youth of Europe, he felt himself reborn ; seeing that youth treading in his footsteps, he clearly saw his own errors and confusion. Looking at his own image mirrored in them he gained a deeper insight into his own nature. After a long period full of difficulties and obstacles he now saw the results of his past work emerging, and his contemporaries realising his hopes. Now for the first time he felt that together with them he formed one real and complete entity. In all his writings he had thought of his own cultural development, not of their influence on others. And now when that influence was being spontaneously exerted and his example was becoming the pattern for Europe, he was not only deeply moved, but also felt capable of a new cultural influence, the last, the crowning one. It finally completed his idea of world literature. When he coined the phrase world literature in 1827, he merely gave a name to an interplay of influence between himself and the rest of the world, which was already in existence.

To sum up, we may say that it was European Romanticism that brought Goethe's idea of world literature to completion, and that the most important stages on the way—if indeed particular moments can be distinguished in this ever-flowing stream of development—are fixed by the names of Mme de Staël, Byron, Manzoni, Carlyle and the French journal *Le Globe*. Goethe realised that all these owed their status in some degree to him ; he was the subject of appreciative dedications from the greatest writers of other countries ; he exchanged letters with them, he was made a member of the Academies of Europe ; he saw his works translated into every language ; he received visitors from all over the world and Weimar became a spiritual centre of Europe, a place whose " gates and roads led to all the ends of the earth ". He particularly noticed how the quarrel between Classic and Romantic spread from Germany through every literature, and that he himself was not without his share in awakening the Romantic movement in Europe. And all this happened in the last twenty or thirty years before 1827, when the idea of world literature crystallised and got its name.

This brought with it the realisation that his influence on the literatures of Europe was by no means an unmixed blessing to them, and might even become, in his sense, a dangerous " Influenz ". This did not confuse his idea of world literature, however. He felt certain that even the false tracks and byways along which Europe was then moving, in his and other German footsteps, would lead to a happy end, as had been the case with him. " Man strays as long as he strives." But it clouded his pleasure in his authority throughout Europe, and even veiled the brightness with which he lit up the world. In particular the world-shattering influence of his *Werther* could give him no happiness, and whenever he spoke of it he tried to deny responsibility for the Werther-sickness that had seized Europe. His *Werther*, he said, had not excited this fever, it had only revealed what lay hidden in the youth of the period. On another occasion he declared it to be only a phase common to the youth of all the world with which the traditions of culture have nothing to do. It must be admitted that it is quite impossible to draw a clear line dividing what Goethe infused into the age from what he as its representative merely precipitated. A Danish writer, Rahbek, once said he did not know " whether he was an enthusiast because he always carried *Werther* in his pocket, or whether he always had *Werther* with him because he had become an enthusiast ". In any case, Goethe could not reckon his *Werther*'s influence among the phenomena which made him consider world literature desirable. And it did not help to further his own development, which was always an essential point with him. In 1790, in the *Venetian Epigrams* he writes :

Hat mich Europe gelobt, was hat mir Europa gegeben ?
Nichts ! Ich habe, wie schwer ! meine Gedichte bezahlt.
Deutschland ahmte mich nach, und Frankreich mochte mich lesen.
England ! Freundlich empfingst du den zerrütteten Gast.
Doch was fördert es mich, dass auch sogar der Chinese
Malet, mit ängstlicher Hand, Werthern und Lotten auf Glas ?

When the first wave of *Werther*'s influence broke, Goethe himself was no longer the author of *Werther* that Europe thought him ; later on, during the European Romantic period, it was with amazement that Goethe saw himself considered everywhere in Europe as a Romantic writer.   It was the works of his youth that fostered the European Romantic movement, and he was claimed as an " anti-Classicist ".   And even now, in the Werther-period in Europe, the strangeness of his position must have struck him.   For when he had finished writing *Werther* he had already passed beyond him.   By giving expression to the sufferings of his youth he had freed himself from them ; and all his works had something of this quality.   During his Swiss travels in 1799, when he learned in Geneva for the first time that the French too were charmed with his *Werther*, he protested, writing to Frau von Stein in Weimar that this was totally unexpected. And when they asked him in Geneva if he was not writing some more works like *Werther*, he answered " God forbid I should ever again find myself in the position of writing or being able to write one."   And the shadow of *Werther* followed him even to Italy, where his cure was completed.

In 1781, Goethe received—from Michael Salom—the first Italian translation, and he was interested then to retrace his thoughts and feelings in the Italian language of which he was so fond, to see them again in a new form.   He found, however, that the passionate expression of grief and joy constantly consumed in their own fire had vanished, and that his favourite name of Lotte had been changed to Annette.   He wrote then : " What a commotion this will-o'-the-wisp has made," and indicated that the commotion was not to his liking, because he had by then outgrown the Werther-sickness.   So when *Werther* met with opposition in Italy from the Catholic church, and the Bishop of Milan bought up the first translation in order to be rid of it, Goethe fully approved this step.   He was rather pleased with the perspicacity of the man who had seen at once that *Werther* was a bad book for a Catholic, and admired him for taking the most efficient means of quietly doing away with it.   But even the Catholic church was not able in the long run to prevent Werther from over-running Italy, and by the end of the century four Italian translations had appeared.   Goethe himself met " the angry shade of the unhappy youth " in a drama *Aristodemo* that the Italian writer Monti read to him in Rome.   " It is a misfortune that would pursue me to India," he once wrote.   It would certainly have pursued him to China, for *Werther* had arrived there. An Englishman, recognising Goethe in Naples, greeted him with : " You are the author of *Werther*," and in Palermo a native of Malta who failed to recognise him and asked him about the author of *Werther*, was vastly astonished when Goethe made himself known. "You must have changed very much," exclaimed the Italian, and Goethe replied : " Oh yes, I have changed a good deal between Weimar and Palermo."

So it was particularly in Italy that Goethe, who had by then written his *Iphigenie*, was obliged to admit that he owed his influence, his fame in the world, to this work of his youth which he had long since outgrown ; and so it went on. As late as 1800, when he had already written his Homeric epic *Hermann und Dorothea* and also *Wilhelm Meister*, Mme de Staël wrote in her book, *On Literature considered in its Relation to Social Institutions*, that *Werther* was the book *par excellence* that the Germans can produce for comparison with the masterpieces of other languages, a book of enthusiasm, of passion, of revolt against society, containing the most striking expression of the German national character.

In 1802 the Italian writer Ugo Foscolo sent Goethe *The last letters of Jacopo Ortis* with a letter " To Signor Goethe, the famous German writer " in which Foscolo himself acknowledged that his work might have owed its origin to *Werther*. On the other hand, it has been proved that Foscolo began his novel before he had read *Werther*. Yet the strange " perhaps " in Foscolo's letter surely means that he himself thought it possible that before reading Goethe's *Werther* he had been infected by the Werther-fever then rife in Europe.

In 1804, when Mme de Staël paid her memorable visit to Weimar, Goethe was highly indignant at her insistence on the contrast between German and French literature. She behaved, he wrote at the time to Schiller, as if she were visiting the country of the hyperboreans whose grand old pines and oaks, whose iron and amber, might yet be profitably turned to use and ornament. She persisted in trying to discuss with him the difference between German and French literature. But Goethe, whose development had already been so profoundly influenced by French literature, and who was engaged at that time in raising the German theatre with the help of French Classicism to a higher artistic plane, could no longer recognise this difference as still existent. He, at least, stood outside the bounds of nationality, and felt himself to be a European, for whose spirit national limits no longer existed. But Mme de Staël was determined to regard him as the representative of the specifically German cast of mind. In a letter to her father she wrote that Goethe, she was sorry to say, ruined her idea of Werther. Europe did not realise that he had long since changed and had become a Classicist, at least by German standards. In her book, *De l'Allemagne*, Mme de Staël positively denies the existence of German Classicism, and Sainte-Beuve, the great critic of the French Romantic period, once declared that the word Classicist could not be applied in connection with some literatures. Who would be inclined, for example (he wrote) to write of German Classicists? Nietzsche was later to record this statement with satisfaction.

This European view of German literature tells us much about its nature, and Goethe, who believed that distance made it possible for a foreigner's eye to see more clearly than his own, got many new sidelights on himself. Quite apart from these facts, however, one may say of the Werther-sickness with which the " mal du siècle " began, that it gave the first signs (as feverish conditions in the intellectual life are symptoms of a cure) of change and development, that crises like these become inevitable when the time comes to alter a state of things that has become intolerable. It is important to bear this in mind when considering every later form of Goethe's influence, especially in the case of *Faust*. It concerns the whole of life, and this is particularly clear in the example that Napoleon affords.

Goethe was taken by surprise when he learned from his memorable conversation with Napoleon how deeply the latter had studied and absorbed *Werther*. We know that Napoleon read *Werther* seven times. He read it in early youth when he too wrote novels and tales in the *Werther* manner. He read it in Egypt at the foot of the Pyramids, and he read it again on Saint Helena. *Werther* was his constant companion. And what does this mean? Why does Napoleon come to Werther, the most ebullient hero to the sentiment-ridden fanatic, the most active spirit to the ineffective dreamer? Goethe himself has suggested that Napoleon's predilection for Werther was founded on the great contrast between the two natures. Napoleon liked melancholy, sweet music and the sad, moonlit laments of Ossian and Werther. The effect that *Werther* had on Napoleon was to dissolve what was too rigid in him, to ease what was too tense and highly strung. *Werther* brought him the comfort of relaxing, mitigating, softening—precisely what a man of heroic temper needs. But it is perhaps permissible to view the matter differently. Napoleon himself often remarked what a vast influence a poem may exert on a receptive nature ; and he had that receptive quality. His nature was attuned to poetry. Did *Werther* perhaps, through its influence on Napoleon, acquire a real significance in the history of world literature and play its part in the creation of a new Europe ? This lament for lost nature, this railing at existing society which seeks to force a nature-loving man into the restrictive bonds of an ageing world, this destiny of a man full of energy and athirst for fame but denied scope for the expansion of his power, pouring all his pent-up energies into the passion of love, and, when this too failed him, having nothing else to live for. Was it all this, perhaps, that awoke in Napoleon the disillusionment from which great deeds can spring ? Did *Werther* perhaps open his eyes to the falsity and inadequacy of existence in Europe, in which the latent powers of a young man would be stifled by prejudices, traditions and conventions ? The grief that drove Werther to his death drove Napoleon to act, to change this static world, to break down the narrowness of existence. And the German poetic dream called on him to create a political reality. Napoleon often blamed Racine's tragedies for making love the whole content of man's life. That, he said, was not enough to inspire the greater-hearted men that had come to the fore with the Revolution. Had he perhaps discovered in *Werther*, long before the Revolution, the deeper cause why love *could* in those days make up the whole destiny of a man—because it was a substitute for the release of his energies which was denied him ? In his conversation with Goethe, Napoleon certainly criticised his adding the motive of wounded ambition to that of unhappy love in Werther, when love alone could amply have motivated his suicide. But it may be that he considered ambition was too big a theme to be used merely as a secondary motive. In short, it is possible that *Werther* set in motion Napoleon's vital urge towards greatness in action, and helped it to move on a higher level. His impulse to action was fired. His revolutionary urge for transformation found a deeper cause and a sharper spur in a general disillusionment. It was a spark of the Faust-spirit from *Werther* that flared up in Napoleon. Goethe himself clearly saw this Faustian idealism in him. Napoleon, he once said, lived in the realm of the idea. He wanted the absolute, and this was his undoing. Thus his life became a tragedy, an example of how dangerous it is to aspire to the absolute and to sacrifice everything to an idea. Goethe went so far as to call him the realist, and enthusiast and a visionary. Goethe recognised Byron (who has so many points of similarity with Napoleon) as his spiritual son, because it was Byron who had lit the fire of the Faust-spirit in him ; and it may be that Goethe had a similar feeling towards Napoleon. Euphorion, in the Second Part of *Faust*, the son of Faust and Helen, who casts himself recklessly into the air and perishes a victim of his desire for warlike adventure in war, may refer not only to Byron but to Napoleon also.

Werther exerted, then, a stimulating influence on Napoleon ; and now we have to consider what Napoleon meant to Goethe. Friedrich Nietzsche once said that it was Napoleon who caused Goethe to reconsider his *Faust*, indeed the whole problem of man. That is certainly an exaggeration, for there can be no question of his reconsidering them. The Earth-spirit, which Goethe himself interpreted as " genius of action ", had already appeared in the *Urfaust*. Faust falls powerless before him, because Faust is not his equal and consequently cannot understand him. But the call to action continues to sound in Faust's ear from so many sides that one cannot doubt that in the end Faust would reach equality with the Earth-spirit, the genius of action. But Goethe could reproduce only what he himself had experienced. So he was able to transform Faust from one content with passive experience to a man of action, only after the spirit of action personified in Napoleon had actually appeared before his eyes. Goethe once called Napoleon one of the most productive men who have ever lived. For, as well as poems and dramas, he produced deeds of greater significance which had permanence and stimulating power comparable with the works of Mozart or Phidias. At the end of his earthly course Faust grew to be a productive man of action of this type. That the second part of the work introduced Faust into the great political world at an Imperial court, may perhaps have owed something to Napoleon's strong influence on Goethé. Of course he may have found this detail already in the chapbook. But it was his own experience which gave flesh and blood to shadows. For, at that momentous meeting, Napoleon had invited Goethe to his court in Paris and Goethe had considered the idea if only for a short time. He did not accept the invitation, nor did he act upon Napoleon's suggestion that he should write a tragedy about Cæsar. But the mental picture of himself, Goethe, at Napoleon's court, advising the Emperor and writing at his suggestion, certainly influenced his composition of the Second Part of *Faust* at the Imperial court. And there is definite proof that Goethe had Napoleon in mind as he portrayed the last stage of Faust's life. In a poem to the Empress of France he thus described the figure of Napoleon :

> Worüber trüb Jahrhunderte gesonnen,
> Er übersieht's in hellstem Geisteslicht,
> Das Kleinliche ist alles weggeronnen,
> Nur Meer und Erde haben hier Gewicht,
> Ist jenem erst das Ufer abgewonnen.
> Dass sich daran die stolze Woge bricht,
> So tritt durch weisen Schluss, durch Machtgefechte,
> Das feste Land in alle seine Rechte.

This described precisely what Faust did at the end of the tragedy : reclaimed coast-land from the sea and gave the earth back her rights. This was the moment of which Faust would say : " Ah still delay, you are so fair."

There existed between Goethe and Napoleon, then, that reciprocity which is the basis of world literature. But the first influence came from the work of art, *Werther*.

It was a Frenchwoman who most clearly recognised the positive side of the disillusionment which by means of *Werther* and *Faust* penetrated the European mind and was known in England as " Satanism ". In the Preface to her novel *Lélia*, which deals with a feminine Werther and Faust, George Sand interpreted the European poetry of despair represented by Byron, by the Polish Romantic writer Mickiewicz, by Musset and George Sand herself, by Heine and Lenau. The doubt and despair, she declared, are maladies that mankind must undergo in order to hasten its progress in religion, and lead it to its goal. The doubt is (according to Herwegh's translation) a sacred right of the human conscience, which may determine whether to adopt or to reject a belief. The despair is the fateful turning point, the crisis in the fever of doubt. But how magnificent is this despair ! The task of this life and particularly of this century is not to sink into a self-indulgent slumber, closing the heart to the noble suffering of doubt. We have something better to do ; we must fight and overcome this suffering, not only in order to regain the dignity of man for ourselves but still more to make smooth the path for the coming generation. There is a great lesson for us in the sublime lines in which René (by Chateaubriand), Werther, Obermann (by Sénancourt), Conrad (by Mickiewicz) and Manfred (by Byron) pour out their souls' grief. These lines were written in their hearts' blood and watered with tears, and belong to the philosophical rather than to the poetical history of the human race. We ought not to feel ashamed of having wept with these great souls. Posterity enriched with a new faith will reckon them its first martyrs. And in the essay on the drama of fantasy where she compares Goethe's *Faust* with Byron's *Manfred* and Mickiewicz's *Conrad*, George Sand glorifies doubt, even when it leads to despair, because it is mankind's path to progress.

The influence which Goethe's *Werther* exerted on the literatures and life of Europe is, in its vast significance, a phenomenon unique in world literature. We must conclude that its influence was due less to its literary worth than to other factors. With Werther there appeared in Old Europe a new man, one who made youth conscious that the European sphere had grown too narrow, too dull ; it was no longer possible to breathe or move within it. Werther's influence joined hands with that of Rousseau. This young man, Werther, applies the standard of Nature to society and to art. He is an artist, a painter who has perceived a new truth :

> It is Nature alone that makes the great artist. There is much to be said in favour of rules as there is of middle-class society. The man who models himself on them will never produce anything crude or bad, just as the man who is governed by precepts and decorum will never be a tiresome neighbour or a thorough-going villain. But on the other hand rules will destroy the real feeling for nature and its expression.

Socially this new type of man is hindered in the exercise of his gifts and powers by rules, injunctions, prohibitions, obsolete customs and forms. He cannot help where he would, as he cannot do what he feels he must. As one of the middle-class he is not accepted in aristocratic society. Only children and the common people understand him. He is denied a sphere of activity. All that society affords is " the permission to paint the walls of one's prison house with gay figures and nice views ". So it remains a prison. All this breaks out in a catastrophic explosion when his ardent love is denied fulfilment because the conventions forbid it. It is too much, too intolerable, to thwart nature and destroy freedom thus, and so he chooses death. This novel is not merely a love-story but is the history of a new type of man in a Europe grown old and cramped. It does not represent the isolated lot of a super-sensitive youth unequal to the business of living. Werther represents the youth of Europe that can no longer live and breathe in its former sphere. This whole novel is written in a pre-revolutionary key. So we can understand the sensation that it caused everywhere, most of all in France, not only because the ground was already so far prepared by Rousseau's *Nouvelle Héloïse*, but because it was the world of French civilization against which this work revolted. For it was France that in those days determined the conventions of Europe. Here we must distinguish between two waves of Werther-sickness in Europe : a pre-revolutionary and a post-revolutionary wave. In serious literature the second was of greater importance. The revolution failed to bring what had been hoped from it : a new life, a new sphere of life, for young, sensitive, enterprising men of genius. Goethe's *Werther* helped to prepare the mind for the Revolution, but it aimed at a different revolution from the one which actually followed. It was the ensuing disillusionment which led to the immense influence of *Werther* in the literatures and indeed in the whole life of Europe.

It was not revolutionary France, but the *émigrés* driven out by the Revolution and living in Switzerland or Germany or England, that exhibited this influence in its highest degree. The literature of the *émigrés* has a Werther spirit and there is evidence that it owed this directly to Werther itself. When Mme de Staël sent Goethe her novel *Delphine*, in which she pictures the revolt of a passionate woman against society, and champions the right of the individual against the rules of conventional morality, she wrote these words : " La lecture de *Werther* a fait époque dans ma vie comme un événement personnel." Chateaubriand, whose *René* is also written in the Werther spirit, once reproached Byron for never mentioning him or what his *Child Harold* owed to *René*. He, Chateaubriand, would have acted differently, he wrote : he would not have failed to mention that Ossian, *Werther* and Saint-Pierre had influenced the formation of his ideas. Charles Nodier, in the Preface to a new edition of his novel *The Painter of Salzburg*, declares that the government of the Directoire was anything but sentimental. The language of musing and of passion, for which Rousseau had won temporary popularity thirty years before, had come to be considered ridiculous by the end of the century. It was different in Germany, that wonderful Germany, the last Fatherland of European works of literature, the cradle of a great society, which was to come—if indeed any society could still exist in Europe ; and Goethe's influence could be effective. We read *Werther, Götz von Berlichingen* and *Karl Moor*. Nodier draws attention to the fact that the hero of his novel is " a German ". George Sand in her Preface to Sénancourt's *Obermann* compares that novel with *Werther*, and admits that the German work with its strange speculations has wrought a change in the spirit of France. All these novels, *René, Adolf, The Painter of Salzburg* and *Obermann* have this in common, that their heroes are Werther's spiritual brothers. Their inner world, like Werther's, is too rich compared to outer reality, their own nature too different, their thoughts too profound, to exist in society as it is. They find in it no scope, no chance of influence, no fulfilment for their being. They are useless and superfluous. In despair at the dullness and narrowness of the social sphere, they flee like Werther to the solitude of nature, Obermann to the Swiss Alps, René to the primeval forests and the savage races beyond the ocean. In Constant's *Adolphe* it is the woman who plays the part of Werther. Under the pressure of social convention, Adolphe dissolves his relationship with her, and she reacts by revolting against society. Many of these Werther-like figures discuss, as Werther does, the right to commit suicide and defend it. And there is ample evidence that it went further than literature, that in Germany and also in France the Werther-mood led to an outbreak of suicides. Werther, writes Mme de Staël in her book on suicide, has been responsible for more suicides that the most beautiful woman. It is really true to speak as George Sand did in her Preface to *Obermann*, of a change in the " spirit of our nation ". The rights of the individual are pitted against social convention. The need for solitude takes the place of social requirements. Emotion and passion revolt against reason, and melancholy breaks into the Rococo's serene enjoyment of life. The world of dream asserts its rights against the world of reality, the inner against the outer. All that had up to now been harmonious, was disrupted. Civilisation, the boast of France, was felt to be a sickness. This Wertherish literature strikes the first note of French Romanticism, and the word Romantic occurs in it frequently. In *Obermann* there is a section " On Romantic expression in the Swiss cow-herds' airs ", and whatever fits in with deep perception and true feeling is called Romantic. Nature and music are Romantic, and René is a " Romantic spirit ". Goethe's Werther stands godfather (with others, of course) at the cradle of French Romanticism, and Lamartine still roamed with Werther and Ossian through the autumnal countryside. Even the " taste for Ossian ", then fashionable in Europe, can be ascribed in large measure to Werther, if we are to believe the Englishman Crabb Robinson. And Goethe did not contest the truth of it with his English guest and interpreter (1829). He only remarked that people had overlooked the fact that Werther while in his right mind had read Homer, and had turned to Ossian only in his disordered state.

It seems curious, however, that in England, the country to which *Werther* owed so much, the book made possibly less impression than in any other country in Europe, at least as far as the more serious forms of literature are concerned. Here the Werther-sickness did not break out, although there was certainly no lack of translations (from 1779 on), imitations, sequels and dramatic versions. But resistance held firm ; and there are reasons enough for this. The English mind had compensations to save it from the mood of disillusionment and melancholy which Goethe had noted as the keynote of English literature ; and this mood was therefore never allowed to gain the upper hand. In England life took on fixed forms, which imposed a check on individual fancies. There was for instance public activity and efficiency, directed outwards into channels of world-wide range, service of the English state, of the British Empire, of Britain's power and wealth. In Germany there was no such sphere of public activity. Here the middle-class man was driven in upon himself by political dispersion and absolutism. In *Dichtung und Wahrheit* Goethe derives the mood of Werther from this fact. England possessed a society with well-defined forms, customs and views, which did not permit a man to give himself up entirely to his personal longings or visions. And in addition to state and society a third compensation existed in the Puritan church, that strict, restraining, life-regimenting institution, while, in Germany, mysticism and piety made religion an intimate and individual matter, purely a matter of emotion. We must remember, too, in this connection, English empiricism : the recognition of the world as it is, even though it should fail to correspond to one's own dream of perfection. Compare from this point of view Hamlet and Faust, two men smitten with disillusionment. Hamlet accepts reality as it is although he sees its frailty. But the English Hamlet, though sceptical and pessimistic, is determined to look reality in the face. Faust, on the other hand, tries to free himself from the limitations set by the world, and to shape reality in accordance with his vision. The same difference is to be found in English and German types of humour. In spite of all his humorous discernment of the vanity of the world and of life, Jean Paul cannot renounce his instinctive Faustian urge towards the realisation of absolute values ; and beyond his simpletons and fools there lie his fantasies and visions of man's absolute perfection. There is always a yearned-for vision of an idealised world by which reality is measured, and whose inaccessibility makes of life one incurable grief. One can perhaps give this vision more precision ; it is the vision of an absolute and unconditional freedom. Contrast this with Sterne's wryly-smiling recognition and tolerance of the existing world. So disillusionment, to which the English mind was particularly liable, was kept within bounds. Young Goethe, the author of *Werther* as of *Götz von Berlichingen*, the Goethe of disillusionment and revolutionary ardour, could not gain a firm footing in England. The periodical *Antijacobin* opposed him and the whole German movement of Storm and Stress as fiercely as it did the French Revolution ; and it was *Werther* most of all which they denounced as immoral and atheistic.

Everywhere else, however, the Werther-fever became a European sickness, and it is sad indeed that this was the beginning of the world-wide influence exerted by Goethe and by German literature. One has only to read in his *Confessions d'un Enfant du siècle* how Musset regarded this devastating influence : Goethe, the patriarch of a new literature, having personified in Werther the passion that leads to suicide, then depicted in his Faust the darkest figure that ever stood for evil and misfortune. His writings began to travel from Germany to France. From his study, among his pictures and statues, rich, fortunate and serene, with a paternal smile he watched his work of darkness approaching us. Byron answered him with a cry of grief, and made his Manfred peer over the abyss as if nothingness were the answer to the riddle.

Pardon me, mighty poets, you are demi-gods and I am but a suffering child. But I must curse you. Why did you not sing of the scent of flowers, the voices of nature, the vine and the sun, the blue sky and beauty ? Granted, you knew life and had suffered ; the world fell in ruins round you and you wept over its ruins ; you despaired and your loved ones betrayed you, your friends maligned you and your fellow-citizens misjudged you. You have a void in your heart, death before your eyes, and you were giants in grief. But tell

me, noble Goethe, was there no comforting voice in the heavenly
music of your ancient German forests ? You, to whom poetry was
the sister of science, could she find in immortal nature no healing herb
for the heart of her favourite ? You were a pantheist, a Greek poet
in the Classical manner, a lover of consecrated forms ; could you not
put a little honey into these fair vessels which you knew how to fashion ?
You, who surely had reason to smile, and who could let the bees sip
from your lips.

Musset tells us how despair, scepticism, complete negation took
possession of youth when these German and English ideas crowded
into their minds. All things lost their value—reputation, love,
religion. The abyss yawned. Gautier, in his poem, " Pensée
de Minuit ", witnessed in much the same way to the influence of
Werther on his youth.

> Et puis l'âge est venu qui donne la science :
> J'ai lu Werther, René, son frère d'alliance,
> Ces livres, vrais poisons du cœur,
> Qui déflorent la vie et nous dégoûtent d'elle,
> Dont chaque mot vous porte une atteinte mortelle ;
> Byron et son Don Juan moqueur.

In Gautier's case, however, Goethe as a worker in Classical
forms had the power to free him from Wertherism—Goethe who
released himself from his own sufferings by giving them expression. But it was not this Goethe who fired the imagination of
the French Romantics. The " mal du siècle " spread because
of him. But Musset's confession also shows how the French
mind yielded only unwillingly to this mood, which was neither
suited nor natural to it, and to which it would never have come
had it not looked to the North, to Ossian, Goethe and Byron. In
France it was repeatedly asserted that German literature, through
Werther and *Faust,* had exerted a paralysing, even a fatal, influence
on Europe. But it must be added that the Werther-sickness had
also a positive value and was in some ways salutary and stimulating. It prepared the mind for the Revolution. And after
the Revolution it drew man's attention from life's superficialities
to its deeper aspects. It woke loftier aspirations, and demanded
the solution of new problems. The grievous discontent was a
spur to the finding of a new way of life. Every metamorphosis
implies a crisis. The effect that *Faust* had will show this still
more clearly.

The influence exerted by *Werther* is at any rate more important
than the later attitude to it, when *Werther* was regarded only as
a manual of love, a psychological love-story of a new and specific-

ally German type. In 1796, in her book *De l'Influence des Passions sur le Bonheur des Individus et des Nations*, Mme de Staël defended *Werther* against the reproach (later made by Napoleon also) that Goethe gave his hero another great sorrow besides love, namely the humbling of his pride through his social position ; society had to inject its poisons into the wounds inflicted by nature, in order that the sharpest pitch of despair, leading to suicide, might be reached. In so doing, Mme de Staël had at least a more profound insight into the historical significance of *Werther* than for instance Villers in his " Erotique comparée ou sur la manière essentiellement différente dont les Poètes françaises et les allemands traitent l'amour ". This contrasts Werther's idealistic rarified love with the wanton, frivolous, purely sensuous love found in French literature. She had more perspicacity also than Stendhal, who compares the superficial physical love in France which avoids extremes of passion or danger, with the German profound Werther-like love which is passionate and heroic, a metaphysical cult—or than Balzac who regards *Werther* as a manual of love that gives a key to almost every situation of the human heart in love—or than Gautier who describes *Werther* as the forerunner of the " roman du cœur ", the " roman ardent et passionné " to which his *Mademoiselle de Maupin* belongs. Balzac and Stendhal protest in the name of active humanity against the passive melancholy of *Werther*, which is no longer suited to the age. But it was this passive melancholy of *Werther* that by the grief it fostered in old Europe first ushered in the new age, the age of action ; and in this fact lies the real significance of the novel.

CHAPTER 12

THE NORTH

The literatures of the North were the first to come under the influence of German Romanticism. Ten years before Mme de Staël's book was published, Romanticism had begun to flower in the North. It was here that the first breach was made in the resistance of the French type of Classicism which in the 18th century had predominated in the North as elsewhere. And this is by no means an accident of history. For German Romanticism had discovered the source of all Romantic poetry in the old Nordic myths and hero-legends. Friedrich Schlegel believed this to be the case ; and Novalis, in the tale which occupies the central place in his novel, *Heinrich von Ofterdingen*, symbolises the polarity between enlightenment and Romanticism, reason and imagination, prose and poetry, in the polarity between day and night, between North and South. The sun has bound the King of the North in fetters of ice and has usurped command over the world. But Poetry, imagination's daughter, whom the compass guides to the North, rescues the rightful ruler of the world. The sun's empire fades and that of Romanticism begins. Heinrich, the Romantic poet, sees in a dream at the beginning of the novel a blue flower which he sets out to seek. He finds it, and in it finds his lost love, with whom he is to govern the world. The name of the blue flower, the symbol of Romanticism, is Edda. This novel by Novalis, himself the essence of Romanticism, illustrates its leaning towards the North which was its source. Thus it came about that the North was able to celebrate in Nordic Romanticism its national rebirth, just as the South had celebrated in the Italian Renaissance, the rebirth of Classical Antiquity. This Nordic rebirth resulted in part spontaneously through Denmark's great poet Ewald, and in part through Klopstock, who had spent many years in Denmark and while there had severed his connection with the literature of Classicism. It was Klopstock who more than any other led the North to study its own traditions.

In estimating Goethe's place with regard to the North, it is important to notice that northern Antiquity was not felt to be contrary to Christianity but rather to pre-figure it. Nor was it opposed to the modern scientific view of life, at least in so far as that was a Romantic philosophy of nature, and not mechanistic and materialistic. This philosophy of nature brought to the North a confirmation of its own myths. The contrast was rather with the paganism of Greece, a contrast between North and South. The North felt the urge to break free from humanism and to recover its independence, and it led Klopstock to this view. Humanism had of course penetrated also to the North, and in the 18th century, in the form of Classicism, it governed Nordic literature.

A Dane of Classical education, such as Jens Baggesen, could never turn his back on his early culture as his native land had already done ; and there resulted the first clash between Goethe and the Nordic spirit. For in the North it was *young* Goethe with his *Werther*, *Götz* and *Faust* who was endangering the Classical tradition. Werther was not translated into Danish till 1832, but all Danes read German. In Denmark as everywhere else in Europe, the older generation who had been brought up on Classical lines, fiercely opposed Goethe as a fanatic, an atheist, an immoral writer, and Baggesen was the mouthpiece of that generation. In 1803 he wrote an abysmally unintelligent satirical poem on Goethe, though by that time Goethe had already become a Classical poet. The following year he composed a double drama in the style of a parody by Aristophanes : *Faust Part I Completed : The Philistine world or Romania at the Inn*, and *Faust Part II Completed : The Romantic world or Romania in the Mad-house*. This second part takes place in Weimar when Mme de Staël is visiting it, and it tells how *Faust* is acted there in a mad-house by lunatics, while Goethe, Mme de Staël, Jean Paul and Wieland are among the audience. It must be admitted that Goethe himself, who appears under the name of Opitz, is represented as being above this mad-house level. But he is parodied as the father of the Storm and Stress which he precipitated, and of Romanticism, represented by Ludwig Tieck. In the first version of this strange *Faust*, Goethe was certainly subjected to much ruder parody than in the modified version which appeared after Baggesen's death, in · 1836. In the meantime Baggesen had undergone a change of opinion. Oehlenschläger's sister, to whom he was devoted, had succeeded in converting him to Goethe, and in 1806 he wrote a " Palinode " which appeared in 1808 in his collection of poems, *Heath Flowers*, and which was a recantation of the former satirical poem on Goethe. Goethe read this poem also. But the change did not go very deep, and it was probably only because a rift had opened between Goethe and Romanticism that Baggesen, its fanatical foe, was able to call Goethe as a witness on his side. How superficial the change was, is shown in his poem, " The Origin of Poetry ", which in its first form (1785) paid homage to Voltaire. In the second version (1791) Wieland had taken the place of Voltaire, and in 1807 Goethe replaced Wieland. But it was only the name that had changed, and the description of Goethe was word for word the one formerly applied to Wieland. And it was not long before Baggesen's old antipathy to Goethe cropped up again, and Oehlenschläger, who had already objected to the satirical poem and the parody of *Faust*, suffered increasingly at Baggesen's hands as his allegiance to Goethe became more definite and obvious. Baggesen was the representative of the previous generation, the age of Classicism in the North.

But it was not Adam Oehlenschläger, but Henrik Steffens, who established Nordic Romanticism. He was born in Norway of German extraction on his father's side, and grew up in Denmark. His great love of nature led him to become a naturalist. Modern science, however, left him dissatisfied because it merely killed and dissected nature, treated it as a mechanism, a mass without spirit or soul. At this point he became acquainted with Goethe's *Faust* (the 1790 Fragment). In his autobiography, *What I Experienced*, and in his tale, *The Four Norwegians*, he records the first impression which the work made upon him. In the North, as elsewhere, Goethe's *Faust* brought about a spiritual transformation which although fortunate in its results, had to be bought at the cost of some sacrifice in happiness and contentment. It cost Steffens his religious convictions. The effect of *Faust* on him was to consume him with an inner torment, to goad him with a longing for complete understanding, an insatiable thirst for nature's springs, her unity and universality. This irrepressible, Faustian urge towards experience was assuaged for the time being by Schelling's philosophy of nature, which conceived nature as embodying a process by which the spirit tends to rise gradually to consciousness of itself. The letter of acknowledgment which Steffens addressed to Schelling [1] gives proof of this. In 1799 he went to Germany, as painters went to Italy or pilgrims to Jerusalem, and became Schelling's pupil in Jena, where he lived among the Romantic writers. His introduction to Goethe was marked by the feeling with which one meets someone who has exerted a decisive influence on one's life.

His first impression of Goethe, like that of many others, was one of disappointment at his cold formality and reserve. But later, when he stayed for some days in Weimar on Goethe's invitation, the latter, who was anxious to convert this young naturalist to his way of thinking, proved most communicative. The time flashed by in talks on natural science, which enabled Steffens to realise the fundamental resemblance between Goethe's and Schelling's conceptions of nature. The outcome of this change in the Nordic spirit, effected by Schelling and Goethe, was Steffens' work : *Contributions to an inner Natural History of the World* (1801). In this book the world is endowed with a power of organisation which raises it from the mineral kingdom to the vegetable and the animal, finally reaching its aim in man as personality in a state of freedom. In the history of mankind this tendency of the world is continuous, till it reaches the creation of increasingly individual beings. The book culminates in the glorification of the creative man of genius, the poet : " To whom nature grants to find within himself her harmonies, and who bears infinity within himself. He is the most individual creation, the great high priest of Nature." It is obvious that this refers to Goethe, and the book is dedicated to " Privy Councillor von Goethe ". Steffens ventures, he says, to dedicate to him Nature's answers to his questions. For, as she answers none but the poetic spirit, only such a spirit can understand his book. With reverent awe, therefore, he places his writings in the delphic temple of sublime poetry. Goethe was gratified by this magnificent gift, thanked the author for recognising him as a collaborator, and expressed his satisfaction that after having been quite alone in the world in his work of investigating Nature, now in his old age he had found companionship with youth. What interested Steffens particularly in Goethe's letter was his report of an experiment he had made with a French naturalist, to see if he were capable of following the course of an investigation, and how the attempt had been a complete failure. Goethe maintained that the French mind was devoid of intuition, and went on to prophesy the fate that a philosophy of nature in general, and Steffens' investigation in particular, would meet with in France, and not only there but at the hands of every empirical naturalist.

Steffens returned home, there to extol Goethe and German Romanticism, for between them he knew no difference. The link that bound them together was Schelling. He felt, too, that the new natural philosophy was a modern rebirth of the

old Nordic mythology, not of the Greek. But it was by arousing
the interest of Adam Oehlenschläger, whom he introduced to
Goethe and Romanticism, that Steffens became the founder of
Nordic Romanticism.

To understand fully the intensely interesting but variable
and complex relationship between Goethe and Oehlenschläger,
we must first consider Goethe's whole attitude to the awakening
of the Nordic world of gods and heroes. This awakening had
spread, after Klopstock, to German literature, and its greatest
representative was Oehlenschläger. The gods of Greece and
Rome were threatened by those of the North. It is most curious
to note how early this Nordic invasion was repelled by Goethe
at a time when his generation had almost without exception
succumbed to it. Goethe's Classical turn of mind is already
noticeable in his Storm and Stress period. He was familiar with
the Nordic world through the Edda, through Mallet's Danish
poems, through the works of Resenius, and through Herder.
But he could not bring it into the sphere of his writings however
much it excited his imagination. It was too remote from visual
perception, whereas Greek mythology was placed before his eyes
in visible form by the greatest artists and poets of the world.
To him the gods appeared to dwell outside the Nature which
he could counterfeit. So what inducement could he have to
introduce into his writings, in place of the pleasant concrete
figures of the South, the Nordic phantoms of the mist—mere
sounds? They seemed to him akin on the one hand to the
Ossianic and amorphous heroes, only they were cruder and more
gigantic, and on the other hand to the merry fairy-tales, full of
humour and parody. For Goethe saw a vein of humour running
through the whole mythology of the North,[2] and his attitude to
it remained the same all his life. He felt towards it as he felt
towards the Indian gods whom the Romantic writers tried to
introduce into German literature ; he could make nothing of
them, because they seemed to him to be formless monstrosities,
inartistic phantoms which offended his classical sense of beauty.
The European struggle between Classic and Romantic largely
resolved itself into Greek versus Nordic myths, and Goethe, the
creator of Faust, was from the time of his Italian journey ranged
on the side of the South. This greatly delayed the completion
of the first part of *Faust*, whereas he found it much easier to
complete the second part, with its presentation of Helen and of a
Classical Walpurgis-night.

And yet Goethe, who was always ready for change and development, did for a time keep an open attitude towards Romanticism. (This was his usual attitude towards really important things, even when they lay outside his own sphere.) Romanticism aroused his interest in Nordic history, and this was probably increased by the fate which Napoleon had in store for Goethe's native land. The Nibelungen epic began to fascinate him. He gave readings from it. He was even not averse to the suggestion that he should write a new or revised version of it. A certain leaning towards the North is noticeable in Goethe from about 1805.

It was at this time that Adam Oehlenschläger came to Weimar. If there is any truth in Ernst Moritz Arndt's words : " We are your ' South '. With us you shall first learn to know some measure of the life of the South, before you go to France and Italy "— they are surely true of the Danish writer who intended to pass through Weimar on his way to Italy. As Goethe was inclining then, to the North, Oehlenschläger was turning to the South, and this is doubtless what made it possible for them to meet midway. For Oehlenschläger then (1805) got the same friendly and paternal reception that Goethe later gave to the youthful Byron, Carlyle, Ampère and others. This young Dane, who was afterwards to reawaken the poetry of Nordic antiquity, was soon fascinated by Goethe, the " great Goth ", as Oehlenschläger once called him. The play upon words, first made by Herder, occurs both in Danish and in Swedish Romantic writers. In the latter the " gothic confederation " was formed under the leadership of E. G. Geijer, who in his *Recollections* calls Goethe's influence on himself boundless, and declares that he learned nothing from anyone else. Gothic was equivalent to Nordic and Mediæval. Oehlenschläger was trying to awaken to new poetic life the national antiquity of his land. But Goethe's *Götz von Berlichingen* which Oehlenschläger translated (stressing its similarity with the old Nordic heroes) certainly influenced him. Henrik Steffens helped to bring it about that Goethe became for Oehlenschläger the one spirit of his age whom he revered and recognised as teacher and master, whom he loved and admired as he did no other writer. He championed Goethe against Baggesen's satiric poem and his Faust-parody. But Goethe had changed. He was no longer the great Goth, but Goethe the Classical writer, the object of Nordic longing. Oehlenschläger decided to remodel Nordic-mediæval barbarity

" into poetry after the manner of Goethe ", to " classicise Nordic nationality ". He even speaks of Nordic Classicism and Nordic humanism. His dramas taken from Nordic history, such as *Hakon Jarl*, are in the German Classical form. His mythical drama *Baldur's Death* even approaches the sublime form of Greek tragedy with its Classical rhythms and choruses and the noble simplicity of its action. He utilised Greek tragedy freely, without abandoning the Nordic spirit. The Classical form now seemed to him perfectly suited to the Nordic sagas of heroes and gods. Oehlenschläger once even named Sophocles as one of his masters. Obviously the Nordic spirit was to be tempered and humanised in this kind of writing, and the writer specifically refers to Goethe's *Iphigenie*. The Nordic writer's leaning towards the South is unmistakable. Nordic strength was to mate with the beauty of the South. It was this leaning that took him to Weimar where Goethe received him in the most friendly way. As we have seen, Goethe was at that time turning towards the North, and Oehlenschläger had to give an extempore German translation and read aloud from his manuscript the whole of his *Hakon Jarl* and his *Aladdin*. In doing so he fell into many Danish turns of phrase, but Goethe, far from rejecting these, said that the two languages being cognate could usefully adopt expressions from each other. In his turn Goethe read aloud to the company, of which Oehlenschläger was a member, some cantos from the *Nibelungenlied*. As much of the Old German was related to words in Old Danish, Oehlenschläger was able to interpret a good deal which would otherwise not have been understood. Goethe also intended to give a performance in Weimar of the " meritorious " tragedy, *Hakon Jarl*, and costumes and scenery were selected for it. " But later it seemed to him hazardous, at a time when crowns were at stake in real earnest, to make sport with these sacred emblems." [3] The drama *Aladdin or the Magic Lamp* was also well received by Goethe, although he did not approve of every detail, especially in the working out of the plot. He even considered openly announcing the publication of *Aladdin*, when this " problematic work " was printed, in 1808. [4] But nothing came of this. In a letter to Goethe, Oehlenschläger admitted that, in working on a new version of *Aladdin* for publication, he had acted on many of Goethe's hints, and that he had also rewritten *Hakon Jarl* in accordance with Goethe's suggestions. [5] Although in this case Goethe did not go so far as to take any public interest in the Danish writer, there was certainly some stimulating influence. Oehlenschläger dedicated " the German version of *Aladdin* " to Goethe, with a poem (1807) which expresses his thanks for the reinvigoration and almost rebirth which he, the poet of Nordic strength, had experienced through the beauty of Goethe's works. This was the meeting, rich in hope and promise for the future, between Goethe as he was turning towards the North and Oehlenschläger as he turned towards the South.

But in 1809, when Oehlenschläger on his way back from Italy once more visited Goethe in Weimar, he was received politely, indeed, but coldly and distantly. It was the greatest disappointment of his life. He wrestled with Goethe as Jacob wrestled with the Angel but in vain. He hoped to restore the old relationship by giving a reading of the drama about the artist Correggio which he had written in Italy ; but Goethe refused to have it read to him. He preferred to read it for himself. Thereupon Oehlenschläger took leave of him with bitter resentment. His exaggerated expression of this feeling further alienated Goethe. Later, they occasionally exchanged greetings. But they did not correspond or make any exchange of their works. And Oehlenschläger's estimate of Goethe dropped considerably. He now declared that he had always loved in Goethe only the great Goth, and was repelled by Goethe's pompous predilection for everything Greek and his hatred of the North. Oehlenschläger clung to his admiration for the works of Goethe's youth. But Goethe the Classicist was now too prudent, too rarefied, too universal, above all too objective. He had lost the enthusiasm and fire of youth and the Second Part of *Faust* was haunted only by the melancholy ghost of Goethe's metaphysical self.

How did all this come about ? Why did an acquaintance between the German and the Nordic spirit, begun with such promise, end so badly ? First, if we note how different was the frame of mind in which Goethe reached and left Italy from that in which Oehlenschläger did so—this will explain a good deal. When Oehlenschläger was leaving for Italy he wrote " to a friend ", a vindicatory poem explaining why the journey was a necessity for him. He needed education, experience, a knowledge of the world. That it was not Nordic to forsake his native land in this way was an unjust reproach. For he would take with him to the South the moral standards, and the gods, of the North and the Nordic way of thinking. Goethe, on the other hand, when he went to Italy, sought to leave the North behind him and to forget it. On his return from Italy, Oehlenschläger wrote the poem " On the Simplon ", in which there is certainly nothing resembling Goethe's sorrowful leave-taking. Oehlenschläger, he wrote, breathed more easily and freely, since finding himself once again amid northern scenery, and no longer surrounded by laurels and myrtles, doves, roses, soft breezes and a cloudless sky. He had indeed been charmed by the South and could call upon the Greek god Apollo to witness to this. The art of the South had conferred on him " immense benefit ". But the god of Nordic poetry called him back to his true home. To Goethe, on the other hand, his return from Italy " land of plastic beauty " to " amorphous Germany " seemed a banishment. After his third journey to Switzerland, his return from the " winter landscapes of the St. Gotthardt " to his " museum " in Stäfa, which was stocked with Italian and Classical works of art, delighted him by its change from the most shapeless to the most shapely. Goethe's turning to the North at the moment of his meeting with Oehlenschläger as he was turning to the South was only temporary.

The compass-needle shifted, and Oehlenschläger once more turned to the North, while Goethe again moved southwards.

Oehlenschläger's drama on the artist Correggio was written in Italy. By his own admission, it was not without reference to the drama of Goethe's youth, *Künstlers Erdenwallen,* which Oehlenschläger translated into Danish, and also to *Tasso.* Why had Goethe been so firm in his refusal to have this drama read to him ? Did he feel perhaps that there would be something in it of that Christian-mystic conception of art which he condemned so strongly in the Romantic writers, and against which, in collaboration with the Swiss Heinrich Meyer, he launched his famous manifesto ? It certainly contains traces of the *Herzensergiessungen eines kunstliebenden Klosterbruders* and the *Phantasien über die Kunst* of Wackenroder and Tieck. So Goethe's reviving dislike of Romanticism was probably one of his reasons for refusing. Perhaps he feared, too, a renewal of that conflict between the artist and the world which he, who had made his peace with the world, had long since outlived. He always rejected anything that might disturb his hard-won equanimity. As for the similarities to Goethe often traced in Michelangelo, the acknowledged master, conscious of his position, cultured and yet aloof, we may suggest here that these touches were added to the picture later, under the influence of Oehlenschläger's intense disappointment. Otherwise he would hardly have dared to ask Goethe to listen to his play.

Oehlenschläger's chief work, his *Aladdin*, is known as the " Nordic Faust ". It displays a contrast which, when Oehlenschläger read it to him, Goethe failed to recognise fully, although the work seemed even then " problematic " to him. When he was writing *Aladdin*, Oehlenschläger was already familiar with Goethe's Faust-Fragment, and its influence is unmistakable. But what a difference ! We cannot here determine whether this is a general difference between the German and the Scandinavian turn of mind. But the Danish writer Georg Brandes describes *Aladdin* not only as the figure that represents the spiritual life of Denmark in the 19th century, but also as the representative of the northern spirit in general. This spirit was rooted in belief in the creative power of the imagination, and the genius which was the gracious gift of Nature. The northern spirit, he writes, is not the spirit of labour and research ; it is carefree, childlike, instinctive, naïve and full of genius. It is typically Nordic to contrast the inspired, creative genius with modern civilisation based on labour ; and that is what Oehlenschläger has done in his *Aladdin*. The same idea is to be found in Ibsen's work. In his *Pretenders* it is the man of inspiration, singled out by nature and born for kingship, to whom the crown falls, while all his rivals are powerless against him in spite of their cunning, their arts and their abilities. Ibsen's *Peer Ghynt*, too, is closely related to Oehlenschläger's *Aladdin*, and *Peer Ghynt* is frequently called the Nordic Faust. In *Peer Ghynt*, however, Ibsen sits in judgment on this Nordic spirit, in whom imagination easily runs to caprice with the loss of all sense of reality. At any rate the difference between Faust and Aladdin is quite clear : Aladdin is an imaginative, creative character, in sympathy with nature and men's hearts, to whom everything comes—love, riches, and power, without his having to do anything about it. His opponent, the magician Nureddin, is a man of intelligence and determination who, in spite of all his work and research, achieves nothing and succeeds in nothing. It is obvious that Aladdin is an inverted Faust. He represents the apotheosis of the inspired, carefree, serene and chosen genius, the ideal human type of the Romantic movement. Indeed, the whole work can be considered as an apotheosis of Romantic poetry, like Ludwig Tieck's *Emperor Octavian* or Novalis's *Heinrich von Ofterdingen*. But Faust is no such carefree spirit to whom everything comes naturally, and in Oehlenschläger's work it is obviously Nureddin who plays Faust's part. For Oehlenschläger was nearer in feeling than Goethe to the Romantic writers. They felt he had brought northern Antiquity to life again. What Goethe missed in Oehlenschläger's work was the same factor that he missed in the work of the Romantic writers. In 1808, in a letter to Zelter, he classes together Zacharias Werner, Arnim, Brentano and Oehlenschläger, and reproaches them all for letting all their works degenerate into absence of form and character. None of them grasped the fact, he wrote, that the highest and most important task of nature and art is the creation of form, and in particular of new species, so that each form becomes and remains something specific and important. Later, in 1828, he seems to indicate that he did not think Oehlenschläger's turning towards Italy had been either fundamental or productive. And Goethe was in a position to observe this in person. "These sons of the North go to Italy and only get as far as planting their bear on his hind legs ; and if he learns to dance a bit, they think him perfect." And in the introduction to the *Propyläen* Goethe notes that it is particularly difficult—indeed almost impossible—for a Nordic artist to make the transition from the formless to the definite or, if he reaches this stage at all, to remain there. He himself had found the way. For him Oehlenschläger became the example of the Nordic artist who failed to do so.

On the other hand, Goethe was able to approve a work which was the outcome of Swedish Romanticism and which gave classic form to the Romantic material of national myths and heroic legend. In this way it attempted a synthesis of Nordic and Classical antiquity. This was the epic of a poet who, like Oehlenschläger, belongs to world literature, the *Frithiof Saga* of Tegnèr. Now this follower of Schiller's was no Romantic writer. He once described the vague, insatiable longing which pervades all the works of Romanticism as a spiritual tuberculosis and a German invasion. His dislike covered all mystical obscurity, every vagueness and blurring of form. It must be admitted that it was not Goethe whom Tegnèr acknowledged as master. He once wrote of him : "I always see the poet but nowhere can I find the man." He acknowledged Schiller and the German idealism of Kant and Fichte. These are the sources of the philosophical and ethical elements that he read into the old northern sagas just as Schiller had read them into Classical mythology. It was the conception of a noble, serious morality, singleness of purpose and humanism. The *Frithiof Saga* obviously aimed at ennobling Nordic heroism, restraining and humanising its power, and thus reconciling Nordic with Christian morality. So we find that, after Frithiof has set fire to the temple of the ancient gods, a temple is raised to Baldur who is expected to rise again as the god of peace, love and reconciliation, the god of gentleness and light. At the close of the epic, the priest of Baldur utters what seems a Christian message, proclaiming that this mild god of love will resolve the ancient Nordic hate and revenge. The last canto is entitled " Reconciliation ". It was a reconciliation of the Nordic heroic spirit with the Christian ideal of man, and also with the Classical ideal of beauty. For the Nordic priest of Baldur's Christian message is expressed in Classical form. Tegnèr's epic is like a Greek temple in which a Nordic priest serves the Christians' God. Here we touch upon a significant problem, perhaps the most significant of all for the Nordic spirit. Ought this spirit to keep itself unsullied, to guard or acquire once more its peculiarly Nordic quality as Grundtvig advocated ? Or should it unite with the other powers on which the culture of Europe is founded, the Christian spirit and Classical form ? Tegnèr solved this Nordic problem entirely in the spirit of German Classicism, whose most earnest aim was to reconcile the Germanic with the Classical and with the Christian spirit. In this he was guided more by Schiller than by Goethe, and his form, too, reveals more of Schiller's style of rhetorical solemnity. But in spirit, and in the idea of humanising the North, he has a close relationship with Goethe. It is therefore quite natural that one of Goethe's followers, Amalie von Helvig, should dedicate to Goethe her translation of the *Frithiof Saga* (it is the Classical translation in which the Saga became a permanent part of German literature) with a dedicatory poem (1826) :

Your hand plucked the most precious fruit of every region ; the supreme favour of the gods wove your wreath from the crowns of all the poets ; to the laurel, caressed by southern breezes, was joined the myrtle, and against the roses of the East were pressed the richly-swelling splendour of the purple grape.

Turn then your kindly gaze towards the heroic tale to which you, in the rôle of Bragi, inspired me—let it be dedicated to you !—The virtue of Iduna's fruit is proved, and the goddess of everlasting youth offers the poet the golden apples of immortality !

In *Kunst und Altertum* (1823) Goethe wrote an extremely favourable article on the " highly-gifted Tegnèr ", as far as his work had then appeared in Helvig's translation. He stressed particularly the fact that "we meet with the old, vigorous, titanically barbaric species of poetry presented very pleasantly in a new, thoughtful and delicate manner".

Where Goethe was able to achieve any real influence in the North, it naturally was quite different from his influence in France or Italy where he helped to awaken the Romantic movement.

But he never influenced the North so deeply as he did other European literatures. There were of course Goethe-enthusiasts such as Oehlenschläger and Tegnèr, but theirs were isolated cases. The resistance that Goethe met with in the North was of two kinds. It was Goethe's Classical and therefore anti-northern tendency that was vigorously opposed in particular by Grundtvig, a man of great influence who has been called the northern Jakob Grimm. Like Oehlenschläger, Grundtvig, who was also inspired by Steffens, achieved his ambition : this was to free the individuality of the North from any foreign admixture, to give it its own particular character and mission which was to be found in strength, not in beauty. He therefore wanted to close all the gates to the South. Northern mythology, northern Saga and history were to be scientifically handled and were to become the foundations of northern culture and life. For this reason Grundtvig opposed Goethe's Hellenising and also his scientific tendencies. Wherever Goethe's science becomes the queen of the age, Sage is ousted from its throne. Grundtvig also blamed Goethe for turning disdainfully away from history and writing novels more to the reader's taste. History would in revenge turn as disdainfully away from him as it had from Voltaire, and he would be robbed of his fame.

The second motive for the resistance which Goethe met with in the North, was his attitude to Christianity. To make this clear by a typical example we must go beyond the span of Goethe's life. For it was Kierkegaard who, in the middle of the 19th century, considered Goethe from this standpoint. He did so many times, particularly in the second part of his *Stages in Life's Way* and in *Either—Or*. This champion of radical Christianity, no longer fashionably liberalistic in tone, insisted upon an absolute decision. He was forced to repudiate Goethe on the grounds of strict morality and of the beliefs which he himself held. This was not because of Goethe's allegiance to the pagan spirit of Greece. That would at least rank as a decision in *Either—Or*. It was because Goethe made no decision at all, because he was not even Antichrist but rather a modern liberalist, that Kierkegaard blamed him for not opposing this development of the modern spirit but actually making himself its herald. The quality that chiefly repelled this Danish Christian was Goethe's Olympian objectivity. It made him in Kierkegaard's eyes an example of modern characterlessness. He was a typical artist, resolving every conflict by giving it æsthetic form. Thus Kierkegaard reproached him, for instance, because when his love affair with Friederike threatened to overwhelm him, he rescued himself by seeking salvation—as a poet—by giving this experience an artistic form. Goethe, the epicurean, who always evaded a decision, had only a chance relationship to what is good, noble, selfless. He could indeed give these qualities artistic expression in the realm of imagination ; but in fact he remained an egoist. He who could create examples of noble devotion never himself made any sacrifice. He adopted the semblance of holiness, yet beyond this mask he gratified only his cold selfishness. Goethe the æsthete had only an æsthetic connection with Christianity and morality. Kierkegaard took particular exception to Faust's relationship to Gretchen. Of course these were not new accusations that were here levelled against Goethe. For selfishness, Olympian objectivity, the outlook of the æsthete—those were Goethe's principal characteristics as pictured by the " Young Germany " movement. But what was felt to be lacking in Goethe was a social conscience. It was the Nordic philosopher who first made the author of *Iphigenie* a symbol of modern man, of one who has lost the power of making decisions.

CHAPTER 13

FRANCE

We learn from the letters that Wilhelm von Humboldt wrote to Goethe from Paris what the position was at the turn of the century with regard to a knowledge of Goethe. Humboldt was able to inform him that Bitaubé's translation of *Hermann und Dorothea* had reached a fairly wide public and had been mentioned at the last meeting of the Institute. He also wrote that in Paris it was fashionable to appear to know a good deal about German literature. German names were constantly on people's lips, and they considered they knew and appreciated Goethe in particular. But Humboldt was forced to call this familiarity with German literature in Paris purely imaginary, and the predilection for Goethe an illusion. One had to look closer to discover how things really stood. The French were still too far removed from us to be able to understand us at the moment when we were just beginning to develop our originality. They were so far from us that the difference of language was a relatively small obstacle.[6]

French *émigrés* were the first to have some success, when they tried to enliven French literature by an infiltration of the German spirit, and indeed to prepare for its rebirth. In the history of thought, one constantly finds *émigrés* playing an important part in intercourse between the cultures and literatures of different peoples. The Protestant *émigrés* from France during the 16th and 17th centuries, the Huguenots, brought French culture to Germany and contributed largely to the beginnings of the German Renaissance. Now we see the opposite taking place, showing at once the great development and increased independence of German literature and the striking difference between the two periods in history. At this time the French *émigrés* came under the powerful influence of German thought, philosophy and literature. They were able to gain a greater insight into it than ever before through getting to know the country and the people, and by having personal intercourse with German writers and thinkers. Having been driven from their country by their opposition to the existing régime, whether revolutionary or Napoleonic, they considered it their mission to take the German spirit to France and thus to prepare for a rebirth of French literature and of France herself. Although they had fled before the Revolution broke out, they carried within themselves the spirit of the Revolution and its need of change, and of liberation from forms and traditions now grown rigid. This prepared the way for expansion and refreshment from other, younger sources. In this connection we must mention three French writers. Charles Villers, who came to Germany before the Revolution, steeped himself here in German literature and philosophy, consorted with the finest minds in German, and both knew and corresponded with Goethe. In a letter to Goethe (1803) he named as his most important concern the struggle against the " culture matérialistique " and the " inphilosophie française ". " Puisse le noble esprit de la sagesse et de la poésie germanique vaincre le pernicieux démon de l'immoralité et de la superficialité française." [7] In this spirit and with this aim he wrote *La philosophie de Kant ou principes fondamentaux de la philosophie transcendentale* (1801), a work directed against French rationalism and materialism, and one which looked to Kantian idealism to bring about the salvation and rebirth of France. He opposed Napoleon's Concordat with Rome in his " Essay sur l'esprit et l'influence de la réformation de Luther " (1804), which sees in the German Reformation the source of true religion and morality. There followed in 1806 the " Erotique comparée ou Essay sur la manière essentiellement différente dont les poètes français et allemands traitent l'amour ". This work deals with love in German works, principally those of the type of Goethe's *Werther*, and represents it as pure, ideal, spiritualised love in contrast to the shameless, lascivious, unrestrained eroticism of French works. Goethe wrote to thank Villers for having introduced him in this way to Villers' fellow-countrymen. He liked to call Villers, who faced both France and Germany, " Janus bifrons ".

Another interpreter of German literature to France was Benjamin Constant, who was by birth a Vaudois, but was descended from Huguenot emigrants. He lived in France during the Revolution, but fled when Napoleon became First Consul and toured Europe with Mme de Staël. His sensitiveness to German poetry was remarkable. In connection with some of Goethe's poems he makes some arresting observations in his diary (1804) on the difference between the tendentious, rationalistic, reflective verse of France and Germany's dreamy poetry, with its absolute surrender to Nature. He translated or rather

re-wrote Schiller's *Wallenstein* (1809), and in the preface to it
he demonstrates the difference between the German and the
French theatre. The aim of his version was to free and refresh
French Classicism by introducing German influence. He sought
to bring about a co-ordination of German with French tragedy.
This attempt, surely not far removed from Goethe's aim, cannot
be said to have been successful, and in 1809, Goethe wrote the
following short poem.

> Der du des Lobs dich billig freuen solltest,
> O ! guter Constant, bleibe still ;
> Der Deutsche dankt dir nicht, er weiss wohl, was er will,
> Der Franke weiss nicht, was du wolltest.

Yet the preface to *Wallenstein* left almost as great and lasting
an impression in France as did Mme de Staël's *De l'Allemagne*, and
it certainly shaped the French conception of the German mind
for many years to come. When Constant visited Weimar with
Mme de Staël, he managed to afford Goethe some " hours of
instruction " and intimate conversation and to be of great use to
him ; for, in seeing how Constant took up his remarks on nature
and art and tried to approximate them to his own, Goethe was
able to note in what respects his own treatment was rudimentary,
confused, incommunicable and unpractical.

There were of course *émigrés* of a different stamp, who widened
rather than bridged the gap between German and French minds,
and one of these lived from 1793 onwards in Weimar itself. This
was Mounier, about whom Goethe remarked ironically that he
had undermined Kant's reputation and was about to " blow him
up ". Conversations with him, which obviously irked Goethe,
brought out certain essential differences which Goethe had known
all his life as existing between German and French thinkers.
" The French ", he wrote on this occasion to Humboldt, " have
no idea there can be anything in a man besides what he has
absorbed from outside." He wrote this in reply to Mounier's
assertion that the Ideal is " composed " of various beautiful
parts. This was diametrically opposed to Goethe's conception
of totality and his view of the nature of an organism. Indeed,
he often expressed a violent dislike of that " truly base ex-
expression ", " composition ", introduced from France : artists
do not compose their work from parts any more than nature
does ; they reveal an image which dwells within their spirit.
" Composition ! " a conversation with Eckermann records (1831)
" as if it were a piece of cake or biscuit, got by mixing eggs and

flour and sugar together ! '' Any creation of the spirit is the work of *one* spirit and is cast in *one* mould, pervaded with the breath of *one* life, *one* soul ; the artist does not arbitrarily experiment and juggle with parts ; the demonic spirit of his genius holds him enthralled, so that he must carry out its commands.

His connection with Mounier seemed, then, to open up a positive gulf between the German and the French mind, and this was really a fundamental problem affecting their attitudes to art and nature.

But the work which had by far the greatest influence in the establishment of intercourse between French and Germans was Mme de Staël's *De l'Allemagne*.   This introduced Goethe and German literature not only to France (naturally her first concern), but also to England, Italy, Spain and elsewhere.   Mme de Staël seemed to be predestined by her very origins to this work.. Her father, Necker, was a Genevan of German extraction, her mother a Vaudois, and she herself was born and brought up in Paris. She was an *émigrée* when she wrote this book, a fugitive from Napoleon.   Long before she visited Weimar, Goethe had expressed great interest in this woman and her works.   In 1796 he translated her '' Essai sur les Fictions '' for the *Horen*.   In Mme de Staël Goethe saw for the first time a definite influence exerted by German literature and thought, and an appreciation of it which had hitherto been very rare.   The essay that he translated shows a striking similarity with his own ideas on the nature of poetry.   So does her book *Del 'Influence des Passions sur le Bonheur des Individus et des Nations*, with which Wilhelm von Humboldt had made Goethe familiar, and from which he planned to translate at least some extracts for the *Horen*.   Goethe wrote that in this book Mme de Staël had considered foreign literature solely from the French point of view, but had nevertheless made some observations on German literature which were remarkable for that period.   She had referred to its obvious idealism, its enthusiasm for the highest ideals of morality and beauty, the love of freedom in religion, philosophy and society—remarks which almost anticipated the later book *De l'Allemagne*.[8]   Observations like these were bound to arouse Goethe's intense interest.   He had the impression that the French system of upbringing and education had been too narrow for her, that she was trying to break free from its restrictions.   Perhaps that was why he considered making a translation of her book.   It showed him that in the '' remodelled '' France, in the '' fierce, refiner's fire '' of the

Revolution which was raging there, another Revolution affecting its relations with the German spirit was in the making. He certainly meant to foster this symptom of a better understanding between the spirits of France and Germany by translating the " Essai sur les Fictions " and some extracts from the longer work. During the same period, his " fairy-tales " were similarly intended to further a political reconciliation. He also wanted Schiller, as editor of the *Horen*, to append to the translations some remarks as " clear and courteous as possible ", about Mme de Staël, so that they might be sent to her, and a beginning thus made towards leading the " dance of the Horen " into France, even in its remodelled state.

When Mme de Staël came to Weimar in 1804, it must be owned that her visit caused a certain amount of embarrassment. Quite frankly, her tireless loquacity, although invariably .clever and stimulating, upset Weimar society. After a meeting with her, Goethe made the following comment : " It was an interesting hour. I could not get a word in ; she speaks well but a great, a very great deal." (Yet Mme de Staël is said to have remarked —after the same meeting—that she could not get a word in, but that she listened with pleasure to anyone who spoke as well as Goethe did.) She always wanted to impress and to build up her reputation by talking, reading aloud and reciting. She made no secret of her intention to use her conversations with Goethe in her forthcoming book on Germany, and it could not be pleasant to see this intention in every question, and to know that every statement would be utilised. Goethe became cautious and to a certain extent reserved. Any free and easy relationship was out of the question in these circumstances, and the visit suffered accordingly. Besides, Mme de Staël was particularly anxious to talk to Goethe about the differences between German and French literatures and this subject was distasteful to him, for at that time he had passed the stage of contrast and quite justifiably felt himself a European. She behaved as if he were still only the author of *Götz* and *Werther*. Also, her especial delight was to discuss insoluble problems in society, and here she ventured on questions of thought and feeling " which ought to remain a matter solely between God and the individual ". Even in private conversation, she claimed " even on the most important topics to be as quick off the mark as if it were a question of catching a shuttlecock ". This quotation is from Goethe's diary and yearbook for 1804. We need not make too much of isolated misunderstandings.

Mme de Staël read him her translation of "The Fisher" in which for the last word in "was lockst du meine Brut hinauf in Todesglut" she had put "air brûlant". Goethe explained that he meant the heat of the embers in the kitchen grate, where fish were roasted. Mme de Staël thought this excessively "maussade" and lacking in taste, finding herself suddenly relegated to the kitchen in the midst of her fine burst of feeling. That, she considered, was just what German poets lack, τὸ πρῶτον, a fine sense of what is fitting. Besides, Mme de Staël unduly prolonged her visit to Weimar. She could not hit upon the right moment to make her farewells. It resulted in Goethe often avoiding her. He even excused himself one evening when she was to give a reading of *Phèdre*, and his "evil spirit" drove him to contradict her at every turn.

Yet, in spite of everything, he was genuinely interested in her project of writing a book on Germany. In 1808 he wrote urging her to publish it soon. "We deserve encouragement," he wrote, "we deserve to be fostered by the good will of a friendly neighbour, herself half a compatriot, and to see our own image in such a flattering mirror." From 1812, Goethe began to read extracts from her work in manuscript, which pleased him greatly.

It is most instructive to see one's own people justly and favourably depicted from a foreigner's point of view. We Germans are usually unfair enough to each other, and foreigners are not always inclined to do us justice. It is fitting that such an intelligent woman should rate us highly enough to take trouble with us. And I hope that this work will eventually be published for the benefit of us all.[9]

And as it began to appear in instalments, Goethe read it (1814) with "growing interest".

The book has the pleasantest way of encouraging one to think, and one is never at variance with the author even if one is not always of her opinion. All that she says in praise of Parisian society can surely be said of her work. The extraordinary fate of this book is probably one of the strangest happenings of the present time. The French police, clever enough to know that a work like this will increase German self-confidence, wisely had it pulped. The few copies that were rescued sleep on, while the Germans themselves wake up and save themselves without the need of this intellectual stimulus. At the present time the book exerts a remarkable influence. Had it appeared sooner, one would have thought it contributed to bringing about the great events which followed : it is like a lately discovered prophecy and a challenge to fate ; indeed it sounds as though it had been written many years ago. The Germans will hardly recognise themselves in it, but this will enable them to gauge all the more surely the great step forward they have taken. It is to be hoped that they will take this opportunity to widen their self-knowledge and will take the second great step of acknowledging each other's merits in art and science, instead of, as formerly, constantly opposing each other. Let them at last decide to work together and, just as they are now eliminating slavery abroad, overcome the tendency to envy and disparagement among themselves. If they do this, no contemporary nation will be their equal.[10]

Goethe expected that the work when completed would lead to useful observations on Germany and France, especially as it was appearing at a time when such vast changes, destined to modify both internal and external conditions, were taking place. " We Germans would have found it hard to sum up our character as neatly as is done in this work by Schlegel and Mme de Staël. When one has lived and worked through much of the period with which it deals, one feels one can appreciate many points if not better, at least differently." Lastly, in 1823, he writes " we can regard that work on Germany as a mighty battering-ram that made a great breach in the antiquated prejudices which stood like a Wall of China separating us from France. Now at last we have become better known beyond the Rhine, and therefore also beyond the English Channel, and so have achieved some actual influence on the lands of the remoter West." [11]   We can understand this opinion of Goethe's when we remember that it was written when he was intensely occupied with the idea of world literature, although he had not then coined the expression. He was bound to welcome an attempt of this kind to open the gates of France to German literature. He was bound to welcome such justice paid by a Frenchwoman to German writings. It fully corresponded with his idea that, through their literatures, the peoples should learn to know and draw closer to one another. And even then he noticed that no second attempt of the kind was made with equal vigour or equal success. For by then (1825) Europe was caught up in the Romantic movement, a movement which would have been unthinkable but for this book by Mme de Staël. It is understandable that Goethe was now indulgent about all the embarrassments and the " clash of national mannerisms " which had troubled him so much during Mme de Staël's visit to Weimar, and seemed to serve no useful purpose.

The appearance of this book was followed by several indications that France was ready to be interested in German literature. One of its consequences was that when, in 1821, Goethe read the

translation of his dramatic works by Stapfer and others, he could
see the freedom from prejudices French literature was acquiring,
as well as the deep insight into his work which Stapfer displayed
in his introduction. Another consequence was that in 1824 he
could speak of the daily increasing interest of the French in
German works. In 1825 he declared it impossible to form any
judgment on contemporary French literature, because the elements from German literature infiltrating into it were having such
a disturbing effect that the results would be distinguishable only
after a score of years. Indeed, when he read the translation of
his notes on Diderot's dialogue *Rameau's Nephew* and considered
the arbitrary treatment they got, he once more gravely doubted
the possibility of any real understanding between German and
French minds. In his published review he expressed himself
with great dignity and mildness. He said it was most instructive
to see how these good young men, who were passionately devoted
to German authors, often unconsciously expressed the cleavage
between the French and German ways of thinking by their
individualistic interpretations. There were some things to which
they constantly returned, others which they could not assimilate ;
yet everywhere their judgment sought some kind of reconciliation.
Mme de Staël's ideas were discussed, some accepted and some
rejected ; but throughout the whole work the aim was clear ;
it was to convey to both nations one common, although limited,
conception. He advised them, too, to acquire a more intimate
knowledge of German writers and their works. Then, if they
retained their goodwill towards him and his nation, a mutually
useful and satisfactory relationship might be established. In
private, however, Goethe's judgment was much more severe. He
was not at all pleased to find his earlier works now swept into the
whirlpool of French literature ; hardly more than his name still
clung to any of them.

The French have an extraordinary attitude to German literature.
They are exactly in the position of the clever fox, who cannot get
anything out of the vessel with the long neck ; even with the best
intentions they do not know what to make of our products. They
treat all our artistic productions as raw material which they have to
handle. How miserably they have distorted and confused the notes
to *Rameau* ! Not a thing is left in its original place (1825).

It was only after Goethe had become acquainted with *Le Globe*
(1826), the organ of French Romanticism, that he could persuade
himself that France really was capable of absorbing German

literature with understanding and eagerness. For this journal, founded in 1824 by Dubois and Leroux, aimed at making known to the French public all important scientific, literary and philosophical works, " in the great peaceful movement which was beginning to sweep over all the civilised world ". This journal gave German literature pride of place, and Goethe realised that it was fulfilling its task with an understanding, a ripe judgment, a breadth of vision and from a lofty standpoint, such as he had hardly thought possible. Mme de Staël's book was justified in its happy consequences.

On the advice of Schiller, Wilhelm von Humboldt and particularly A. W. Schlegel, Mme de Staël had based her book on the difference between Classicism and Romanticism. French is declared to be the most Classical of all modern literatures, while German is the most Romantic. The Classical literature of France is based on the Græco-Romans, the Romantic literature of Germany on the Christian and Germanic Middle Ages. But the essential difference—and this is the main theme of the whole work and the specifically French interpretation of a distinction taken over from Germany—is that French literature is fundamentally social, whereas German literature is individualistic. In French literature, therefore, we find the authority of traditionally determined and binding rules, but in German literature the freedom of a creative individuality. The German writer works by and for himself alone. Each one goes his own way, speaks his own language, creates his own form, his own law. The merits which count in French literature are social merits : beauty, charm, grace, wit, taste, reason, order, propriety, clarity and proportion. But the merits that rank highest in German literature are imagination, passion, feeling, depth, enthusiasm and in particular the gift of dreaming. For of all emotional states dreaming is the loneliest. We can scarcely tell our nearest friend the content of our dreams ; how then should we be able to impart them to society ? French literature keeps to the world of experience and reason. But the German writer and thinker penetrates beyond this limit of experienced and familiar reality to distant and unknown spheres. He seeks to fathom the riddle of the universe. He will not let his imagination's wings be cut by tradition, experienced convention, reason and rule. That his limitless urge towards truth halts at no dogma, however sacrosanct, is seen in the course of the German Reformation and German mysticism. The German writer loves untrodden ways and travels alone towards unknown goals even if they are infinitely remote. For what he seeks is nothing short of infinity. This explains why melancholy is the keynote of German poetry (Goethe heard it as such also in English literature). For the constant measuring of time by eternity, to which it can never correspond, inevitably leads to melancholy. The German poet is thus the born idealist. It is the ideal for its own sake that excites his enthusiasm—that most German of qualities, while French society, concerned with pleasure and profit, makes use of ridicule and scepticism to stifle enthusiasm for ideas. Mme de Staël's work ends with a eulogy of this German enthusiasm. It is the way of ennoblement for humanity, the path into the future, which the German spirit has pointed out and which France is now about to take. Mme de Staël does not deny that Germany too should learn from France. Mutual interaction is a necessity. The Frenchman ought to grow more religious, the German more worldly. The French writer ought to realise that good taste is not the only standard, and that an offence against the laws of Society is not a crime, if noble ideas and genuine feeling are concerned. Writers in Germany ought to guard against offending good taste, and to strive more for proportion and order, clarity, definition and precision. The Frenchman could make use of German profundity to guard him from frivolity, and the German of French form as a safeguard against lack of restraint. Each nation should serve as guide to the other, and they would be guilty of grave injustice if they deprived each other of the valuable ideas that they could exchange. It is Goethe whom this book of Mme de Staël's represents as the essence of German literature ; yet not the Goethe who had already achieved within himself the synthesis of the German and the French spirit, but Goethe as the focus of all German qualities, and the representative of Romanticism. She finds in his lyric poetry the expression of Romantic feeling : reverie and melancholy ; in his *Götz* and *Egmont* she sees freedom from formal restraint, from the substitution of rules, and national history instead of ancient mythology ; and in *Tasso* there is the conflict between the genius and society. *Iphigenie* and *Hermann und Dorothea*, written in the manner of the Græco-Romans, only go to prove, in her view, that Goethe held no universally applicable criterion of art. As opposed to French writers he was always seizing upon new modes of expression, always revealing himself as unexpectedly different ; on this occasion he made use of the manner of the Græco-

Romans ; but he was never static. (Ampère in the *Globe* also stressed this protean capacity for metamorphosis on Goethe's part.)

For Mme de Staël, then, *Faust* represented the most comprehensive incarnation of Goethe's spirit. She analyses it minutely : in *Faust* nothing is constant ; it alternates between the heights of rapture and the depths of despair, the longing for spiritual perception and desire, for purely sensual gratification, between the rhythms of the tragic and the comic. His ideas move at bewildering speed, his devils and witches flout all reason. He breaks down man's limitations as he does those of poetry and of art. Mme de Staël criticises in *Faust* the lack of form, the absence of taste, of proportion and of moderation. She hopes that no further attempts of this kind may be undertaken. Yet her detailed analysis of *Faust*—the most detailed in the whole book— and her translated quotations from it, made it known in France ; and it is quite obvious that the German spirit, with Goethe as its representative, was felt by her to be essentially that of *Faust*. And that is what distinguishes this new image of Goethe from the former one, so completely conditioned by *Werther*. It is most striking to note how *Werther* falls into the background in Mme de Staël's work, and this is certainly deliberate. She wishes to ensure for Goethe and for German literature a new and more positive influence. Its old crippling, suicidal pessimism is no longer its most prominent feature. Disillusionment with life, discontent, insatiability—these are now shown to be the most effective motives. Their source is traced to *Faust*'s idealism, to the German enthusiasm for ideas, to the longing to surmount the limits laid down for man and heighten his powers, and in this way to attain a better future for humanity. The German spirit now appears braver, bolder, more heroic. Its essential quality is felt to lie no longer in a " return to nature ", but in the way it keeps its eyes on the future. Its representative expression in literature is seen no longer in *Werther* but in *Faust*. This book of Mme de Staël's aims at imparting new courage and hope to France, and, by opening up springs of fresh youth such as these, to direct its future course.

It is impossible to estimate the new impetus that this access to *Faust* gave to the French spirit, to whom the world so secure, so clear, now deepened into mystery. The solution demanded powers other than reason and empirical knowledge. It needed something more occult, visionary and imaginative, and the great impulse towards superhuman exaltation awoke. Enjoyment of the present gave place to an urge towards a limitless future.

This is not the place in which to refer to passages in various works which recall parts of *Faust*. And it would be a mistake to lay too much stress on the fact that pacts with the devil and similar themes, hitherto rare in French literature, now became a commonplace. It is a question rather of the spirit of *Faust*. All the same, pacts with the devil, witchcraft, sorcery and magic, which, after the appearance of *Faust*, replace Classical mythology in the works of French Romanticism, do constitute a definite expression of a spiritual change. For it is one of the most crucial points of contention between European Romanticism and European Classicism whether the world of the Greek gods and heroes or that of the mediæval northern devils and spirits is to be considered the source of modern poetry. It often seems almost as if this were the most important difference—after that of the Rules. For in this difference there lies a profound significance. Fundamentally, the question is whether a simple ideal of beauty, clarity and grace, or gloom and a misty half-light, shall govern poetry : whether it is to have a content common to all men or a national one : whether it is to be inspired by the Græco-Romans or by the Middle Ages : in a word, whether it is to be Classical or Romantic. The first article that Goethe translated from the *Globe* and published in his journal *Kunst und Altertum* was a French defence of the use by modern poets of mediæval diablerie against Classical criticism. It was in fact a defence of two German works, namely the *Freischütz* and *Faust*, in which the element of " improbability " was certainly no greater than in that of the Classical myths of antiquity which only custom has made more credible to us. But the time had now come to disregard the authority of custom. A more important point is, of course, that the Faust-spirit was creeping into French writings. It is dissatisfaction, the insatiable urge to experience every height and every depth, to exhaust every grief and every joy of life, which never finds fulfilment, and is driven even beyond its highest aim by a longing for one that is unattainable. It is a boundless thirst for knowledge, no longer content with the conception of the world that had been till then so secure and so unquestioned because based on reason and experience. It seeks to pierce this mystery by using other obscurer, more hazardous means of raising the world's veil. A metaphysical longing is awakened, a courage to adventure into dark, unknown, dangerous regions. French poetry, formerly of so social a stamp, loses itself in the melancholy satisfaction of infinite loneliness. It bursts the bonds of its previous formalism, so strict, so precise, so clear and well proportioned. For, to the Faust-spirit, every form is a prison, every limitation an intolerable affliction. Instead of the unity of place, we now find the limitlessness of all space ; instead of the unity of time, eternity. The traditional fixity of French form is broken up, partly by the instrumentality of *Faust*. We can hardly appreciate how Goethe's *Faust* must have affected a spirit which had been accustomed for centuries to Classicistic notions. George Sand once wrote an " Essai sur le drame fantastique " (in the *Revue des Deux-Mondes*). Its subject was Goethe's *Faust* and the Faust-dramas which it inspired : Byron's *Manfred* and Mickiewicz's *Conrad*. She diagnoses the difference between them thus : Faust, the German, wrestles with God for truth, Manfred, the Englishman, for the power to forget, and Conrad, the Pole, for the liberation of his fatherland. But they are all " metaphysical dramas ". George Sand thought they were bound to arouse opposition in France because France was " too Classical ". When *Faust* appeared, the academic spirit of France was outraged by the disorder and obscurity in this masterpiece. Its form was so novel and the plan not adapted to the French traditions hallowed by the rules. *Faust* could not be acted on the stage ; and reason was powerless to comprehend this medley " of metaphysical and actual life ", in which the novelty of *Faust* consists.

Now it is most interesting to observe the attempts to overcome these difficulties. First, the help of music was enlisted. The Faust-spirit appeared to need music if it was to penetrate into the world lying beyond reason and experience, and to create an atmosphere in which it would be possible to understand what seemed so extravagant, and by all rational standards so improbable. Again and again the attempt was made to achieve this atmosphere by means of music, and it is unlikely that France would have succeeded had it not been for Berlioz's magnificent Faust-music and the less magnificent but highly acceptable music of Gounod. The German spirit, on the other hand, is naturally at home in these Faust-like regions, and has no need of music. Berlioz himself sent the score of his *Faust : Eight Scenes from Faust, a Tragedy by Goethe ; translation by Gérard (de Nerval)* to Goethe with a letter of homage. In his memoirs he describes the effect that *Faust* had upon him. He considers it one of the greatest pieces of good fortune of his whole life. The impression it made

was strange and profound. The amazing book fascinated and
haunted him from the first moment. In the letter to Goethe he
wrote that for some years he had constantly re-read this astound-
ing work. He begged Goethe to pardon a young composer who,
his heart being stirred and his imagination inflamed by Goethe's
genius, could not repress a cry of admiration.

Another way in which France tried to draw nearer to *Faust*
was by calling in the aid of graphic art in an attempt to fix this
elusive figure in visible form. The attempt had a stupendous
success vouchsafed to no German artist—neither Retzsch nor
Cornelius nor Kaulbach. It was a French artist, Delacroix, who
succeeded in creating illustrations to *Faust* which are works of
genius, and which accompanied Stapfer's translation. It is true
that Ary Scheffer's Gretchen-pictures were more popular with
the French public. But they are insipid daubs, whereas
Delacroix's pictures, with their gloomy, savage genius are particularly appropriate to their subject ; indeed Goethe, when comparing the *Faust* pictures of Delacroix with those of Cornelius,
declared the former's to be the more German in character. He
was obliged to admit that this tempest of ideas, the confusion in
the composition, the violence in the attitudes, and the crudeness
in the colouring, although not entirely to his liking, yet revealed
Delacroix's ability to merge himself in *Faust*. He had become
so intimate with the work that he had realistically conveyed its
gloom, and had matched with his restless brush a restlessly
striving hero.[12] At any rate these pictures facilitated the understanding and appreciation of *Faust*.

The third way was afforded by the French language itself,
whose native precision and lucidity lit up what was obscure in
the work. Goethe himself was conscious of this when he read
French translations of *Faust*. In 1808, Lemarquand, while on
a flying visit to Weimar, translated some passages from *Faust* with
the book in his hand. Goethe was struck by the freedom, the
charm, the serenity of his translation, and approved Lemarquand's intention to render the whole work in this way. The
result would certainly be remarkable " for the French and German
spirits have perhaps never before engaged in such a keen contest ".[13] It was rumoured that Goethe, in a letter to Gérard
de Nerval, said that it was only in de Nerval's translation that he
had first understood his own *Faust*. This is a myth of which
French Romanticism was inordinately proud, and which still
haunts the Faust-literature of both Germany and France. There

exists, however, an attested verdict of Goethe's on Gérard de Nerval's translation. Goethe said it gave him a very strange feeling to realise that *Faust* had now gained a place for itself in a language dominated fifty years earlier by Voltaire. He had no wish to read his *Faust* in German : but in this French translation it all seemed quite fresh, new and sparkling. The letter, as we have mentioned, is a myth. But Goethe really did say about another translation (Stapfer's) which appeared with illustrations (by Delacroix) : " Although this drama is played out on a confused and darkened stage, its theme and its purpose seem infinitely clearer when rendered into French—that exhilarating language which is so good a vehicle for ideas." [14] Théophile Gautier's pride is therefore partially justified. He writes in his *History of Romanticism*, on the subject of Gérard de Nerval's translation, that it was a hard task to transpose the strange, obscure beauties of this ultra-Romantic drama into the French language which had grown so timid. But the attempt was successful, and the Germans, who claimed to be beyond the understanding of the ordinary man, had to admit defeat ; the French Œdipus had guessed the riddle of the German sphinx.

We have still to consider some works of French literature which belong to the tradition of *Faust*, although with a few exceptions their writers could not have known Goethe. In two of Alfred de Musset's works, the dramatic poem *La coupe et les lèvres* (1832) and the epic *Rolla* (1833), a type of humanity unfamiliar to France was presented. Here we have two heroes whose insatiable thirst for life is their undoing. Rolla plunges into every sensual excess, is never satisfied, and his very enjoyment is poisoned by desire until in the end he compasses his own death. And this work contains a long invocation to Faust. The hero of the drama is of the same type. He seeks to drain the cup of life. But an insuperable obstacle keeps his mouth and the cup apart. The curse that he hurls against God and nature for endowing man with this thirst, and yet denying him the means to slake it, echoes Faust's curse almost word for word. It really seems as though with this drama Musset is aiming at giving France a work analogous to *Faust*. Although of course in significance it cannot seriously be compared with *Faust*, yet in theme it can. And now a new note is sounded in French literature ; George Sand creates in *Lélia* a female Faust, whom no love-affair can completely absorb and no moment completely satisfy. Balzac notes his interest in " le monde nocturne et fantastique des ballades allemandes ", in *Faust*, and in E. T. A. Hoffmann. He calls the Germans the people of the occult sciences, and typical Germans are, in his view, Jakob Böhme, Agrippa von Nettesheim, Paracelsus, Faust, " les grands chercheurs de causes occultes ". He himself ransacked every science, every philosophy, every religion, indulged freely in occultism, in order to gain a deeper insight by these Faust-like means, to raise the world's veil, to fathom her secret. He no longer trusted to reason, that instrument of knowledge to which the French spirit had hitherto owned allegiance. His novels are full of these " chercheurs de l'infini ", " chercheurs de secrets ", magicians, occultists, alchemists, men of mystery, so new and so incongruous in French literature. And those of his characters who are not questing along dark paths are yet driven by an inner urge, " le désir ", desire worked up into a wild chase after love, riches, power. His inventors, artists and thinkers are possessed, devoured by the Idea. Everywhere we find this ever-insatiable demon, everywhere these seekers after infinity. This is the Human Comedy. Balzac was the chief of the " satanic school " in France, as Byron was in England, and this whole movement had its origin in Goethe's *Faust*. Twice in his novels, *La Recherche de l'Absolu* and *La Peau de Chagrin*— particularly in the latter—Balzac actually appears to have entered into competition with Goethe's *Faust* (and with E. T. A. Hoffmann). But in this work of his youth the resemblance is merely external, limited to a pact with the devil. Balzac, in sending this work in 1831 to Weimar with a large consignment from among the works of French Romantic writers, may have wished to show that *Faust* was one of his spiritual ancestors. But Goethe, who certainly saw in it the product of an outstanding brain, found too, that it displayed an incurable perversity in the nation's disposition, one which would gain ground " if the Departments which at present cannot read or write do not so far as is possible restore it to health ". At that time Goethe was busy with the Second Part of *Faust*.

We must repeat that *Faust* certainly did not bring happiness or blessing to the young writers of France, and in his *Confessions* Musset curses not only *Werther* but *Faust* also. But that *Faust* caused a tremendous expansion of France's cramped range is undeniable, and at this point we find a whole series of French works, influenced by *Faust* yet giving a more hopeful and comforting picture of both the present and the past. Articles on

Faust written by French Romantic writers frequently state that the drama is more than the history of one man. It is the history of the spirit of man as a whole, and *Faust* symbolises the history of mankind. It reveals the meaning and the aim of history, which is working itself out according to a mighty world plan. The course of mankind's history is a succession of griefs and errors. But these trials transform and purify man's spirit. *Faust* was now interpreted as a philosophical work, a philosophy of history couched in poetic form.

It should be noted, too, that besides Goethe's *Faust* another German literary work encouraged a mental attitude akin to *Faust*'s. This work is Herder's *Ideas towards a Philosophy of the History of Mankind*, in which history is seen as the development of all the possibilities inherent in man's nature which aim at an ideal. These possibilities expand according to the differing genius of the nations, their varying circumstances, and the extent to which the peoples co-operate. It represented the history of mankind as the gradual realisation of the ideal of humanism, and this had much in common with Goethe's idea of *Faust*. Goethe had contributed to Herder's work ; one might even call it a work of collaboration. Goethe and Herder believed mankind to be a living organism in which every people had a definite function to perform by means of which mankind's natural vocation would be gradually realised. This idea caught fire in the period of French Romanticism. The philosophical writer and philanthropist Degérando had already drawn the attention of Frenchmen to Herder, had published articles on him, and had translated extracts from his *Ideas*. But his efforts had had no success. Degérando had however induced Edgar Quinet, then a young man, to translate the whole of the *Ideas*. The translation was published in 1825 with a long preface : " Introduction à la Philosophie de l'Histoire de l'Humanité ". Two years later there followed Quinet's " Essay sur les Œuvres de Herder ". When it appeared in a new form in 1857, Quinet dedicated this translation to the shades of Goethe. It was only after Goethe's death that Quinet discovered that he had recommended it in *Kunst und Altertum* to the attention of the German public. For Goethe, of course, it was a welcome sign of the world literature then coming into being : a spirit which had completed its period of influence in Germany was now rising to new life in France. Quinet himself tells how, in his early youth, Herder exerted over him a helpful influence which decided the whole course of his life. The *Ideas* revealed to Quinet, in the midst of the hopeless and bewildering chaos of historical event, a guiding principle : namely, that the seed of the humanist ideal of freedom, justice, moral uprightness and beauty is planted by nature in man, and blossoms in the universal history of mankind through the corporate effort of men and peoples. In this idea he found man's vocation and also his own. Man, according to his strength and his circumstances, helps to build up this future empire of humanism which reaches out beyond his own individuality, his age and his race. The triumph of humanism means the reign of the spirit, of freedom, justice, morality and beauty in man's relations with his fellows. In this way the French philosopher of history claimed to overcome Helvetius's egoistic philosophy, Voltaire's mocking scepticism, and English utilitarianism.

What is it in Herder, then, that effected such a change in the French spirit ? Quinet himself makes this clear in the preface to his translation, and in his essay on Herder. A moral transformation was wrought within him by the idea that man was called to serve the highest ideal for its own sake, not for the sake of personal happiness or individual aims and interests. This " for its own sake " was felt in other countries to be a particularly German trait. It is even demonstrable that in France the origin of the principle of " l'art pour l'art " is considered to lie in Germany—in Kantian philosophy and the art of Weimar. The second effect was the formation of a historical conception of the world, seen in terms of continuous development. For it is in the nature of an ideal that it can only be approached, and never attained. But this approach—here we have the third effect—can be achieved only by men, peoples and ages working in harmony together, and this eliminates any isolation of one man, one people or one age. A new ethos is here proclaimed. There dawned upon the French mind in particular (which hitherto had tended to isolate itself and be self-sufficient) the perception that accessibility, influence and confluence are necessities. It must co-operate with other peoples to link up with the past and keep in mind the future. It is no accident that Herder's follower, Edgar Quinet, was one of the first French writers to proclaim the idea of world literature. He does so in his essay " De l'Unité des Littératures Modernes " (1838). In it he looks to a new science which shall see all literatures as one indivisible unity, and he demands that no literature shall shut itself off, but that each shall be correlated with and accessible to, others. It is only through the corporate effort of all peoples that the development of the humanist ideal can be achieved.

These ideas from Herder merged with those in Goethe's *Faust*. Quinet himself, Herder's follower, his translator and mouthpiece in France, formed a plan to embody this philosophy of history in a mythical figure. His epic poem *Ahasuerus* (1833) cannot be said to have much intrinsic significance as a work of art, but it plays an important part in the history of French literature, for it initiates a series of Faust-like works concerned with the history of mankind. A figure like Ahasuerus, already frequently compared with Faust, appeared at this point in French literature quite as a stranger, not only because he did not belong to Classical mythology or history, but because he was a man constantly goaded, hounded along. In this mythical figure, in the ceaseless wanderings of the Jew through all ages and peoples, the writer symbolised the history of mankind and thus set a fashion which many were to follow. In 1838 Lamartine wrote the epic poem *La Chute d'un Ange*. This aimed at representing the development of the human spirit, the phases through which it passes to fulfil its heavenly mission, and, led by Providence, to reach its goal after many earthly trials. Laprade's *Psyche* (1841) dealt with the soul's decline from God through its desire for knowledge, its banishments, its temptations, and its ultimate purification and union with Amor, the god of love. The many volumes of Victor Hugo's *Légende des Siècles* (from 1859 onwards) were to tell the story of the development of mankind in succeeding epochs, the monotonous and hard ascent towards the light from Eve the mother of men to the Revolution the mother of the nations, from barbarism to civilisation. Each epoch is represented as a fresh change in the physiognomy of mankind. The clue which guides us through the labyrinth of history is progress, " le progrès ", by which man mounts from darkness into enlightenment, " la transfiguration paradisiaque de l'enfer terrestre, l'éclosion lente et suprème de la liberté ". It was a kind of religious hymn in many verses, combining the history, mythology and legends of many peoples and ages. The Second Part of *Faust* was certainly known to these writers for whom the Faustian idea of development, the ascent from darkness into light, now stood in the foreground. In Vacquerie's *Futura*, the Faust of the Second Part is actually the hero. From the union of Faust (here representing unhampered thought) with Helen (who is beauty) there springs Futura, the future, who founds the kingdom of God on earth, the kingdom of love, kindness, justice and humanity. French drama as well as epic poetry, was touched with the Faust-spirit. To this period belong dramas in which Albertus Magnus, a legendary Faust-like figure of the Middle Ages, is shown as a hero tormented by an insatiable thirst for universal knowledge. He is in danger of succumbing to the devil's wiles but is saved, like Goethe's Faust, by a process of purification and a woman's love. We find the same theme in George Sand's " Drame fantastique ", *Les sept Cordes de la Lyre* (1839). George Sand wrote an essay comparing Faust with Byron's Manfred and Mickiewicz's Conrad, and in this drama Mephistopheles calls upon Faust as an ancestor of Albertus and also Gretchen, though he chooses a new way of tempting this new Faust and his Helen. The work thus reveals its descent from Goethe's *Faust*, and not only from the First Part but also from the Second. This is indicated by the name of the girl, " Hélène " and also the mystical symbol of the lyre, the rescue by the heavenly powers and the apotheosis of Helen. Théophile Gautier, too, wrote an Albertus Magnus and there are, besides, French dramas in which Faust himself appears as the hero. In his *Comédie de la Mort*, Gautier contrasts Faust in his old age with Don Juan—a theme which became common in both French and German literature. In his drama *Fin de la Comédie ou la Mort du Faust et Don Juan* (1836) Adolphe Dumas depicts the transformation of Don Juan from a Lovelace to a man of Faust's perception, while Faust as a character evolves from perception to love.

Such were the works of the French Romantic writers dealing with Faust. They show the power of Goethe's *Faust* to open up new horizons. At the same time they remain typically French, for in most cases everything is regarded from the viewpoint of human society, and the idea of development is shown to be that of social progress. Although Goethe's *Faust* ends by being an instrument of civilisation, wresting from the sea new land for men to settle upon, this is only the last stage in the perfection of his personality, the stage of action. But in the French works dealing with Faust we are led towards the kingdom of God on earth, a kingdom of justice, freedom and humanity, an ideal society. Here then is another proof of the difference between German literature, based on the idea of personality, and French literature, based on that of society. This difference outlives the period of Romanticism, and reappears in the Parnassian, Sully Prud-homme's epic drama dealing with Faust, *Le Bonheur* (1888). It

may be regarded as a continuation of the Second Part of *Faust*.
Faust, waking after death to find himself upon another, better
planet, lives there a blissful existence full of peace, beauty and
harmony, with Stella, his loved one transfigured. But he wearies
of it. His Faustian restlessness possesses him again. He plunges
into the study of Classical and modern philosophy and the natural
sciences, hoping to discover the secret of the Godhead and creation.
But when voices from the earth rise to his ears, begging his help
in their sufferings, he returns to earth with Stella, and there
(mankind having meanwhile become extinct) becomes the
ancestor of a new human race which is to bring about universal
happiness by means of justice and brotherly love. It is quite
obvious that the end of Goethe's *Faust* appeared to the French
writer—even of that day—to be a monument of human egoism.
He was substituting for it the Utopia of a future community
founded by Faust, an earthly paradise, not—as in the last vision
of Goethe's *Faust*—an endless struggle against chaos, but everlasting peace. By wide-spread socialising of German ideas, the
French Romantic movement guided German literature to a stage
beyond Romanticism. " Young Germany ", a thoroughly social
and political movement, occupies the place in German literature
that French Romanticism does in French literature, and it is
profoundly influenced by the latter.

During the period of French Romanticism the conflict of
the personality—particularly that of the genius, the poet—with
society became a favourite theme ; and this development is
attributable to the influence of Goethe.

It is in Goethe and his work that, for the first time in world
literature, the relationship between the poet and society is shown
to be profoundly problematic, and it is Goethe who for the first
time in world literature wrote tragedies whose theme is that of
the creative artist. He did so in his youthful work *Kunstlers
Erdenwallen* and later in *Tasso*. The English drama, *Tasso's
Melancholy*, by an unknown writer, which was acted at the end
of the 16th century in London and is now lost, was certainly no
tragedy about the creative artist. But Goethe's *Tasso* states the
problem of the poet and society. It is the tragedy of a poet who,
living in the kingdom of his dreams and insisting on his own
standards and privileges, finds in society no room to exist, no
breathing space. And because he rejects the traditions and the
standards of society he is in his turn rejected and ostracised by
it. In *Werther*, Goethe had not limited himself solely to the

motive of love, but had added a social motive, and here in *Tasso* he does the same. When Goethe completed this work, he certainly no more resembled Tasso than he had been identified with Werther when he completed it. In Weimar he had learnt to take his place in the order of society, and his *Tasso*, which was finished in Italy, was thus a kind of self-judgment. Once again, however, the world failed to see the Goethe who was stronger than his own inclinations. It saw in Tasso and in Goethe the lonely poet who, because of his gifts, comes into conflict with society, and judges it by his own poetic genius. It is no exaggeration to say that Goethe wrought a change in the world's conception of the nature of the poet, and indeed of any type of artist. It was through him in the first place that the relationship of the poet and society was seen as a tragic problem. We find the poet thus freshly interpreted in every European literature : in the *Correggio* of the Danish Romanticist Oehlenschläger, who refers in his autobiography to Goethe's melodramas on the theme of the creative artist ; in Mickiewicz's *Conrad* ; in Byron as a figure as well as the author of a *Tasso* ; in Shelley (and it was certainly no coincidence that he planned a Tasso-tragedy, of which some fragments remain) ; in Felicia Hemans's *Tasso's Coronation* ; in the Russian drama *Torquato Tasso* by Nestor Kukolnik (1830-1). Shelley and Byron, moreover, were ostracised by English society, banished from England, and bore as it were the poet's mark of Cain upon their brow. In his epic *Alastor, or the Spirit of Loneliness* (1815) Shelley makes his hero a Faustian figure, but a Faust who is a poet, and indeed a poet of Tasso's type. It is the history of a poet whose imagination is filled by such a sublime vision that he seeks in vain its counterpart in reality and so he languishes and dies, a lonely figure.

This change in the conception of the poet is most noticeable, however, in French literature. The French poet had hitherto felt himself to be thoroughly representative of society, and his judgments had conformed to its standards and usages. The cult of form in French literature, for instance, was essentially a cult of social form, of form as the genius of society. It was Mme de Staël who drew the attention of the world to the contrast between German and French literature in this respect. It was she, too, who first saw in Goethe's *Tasso* the tragedy of the conflict between poet and society and pointed it out in her book *De l'Allemagne*. It was through her, one may say, that Goethe changed the conception of the nature of the poet in the minds of the French

Romantic writers. We need not confine ourselves here to that French version of Goethe's *Tasso*, Alexandre Duval's *Le Tasse* (1826) about which Goethe wrote in *Kunst und Altertum* that it had aroused the whole nation's attention and had a striking success. This work, however, transforms Goethe's *Tasso* into a highly conventional tragedy of courtly love and jealousy. There is no trace in it of a poet's tragic fate. But one of the first and decisive victories of French Romanticism was a drama by Alfred de Vigny, *Chatterton* (1835). This portrays the martyrdom of an English poet who is filled with so lofty a conception of poetry and poetic genius that in his own poetry he ignores the demand of society. Society, however, takes its revenge on him for this attitude, and drives him to penury, hunger and death. It is quite clear that in this drama Chatterton resembles Tasso, and we may assume that Alfred de Vigny had read Goethe's drama. He knew it, at all events, from Mme de Staël's detailed treatment in her book *De l'Allemagne*. In his novel *Stello* (1832) he calls up three figures of poets : Gilbert, who became insane, Chatterton, who took poison, and Andre Chénier, who was guillotined ; and he uses them to prove that the poet, as such, belongs to a race for ever cursed by the forces of this world, the state and society.

It is no wonder that his originality and his power to portray himself are among Goethe's most prominent characteristics as he appeared to French Romantic writers. These are the foundations of the truly profound character-study of Goethe which Ampère wrote for the *Globe*, and which Goethe himself translated. Ampère attributed to Goethe's originality the fact that he was so slow to find favour in France ; and what particularly amazed Ampère was that Goethe sought the material for his productions so exclusively within himself, that he would write of nothing but what he had himself seen or felt. In every work of his, even his dramas, he expressed what had pleased, grieved or in some way occupied him. In reading him, one must start from the standpoint that every one of his works refers to a certain stage in the development of his soul or of his spirit ; one must see in them the history of his feelings as well as the events which made up his existence. What a spectacle it is, a bold spirit relying on itself alone, listening only to its own inspiration ! This was Ampère's main thought, that he would find Goethe and his whole personal experience in his writings ; and Goethe himself witnesses to his success. To the German reader, all this seems self-evident. But for France it meant a new revelation—that a great poet need not be merely the mouthpiece of society, but may disclose in a poem his most intimate personal experiences. It may be this revelation that gave some of the French Romantic writers, Musset for instance and Lamartine, the courage to strike out along the same path.

Naturally it was in French lyric poetry that this change was first felt. The whole conception which the French Romantic writers formed of Goethe was that of a lyric poet, revealing himself also in drama and epic poetry, and drawing upon his own personal experiences. But it was his lyrics that had the greatest influence. They contributed more than anything else to the change-over from the purely social French chansons to those lyrics of French Romanticism which sound deeper, obscurer, more intimate notes—the voice of solitude and longing, tones of grief and of happiness, of harmony not with society but with nature, and of a love which is no longer gallantry but deep emotion. To French Romantics, as to others, Goethe became the pattern of the lyric poet ; and in France Heinrich Heine is the only lyricist who can compete with him in this field. More than this, after Mme de Staël made public her conception of Goethe the word " lyric " became synonymous with German, just as for Musset " Romantic " and German were identical notions. It was Musset who called Romanticism " Germany's daughter " ; it was he who spoke of the " douce obscurité que le Romantisme importa d'Allemagne ". La douce obscurité . . . How strange that sounds in the land of clarity and reason. " Le Romantisme," writes Musset, " c'est la poésie allemande." And in André Suarès's work, Goethe le Grand Européen, which appeared to mark the Goethe Centenary in 1932, and which calls Goethe the greatest man of modern times and the master of us all, the author declares his lyrics to be the most moving and the finest of his works ; even in Faust he finds the lyrics more wonderful than anything else. For in them thought has found its musical expression. It is in Mignon's song and that of the harpist that for Suarès the climax of beauty in Wilhelm Meister is reached. Romain Rolland thought much the same. But this is all the more astonishing during the Romantic period, when we remember that at that time the translations of Goethe's lyrics were poor ; even Gérard de Nerval's Poésies Allemandes (1830) was no very striking exception. Besides, at that time, Goethe's lyrics and ballads were chiefly translated only into prose, and were thus from the beginning robbed of their soul. And the language of French poetry was then completely lacking in the tones which Verlaine was the first to give it, and which would have made possible an adequate rendering of Goethe's lyrics. We must remember also that lyric poetry as a whole presents special difficulties to the translator, and that its fragrance, its bloom, its mood, its music vanish all too easily. It is all the more astonishing, then, that Goethe's lyrics (and those of other German lyric poets such as Bürger, Schiller, Uhland and Heine, as well as English lyrics) had so much effect on French lyric poetry. For they accomplished this actually in translation ; the writers of French Romanticism, with few exceptions, were limited to translations. The *Poésies de Goethe, auteur de " Werther "*, traduites pour la première fois de l'allemand par Mme E. Panckoucke* (1825)—in reality by various collaborators of the publishing firm of Panckoucke, including Aubert and Loeve-Veimars—were at once criticised by Goethe as having "paraphrased, and destroyed the poetry". We may perhaps see an explanation in the fact that Goethe's lyrics were carried to France on the wings of the music of Beethoven and Schubert. We ought never to forget what enormous help German music, in its world-wide advance, gave to German poetry. It was music and not poetry that from the days of European Romanticism onwards was the real universal language of Germany, and the natural expression of the German soul—its breath, as Victor Hugo described it in his panegyric of Germany, and "la grande communication de l'Allemagne avec le genre humain", as he calls it in his Shakespeare book. "C'est par la musique que ces idées qui pénètrent les âmes sortent de l'Allemagne." Beethoven's declaration, that music is the universal language, which needs no translating because it speaks directly from one soul to another, is particularly apt in the case of Germany. On his death-bed, in his last delirium, Musset thought he heard German music, Beethoven, Mozart, Schubert. In his *Lutetia*, Heinrich Heine tells us how German music captivated France and was also destined to further an understanding of German literature. But even though the harmony was lacking, the French lyric poets heard in Goethe's and Heine's poems (even in mere translations) the inner music ; and in it they felt the contrast to the lyric poetry of France, which hitherto had been so rhetorical, so reflective, so rationalistic. Any poem by Goethe, on the other hand, in fact any German poem (it was now realised in France) called essentially for a musical setting, and all the composer had to do was to listen to the poem's immanent melody.

This poetry, destined by its nature for expression in song—the outpouring, in musical language, of the soul, the heart, the feelings —in a word, the lyric, was recognised as the specifically German art, or better still, the specifically German nature. It dawned upon men that the lyric is born of the spirit of music. Musset, who had translated Goethe's lyric poem " Selbstbetrug "—" Le rideau de ma voisine, imité de Goethe " and had written " Chansons à mettre en musique ", realised this. Otherwise he might not have written his famous poem " Rappelle-toi, Paroles faites sur la musique de Mozart ". (It seems to be taken from a German song, its music not originally by Mozart.) During this period, French operas were frequently written on the themes of German dramas and ballads. From Goethe's works there are *Faust* by Berlioz and by Gounod, the *Bride of Corinth* which Scribe adapted for Auber, *Mignon* by Thomas, *Werther* by Massenet ; and Théophile Gautier even planned to compose a ballet on the " Erlkönig " theme ! But nothing exemplifies German influence in French literature so well as this fact : the actual German word " Lied " came into use to denote French poems which had this quality of immanent music. It was first so used in the period of French Romanticism, by Musset, Gautier and Sainte-Beuve, was continued in the Symbolist period, and today the designation " Lied " is still in ordinary use in the French language, along with other untranslatable words such as " Gemüt " and " Stimmung ". To realise the transformation that took place in the relationship of the two peoples between the 18th and 19th centuries, one has only to recollect how often in the 18th century the gay social song intended to be sung in company was called by German writers a " Chanson ".

This points, however, to a further difference between the voices of the two peoples, and to still another development of the French lyric. For in France the " Lied " was taken to mean not the cheerful poem, but the melancholy, visionary, dreamlike one, absorbed in nature and in itself, not the social but the folk-song type ; and Goethe was partly responsible for this. What particularly astonished the French mind about Goethe was that a creative artist of such eminence, of so select and universal a culture, of so splendid a position in society, should yet venture to sing the music of his own soul in the strain of the folk-song, just as he was not ashamed to owe the theme of his greatest work, *Faust*, to a chapbook. To the France of that day this was as new as the poetry of experience. In French

literature the folk-song was not considered fit for educated
society, yet here in the mouth of so great a poet they heard
lyrics in the spirit of the folk-song.   It is significant of the understanding of German poetry which had now awoken in France
that this image of Goethe's, derived from his poetry of isolation
and confession, should accord so well with the image of Goethe
the poet of the people, the poet of the Gretchen, Mignon and
Harpist's songs.   In the same way Edgar Quinet saw in Faust,
and in Gretchen, two sides of the German character which
always co-exist in the German people : " L'extrême reflexion et
l'extrême naïveté, tout l'héritage de science du genre humain et
toute la poésie virginale d'une race nouvelle."   Nothing is more
truly the product of the spirit of isolation than is a German folk-
song.   It can be sung with real meaning only when one is alone,
in complete contrast therefore to the French Chansons.   Goethe,
who was a great admirer of Béranger, that master of the Chanson,
and who repeatedly tried to make him known in Germany, was
forced to admit to Eckermann that political songs like these were
out of place in Germany.   There was nothing capable of arousing
the enthusiasm of the whole nation.   They would become the
songs of one particular party.   It is fitting, then, that it should
be left to Chamisso, a Frenchman by birth, to naturalise
Béranger's songs in Germany and to write his own German
Chansons in the same style.   Yet, with the echo which they
called forth in France, Goethe's lyrics sounded completely new
notes within the hitherto so exclusive and socially selective confines of French literature, and signified—even compared with
Béranger—something new.   In imitation of the collections of
German folk-songs, the old folk-songs of France were now
collected, and they too were called " lieder ", the lieder of
France.   During the Symbolist period, so strongly influenced
by Richard Wagner (the cult of whom was something quite
without precedent), a new wave of enthusiasm for the German
lyric swept over his followers in France.   To this period belongs
the work of that fanatical Wagnerian, Camille Mauclair.   *La
Religion de la Musique*, in which he calls the oldest, truest poetry
" le lied ", speaks of the " lieder " of the Bible, of the Chinese,
Persians and Japanese.   He applies the German name to this
oldest, most original and most natural type of poetry, because
in Germany it owed its resurrection in the first place to Goethe,
Heine, Schubert and Schumann.   But Mauclair also gives the
name to the poems of Baudelaire and Verlaine, because they too

express pure feeling in musical language. " On reconnaît un poète à ce qu'il a du sens du lied, c'est-à-dire de la racine du sentiment." The link with the tradition begun through Goethe's influence in France is obvious.

To estimate the stupendous range of Goethe's sphere of influence, we must remember that with his *Götz von Berlichingen* and his *Egmont* he sponsored the beginnings of historical drama, or rather dramatised history, in France. During the last years of his life Goethe remarked that French literature was beginning to experience a change which German literature had experienced more than fifty years before, and whose origins were to be found in *Götz*. Of course, besides Goethe, Schiller and still more Shakespeare influenced (for instance) Vitet's dramatised historical episodes : *Scènes historiques, Les Barricades* (1826), *La Mort d'Henri III* (1829). These were dramas which owed their themes not to mythology but to mediæval and more recent history. They observed historical accuracy, and tried to preserve the colour of the historical period instead of the more abstract atmosphere of the Classical tragedy. In this way they gave new colour and variety to the theatre, which finally abandoned Classicistic rules and thereby made an end of the older form of tragedy. A drama of this type is only a loosely-strung succession of scenes ; and, when we bear in mind that the quarrel between Classicism and Romanticism in Europe was to a large extent a quarrel about the rules of the Unities, we can appreciate how far French Romanticism was responsible for the downfall of French Classicism. The effects which Goethe had : the awakening of the French spirit, the opening up of fresh sources such as the Nordic sages and national history, the quickening of the soul of lyricism through music, liberation from stereotyped forms ; all these tended towards the overthrow of the Classicistic traditions and conventions in France.

It was natural that changes such as these could be accomplished only after a struggle against the most violent opposition. At the time when Mme de Staël's book appeared, clearing Goethe's path to France, French literature was completely under the domination of the Academy, and this body regarded it almost as a religious duty to uphold French tradition, good taste and the sacred doctrine of the Rules. To the French, Germany was still the land of barbarians, of hyperboreans. In their eyes, Mme de Staël's book amounted to a crime against the state, an attempt to open the gates of French culture to the most dangerous of enemies—and it was a Frenchwoman who had done this ! The country is in danger ! Hannibal ante portas ! Faust is at the gates of Paris ! At the opening of the " Société des Bonnes Lettres ", in 1823, Lacretelle said :

> Oh shame and dishonour ! Against our Classicism is cited the authority of a woman who is better known for the liveliness of her mind than for the sureness of her taste, and who dares to venture on comparisons between Corneille and Schiller, between Racine and Goethe. Are we really to sacrifice to strange gods, really to lay France's fairest crowns at their feet and like a conquered people cry : Vive la Germanie, Vivat Teutonia ? To what extremes would the German invasion not lead, not only in our literature but also in our state and in our society ! The robbers, those favourites of Romanticism, would infest our woods, our roads, our towns.

The Academy issued an official manifesto, Auger's " Discours sur le Romantisme " (1824) against the formless monstrosities then making their way into France from Germany, against the barbarians who would exchange Racine's *Phèdre* and *Iphigénie* for *Faust* and *Götz von Berlichingen*. When *Faust*'s translator, Gérard de Nerval, became insane, it was seriously imputed to the fact of his having ventured into regions of Faustian irrationalism, and become the first victim of German overheated imagination, on whom French rationalism was now taking its revenge. French Romanticism triumphed in spite of opposition of this kind. But it did so, and at the same time Mme de Staël's picture of German literature, and of Germany as a whole, enjoyed great popularity. It depicted a people of poets and thinkers, musicians, dreamers, visionaries, enthusiasts and idealists, kings in the realm of imagination. This picture survived until the war of 1870–71, when France was forced to realise that Germany contained not only poets and thinkers but also soldiers, not only Romantic poetry and music but also cannon, and that it would not be content with a mere dream-empire in the clouds ; it was bent on establishing one very firmly on earth. Then Mme de Staël's picture was shattered, and people began to accuse her of being responsible for the defeat of France, because, with her picture of Germany, she had lulled her country into a sense of security ; and the intellectual invasion for which she had cleared the way had prepared the ground for the real one. At this point, the French writer Barbey d'Aurevilly made his famous attempt to unmask and destroy French conception of Goethe as a false idol. This procedure was repeated in the 1914–18 war, when Jacques

Bainville (in his work *Cent Ans d'Illusion sur l'Allemagne*) called German idealism " une mystification abominable et dangereuse, la pure légende staëlienne ", and Péladan, the Wagner enthusiast (in his book *L'Allemagne devant l'Humanité et le devoir des civilisés*), brought against Mme de Staël the same accusation of treason. When passions had stilled, and the outlook was once more clear, it was obvious that Goethe had survived the storm, indeed that he was now seen more truly because more completely. Although he was regarded as a German prodigy, he was seen also as a European, as a bridge between the nations and a link between peoples, as the synthesis of the Romance and the Germanic, of the Classical and the Romantic spirit, as Faust wedded to Helen.

Goethe was in very truth all that by the time he inspired the French Romantic movement, and it is thus understandable that he was not altogether content with his powerful influence and the honour paid to him. It is true that the change in French literature took place in the spirit of his idea of world literature, and showed him the benefit that one literature may receive from another. He saw fresh life coming into an ageing literary tradition, flexibility into rules grown rigid, liberation from limitations grown too narrow, a breaking down of national limitations, enrichment in the matter of materials, forms and themes. But he was appealed to by the French " anti-Classicists ", who in his name fired the sacred precincts of the old temples of the gods ; and this amazed and also alarmed him. For he had already left far behind him all trace of Herostratus's zeal.

He therefore felt the need to sound a note of warning. While he was translating from the *Globe* and publishing in *Kunst und Altertum* an article playing off the Nordic spirit world of his *Faust* against Greek mythology, Goethe added his own observations. The poet must certainly be allowed, he said, to find his materials in an element of this kind, but Greek mythology, the incarnation of humanity at its noblest and purest, was surely preferable to a hideous company of devils and witches which were the outcome of gloomy, fearful epochs, and of confused imaginings that fed as it were on the lees of human nature. It was Faust's creator who spoke thus. In spite of a certain admiration for Delacroix's grandiose illustrations to *Faust*, Goethe still objected to Delacroix's wild manner, the vehemence of his conceptions, the confusion in his composition, the violence in the attitudes and the crudeness of his colouring. He admitted that this manner was certainly well suited to the First Part of

Faust. But he himself had far outstripped this *Faust.* Here we have another clear instance of how the French and the Germans had in spirit exchanged the parts each usually played. Goethe did not deny that the revolutionary change in French literature had brought many advantages. He was certainly pleased that the *Globe* defended liberation from the fetters of meaningless restrictions. " What is the sense of all this frippery of rules belonging to a formal obsolete age ? " we read in a conversation with Eckermann, " and all this fuss about Classical and Romantic ! The vital point about any work is that it should be good and sincere, and then it will turn out to be Classical." In a conversation with Napoleon Goethe had already made the reply : " Rules are not for us." Napoleon was amazed that such a great mind as his should ignore rules. But Goethe approved the biased tendentiousness of the French Romantic writers as little as the narrow pedantry of certain Classicists. He would be shocked, he declared, if any form were rejected without qualification ; great works constructed in strict accordance with the rules are essential for certain subjects which demand the style of Classicism. He himself affords an example of this. He used the strictest Classical methods when dealing with material which had to appear in the style of the ancient Greeks if it was to retain its intrinsic truth. It would have been madness on his part to have tried to keep his *Götz* within the three Unities ; but it would have been no less a sin against the Holy Ghost of beauty to have decked out his *Iphigenie* in the style of Romanticism. " In short," writes Soret, " in this futile and stupid quarrel, Goethe is completely impartial." We must admit, however, that *Götz* and *Iphigenie* belong to two quite different periods in the development of his style, and that the difference in the material of each, which called for such different forms, is not fortuitous. Regard for rules, or lack of it, is not dependent only on the type of material. It is a question of style. But this dubiously valid argument of Goethe's conceals a deeper reason. It is this : that the French Romantic writers confirmed his opinion and experience that no revolution can avoid extremes. At first, he wrote, they aimed at no more than a rather freer form. But, not content with this, they next rejected both the form and the content of previous works. The representation of noble sentiments and actions began to be considered tedious, and experiments were made in the treatment of all kinds of repellent themes. Instead of the pleasing content of Greek mythology, we had devils, witches and vampires, and the noble heroes of old gave place to swindlers and galley-slaves. For such people are fascinating, stimulating ! Goethe called Victor Hugo's novel *Notre Dame de Paris* the most odious book ever written. Only Mérimée, he conceded, treated such ultra-romantic things in a tolerable manner, for none of these repulsive objects affected him much, and he was able to remain objective while creating them. In all other cases it was precisely this lack of objective, artistic creation, this arbitrary subjectivity, this inability to lose sight of oneself in any composition, that Goethe criticised in the French Romantic writers (and in the whole Romantic movement throughout Europe). A further reproach was the exaggerated disregard of rules. It was in connection with the French " ultra-Romanticism " that Goethe made his often-quoted and often misapplied statement : Romantic is what is ailing, Classic is what is healthy. He even spoke of corruption and decay. All this alienated him in his old age from his own times, and he must have been disquieted when he saw in this European development his own influence, indeed the impetus given to it by the works of his youth and by his *Faust*. The European Romantic writers, too, never tired of assuring him that they regarded him as their spiritual ancestor. And the fact that the influence of German literature as a whole (particularly that of E. T. A. Hoffman) enhanced these effects, involved the possibility of jeopardising his theory of world literature. He himself had longed for France to adopt an open attitude to the works of German literature, and now he saw consequences which he considered disastrous, and had to admit that German literature could not always feel proud of its influence on the world. He only hoped that these extremes and exaggerations would gradually disappear and leave only the great advantage that, with a freer form, a richer, more manifold content had been achieved, and that nothing in all the diversity of life was now excluded as inherently unpoetical. He looked upon French Romanticism as a severe attack of fever, which, with good fortune, would lead to a better state of health.

He hoped, too, for a favourable reaction on German literature. For the " Globists " seemed to him to be a perfect example of a concentration of a nation's intellectual strength. In Germany, on the contrary, he saw only individuals, each of whom held the opinions of his province, his town, his own personality. And it naturally gratified him to see that German literature was now highly esteemed in France. His interest in the French Romantic movement remained extremely lively. The *Globe* was his favourite reading-matter. It charmed him from the beginning. He would hardly read anything else, and he made extracts from it to which he added his own notes. He also translated entire articles which he published with his own remarks in *Kunst und Altertum*. He kept the German public constantly informed of all the opinions he found there on himself, Schiller, Herder, and on German literature in general.

Is it really so strange to see Goethe, the German Classicist, as a medium of French Romanticism in Germany? For one thing it must have given him a great deal of pleasure to find himself so thoroughly understood. It is true that he expressed to Riemer his great dissatisfaction with Mme de Staël's judgments on his works in her *De l'Allemagne*. She saw them as completely detached and isolated, and seemed to have no conception of their underlying homogeneity, and their origin. But when he read the essays on himself by Stapfer and Ampère, Goethe felt that these French writers possessed a deeper insight than anyone in Germany. He admired their ability to diagnose the state of his soul from his works, to read between the lines what he had not put into words. But that was not all. He could recognise from the statements in the *Globe* as well as from private evidence that the young poets of France loved and honoured him as their spiritual leader. A letter from Deschamps showed clearly what an influence he had had on the new life of French literature. It was like the influence of Shakespeare on Goethe's own youth, Eckermann adds. Stendhal, by taking up a totally different attitude to Goethe, practically isolates himself within French Romanticism. As Goethe himself noted with surprise and a certain amount of irony, Stendhal makes use (in his book on Rome, Naples and Florence) of quite a few points from Goethe's *Italian Journey*, and presents them under the guise of his own experiences. But that did not prevent him from making his well-known remark about *Faust* : that Goethe gave Dr. Faust the devil for a friend and with the aid of so powerful a helper Faust did what we all do at the age of twenty : he seduced a " modiste ". Stendhal considers it supremely ridiculous that Goethe thought it important enough to mention in his four-volume autobiography how he dressed his hair at the age of twenty, and that he had an aunt called " Anichen ". If we reduce these opinions to a common denominator and interpret them, we see that to this writer, filled with enthusiasm for the Renaissance and often not unjustly described as one of Nietzsche's forerunners, Goethe's poetic and literary style was too commonplace and not sufficiently heroic. Goethe on the other hand was fascinated by Stendhal. The book on Italy both attracted and repelled him, so that he could not get away from it. He considered *Le Rouge et le Noir* to be Stendhal's finest work, and admired his accurate observation and psychological insight. But to Eckermann he declared that some of the female characters seemed a trifle too Romantic. This, however, compared with Goethe's verdict on the exaggerations of French ultra-Romanticism, was an extremely mild observation. Admittedly it seems strange that Henri Beyle, the admirer of Winckelmann, from whose birth-place he took the name Stendhal, did not see that it was Goethe who translated Winckelmann's gospel into poetic reality. The explanation seems to be that Stendhal, like all his contemporaries, failed to discern the Classical element in Goethe, because such an element could have no importance for those who needed Goethe's help in the struggle against Classicism. But, as we have already said, Stendhal in his bold attitude to Goethe was an exception within French Romanticism. Otherwise Goethe received from all sides nothing but signs of homage, and the traces that his works left in those of the French Romantic writers are of much greater importance than the meagre and inconsiderable ones we find in Stendhal.

The French sculptor David sent Goethe a consignment of plaster casts of Mérimée, Victor Hugo, Alfred de Vigny and Deschamps. David had himself come to Weimar in 1829 to make a marble bust of Goethe, and, backed by recommendations from Ampère and Cousin, he succeeded in inducing Goethe to sit to him. When the finished article arrived in Weimar in 1831, Goethe accepted it " with feelings of lively gratitude ", " as showing the goodwill of one nearly related in spirit, as proving that the limitations of strict nationalism had been abolished : and in this we believe we have approached the lofty aim of the donor ". This quotation is from Goethe's letter of thanks to the artist. Sainte-Beuve, Ballanche, Hugo, Balzac, Vigny and Janin sent him a number of their works, and this homage gave Goethe intense pleasure. He remarked to Eckermann on this occasion that the young poets of France had been occupying his attention for that whole week, and had put new life into him through the fresh impressions he had gained for them. He gave a place of honour in his art-collection and his library to these gifts, and made a catalogue of them. He had visits from Ampère, the *Globe*'s leading critic, and from Stapfer, the translator of *Faust*. Ampère spoke to him of Mérimée, Vigny and Béranger. Goethe told his French guests of his plane for a " Tell " and they conversed about Tasso and Helen. The " slight indiscretion " and " platitude " of which Ampère was guilty in an article telling the French public of this visit to Weimar did not lead to any interruption in their cordial relations.

What Goethe gave to the French Romantic movement turned to his own advantage. He was able to see his own image in this foreign mirror and to realise how he, the Olympian, who had outgrown Romanticism and learned to control his Faustian spirit, reacted on the world. This had taken place in quite a different way, and with quite different sides of his character from those which now at the final stage in his development he considered to be essential and characteristic of himself. He could not avoid noting that it was the " anti-Classicists " who found him useful as an example. It was not *Iphigenie* but *Götz von Berlichingen*, *Werther* and the First Part of *Faust*, works which he had left far behind him, that stirred the world. This fact occupied him intensively, and may well have suggested to him that these were the works that contained that contribution of the German spirit to world literature of which the world stood in need ; and that, although the effect was not entirely agreeable, it might prove salutary. It may have made him conscious that here were to be found the truest springs of his own and of the German character. His Classical works he owed to what he had learned from the Græco-Romans and the world of Romance culture. But here was what he himself had to give to the world. That with which he himself had no further concern was now proving of service to the world. He saw that a people that had been refined through so much suffering as had been the lot of the French, when looking round for fresh sources to quicken, strengthen and restore it, turns, not to a finished and established neighbouring people, but to one still caught up in struggle and stress ; " the freedom, even the licence, in our literature was particularly welcome to these extremely active men (of the *Globe*) who were still at grips with Classicism, whereas we have more or less reached the stage of equilibrium again ". Particularly in the theatre, where traditional form had grown rigid and the need for liberation was felt most urgently, the example of Germany was beneficial to the French. They began to appreciate more justly, and to use more wisely, the German productions which had so long been jibed at. Liberation from rules was attained on German lines. But French literature was also limited by too narrow a range of material, and was obliged to turn to other countries, and to take new themes from German literature which is superior to French in wealth of material and themes. France was able to spread social culture over the whole world. But in what concerned higher types of culture it could not itself escape foreign influence. The French found much in German philosophy that helped to open up to them the world of ideas. More idealistic forms began to be used, and these in their early stages were called Romantic. The French Romantic movement gave Goethe a new light upon himself, while, to the movement, he stood for liberation from traditional forms and restrictions. Although his own later development was on different lines, he felt his youth revive as he watched the developments in France. He no longer felt himself alone, he was at one with his contemporaries, and this was what he expected from world literature. And world literature is the idea running through all that Goethe writes in *Kunst und Altertum* about the French Romantic movement. Apart from his letters to Carlyle, this is the most important clarification of the idea. He was able too to assure his friends that his idea was finding in France, as in England, an echo from which much could be hoped. In an essay " Bezüge nach aussen " (1828) he announced with satisfaction that his confident statement (that in this present age of movement and greater ease of communication there was immediate hope for a world literature) had been favourably received by his western neighbours. They were in a position to do great things in this respect, and had made the following statement in the *Globe* : Truly every nation in its turn is conscious of the power of attraction which, like that possessed by physical bodies, draws one towards another, and which in time will unite all the races of mankind in one common harmony. The endeavour of scholars to understand one another and to link up their works has nothing new about it, and the Latin tongue used to serve this purpose admirably. But, whatever pains they took the barriers dividing one people from another led to a separation between them and hampered intellectual intercourse. Even the medium which they employed was applicable to only one succession of ideas, so that they communicated with one another only by means of the intelligence, instead of also by means of the heart and of poetry. Travel, the study of language, periodical literature, had taken the place of a universal language, and brought about much more intimate relationships than such a language could ever establish. Even nations which are principally concerned with trade and commerce have their own traffic in ideas. England, whose internal activities are so great that it seems almost self-sufficient, is now showing symptoms of this need to expand and to widen its horizon. Its Reviews, with which all are familiar, no longer satisfy it ; two new journals specially devoted to foreign literatures are to collaborate regularly.

Goethe counted it among the benefits of world literature that quarrels and differences within one literature might be settled and appeased by another, and he himself tried to do this for France. His whole attitude to French Romanticism was clearly one of mediation between the Romanticists and the Classicists. But the most obvious and the most conscious efforts of this kind were in the realm of science, while in that of philosophy he needed only to give his glad approval to a spontaneous effort within France towards a synthesis.

As late as 1798, under the influence of Mounier's attack on Kantian philosophy, Goethe had written about the French : " They have no idea that there can be anything in a man but what he absorbs from outside." Since then, however, Victor Cousin had brought about a decisive change in French philosophy which sought—as did creative literature—renewal and completion from German sources. Goethe made a contribution to this change when Cousin visited him in 1817. Cousin had come to Germany to gain a more intimate knowledge of German philosophy, and Goethe made an outline of it for him. He did this with such clearness, accuracy and simplicity, and at the same time with such " Magie de l'infini ", while himself acknowledging the Kantian principles, that Cousin was satisfied and convinced.

When Goethe later became familiar with Cousin's mature philosophy, he welcomed the latter's attempt at uniting German idealism with French sensualism and English empiricism. To speak of these things to Frenchmen, he wrote, was now much easier than formerly, for at the present time (1828) M. Cousin, taking the German school as his starting-point, was seeking to deal clearly with the chief questions underlying each method. It is a case of the old mutual influence, constantly renewed, contradictory yet always unconsciously helpful, indispensable in theory and in practice, an influence in which perfect equipoise is always sought and never achieved.[15] The French have renounced materialism and have conceded the existence of more spirit and life in the beginnings of things ; they have thrown off sensualism and acknowledged a spontaneous development in the depths of human nature ; they no longer deny her productive power, and they do not seek to explain all art as imitation of something perceived by the senses. They acknowledge a higher philosophy which gives its due to what lies within, and distinguishes it from what we apprehend from without.

With Cousin, then, there is an attempt to introduce German idealism into France and to reconcile it with the French spirit— an attempt which seems analogous to that which sought to communicate German Romanticism to France. For Cousin thought of Kantian philosophy as a product of Romantic literature, claiming that the imagination, the inner vision, the creative power of fancy are the sources of reality, that an understanding of the spirit is not to be reached by way of sensory impressions and experience. This interpretation of Kant is highly questionable ; but Cousin attempted to reconcile it with France's strong tradition of psychology, by trying to found Kant's *a priori* forms of perception on the empirical observation of human nature and to use it as a clue to them. In his scheme for a projected essay " Teilnahme der Franzosen an deutscher Literatur " Goethe says it is typical of France to attempt in this way to unite idealism —which in French literature is conceived of as pure abstract speculation—with realism, sensualism and empiricism. He approved of the intention, and blamed only the name of " eclecticism " which Cousin had given to his all-embracing philosophy ; Goethe preferred " totalism " or " harmony ".[16] Schelling, moreover, also greeted Cousin's attempt at reconciliation. Cousin, in Goethe's opinion, had little to give the German spirit, for the philosophy which he brought to his fellow-countrymen as something new had been known in Germany for many years. But for the French he was of great significance. He would give their thought an entirely new orientation. But Goethe's chief reason—expressed to Eckermann—for welcoming Cousin and his school, was that their efforts were directed towards bringing France and Germany closer together, by evolving a philosophical language pre-eminently suited to an exchange of ideas.

But, although in the sphere of philosophy Cousin made this attempt at reconciling idealism and empiricism, in the realm of science the quarrel between the two modes of thought broke out openly and with unusual violence. This occurred in the memorable session of the Paris Academy for 1830, in which the two great naturalists Cuvier and Saint-Hilaire opposed each other, and which Goethe held to be much more significant than the simultaneous outbreak of the July Revolution. And he had a personal interest in it. In the early days of 1810 he was not interested in how his theory of colour was received in France. A friendly reception would have surprised him. However, Degérando's discourse " Philosophie expérimental " afforded him a wonderful hope of reconciling French and German attitudes of mind. For in these pages he found nothing contradictory to his own way of thinking.[17]

In his scientific researches Goethe himself had reconciled the principles of idealism and empiricism, and had thus given a new and powerful impetus to science. Empirical experience, he realised, can apprehend each phenomenon only in isolation. But in nature everything is part of a larger whole. This whole is apprehended not by experience but by the creative, formative power of the mind. The mind combines empirical phenomena according to ideas viewed in an *a priori* form ; it arranges and combines them in the unity of nature as a whole. Thus it may be said to re-create nature, which itself frames the separate phenomena in accordance with an idea, and develops them out of its own integrity. In the quarrel between Cuvier and Saint-Hilaire, in which Saint-Hilaire defended the proposition that nature possesses one uniform plan of organisation for all creatures, the whole struggle was between two conceptions of nature : the analytical and the synthetical, the empirical and the transcendental, the separating and the combining principles ; nature viewed from the standpoint of the single phenomenon and from that of the whole. It is true to say that in the whole course of his scientific studies nothing gratified Goethe so much as the fact that at the end of his life he found a close ally in Saint-Hilaire. For fifty years he had been fighting for a synthetic conception of nature, and, after a long period of loneliness, he had found a few comrades such for instance as Schelling, Steffens, Oken and Carus. But now he was able to exult over the victory of that to which he had devoted his life, and which was pre-eminently his own. This event was of incalculable importance in his eyes :

From now on [he told Eckermann] the mind will govern science in France also, and will have mastery over matter. They will catch glimpses of the great principles of creation, in God's mysterious workshop ! What after all does any traffic with nature amount to, if we only concern ourselves analytically with isolated fragments of matter and do not feel the breath of the spirit, assigning its direction to each part and controlling every deviation by the law that dwells within it.

And once more Goethe was able to rejoice whole-heartedly when Saint-Hilaire referred to German science and to Goethe who had stimulated it so effectively. In Saint-Hilaire's report to the French Academy on Goethe's *Metamorphosis of Plants* we read : When Goethe published his article in 1790, it attracted little attention and indeed was almost written off as a misconception. It did start from a false conception, but one such as only genius could arrive at. For Goethe was mistaken only in publishing his treatise almost a half-century too early, before there were any botanists capable of investigating and understanding it.—Once more it was a kind of Romantic radiation proceeding from Germany. Goethe himself speaks of " more ideal forms " in which French science was now beginning to work and which " in their empirical and imperfect manifestations are called Romantic ". He compared the difference between the modes of scientific approach with Schiller's differentiation between naïve and sentimental poetry, with which he laid the first foundations of a whole new æsthetic theory. " For Hellenic and Romantic and all the other synonyms can be traced back to the first mention of a preponderance of realism or of idealism in the treatment." [18] In actual fact it was the idealistically synthetic conception of nature that linked Goethe with Romantic philosophy of nature. True, he believed himself obliged to conclude that because Carus's philosophy of nature, in spite of its accompanying French translation, had remained totally unknown to his western neighbour, whole stretches of a " Wall of China " separating scientific and artistic Germany from France were still apparently intact. But he now hoped that these would gradually be demolished, and that, from now on, German science would enjoy the benefits of constant and sympathetic collaboration on the part of the French. And in more recent times it has never been to France's disadvantage to take cognisance of the results of German research and endeavour. [19]

Goethe was far from wishing, in an eclectic manner, to reconcile everything with everything else. The subject for a prize essay in Physics, issued by the St. Petersburg Academy of which he was an honorary member, was one which had a special interest for him. It was : " The various theories of light ought to be reconciled with each other." In a critical article Goethe declared the problem to be completely insoluble.[20]

But, just as in his researches in the field of science Goethe had harmonised the synthetical with the analytical conception of nature, so he now took his stand between, or rather above, the French parties, in an attempt to reconcile them. He did this in his great article : " Principes de Philosophie Zoologique par Geoffroy de Saint-Hilaire", which gave significance to the quarrel which had broken out in the French Academy. Why, he asks, ought the German mind to give close attention to this quarrel ? Because every scientific question, whenever expressed, must immediately arouse the interest of any nation of culture. Scientific work ought to be regarded as one single body, and Saint-Hilaire looked to German science, while Cuvier rejected it specifically as a " pantheistic system " ; " which they call the philosophy of nature ". Now Goethe surely had no real hope of composing his neighbours' quarrel :

Here we have two different ways of thinking which usually exist in the human race distinct from one another. They are so distributed that in the sciences as elsewhere they are very rarely found in combination, and are not easily united. This is so much the case that one part, where it can make use of some portion of the other, admits it with a certain degree of distaste. The history of the sciences and personal experience lead one to think it unlikely that human nature will ever be cured of this dissension.[21]

According to Goethe, then, this dissension is irremediable. There will always be Guelfs and Ghibellines, even in the sciences. But Goethe did entertain the possibility of a certain approximation, which might lead to a reconciliation and perhaps even to collaboration. " For each of us might say in this connection that, in life, analysis and synthesis are two inseparable actions. It would perhaps be better to say that whether one wills it or no, one cannot help passing from the whole to the individual, from the individual to the whole ; and the livelier the connection between these functions of the mind—like breathing in and out— the better it will be for the sciences and their friends." [22] In another place, Goethe says that in the mind of a true scientist there must always be a kind of regular, balanced alternation of systole and diastole, and in this way the empiricist with his tendency to separate and distinguish things may collaborate most beneficially with the idealist who tends to combine them in accordance with an intuitive vision and theory. The quarrel between Cuvier and Saint-Hilaire roused Goethe to add to his *Metamorphosis of Plants* a translation furnished by Soret, and to send (in 1831) a dedicatory copy of it to Saint-Hilaire. The latter presented it with a short report to the Paris Academy, because the French translation led him to suppose that Goethe's intention was to express his high regard for the Academy in this way. He also sent this report to Goethe. Cuvier, in his capacity as secretary, expressed the thanks of the Academy in a letter to Goethe who made a step towards a kind of reconciliation by assuring Cuvier of his gratitude and admiration. In the course of his long life, he wrote to Cuvier, no event had moved him more pleasurably than the discovery that the study and research which he had undertaken in the first place solely for his own further education had also exerted a beneficial influence on others. Now, at the close of his life, he realised with heartfelt gratitude that a famous society was taking sympathetic notice of his investigations and accepting in a friendly spirit the assurance of his esteem. "How much I personally owe to you, Sir, how often your invaluable works have been a guiding star in my researches, I cannot adequately acknowledge." This letter was translated into French by Soret. [23]

So, at the very end of his career on earth, Goethe appeared as a mediator and a peacemaker not only between the nations but also within the nations. He would have been justified in giving himself the name he gave to the leader of the world league in *Wilhelm Meister*: the Link.

Ten years previously he had played a similar part as a mediator in Italian poetry. For on the Classic soil of Italy the war between "Guelfs and Ghibellines", between Classicists and Romanticists, had broken out.

CHAPTER 14

ITALY

In France, a Germanophil tendency which gave to the French mind fresh powers of renewal and of transformation had been noticeable as early as the sixties of the 18th century. In Italy Bertola (with his work *Letteratura allemanna* in 1779 and his *Idea della Letteratura allemanna* in 1784) was the first to draw attention to the recent and hitherto unknown literature of Germany. He did not do so, however, with any idea of applauding the German Storm and Stress, which was then in its prime—or because a new spirit was stirring which might have had a stimulating effect in Italy. He did it because German literature, which in Italy had hitherto been considered utterly barbaric, had mastered the Classical form. Bertola saw on the banks of the Elbe and the Spree a new Parnassus rising, on which Gleim played the part of Anacreon, Günther that of Horace, and Klopstock that of Homer. And when Bertola translated Gessner, it was because his idylls might be compared with the Classical works of Virgil and Theocritus. But against young Goethe, against the Storm and Stress as a whole, Bertola uttered a warning, if that tendency should prevail—and it represented a relapse into barbarism—German literature would be lost. What fame Herr Goethe could win, exclaims Bertola, if one day it dawned upon him that his disregard for the rules could deceive only for a little while.

But in Italy, as all over Europe, the German invasion could not be stayed. There is always in Europe a general movement of literature which, although the point of time may vary, over-runs all frontiers. It was Goethe's *Werther* that opened the way into Italy for German literature and, in spite of all the attempts of Catholicism to suppress it, held its ground and headed the Romantic movement in Italy. Ugo Foscolo himself acknow-ledges that his novel *Le ultimi lettere di Jacopo Ortis* may have been written under the influence of Goethe's *Werther*, although he was thinking of the Werther-feeling rather than of the actual reading of the work, for he had begun his novel before he read *Werther*. He sent his work with a letter to Goethe, who at once recognised its affinity with his *Werther* and considered translating at least some of the letters. Foscolo also told Goethe that Countess Antonietta Aresi was translating *Werther* in the style of the *Ortis* letters, and this translation, wrote Foscolo, would be the only one in Italian that the ignorance of the translators, or the arbitrary interference of the Government, had not mutilated. It may be added that when Foscolo wrote his novel he knew *Werther* only in a French translation. At that time German literature was as a rule not brought directly into Italy in the German language, but followed an indirect route by way of French. On title-pages one often finds this note : " Translated from the German into French and from the French into Italian." In taking this indirect route, however, German works suffered considerable change. For in France they were made to conform to the rules, were arranged in a more orderly manner, were purified from offences against good taste, in a word : they were " Europeanised " or, as the French expressed it : " réduits aux usages communs de l'Europe."

Foscolo's work, which marks an epoch in Italian literature, also formed the beginning of, or rather the prelude to, Italian Romanticism. This really made its appearance after the publication of Mme de Staël's book *De l'Allemagne*, which did much in Italy to prepare the way for German literature. In Italy Mme de Staël was already well known and had a high reputation. In 1807, before her book on Germany, she had already published her novel *Corinne ou l'Italie*, and this book acquired as great importance for the cult of Italy in the European Romantic movement as did the book on Germany for the Romantic cult of Germany. Italy was thus predisposed to lend a willing ear to Mme de Staël. And through Corinne, whose blood is half Nordic and half southern (thus affording an opportunity for the lengthy observations on the mixture and conflict of races) the Italian mind was prepared for the problem that was to play such a decisive part in the Romantic movement. But still greater effect was achieved by Mme de Staël's direct challenge and exhortation to Italian literature, in her essay " Sulla maniera e la utilità delle Traducioni " (1816). Italian literature, she wrote, ought to rouse itself from its indolence and apathy and reinvigorate itself by mingling with the Nordic, Germanic spirit ; it ought to study the example set by German translators, especially Schlegel's translation of Shakespeare. In Italy as in France this roused the indignation of the academic party of Classicists and Francophils. They replied to Mme de Staël in their journal *Il Spettatore* ; a remedy for Italian decadence was to be found, not among Nordic barbarians, but through a profounder study of

the Greeks and Romans. For the rebirth of Classicism was
the national rebirth of Italy. The Latin world was urged in the
name of good taste and good sense to resist the conspiracy of the
Teutonic spirit, with Mme de Staël and A. W. Schlegel at its
head, and to deny Nordic vandalism admittance into Italy.

But this admittance could no longer be withheld. In 1816
Giovanni Berchet wrote his letters on Bürger's " Wild huntsman "
and " Lenore ", adding a translation of these German ballads,
which, it may be noted, have materially contributed in every
European literature to the awakening of the Romantic movement.
(It would be worth while to undertake the task of giving a connected account of the great influence of Bürger's " Lenore " on
the genesis of European Romanticism.) Berchet's work was the
first manifesto of Italian Romanticism. It urged Italian literature to cease taking themes from Classical theology which were
familiar only to educated people, and instead to draw upon the
resources of the popular legends of the North, which were still
alive. " Classicism ", it said, " is a poetry of the dead, feeding
upon the past alone. But Romanticism is a poetry of the living,
whose sources are nature, life and the present. Become the
contemporaries of your own age and not of the vanished
centuries."—The struggle had broken out in Italy between
Classicists and Romanticists. Monti, the translator of the *Iliad*,
rose in opposition to Berchet : in spite of the influence which
Goethe's *Werther* had exerted upon him, Monti can be considered
the chief representative of Italian Classicism. In his *Sermone
sulla Mitologia* (1825) he champions the Græco-Latin world
against the " audace scuola bureal ". Are the beautiful figures
of Classical mythology really to give place to a love-sick girl
(Lenore) who rides at night through the moonlight in the arms
of a hideous skeleton on a black horse ? the gods of Greece to
Nordic witches and spirits ? the blue of the Italian sky to the
gloomy half-light of the arctic polar regions ? southern serenity to
northern *mal du siècle* ? Is only the dark, the gloomy and the
horrible to be considered beautiful ? Surely life held more
splendour when art and poetry breathed a soul into all things on
earth and in Heaven, when dryads dwelt in the trees and naiads
in the fountains, when Pan's pipes were heard among the reeds,
when the sun's golden chariot brought the light and the Hours
danced ? But Monti was opposed by Tedaldi-Fores ; the
latter's *Meditazioni poetiche sulla mitologia difesa da Vincenzo Monti*
(1825) defends the formless, the infinite, as the true realm of the

poet's imagination, in contrast to the Classical world of plastic figures. Here we have the new range of subject-matter from the Nordic visionary world forcing its way from Germany into Italy.

There were also other fields which Italian Romanticism threw open to creative literature. One was national history. In Manzoni's drama *Count Carmagnola* it takes the place of the world of Classical heroes—which for Classicism was the only valid one—and the example of German dramatic works, Goethe's *Götz* and Schiller's historical tragedies, was cited. The other field was that of the Christian religion of Catholicism, which, with Manzoni's *Sacred Hymns* and Torti's poetic delineation of Christ's sufferings, began to supplant the Greek gods that Classicism had reverenced. But the extent of the part played by the German Storm and Stress, and also by the German Romantic movement, in the initial stages of Romanticism in Italy, can be seen most clearly in the change in dramatic form, in the struggle which now began against the rules of the Unities, which Classicism held sacred. Visconti, who had a special knowledge of German philosophical and literary works, carried on this conflict in his dialogue on the Unities of Time and Place. So did Silvio Pellico in one essay " Sulla nuova scuola dramatica " (1816) and in another—in the *Conciliatore* (1819)—on Schiller's *Maria Stuart*. And Manzoni contributed theoretically by his " Lettre à M. Chauvet sur l'unité de temps et de lieu dans la tragédie " (directed against Chauvet's French criticism of his drama *Count Carmagnola*), and in practice by the tragedy itself. The repeated references of the Italians to Goethe's and Schiller's dramatic work and to A. W. Schlegel's lectures show that this conflict drew its inspiration from Germany. In Italy the scene of conflict between Classicists and Romanticists was Milan which, because of its position, maintained the closest intellectual and commercial connection with Germany. It broke out in the *Biblioteca italiana* and, after its defection to Classicism, in the *Conciliatore*.

Goethe first heard of this through Archduke Karl August, on the latter's return to Weimar from a journey to Milan (1818). Naturally, it aroused his interest at once. Indeed, he saw it as the first beacon of the fire fanned by Germany which was soon to set the whole of Europe ablaze. And this fire had broken out in Italy of all places, the country to which he owed his Classical perfection ! No doubt he was all the more amazed that the conflict had begun precisely on this Classical ground. Whereas up to now the South had penetrated northwards, now the reverse was taking place. He himself stood above party and nation. In him the spirit of Faust had united with Hellenic beauty. The contrast between Germanic and Romantic had been reconciled in his all-embracing Europeanism. He therefore at once made the attempt, which he alone among writers was qualified to make, to mediate between the opposing parties and at the same time to show German literature (which had already come through this conflict and had reached a kind of equipoise) wherein lay its progress and its errors. " Classicists and Romanticists in Italy in violent conflict " is the title Goethe gave to his attempt at mediation in *Kunst und Altertum* (1820), and an Italian translation of it appeared in the *Antologia* (1825).

Romantico ! a strange word to Italian ears . . . has for some time been rousing great excitement in Lombardy, and particularly in Milan. The public is divided into two parties ready to come to blows with each other ; and whereas we Germans quite calmly make occasional use of the adjective " Romantic " for Italians the expressions " romanticismo " and " classicismo " represent two irreconcilable points of view. With us the quarrel, if there is a quarrel, is waged more in practice than in theory ; our Romantic poets and writers have their own contemporaries on their side and lack neither publishers nor readers, and we have long outlived the first indecisive stages. So we can remain calm as we watch the fire which we kindled now burning beyond the Alps.

It is obviously natural that Classical culture should be highly esteemed in Italy. It is consistent for Italians to wish to rely solely on this foundation which has supported their whole edifice. But dependence of this sort easily degenerates into a kind of stubbornness and pedantry. The man who concerns himself with the past alone ends by being in danger of embracing what we should consider a dead thing, a dried-up mummy. So whenever this stage is reached, a revolutionary change sets in. What is enterprising and new gets out of control. It tears itself free from the past, will neither acknowledge its merits nor make further use of its advantages. The modern artists who supply what their contemporaries want, whose tastes conform to those of their century, naturally carry with them the greater part of the public which prefers them to artists who seek to lead them back into the past. This sequence of events now took place in Italy, as it had done in the history of literature and art in Germany. Goethe mentions in this connection the following Italian Romanticists (with whose works he was not yet familiar when he began to write his essay) : Torti with his poetic portrayal of Christ's

sufferings and his tiercets on poetry ; Manzoni, the author of the
tragedy *Carmagnola* and of the sacred hymns ; and the theorist
Hermes Visconti. On the Classical side he mentions Monti,
whose personal acquaintance he had made in Rome and who
had there read to Goethe his drama *Artistodemo* with its tincture
of Wertherism. In 1810 Goethe had produced Monti's Roman
tragedy *Caius Gracchus* in Weimar, using both it and the tragedies
of French Classicism to raise the German theatre to a stage
beyond naturalism and to a more elevated artistic style. Monti's
Italian translation of the *Iliad* which, when set to music and sung,
seemed as if made expressly for Homeric rhapsodies, showed
Goethe the strength of the Classical tradition in Italy. It
was the lack of this tradition that had prevented the German
translator of Homer, J. H. Voss, from making his Homer
comprehensible to everyone. But Monti seemed to Goethe to
be an isolated case. He called himself a Classicist, but his friends
and admirers called him a Romanticist and insisted that his best
works were ⁘Romantic, to Monti's great annoyance. Surely
this must have reminded Goethe of his own case. At this point
his work of appeasement began ; he declared the contradiction
easy to resolve if one reflected on the meaning of the word
Romantic in Italy and on its greatly varying content. By
Romantic the Romanticists in Italy meant something quite
different from what was meant by it in Germany. They sought
to write and to exert their influence purely in the spirit of their
age. They called Romantic whatever lived in the present and
exerted an active influence on the moment. They therefore
accused the Classicists, who wrote in the spirit and form of the
Græco-Romans, of being in a dead and mummified condition
while yet alive, and of writing for the dead. The Romanticists
themselves claimed to be modern in drawing from so many sources,
as for instance the Christian Bible, national history, the world
of Nordic and mediæval phantoms, because they held that all these
were nearer the present day and more fully alive than Classical
antiquity. So, in Italy, Romantic is more or less synonymous
with modern. We may add to Goethe's observation that this
particular identification is also met with in France ; Stendhal, for
instance, in his book *Racine et Shakespeare* (which was known to
Goethe), calls those works Romantic which are written in the
spirit of the age and not of a dead past, and which correspond to
the actual present. From this point of view Stendhal calls even
Racine a Romanticist. " Young Germany ", on the other hand,

which supplanted Romanticism in German literature, contrasted
" modern " works in the spirit of the age with Romantic ones
which incorporated the spirit of the dead past.

The fact that in Italy Romantic and modern were treated
as synonymous may be due to the original conception of the
Romance language as that formed by the mingling of Classical
and newly added Germanic elements—not as the Latin of the world
of learning, but as the living language of the people. Indeed,
Romantic was also originally synonymous with Romance. But
there is a further reason. The Græco-Romans lived on in the
Italians in race and spirit, Roman Catholicism was not fundamentally opposed to the Classical spirit. Italy's national history
was a continuation of Roman history, and the Italian Romantic
movement aimed chiefly at a modern, progressive, reshaping of
an Italy which had fallen behind in the development of Europe,
and was languishing under the yoke of Austria. In reality, the
movement was a modern freedom-movement in touch with
present-day events.

Goethe tried, then, to mediate between the conflicting parties.
If we looked closely, he maintained, we saw there was no contradiction. No one who from his youth up had owed his education
to the Greeks and Romans would deny the existence of a certain
legacy from them. He would always gratefully acknowledge
his debt to his past teachers, even while devoting his mature
talent to the actual present. We were equally unable to deny
the culture that the Bible has given us, though it might be as
remote from us and as strange as any other form of antiquity.
We only felt ourselves nearer to it because of its influence on
belief and morality, while other literatures were directed towards
good taste and " average humane behaviour ". Classical
antiquity and the Bible were equally near and equally far from
us. Together they could be inexhaustible sources of our education, antiquity of our æsthetic and the Bible of our moral
development. Even the past of our own native land lay no
nearer than that of Greece or Rome to our judgment which had
been moulded through the centuries by the traditions of antiquity.
But our own past history was able to give a more definite,
characteristic stamp to the common human content. Later, in
1826, Goethe referred again in a short article " Modern Guelfs
and Ghibellines " to the Italian conflict which was then being
waged between Monti and Tedaldi-Fores, and which in the
meantime had spread over the whole of Europe, and had far

outrun the limits of literature. Once more Goethe attempted to mediate, using new arguments. The literary art of the Ancients supplied the imagination with shape and form, while that of the newer races left it free play and appealed to inner feelings, to temperament, in other words to human nature. But antiquity also presented the " essential human " in certain forms. Each party had its advantages, but both had cause for fear— the Classicists that their gods might become an empty phrase ; the Romanticists that their productions might end by seeming nondescript ; in such a case the two would be equally meaningless.

This, then, was Goethe's finest effort at mediation : the Poet's task was to influence his age and the present as a living man of the present. But to influence was to educate, and only a fully educated man could do this. The sources of education were to be found as much in antiquity as in Christianity or in a nation's own past. A constant human core was hidden deep in all these powers. For that reason all were equally near us, and alive, and were able to effect our education in equal measure, provided they were intelligently used and were not tied down by the limitations of any one age. A man whose education had been the work of the great past common to all men would then influence his contemporaries ; in other words he would be able to educate them. If what Italy (and also France) maintained was true, and Romantic meant whatever belongs to its own age, then every living educative power might be called Romantic. This attempt at mediation obviously sprang from the depths of Goethe's own experience. His was the spirit that had been educated by all these great powers of the past, by Classical and by biblical antiquity, and that—especially at that time—exerted an unrivalled influence on his age. He had begun as a Classicist and ended as a modern. It was he who in his works gave expression to the most urgent problems of his own day, and whose vision offered a solution—Wilhelm Meister's *Wanderjahre* is a case in point. His very activity in the cause of world literature, towards bringing the peoples closer together and uniting them with each other, was one of these urgent and thoroughly modern problems.

When Goethe read the works of the Italian Romantic movement, he must have noticed that the battle so hotly waged in theory was by no means so evident in poetic practice. One often finds the opinion expressed in other literatures that there is no such thing as German Classicism ; contrariwise, the Germans reply that there is no such thing as Italian Romanticism. If one confines oneself to literature and excludes the ories and manifestos, there is some truth in this suggestion, paticularly if one compares Italian with German Romanticism. For one gets the impression that compared with the latter, Italian Romanticism has a Classical look ; more so than is the case with French Romanticism. Classical form never broke up to such an extent in Italy as it did in France, to say nothing of Germany. It was the group of Italian forms, the lyrical sonnet, the epic *ottava rima*, the prophetic tiercet that guided the romantically extravagant, indeterminate, German spirit into safe channels and gave a pre-determined form to Romantic subjectivity. Everything that was shapeless, indeterminate and vague about German Romanticism received from Italy form and outline. From the " novella " of the Italian Renaissance, the narrative art of such writers as Kleist, Brentano and Arnim got its objective attitude and narrative style. And Roman Catholicism gave German Romanticism, which was so strongly attracted to it, all the beauty of religion and religious art. Here too, the somewhat indeterminate and romantic religious element benefited from being subjected to recognised forms. Goethe himself, when taking Faust at the close of the Second Part up into the unexplored spheres that lie beyond the senses, was glad to have access to the " clear-cut figures and conceptions of Catholic Christianity ". The reason for this may be that the Italian feels the inheritance of antiquity too deeply rooted in him for him ever to be able to deny it entirely, that he lives in constant sight of the relics of antiquity, on the same soil, in the same scene, and under the same sky that saw the growth of Classical art and literature. The rebirth of Classical antiquity at the close of the Middle Ages did not occur in Italy by mere chance ; the Renaissance was Italy's national rebirth. So the Classical tradition was a bulwark there against German Romanticism. The second bulwark was Catholicism. This, after all, had grown up on Roman soil and had taken over the inheritance of antiquity with all its temporal beauty and tangibility, its strength and proportion to order, so that Italy never broke with this tradition. In France, on the contrary, Catholicism had not only lost ground through the Huguenots (and it was Protestants in particular, like Mme de Staël, who had introduced German literature into France), but also the French Revolution had curtailed its powers, and it was no longer able to act as a defence. In the German Romantic movement the Catholic religion was no more than an object of a sentimental longing.

Italian Romanticism differed, then, from the German variety to which it had owed its inception. Goethe came to recognise this through a consideration of Manzoni, its greatest representative ; and for this reason there was no Romantic writer in Europe for whom he had such unqualified admiration as for Manzoni. When first writing on Italian Romanticism, Goethe had singled out Manzoni's sacred hymns. They differ from Monti's hymns to the Olympian gods in that his religion and his poetry unify the whole work " although men are at variance concerning many of the events of the age ". Goethe saw that this writer of Catholic hymns was a Christian without fanaticism, a Catholic without bigotry, an enthusiast without intolerance. The mystical content of the hymns, as Goethe later notes, is always treated quite simply ; each word, each turn of phrase has been familiar to every Italian from his youth up. A writer born and brought up in the Catholic faith naturally knows how to handle his Church's articles of faith quite differently from the poets of other creeds ; they, after all, are able to transport themselves only in imagination into a region to which they can never feel they belong. Goethe's remarks here are clearly directed against the catholicising tendency of the German Romantic writers, the great majority of whom were Protestants and whose return to the bosom of the Church was a result purely of sentimental attachment, a kind of nostalgia, or of the æsthetic charm exercised by the Catholic Church. What Goethe meant was that with the Italian Romantic writers Catholicism as a native attribute was artless and real, whereas with the German Romantic writers it evolved merely out of the hankering for a lost paradise, and was an imaginary experience and as such fundamentally Romantic.

In Manzoni's dramas from the national history of Italy in the Middle Ages, *Count Carmagnola* and *Adelchi*, dramas which must have meant a Romantic revolution in Italian literature, Goethe saw another instance of the contrast to the German Romanticism which found its subjects in the German Middle Ages. We allow the mask of the Middle Ages much too large a place in art and life, wrote Goethe, and we treat it as something real. Manzoni on the other hand endows a semi-barbaric age with refinements of sentiment and feeling of which only the advanced religious and moral culture of our own age is capable ; and this is the only correct treatment. Everything in the past that we evoke in order to present it in our own fashion to our contemporaries must invest antiquity with a more advanced culture than it actually possessed. Goethe discerned in the mediæval dramas of Manzoni the same spirit of humanism which in his *Iphigenie* he had given to his own barbaric Tauris ; and he never failed to admire the humane and sensitive feeling of this fine and truly poetic talent.

He saw, too, that Manzoni, though he ranks in Italian literature as Classicism's chief opponent and conqueror, by no means denied the education he had received from Classical antiquity. Goethe found evidence of this education in the choruses of Manzoni's tragedies. " In *Count Carmagnola*, the chorus, by describing the progress of the battle in great detail and yet without confusion, finds, even in the midst of indescribable complications, expressions which explain the disorder and make this wild onrush comprehensible. The two choruses in the tragedy *Adelchi* have a similar effect, calling attention to the immense panorama of past and present conditions."

The only criticism that Goethe had to make of Manzoni was over one isolated point, namely, that in *Count Carmagnola* he had divided the personages into historical and imaginary ones. This certainly represents a Romantic tendency, in contrast to which Goethe adheres to his Classical standpoint, that of Aristotle and of Lessing : " For the poet no personage is historical ; it pleases him to represent his own moral world, and to this end he honours certain personages of history by investing them with the names of his characters." Goethe went so far as to beg Manzoni never to make this distinction again, and Manzoni agreed. For he had to admit, as he wrote to Goethe, that the division of personages into historical and imaginary was his own error, caused by too great a dependence on strict historical exactitude. This had led him to separate the real personages from those whom he had devised to symbolise a certain class, an opinion, or an interest. In a more recent work (*Adelchi*) he had abandoned this distinction and felt gratified that in doing so he had anticipated Goethe's advice. Nevertheless there was a divergence of views with regard to this between Goethe and Manzoni. For Manzoni's further development led him in the direction of history rather than of the imagination, and he made increased attempts to approximate literature to history. Of these attempts in the later novel *I Promessi Sposi* Goethe could not approve. Goethe did not live to read Manzoni's essay " On historical novels and in general on works combining history and the imagination " (1845). In it, Manzoni elaborates the thesis that history and invention can only with difficulty be united in one work, without both losing their own characteristic qualities. " It is only in cases where this union is unconsciously effected that from an artistic point of view it can be justified." Thus in his later years Manzoni condemned historical literature as a mixture of historical truth and imaginative invention. In this respect Italian differed from German Romanticism, and one has only to recall Arnim's *Kronenwächter* or Hauff's *Lichtenstein* to see the difference. What Italy called Romanticism was actually—as in France—the birth of modern realism, while in German literature the true historical novel, as it originated under the influence of Sir Walter Scott, represented a victory over Romanticism. But Goethe found too much respect for history and facts even in *I Promessi Sposi*. In this work the historian gets the better of the poet, and the novel becomes a chronicle. This was far from being a Classical trait, but it was not Romantic either ; it opened up the way towards modern realism in which Goethe could have no part.

In all other respects, however, they were in complete harmony. Goethe was particularly struck with Manzoni's restraint, even when he separated himself from the Classicists's strict regard for rules and from the Unities, citing as he did so the dramas of Goethe's youth, and the reasons adduced by A. W. Schlegel. English criticism also (the *Quarterly Review*) noted this quality of restrained freedom, but disapproved, saying : Manzoni is declaring war on the unities. We, however, are privileged and acknowledged free-thinkers after Shakespeare's fashion, and we shall find that this new convert will scarcely corroborate our Nordic conception of dramatic freedom. We fear that the Italians will demand more substantial infringement of the traditional rules before they can be induced to abandon them. But this time Goethe defended the Italian Romantic writer against this English criticism. This led the French philosopher Victor Cousin, when he visited him in Weimar, to express his thanks to Goethe, and this was a confirmation of his theory of world literature. It was particularly praiseworthy in Manzoni, Goethe wrote, to be so restrained, and to try to reach a laudable degree of freedom only by the methods of peaceful evasion. He had freed himself from the old rules and had proceeded so sincerely and steadfastly on his new course that one could frame new rules on his work.   At this point Goethe makes the decisive remark :   " We can testify that with him every detail shows thought, consideration and precision.   Accurate observation, as far as it is possible for a foreignei to claim this, has shown us neither a word too many nor one too few.   Manly sincerity and lucidity are the governing factors throughout, and we would therefore describe his work as Classical."   Goethe never awarded this epithet " Classical " to any other European Romantic writer.   It was only this one Italian writer who received it. And it is this conception of Manzoni as a Classical writer that explains why, in spite of his being regarded in Italian literature as a Romantic, Goethe made such constant attempts to draw the attention of German and indeed of European readers to him. He did so by discussing his works in great detail, in particular *Count Carmagnola*.   He planned to do the same for the tragedy *Adelchi*.   (" Ah !   Why can one not perform the same labour of love for any German contemporary ! ")   He also did it by translating Manzoni's " Hymn on the Death of Napoleon ", and by getting Streckfuss, the translator of Dante, to make a translation of the tragedy *Adelchi*.   This appeared in 1827 and was " dedicated to Goethe, with feelings of respect, affection and gratitude ".   Finally, and most effectively, he did it by writing an account of all that he had done for Manzoni and of the relationship that had grown up between them.   This was published as " Teilnahme Goethes an Manzoni " and formed the introduction to an Italian edition of Manzoni's works which appeared in 1827 in Jena.   Indeed it was to Goethe that Manzoni owed his fame not only in Germany but also in Italy and everywhere else.   Goethe's article on *Count Carmagnola* appeared in 1825, in the Florentine edition of Manzoni's tragedies, his critique of *Adelchi* in 1822 in *Eco*, and an Italian translation of his article " Teilnahme Goethes an Manzoni " in 1827.   Fauriel included that article on *Count Carmagnola* in his French translation of the tragedies (1823) and in 1827 published it separately in French. In the *Globe*, Victor Cousin put before the French public the conversation which Goethe had with him in 1825 about Manzoni. And yet the time when he was laying the foundations of Manzoni's world-wide fame, Goethe had not yet read that writer's masterpiece, which belongs to the lasting possessions of world literature : the novel *I Promessi Sposi*.   When he got to know it he expressed his warmest admiration, in conversation with Eckermann, and praised the writer's cultured personality and the delightful maturity which seemed almost unique. The treatment was as clear as the Italian sky, and the different localities were described with admirable precision and detail. In a letter to Boisserée in 1827, he even said that the effect on him of this novel had been epoch-making. We repeat, however, that it was not this novel that occasioned Goethe's efforts in the sphere of world literature on Manzoni's behalf. Goethe made no further public statement about him, although he still planned one. He even thought of translating the work. "If I were not hindered by advancing age and so many pressing obligations, I would do for this work what I did for Cellini." The review of the novel for *Kunst und Altertum* was undertaken by Streckfuss. Goethe urged Streckfuss to translate the work. He refused, but at Goethe's suggestion found another translator in the young writer Daniel Lessman, the progress of whose work Goethe, with Streckfuss as intermediary, followed with interest and advice.

Goethe had no need to do more. He had already laid the foundations of world-wide fame for Manzoni, whose character and great qualities he had recognised from the beginning. Now Goethe enjoyed the rare experience of being able whole-heartedly to rejoice in the results of his own influence. For Manzoni himself told Goethe how much he owed him. Not only had Goethe's opinion, expressed in public, helped him to realise his worth and given him energy and courage ; not only had Goethe's criticism assisted his development ; but in addition to this, from his earliest youth and before he had had any kind of contact with him, he had always regarded Goethe as a kind of guiding star. The words which he wrote in the presentation copy of the tragedy *Adelchi* which he sent to Goethe, were chosen with good reason : " You are no stranger to me. It was your name that shone before my earliest youth like a star in the sky ! " When Goethe's review of *Count Carmagnola* appeared, Manzoni sent a letter of thanks to Weimar, in which he wrote : If anyone had told him, while he was at work on that tragedy, that Goethe would read it, it would have been the greatest encouragement and would have held out to him the hope of an unexpected prize. His Italian publisher wrote in French to Goethe, saying that Manzoni was deeply moved by this proof of goodwill from one whom, from his youth up, he had been accustomed " à vénérer comme maître dans sa noble carrière." (The reference is to the article " Teilnahme Goethes an Manzoni ".) And Manzoni was greatly moved when Victor Cousin conveyed to him Goethe's words of praise in the conversation he had with Cousin. Indeed, it was probably *Götz von Berlichingen* and *Egmont* which in the first place had helped Manzoni to detach himself from Classicism, to choose subjects from national history, and to gain historical truth and freedom from hampering rules. In this case, Goethe could take pleasure in the influence his youthful works had had because their effect on Manzoni had resulted in such restraint, accompanied with lucidity and flexibility, that Goethe felt justified in applying to him the epithet " Classical ".

Goethe felt uneasy about the exaggerations of French Romanticism. His effect in that direction no longer corresponded to his own stage of development. The whole thing was degenerating into licence. He also became familiar with works of Italian Romantic writers, " spectral monsters " which inspired him with dread, for instance Grossi's *Ildegarda*. These were extraordinary productions which he had no wish to make known to others. He found them so distasteful with their arbitrary choice of subject, their disregard of law and order, and their obvious self-satisfaction.[24] But these were unimportant. Manzoni, the real representative of Italian Romanticism, this writer of " sincerity, clear thought, keen perception and humane sentiments " did not deny the ancient heritage of antiquity and of the Italian mind. Goethe could be proud of this disciple. Italy, the land that had completed his Classical education, was now opening its gates to northern Romanticism. But the Classical spirit was not lost. Even Italian Romanticism bore witness that it grew up under an Italian sky and on the soil of Roman antiquity and the Renaissance. If Goethe inspired Manzoni, at least it was not the Faust-spirit whose spark caught fire in him, as it did in Byron. Manzoni did not resemble, as Byron did, a fire fiercely flaring up and quickly burnt away and spent. It is a significant fact that Goethe's *Faust* was not translated and did not become known in Italy until later, after the Romantic period. In the seventies, however, no fewer than five translations appeared. Maffei dedicated his to King Johann of Saxony, the translator of the *Divine Comedy*, and thus established a brotherhood bond between the two nations through an interchange of their poetical masterpieces. In Guerrieri's popular version *Faust* became the property of Italian youth. But there is no proof of any deeper influence of *Faust* upon Italian literature, such as there was in France and England. At least Manzoni could never have aspired, as Byron did, to a literary memorial as the son of Faust and Helen. The message within the scope of world literature which Goethe had to give Italy was not the message of *Faust*. Yet we ought not to forget Boito's opera *Mefistofele* (1868). For Boito was not only a composer ; he was also a poet, and his work (in contrast to the other Faust-operas) really is a poem, though the text which unites the First and Second Parts of Goethe's *Faust* suffers from extremely ruthless although necessary abridgement. The Prologue on the Stage, in which Faust is described as an eternal symbol of inexhaustible variety of meaning, shows that Boito had studied *Faust* profoundly. This is also apparent from Boito's discussion of an Italian statue " Faust and Gretchen ". But it is doubtful whether Goethe would have approved of that work. For Goethe, who wished *Faust* to be set to music and who had himself begun to sketch it out in the form of an opera, had in mind the composer of *Don Juan*, or one " who like Meyerbeer had lived for a long time in Italy, so that his German nature had absorbed Italian ways ". While he was in Italy, Italian opera had profoundly affected Goethe, and since his return he had fostered it in the theatre at Weimar. He had himself translated some Italian texts, and had written or at least planned original libretti in the Italian style. This aimed at driving naturalism from the German theatre. And now his *Faust* was set to music by an Italian. But his unbounded enthusiasm for Richard Wagner led Boito too far from the style of Italian opera, although he was faithful to a stricter musical form than Wagner. So we see that, while it was in Italy that Goethe was freed from his Faustian discontent, on the other hand he inspired this opera which led Italian opera in the direction of Richard Wagner. Here we may draw attention to a strange fact : namely, that great works of literature are usually set to music not in the country of their origin but by composers in other nations ; Shakespeare, for instance, not in England but in Italy, France and Switzerland ; Goethe and Schiller in France and Italy. The probable reason is that the original work seems to its own nation too sacred to be exposed to the inevitable alterations, distortions and adjustments. This of course does not apply to lyrics. In musical compositions the distortion of an original work of literature is unavoidable ; and the process of exchange in world literature, by means of setting to music, often leads to the falsification of a great work. Yet this applies less to Boito's opera than to many others, because in Goethe's *Faust* the German

mind had assumed a Southern form, and Boito's Italian min
was following a German direction, so they could meet each othe
halfway with happy results.

In Italy, none the less, Goethe could hear the echo of his ide
of world literature, when in 1828 he got to know the journa
L'Eco. Its aim, like that of the *Globe*, was to make Ital
familiar with foreign literatures and particularly with Germa
literature, and it published translations of some of Goethe
poems. He wrote to the editors that the journal would certainl
contribute in the happiest way, through its content and i
attractive form, to the universal world literature which wa
spreading more and more actively, and that he was much inte
ested in it. The editors asked him which of his works they coul
use, and how they could do so most suitably ; Goethe replie
that they should make use, as they had already done, of h
shorter poems. With his letter he sent the poem " Ein Gleichnis
to which the editors themselves had referred. In this poem h
records how refreshing it had been to read his poems in anothe
language, and this, as he pointed out to the editors, might we
relate to their endeavours in connection with his works. Th
poem was printed in June 1828 in *L'Eco*.

Take note [Goethe then wrote to Zelter] how world literature, whic
like the sorcerer's apprentice I called up, is now pouring in to drow
me ; Scotland and France flood in almost daily. In Milan they ar
publishing a most important daily called *L'Eco* ; it is outstanding i
every way, just like our morning papers but with a wide intellectua
range. Draw the attention of the Berlin public to it ; they migh
profitably season their daily dishes with it.[25]

This recommendation appeared in *Kunst und Altertum*, wher
Goethe praised the serene intelligent independence of the paper
its grasp of recent foreign literature and its high standard through
out. These qualities were founded on antiquity and on thei
earliest literature, but one realised what they sought to impar
to the foreigner—what portions of German literature they like
and could use, and how they could do so, and their attitude t
the Frenchman, the Englishman and the Spaniard. " Thi
paper, continued along these lines, will serve to enrich the idea
and the language of Italy, and will widen its æsthetic horizons.'

CHAPTER 15

ENGLAND

In the Romance literatures of France and Italy, Goethe could watch the struggle between the Classicists and the Romanticists spreading from Germany across their borders ; but in a Germanic literature like English the case was different. Dedicating his *Marino Faliero* to Goethe (in 1820), Byron wrote that in Germany as in Italy a great conflict had broken out over what was called Classic and Romantic, although in England, at least a few years ago, these expressions were not yet in common use. Possibly something of the kind had grown up since, but he had not heard of it, and it would be evidence of such bad taste that he would be extremely sorry to have to believe it. Certainly there was little sign of such a struggle in English literature, and it never took on so acute a form as in France or Italy. The reason is clear. If you investigate the origins of European Romanticism, you find them in English literature. For even the German Storm and Stress, even young Goethe who became of the greatest importance in awakening Romanticism in Europe, had been reanimated by English literature, and under its influence had freed himself from French Classicism. Classicism in England, which had had its representatives in Pope and Dryden, had fallen out of favour long before the decline of Classicism on the Continent. England no longer needed to carry on a struggle which it had outlived. On the other hand, the rising movement had never taken on such radical forms in England as it had in the German Storm and Stress and in Romanticism on the Continent. For in England there were other factors which maintained a wholesome balance of forces between freedom and control. The conservative spirit of England had undergone a democratic revolution which anticipated the French Revolution ; and out of it they had framed a secure political structure, within which the old authoritative powers accommodated themselves to the new freedom of the nation and the individual. The old order of society had not been dissolved but merely relaxed. Goethe heard a note of melancholy and dissatisfaction as the keynote of English literature. But the individual's chance to play an active part in the great sphere of world-wide empire prevented the unfulfilled desires of youth from turning inwards to paralyse it, or outwards to revolt against existing realities. The Anglican church, solid and confident, formed a sure bulwark against collapse of existing standards of morality or any general feeling of despair. The deeply-rooted empiricism of England, its reliance on practical experience and " common sense ", led the English mind to regard with suspicion all Romantic flights of fancy and every overstepping of the limits of experience and reason. Young Goethe met with violent resistance in English literature. But this resistance did not come, as in France, from academic Classicism, but from the political, religious and moral stability that we have mentioned. On no literature, on the life of no nation, did Werther exert so little influence as he did in England. This was not only because so much in *Werther* was already familiar in English literature—which after all provided its ancestry—but also because England was able to hold the balance against it by means of all those compensating forces which were lacking in other countries. Young Goethe was refused entry because he was considered revolutionary, immoral and atheistic. Æsthetic considerations were an unimportant factor. In 1779, when the first translation of *Werther* appeared, English criticism was directed with almost unanimous violence against the immorality and irreligious tone of the novel. In the eighties quite a number of imitations, adaptations and sequels did appear in England and Scotland, but these were all the work of unknown writers. When Rosa Lawrence published the first English translation of *Götz von Berlichingen* in 1799 and sent it along with a letter to Goethe, she stated expressly that the work contained no trace of the immorality to be found in *Werther*. The French Revolution and the rise of Napoleon led to an enormous increase in English conservative feeling ; and the aim of the journal *Antijacobin* was to defend that spirit against any attempted revolution in the fields of politics, religion or morality. It claimed to trace such attempts in the works of young Goethe : in *Werther*, in *Götz*, and in *Stella*. Goethe was branded as an enemy of Church and State as well as of society. Even in the case of a protest against neglect of formal rules, this was made not for æsthetic but for political reasons ; their rejection was taken to be a symptom of the revolutionary spirit. But it was impossible to hold back the influence of the German Storm and Stress literature in England. Henry Mackenzie's famous lecture to the Royal Society in Edinburgh (1788) on the drama of the Storm and Stress, with which Mackenzie had become familiar in French translations, made a sensation and marked an epoch in the literature of England and Scotland. This was the lecture that inspired Sir Walter Scott to make his translation of *Götz von Berlichingen*, and traces of *Götz* and also of *Egmont* can be followed in Scott's epic works. It seems not too much to say that it was through *Götz von Berlichingen* that Scott received the external impetus for his historical romances. Only the outward impetus, however, and there is no question of any revolutionising of English literature through the influence of young Goethe. In imitating *Götz* by treating a subject from the point of view of history and neglecting formal rules, English drama was only getting back what, through Shakespeare, it had already given to German drama. The transformation that *Götz* underwent in Scott's translation is abundantly evident. If it is possible in the case of *Götz* to speak of any revolutionary tendency in social politics, this is completely cancelled by Scott. He was a passionate foe of the French Revolution, and subsequently of Napoleon, and made *Götz* completely conservative in spirit, with due respect for tradition. On the other hand he enriched it out of his own resources and, by portraying old customs and usages and introducing dances, festivals and processions, made it a gaily coloured historical picture of the old days of Chivalry, an ode on the patriarchal, aristocratic feudalism of the Middle Ages. He also tried to keep much closer to historical truth. In translating Goethe's " Erlking ", " The Faithless Youth ", the bandit's song from *Claudine of Villa bella*, or Bürger's " Lenore ", Scott was only taking back what England had given to German ballad-poetry through the medium of Percy's *Reliques*. These German popular ballads would never have been written had it not been for England's initial encouragement ; ·and yet what a change Scott, translating in the tradition of England and Scotland, wrought on Goethe's " Erlking " ! To take the simple, ordinary scene in Goethe's poem a road beside a river bordered by gaunt willow-trees becomes a woodland scene of dreadful wildness, the rustling wind becomes the wild blast of a tempest, the wisp of mist a dark wrack of cloud blotting out the moon, the swift ride a tearing gallop across a wild stretch of country. It is raining. This is not the setting of the " Erlking " ; it reminds us of *Lear* and of Ossian. And it so fills the foreground that the ballad almost becomes a descriptive nature poem of a kind indigenous to England. Obviously this gruesome scene is meant to provide motive and explanation for the child's visions, which become

more colourful and sensuous.   English empiricism and sensualism
come into play, and transfer the accent in Goethe's poem from
within to without.   The rhythm and language become corre-
spondingly wilder, more agitated, more graphic :

Erlkönig

Wer reitet so spät durch Nacht und Wind?
Es ist der Vater mit seinem Kind ;
Er hat den Knaben wohl in dem Arm,
Er fasst ihn sicher, er hält ihn warm.

Mein Sohn, was birgst du so bang dein Gesicht?—
Siehst, Vater, du den Erlkönig nicht?
Den Erlenkönig mit Kron' und Schweif?—
Mein Sohn, es ist ein Nebelstreif.—

" Du liebes Kind, komm, geh mit mir !
" Gar schöne Spiele spiel' ich mit dir ;
" Manch bunte Blumen sind an dem Strand ;
" Meine Mutter hat manch gülden Gewand."

Mein Vater, mein Vater, und hörest du nicht,
Was Erlenkönig mir leise verspricht?—
Sei ruhig, bleibe ruhig, mein Kind,
In dürren Blättern säuselt der Wind.—

" Willst, feiner Knabe, du mit mir gehn?
" Meine Töchter sollen dich warten schön ;
" Meine Töchter führen den nächtlichen Reihn,
" Und wiegen und tanzen und singen dich ein."—

Mein Vater, mein Vater, und siehst du nicht dort
Erlkönigs Töchter am düstern Ort?—
Mein Sohn, mein Sohn, ich seh' es genau ;
Es scheinen die alten Weiden so grau.—

" Ich liebe dich, mich reizt deine schöne Gestalt ;
" Und bist du nicht willig, so brauch' ich Gewalt."
Mein Vater, mein Vater, jetzt fasst er mich an !
Erlkönig hat mir ein Leids getan !—

Dem Vater grauset's, er reitet geschwind,
Er hält in Armen das ächzende Kind,
Erreicht den Hof mit Mühe und Not ;
In seinen Armen das Kind war tot.

O who rides by night through the woodlands so wild?
It is the fond father embracing his child ;
And close the boy nestles within his loved arm,
From the blast of the tempest to keep himself warm.

" O father !   O father ! see yonder ! " he says.
" My boy, upon what dost thou fearfully gaze ? "
" O ! 'tis the Erl-king, with his staff and his shroud ! "
" No, my love ! it is but a dark wreath of the cloud."

" O wilt thou go with me, thou loveliest child?
By many gay sports shall thy hours be beguiled ;
My mother keeps for thee full many a fair toy,
And many a fine flower shall she pluck for my boy."

" O father !   O father ! and did you not hear?
The Erl-King whisper so close in my ear? "—
" Be still, my loved darling, my child, be at ease ! "
It was but the wild blast as it howled through the trees.

" O wilt thou go with me, thou loveliest boy?
My daughter shall tend thee with care and with joy ;
She shall bear thee so lightly through wet and through wild,
And hug thee and kiss thee, and sing to my child."

" O father !   O father ! and saw you not plain
The Erl-King's pale daughter glide past through the rain? "—
" O no, my heart's treasure !   I knew it full soon ;
It was the grey willow that danced to the moon."

" Come with me, come with me, no longer delay !
Or else, silly child, I will drag thee away."
" O father !   O father ! now, now keep your hold !
The Erl-King has seized me—his grasp is so cold."—

Sore trembled the father ; he spurred through the wild,
Clasping close to his bosom his shuddering child.
He reaches his dwelling in doubt and in dread ;
But, clasped to his bosom, the infant was dead !

And surely it was enthusiasm for *Götz* that gave Sir Walter Scott
the idea of portraying Scotland's and England's past in a cycle
of historical novels ; so that in this respect Goethe did stand godfather to the English Romantic movement, and guided it to its
own national past.   But Sir Walter Scott's scholarly studies led
him to use such epic objectivity in his narrative style, and to give
such a degree of realism to his historical novel, that it cannot be
called Romantic in the German sense.   Eventually it became a
European genre, and its influence on German literature took the
form of helping it to overcome Romanticism, to substitute
historical accuracy for a Romantic vision of the past, and thus
to take the decisive step that leads to realism.   In conversation
with Eckermann, Goethe freely expressed his admiration for
Scott.   He admired his accuracy in delineation, which came from
a comprehensive knowledge of human nature whose deepest
secrets lay open to him : the fundamental reality, the striking
truthfulness, and particularly the epic art of his narration, its
precision—in short, his profound understanding of his art.
Goethe did not regard Scott as a Romantic writer.   On the

contrary, he appealed for Scott's help in his struggle against the morbid aberrations of E. T. A. Hoffmann, then passing in Germany for innovations representing an important advance. For Goethe, without knowing Scott's authorship of it, gave a detailed report on his essay " On the Supernatural in Fictitious Composition ". Here Scott uses the example of Hoffmann to show how the imagination, when left to itself without artistic restraint, works itself into a state of feverish dreams, even of madness. This condition should be made known, not as an example to be imitated but as a warning. Goethe could not recommend this article highly enough to his German readers.²⁶ In his later years, after Byron's death in 1827, Scott received a letter from Goethe expressing his thankfulness that in his earlier years he had come to know Scott and his works, and had even called upon the English nation to do the same. Scott, naturally greatly pleased and honoured, answered that ever since 1798 (when 'he had translated *Götz*) he had been one of Goethe's admirers, and that he even now attached a certain importance to that early attempt at translation, although it suffered from his imperfect knowledge of the language. Still, it did at least show his ability to choose an admirable subject. But it must be added that to Shakespeare's native land this subject was no novelty. So it cannot be contended that Goethe exerted an influence on Europe through the medium of Scott and the type of historical novel that he created. This influence came to be exerted through the medium of Shelley, and first and foremost through Byron. For, in Byron's case, Goethe actually did snatch an English mind out of the bonds of English traditions. The spirit of Goethe burst into flame in a genius who exerted the most powerful influence over every literature of Europe, an influence more palpable than Goethe's own. It was the Faust-spirit which flared up in Byron ; and it is significant that both Byron and Shelley, the poets imbued with the spirit of Goethe, were outlawed and banished from England.

To recapitulate : young Goethe overthrew the rules ; in place of Classical mythology he resorted to national history and Nordic phantoms. In other literatures these precipitated the conflict between Classicists and Romanticists ; but this could not happen in a literature that had Shakespeare for progenitor, and owned also Ossian and Percy.

The year 1798 saw no fewer than five English translations of Bürger's " Lenore " appear at the same time ; Monk Lewis,

who in 1792 had visited Goethe in Weimar, translated the
" Erlking ", as Scott had done ; but here English literature was
merely taking back what it had previously given to German. It
is only with Shelley and Byron that one can begin to speak of any
revolutionising of English poetry through Goethe through the
Faust-spirit. English literature can indeed point to Christopher
Marlowe's Faust-tragedy, brought to Germany by English players
and, in its German adaptation for the Marionette theatre, of
some importance in connection with Goethe's *Faust*. As for
Marlowe's own drama, it became known to Goethe too late to
have had any influence on his *Faust*. After Goethe had read it,
he expressed his admiration for the greatness of the design, and
Crabb Robinson reports that he even considered translating it.
But, though Faust was a popular figure in England during the
16th and 17th centuries, though Shakespeare mentioned him in
the *Merry Wives of Windsor*, this can all be traced to an early
translation of the German chapbook of Dr. Faustus on which
Marlowe based his tragedy. This tragedy differs fundamentally
from the old chapbook, however, in recognising for the first time
in the German Faust a noble spirit whose aim, being all too high,
led him to sin against the divine law, and in thus making a true
tragic hero of him. Yet English literature did not absorb the
Faust-spirit, although it was the first of all European literatures
to free itself from Classicism. It was able to evoke, in young
Goethe, Werther's *mal du siècle*, but it was Goethe who threw into
its midst the spark of Faustian revolt. It is a highly significant
fact that the Lake Poets, Coleridge, Southey and Wordsworth,
who in other respects were far from being antagonistic to German
literature, turned resolutely away from *Faust*. When Byron,
Shelley and Scott urged Coleridge, who was translating Goethe's
poems, to translate *Faust*, he refused, although for a short time he
did entertain the idea. He considered *Faust* so immoral and
pagan, its language so vulgar and blasphemous, that he could
not reconcile it with his moral character to pay such a work
the compliment of translating it into English. He even went so
far as to plan writing an Antifaust. He may have been thinking
in this connection of resuming work on an old plan of which he
spoke in his *Table Talk*, and which he conceived before he made
acquaintance with Goethe's *Faust*, but when he was of course
familiar with Marlowe's. This was the idea of a drama whose
hero was a figure akin to Faust, the magician Michael Scott.
The plan is very like that of Goethe's *Faust*, and the close seems

almost to anticipate the end of the Second Part of *Faust*, the rescue. For Michael Scott was to triumph at the last, and to find peace for his soul in the conviction that God's Grace affords salvation for sinners. Yet the difference here from Goethe's idea of redemption is so great that it gives a clear insight into the difference between Goethe and Coleridge. Goethe's Faust is far from finding peace for his soul in the conviction that the sinner is saved through God's Grace ; and to a consciousness of sin he remains to the end a stranger. He is redeemed because he goes on constantly striving and never gives up his endeavour. Southey and Wordsworth adopted a similar attitude, and also turned their backs on Faust. For the conception of Goethe that was still dominant in England was Goethe the enemy of society, morality and religion. Wordsworth openly accused him of egoism, saying he was never able to forget his own personality. The English poet contrasted Goethe's cult of the self with a pantheism which grips the inner one-ness of nature and man, and gives it poetical expression. For Goethe man alone—or rather he, Goethe, alone —comprises the whole meaning of the world. That age failed to realise that the so-called egoism, the result of the most rigid self-discipline, was the fruit of the bitterest sacrifice and renunciation, and that in reality it served the higher development of mankind. Riemer notes in 1811 that Goethe himself had under consideration a plan for a novel *The Egoist*, which was to treat the idea " that self-mastery is taken for egoism ". This is noted, too, in his *Maxims and Reflections*. This novel was obviously designed as an answer to the reproach he heard on all sides. In France, then, *Faust* was rejected by the Classicists on æsthetic and rational grounds, but in England the grounds were moral and religious. Even William Taylor, who translated Goethe's *Iphigenie*, made a violent attack on *Faust* and could not understand how Goethe, who in writing *Iphigenie* and *Tasso* has shown himself a worthy disciple of Sophocles, could write such a wretched drama. It contained such a multitude of absurdities and obscenities that one could not wish for any English translation (*Monthly Magazine*, 1810). The line-drawings for *Faust* by the artist Retzsch appeared in 1820 in London, in the form of copies by Henry Moses ; and these, Goethe learned, aroused great curiosity on the subject of the tragedy ; a new edition of them added long passages from *Faust*, written in blank verse and interspersed with narrations in prose. But those parts which might have shocked the English reader by their immorality and lack of religious feeling were suppressed. The Prologue in Heaven could appear as a drawing, but not in translation ! George Soane's incomplete translation of *Faust* won Goethe's approval, although one can hardly understand on what grounds it did so. In 1822 Goethe received the first sheets with the original printed opposite. He found that his *Faust* had been admirably understood and brought into harmony with the English language and the requirements of the English public. He took it as a sign that the nations were gradually learning to understand each other better.[27] But Goethe was far less satisfied with the Faust-translation by Lord Gower (1823), who visited him in Weimar in 1826 : " Really it was a completely new version, hardly anything was left of the original ; and he therefore was obliged to omit a great deal which he was unable to mould to his fancy." Among the omissions out of " considerations of decency " and on religious grounds, the Prologue in Heaven figured once more ; only the Angels' Songs were translated from it : " There is a tone of familiarity on both sides, which is revolting in a sacred subject." Gower's dedication to Goethe appeared in 1823 in *Kunst und Altertum*.

Since 1826 Goethe had been familiar with Shelley's fragmentary translation of *Faust*,[28] but he never mentions it, though it is the finest translation of *Faust* in English—and not only in English. In Goethe's mind, Shelley was always overshadowed by Byron. Shelley's attention was drawn to Goethe by Mme de Staël's *De l'Allemagne*, and he was so strongly impressed by its references to *Faust* that he learned German and set about making the translation which comprises the Prologue in Heaven, the Earth-Spirit scene, the Easter Walk and the Walpurgis-night. A contemporary account exists, telling how Shelley was found in Pisa, bowed over Goethe's *Faust*, a dictionary in his hand. He read *Faust* with feelings that no other work ever aroused in him. " We, the admirers of *Faust*," he said, " are on the true path to Paradise." One has only to read the opening of Shelley's epic poem, *Alastor, or the Spirit of Solitude*, to be conscious at once of the profound effect exerted by *Faust*. For it reads like a wonderful variation of the monologue " Sublime Spirit you gave me, gave me all for which I prayed ".

Goethe made no mention of this work, and Crabb Robinson expressed his astonishment at this in a letter to Goethe (1829). He had hoped to find in *Kunst und Altertum* an appreciation of Shelley's *Faust*. But in 1817 when Goethe first read Byron's *Manfred*, he at once recognised the son of Faust.

The most wonderful event [he wrote to Knebel] has occurred for me in the appearance of Byron's tragedy *Manfred*, brought to me the other day as a gift by a young American. This unusual and gifted poet has absorbed my *Faust* and has got from it the strangest food for his hypochondria. He has used every theme in his own fashion, so that none remains as it was ; and for this in particular I cannot sufficiently admire his genius. This reconstruction is entirely of a piece ; one could give most interesting lectures on its similarity to the original and its departures from it ; I do not deny, however, that the dull glow of an unrelieved despair will become wearisome in the end. Yet one's irritation will always be mingled with admiration and respect.

Goethe's public review of *Manfred* in *Kunst und Altertum* began with these words just quoted. Byron, who took note of this criticism, was quite justified in declaring, in his dedication of *Marino Faliero* to Goethe, that through one single prose work, *Werther*, Goethe himself had encouraged a scornful attitude to life to a greater extent than had all the volumes of English poetry ever written. Byron denied, too, that his Manfred-tragedy had been inspired by *Faust*. He had known nothing of it, he declared, and did not even understand German. It was not *Faust*, it was the Jungfrau of the Bernese Oberland that had inspired him to write it. But a knowledge of the German language was not necessary, and Byron himself tells us that just before he wrote *Manfred* his friend Monk Lewis read him aloud a *viva voce* and literal translation of *Faust*, and that he, Byron, was greatly moved by it. And Mme de Staël's book, which appeared in London in 1813 and to which Byron owed his first acquaintance with German literature, gave him some idea of *Faust*—a most incomplete one it is true, but interspersed with copious translations. But evidence of this sort is quite unnecessary. For *Manfred* bears within itself the unmistakable traces of Goethe's *Faust*. These traces did not escape any of its European readers, although Goethe himself in his review of *Manfred* drew attention to the fact that everything had been transformed in such an original fashion. The spirit of this tragedy shows the Titan suffering intolerable anguish because God, while creating man in His own image and giving him the divine spark, yet kept him to the dust and made him His slave. For man has mastered the tragic art which makes him lord of all demons, yet he has to realise that even logic cannot release his soul from torment, nor bring him forgetfulness. This spirit is the spirit of *Faust*. There was nothing Byron envied Shelley more than his ability to read *Faust*—" that astonishing production "—in the original. " I would give the world to read *Faust* in the original." He urged Shelley to translate the whole work. He took *Faust* with him on his travels, as Napoleon took *Werther*. Byron himself declared in the preface to his drama, *The Deformed Transformed*, that the work was " partly " based on great Goethe's *Faust* ; and when he was giving it to Shelley, he said he had written " a faustish kind of drama ". (Shelley's opinion, however, was that it was a " bad imitation of *Faust* ".) And in fact the likeness to Goethe's *Faust* is but superficial. Arnold, the cripple, who intends to commit suicide because of his physical ugliness, is changed by the Devil into a most beautiful figure on the model of Achilles, and becomes the leader of the forces attacking Rome, while the Devil himself takes the form of the cripple. But Arnold discovers that even beauty and power do not lead to happiness. The love of the beautiful Roman girl is given not to him but to the cripple. This new life of the hero in beauty and power reminds us almost more of the Second Part than of the First Part of *Faust*. The noble poet takes his Faust at once into the great world of society. But Byron's fundamental pessimism separates him from Goethe. What was to be the end of this drama which appeared only as a fragment? Was the hero to change back into a cripple, and was the end, in contrast to Goethe's Faust whose path is a continual ascent, to be like the beginning, and was everything to prove in vain?

Yet there are other ways in which the Faustian spirit speaks in the works of Byron. His tragedies are storm signals, as *Faust* was, of a new human type, a new Europe. Manfred is forced to realise that the tree of knowledge is not the tree of life, that no spiritual superiority can bring happiness and help ; he destroys himself because he is too proud to accept God's help. To him comes Cain, the accuser of Adam his father who plucked the fruit of knowledge and not the fruit of life, and thus woke a thirst for knowledge that can never be quenched. He is also the accuser of God Who set the curse of work and death upon this forbidden knowledge, and so limited its scope. But when Lucifer breaks his bonds and reveals to him, in his flight through space, the secret of death, of past and future, then there remains for man this last word of wisdom : that God is indeed all-powerful but not all-gracious : He is the constant destroyer of His own creation, the tyrant Who can brook nothing beside Him but dust and helplessness. This knowledge makes it intolerable in Cain's eyes that Abel should offer sacrifice to this cruel deity, and he slays his brother.   The religious play *Heaven and Earth* was another rebellious accusation against God Who forbade any intercourse between the creatures of earth and of Heaven, and punished it with the Flood which engulfed everything. And finally we have the poem " Prometheus ", a hymn to the Titan who, defying God, lit the flame of spiritual power in man and now, bound in everlasting chains and ceaselessly torn by vultures, yet resolutely opposes God with all the power of his spirit.

Works like these Goethe read with foreboding and amazement. He saw how the poet Byron himself, when he found no answer to the questions that tormented him, and was driven like Faust by his thirst for knowledge, plunged headlong into life, to heap upon his own head his own joy and sorrow, together with all the weal and woe of the world.   It need not be stressed further that the reason for the profound effect of Goethe's *Faust* lay in Byron's own Faustian nature ; the spark from Goethe naturally fanned it into flame.   In Faust he recognised himself.   A new and boundless human pride rose up in him against the limitations imposed upon man.   As an English nobleman he commanded wealth and power, as a poet, fame and the favour of women ; he had no need to deny himself the gratification of any wish. But his tempestuous life led him into mysterious guilt and tor- ment.   He sucked nothing but poison even from the sweetest fruits of love.   Like Faust he reeled from desire to gratification, and in the moment of gratification thirsted for desire.   Dis- harmony within himself led to dissatisfaction with the world. On every side he found life suppressed and choked.   He trusted that Napoleon would liberate Europe and awake new life. Napoleon's fall left him with nothing to hope for.   The battle of Waterloo ushered in a period of general reaction in Europe. Absolutism and feudalism oppressed the peoples, the Church robbed the spirit of all freedom, society confined man within the rigid forms of a hypocritical moral code.   Then Byron began to shake all the stable conventions of European life and shattered them by the force of his word and his spirit, his pathos and his scorn.   He called on the peoples to liberate themselves, to serve no longer the tyrants of earth and heaven.   He tore the mask from society.   But his contempt was directed less towards the oppressors than towards the common man of Europe who was willing to go on dragging his miserable chains of slavery, and towards the poets of Europe who—with one exception—entered the service of force. His own poetic writings became a political act. But he did not stop even there. When the Greeks began their struggle to free themselves from the Turkish yoke, he placed himself at their head and fell as a hero shortly before he would have gained the promised crown of Greece.

From his quiet corner in Weimar, the ageing Goethe followed with amazed and ever-increasing admiration the course of the brilliant comet, this new star so completely without parallel in former centuries that there seemed to be no criterion for calculating how far he would go. Goethe did what he could, by reviews of Byron's works and translations from them, to contribute to his European fame and glory. He noted how Byron's radiance actually outshone everything, and how he had no rival anywhere. Byron had obviously found the word that Europe wanted to hear. He gave his name, " Byronism ", to Europe's state of mind. It was a magical, demonic charm that drew Goethe to Byron. He tried to get news of him privately whenever possible, and never tired of speaking of him in letters and conversations ; he called him the greatest genius of the century, the only one that he could place beside himself. Whenever he spoke of the attributes that a true poet must possess, such as demonic impulse and the power to anticipate, Byron served him as an example. He contrasted him with Shelley, although Shelley was possibly the greater poet of the two, and indeed by that time opinion on Byron had altered in his disfavour, even to the point of injustice. At any rate, no other contemporary occupied Goethe's thoughts so continuously and so deeply. In no one of them did he take such a personal interest. No proofs of esteem gave him such satisfaction and sincere gratification as he got from Byron's dedications, letters and greetings. Byron considered dedicating his tragedy *Marino Faliero* (1820) to Goethe. The dedication was not printed, and only reached Goethe in 1830. The conclusion is as follows : " Considering you as I really and warmly do, in common with all your own and with most other nations, to be by far the greatest literary Character which has existed in Europe since the death of Voltaire, I felt, and feel, desirous to inscribe to you the following work . . . as a mark of esteem and admiration from a foreigner to the man who has been hailed in Germany as the Great Goethe." When nothing came of this dedication, Byron decided to offer his tragedy *Sardanapalus* to Goethe in the following terms : " To the Illustrious Goethe a Stranger presumes to offer the homage of a literary vassal to his liege Lord, the greatest of existing writers, who has created the literature of his own country and illustrated that of Europe. The unworthy production which the author ventures to inscribe to him is entitled *Sardanapalus*." But the dedication was delayed, and this drama too appeared without one (it figures in the 1823 edition, London, John Murray) ; Goethe, however, was very pleased to possess a lithograph facsimile of the manuscript which Byron had made. (Medwin's *Conversations with Goethe* record that Byron's reason for dedicating this drama to Goethe was because he looked to him as the greatest genius that the age had brought forth.)

At this point Goethe decided to express clearly and forcibly his gratitude for these manifestations of goodwill by recording how he was filled with esteem for his incomparable contemporary and animated by feelings of sympathy with him. But this task proved too great ; words were inadequate to do justice to Byron's deserts. When a certain young man (Sterling) arrived in Weimar in the spring of 1823 from Geneva, where he had met Byron, he brought a letter of introduction written by Byron himself, and when, soon after, the rumour spread that Lord Byron was about to direct his great mind and varied powers to dangerous undertakings overseas, Goethe hastily wrote the following poem :

> Ein freundlich Wort kommt eines nach dem andern
> Von Süden her und bringt uns frohe Stunden ;
> Es ruft uns auf, zum Edelsten zu wandern,
> Nicht ist der Geist, doch ist der Fuss gebunden,
> Wie soll ich dem, den ich so lang begleitet,
> Nun etwas Traulichs in die Ferne sagen?
> Ihm, der sich selbst im Innersten bestreitet,
> Stark angewohnt, das tiefste Weh zu tragen.
> Wohl sei ihm doch, wenn er sich selbst empfindet !
> Er wage selbst sich hoch beglückt zu nennen,
> Wenn Musenkraft die Schmerzen überwindet,
> Und wie ich ihn erkannt, mög' er sich kennen.
>
> Weimar, 22. Juni 1923.

The poem reached Genoa, but Byron was no longer there. Storms at sea delayed him, however, and he landed again at Leghorn where the poem reached him, in time for him—as he was leaving for Greece—to answer it with a sincere, " sensitive " note which was to be one of Goethe's most treasured possessions. In his letter Byron wrote that as he was just about to set out for Greece, he would only express in hasty prose his sincerest thanks for the lines. Moreover he would not venture to exchange verses with Goethe, who for fifty years had been the unrivalled monarch of European literature. But the poem would prove a

good omen for him ; and, if he ever returned, he would visit
Goethe in Weimar to offer him the heart-felt tribute of one out
of the many millions of his admirers. It was a vain hope, however, and Goethe never had the pleasure of greeting in person
the most distinguished of minds, the friend whom he had been so
fortunate to find, and the most humane of conquerors. Instead
of Byron himself, it was news of his death that reached Weimar.
" The brightest star of the poetic age has paled, and it is the
duty of the survivor to keep his undying memory fresh, in public
as in private." What else could Goethe do but let his Muse
master his grief and sing Byron's elegy :

> Stark von Faust, gewandt im Rat
> Liebt er die Hellenen ;
> Edles Wort und schöne Tat
> Füllt sein Aug' mit Tränen.

> Liebt den Säbel, liebt das Schwert,
> Freut sich der Gewehre ;
> Säh' er, wie sein Herz begehrt,
> Sich vor mut'gem Heere !

> Lasst ihn der Historia,
> Bändigt euer Sehnen ;
> Ewig bleibt ihm Gloria,
> Bleiben uns die Tränen.

In the same year (1824) Goethe wrote for Medwin's book of
remembrance *Conversations with Byron,* his " Contribution towards
the memory of Lord Byron ". In it he spoke of the friendly
relationship which had grown up between him and Byron, which
culminated in the hope that England too, which had exiled its
gifted son, would come to realise what it had possessed in him.
And later, in the Second Part of *Faust,* Goethe raised a memorial
to him for all time in the figure of Euphorion, the son of Faust
and Helen.

How did all this come about ?   Is Goethe's boundless affection
for Byron not very strange ?   After all, Byron is not the type of
man and poet that was Goethe's ideal in his wise old age, and that
he had realised in his own case.   After struggles and painful
renunciation he had accepted the limitations of proportion and
strict form, and had devoted himself to the service of order, law
and the moral code in human society.   But Byron swept through
life, heedless of proportion, law and control, broke with all the
traditions of his own people, renounced obedience to all the moral
codes of society and the accepted standards of Europe.   Goethe

had won through from the universal disillusionment of his youth to a positive acceptance of the world : " In whatever form, life is good." He had made his peace with the world. But Byron persisted in boundless contempt for man and for the world ; his poetry was a poetry of despair and denial. For every sorrow Goethe found solace in his Muse. But Byron had lost faith in pure art : it served him only as a political weapon of revolt. Goethe once called Byron's poems " Repressed Parliamentary Speeches ". Goethe's allegiance was to the gods of Ancient Greece. But Byron called these gods " potters' ware ", and told his guide in Ithaca that he hated antiquarian patter. The cause for which he died was not the rebirth of Ancient Greece, its civilisation and its art, but the political freedom of modern Greece. If any Classical figure inspired him, it was not Apollo, Goethe's god, but Prometheus, the Titan in revolt against the gods of Olympus. But Goethe had long since renounced the promethean Titanism of his youth. To realise that this was the case, one need only contrast the Prometheus-figure of his Storm and Stress period with that of his " Pandora ". Why did Goethe lavish affection on this young poet who by no means embodied his ideal of man or poet ? Was it because, as he himself admits, he regarded the recognition of greatness in others as the surest means towards his own self-education, and did not enquire into the nature of that greatness ? " There is education in all greatness, once we appreciate it," Goethe said to Eckermann, who expressed his doubt whether Byron's writings could yield anything of definite value towards man's true education. " Byron's daring, wilfulness and grandiose manner, are not all these elements of education ? We must guard against seeking it only in what possesses absolute purity and moral value." Was it the demonic power in Byron that charmed and fascinated him whom every demonic spirit moved ?

In Goethe's relationship to Byron another and deeper note was struck besides the desire for education and the honour due to genius. The note was that of love. It was the love of a father for his son, his spiritual son, that bound Goethe to Byron. In him Goethe recognised the son of his Faust, of his own Faust-nature altogether, not only in *Manfred* and in *The Deformed Transformed* but in Byron himself, the man and the poet as a whole. In this most strongly-marked personality, the Faust-spirit had indeed taken on an entirely new shape, but it remained unmistakable to Goethe's prophetic eye. And in his turn he saw the love of a son for his spiritual father in the honour in which Byron held him. " Of Byron he spoke lovingly, almost like a father of his son," wrote Prince Pückler-Muskau. Goethe was unwilling to attribute the dedication of *Sardanapalus* to his own merits. Instead, he saw in it the honour which a younger man enthusiastically pays to the signs in his predecessor of an urge he cannot subdue within himself. In Byron, Goethe's own youth rose up once more before him, with all its griefs and yet in all its glory, with all its errors and yet in all its demonic beauty. There even came a moment when, through Byron, he realised with anguish all that he had had to sacrifice to his own higher ideal of mankind ; and Byron awoke again in the ageing Goethe the youthful spark of Faust. It was England that had once given Goethe the courage to be himself ; and now through the English genius this was happening once more to Goethe in his old age. The seventy-four-year-old poet's love was kindled for young Ulrike von Leventzow, and he was torn by the struggle between passion and renunciation. At this point a letter from Byron reached him, bringing before him this young, passionate genius who knew no renunciation. And again the fire, the pride, the courage of Goethe's youth awoke : he would renounce no more, he could grasp and hold what he so fervently craved. He would seek to win Ulrike. The *Trilogie der Leidenschaft*, the deepest and the finest love-poem that he ever wrote, trembles with Byron's tones, and its first section " To the Shade of Werther " might have been addressed to Byron. When Eckermann deduced Byron's influence from the unusual force of the feelings expressed, Goethe made no denial.

But with this fatherly love that Goethe felt in his old age for the spiritual son in whom his own youth lived again, another feeling was mingled, namely concern, even anxiety. This is what distinguishes Goethe's relationship to Byron so markedly from that in which he stood to Manzoni, to whom he was able to apply the epithet " Classical ". Goethe saw in Byron's case a wonderfully gifted, richly productive mind consumed in the dull glow of boundless despair, acknowledging neither proportion, nor law, nor limit, powerless to distinguish between ideal and reality, resisting every constraint. Speaking to Eckermann, Goethe expressed great satisfaction that Byron, who loathed every limitation, never made a compromise, never consulted any law, did at last (in *Marino Faliero*) conform to the demands of French tragedy, and reconcile himself to its strictly limited form. But Goethe was amused that it was precisely " that most stupid rule of the three Unities " to which he subjected himself. If only he could have restrained himself equally in the moral sphere ! That he was unable to do so was his undoing ; and it is true to say that Byron perished as a result of his defiance of restraint. His heedless struggle against Church and State drove him out of England and would in time have driven him out of Europe. Every place was too narrow for him, and in spite of the widest personal freedom he felt oppressed. The world became a prison to him. His departure for Greece was no spontaneous decision ; his being at variance with the world drove him to it. In breaking free from all tradition, it was not only his personality that he undermined. His revolutionary tendency and consequent mental agitation, the opposition he met everywhere, his negative attitude of mind which ignored his own obligations and had no toleration for others, all militated against it. For a negative attitude is not a productive one. This it was that instilled the drop of wormwood into Goethe's love and admiration. He saw also that through Byron the ground was being prepared in English literature for an atmosphere that was symbolised for him in an ultra-Romantic drama by Maturin. This was *Bertram or the Castle of St. Aldebrabd* and was dedicated (by Iken) in the German translation " to the supreme poet Goethe, with feelings of the profoundest respect ". " Exaggerations necessary to the English stage rage furiously throughout the play." To understand it we must turn back to Shakespeare, who unfolded, clear as day, the most dreadful depths of man's nature. In the course of time and with a decline in serenity of outlook, more and more abstruse elements came to find a place in dramatic works. Misled by this, the public began to think that uncontrolled discontent was a fit poetic subject ; respect was paid to man's violence, no one seeming to remember that such is capable of destroying any art.[29] Goethe may have been very much disturbed at recognising in Maturin's work " typical Germanisms ", elements of German Romanticism. He would not have failed to see the traces of his Götz and Faust, though of a Faust totally misunderstood, and bearing the influence of a sensational Romanticism. These traces are found in Maturin's *Melmoth* and in Lewis's *Monk*, which at the time enjoyed world-wide fame, and more clearly still in *Frankenstein*, the work of Shelley's wife. Of course Goethe did not intend to compare Byron with Maturin. But these phenomena did help him to recognise that Byron's case was not an isolated occurrence.

Not only in England but in all the Romanticism of Europe, particularly that of France, this mood of wild discontent is noticeable.

Goethe's anxiety, then, was not merely for Byron the man and poet, but for the whole of Europe seared by the flame of this genius ; and he had to admit that he himself was not without responsibility for this world-wide mood. Were not the names Byron and Goethe linked like *Manfred* and *Faust*, in every European literature ; and in what sense were they so linked ? In France, for instance, Lamenais denounced Byron and Goethe as unbelieving sceptics, as desperate champions " du mal infini éternel ". In 1830, when both Goethe and the Pope were lying dangerously ill, Balzac wrote in his *Lettres sur Paris* : Goethe and the Pope are both dying : " l'auteur du *Faust* et le vicaire de Jésus-Christ." And Goethe was described as the head of the Satanic school " le chef de l'école satanique auquel nous devons Lord Byron ". Gérard de Nerval, the translator of *Faust*, compared the latter with *Manfred* and *Don Juan* as its next of kin. Pushkin frequently mentioned them together. George Sand wrote an essay in which she grouped Goethe's *Faust*, Byron's *Manfred* and Mickiewicz's *Conrad* together as dramas on the same Faust-spirit, each bearing the stamp of its own nationality. Mickiewicz wrote an article " Goethe and Byron ". It is only exceptionally that we find a comparison between *Faust* and *Manfred* repudiated as it was by Crabb Robinson in conversation with Goethe in Weimar. What is much more important is that the influence Goethe exerted through his *Werther* and *Faust* blended completely with that of Byron, so that after Byron's appearance in European literature Wertherism became synonymous with Byronism, and it is often impossible to say whether Goethe's influence had acted through the medium of Byron, or whether he or Byron together had precipitated the " mal du siècle ".

Here we have another instance of the phenomenon so often noticed already : that the influence that Goethe exerted in the world no longer corresponded to the stage he had himself reached. Was this not the fire that he himself had wished to kindle on the sacred altar of European civilisation, and that now set Europe ablaze and threatened to destroy it ? Nothing could bring so clearly and so poignantly to his mind his own tragedy—for such it is—as the example of Byron, his spiritual son, and the influence which through the medium of Byron he himself was exerting on

European literature. We must go further ; if in Goethe we recognise the most typical representative of the German spirit, we must mention the tragedy of this German spirit, which set Europe ablaze, robbing it of proportion, beauty, order and form, just when that spirit had acquired all these qualities in the person of Goethe. What swept over the world was the German Storm and Stress, and German Romanticism. Almost all cultural influence was denied to Goethe's spirit when it went beyond the merely German.

This tragic experience may have been Goethe's incentive for following up the First Part of *Faust*, after an interval of over twenty years, with the Second Part, although he had almost ceased to think of completing it. When the First Part was finished, Goethe had already begun (in 1800) the drama of Helen ; and he then thought of rounding off a continuation of *Faust* with the marriage of Faust and Helen. For this was the stage in Faust's journey that Goethe himself had reached, and he could create only out of his own experience. But now he was forced to realise that Faust's journey, on which he had taken with him the literatures of Europe in the First Part of *Faust*, took a totally different direction both from his own and from the course he had planned for Faust. He saw that the survival of his influence in the next generation in Europe, as exemplified in Byron, had taken on quite a different aspect from any he had desired or anticipated. By sacrifice and renunciation he had overcome the Faustian longing for boundless and unqualified freedom. Now, however, he was forced to see that all this sacrifice was in vain, as far as his influence in Europe was concerned. He had roused the Faust-spirit in Byron, in Europe indeed, but without being able to guide others along the way of his own Faust, his own way of sacrifice and renunciation. His grief and revolt had developed into a European sickness, but his cure and his recovery had not yet reached Europe. He had wanted to restrain and he had incited. He had wanted to mould, and he had distorted. It was he who had called up the revolutionary spirit of the 19th century, the spirit of revolt and denial, which before his eyes destroyed Byron, a man of genius. And he shares the responsibility for this, the fate of his spiritual son. The son of the union of Faust and Helen, therefore Goethe's own son, gifted and fascinating, captivating and brilliant, destroyed himself by his lack of proportion and self-control, and by his spirit of rebellion. Such was Byron, the incarnation of the youth of Europe. Goethe had of course read

in the German chapbook of Dr. Faustus that Faust and Helen had
a son. But now he had experienced this sonship in Byron, and
the shadow became a thing of flesh and blood. Now therefore he
was in a position to create it, and was impelled to do so. He felt
he must bar Faust's path along which Europe was going astray,
and must point out the path which leads his Faust through darkness and error to truth and the light of day. The Second Part
of *Faust* was begun in 1824, and this was the same year in which
Byron plunged into the Greek adventure and in it lost his life.
Byron's fate may have provided the incentive for the writing of
the Second Part of *Faust*. For not only had Goethe's imaginative
picture of Faust in Greece, fighting to rescue Helen, been realised
in a way by Byron in Greece, fighting to rescue the Greek people ;
the fate of his spiritual son revealed in a flash to Goethe where
Faust's path was threatening to lead the mind of Europe. We
have Goethe's own word for it that the figure of Euphorion, the
son of Faust and Helen, represents Byron. He said to Eckermann:
" I could use no one as the representative of the most recent poetic
age except this man, without doubt the finest talent that the
century has produced. Besides, Byron belongs neither to
Antiquity nor to Romanticism ; he is like the present day itself.
He was just the kind of man I required, with his questing nature
and his predilection for conflict which led to his death at Misso-
longhi." So in Byron's image he created Euphorion, who
inherited from Faust his father his insatiable thirst for the heights,
and from his mother Helen beauty of form, grace of movement
and the gifts of the Muses. But lute-playing, song and dance
were all insufficient to curb his feverish longings. Full of the love
of battle, defying death and eager for danger, climbing higher and
higher, he sees in the far distance and from the highest peak two
hostile armies in conflict, and in order to take part in it he casts
himself, wingless, into the air and falls dead at his parents' feet.
The chorus's dirge for the dead Euphorion is Goethe's lament for
his spiritual son, and for the whole youth of Europe, then in
process of destroying itself. Now it is certain that for Faust
Euphorion had a noble vocation. For it is Euphorion whose
heroic death separates Faust from Helen and, acting as a warning,
guides him beyond the stage of beauty won, that is to say beyond
the noblest stage of contemplation to a higher one, the last of his
earthly course, the stage of action. For, in his union with Helen,
Faust ran the risk that possessing beauty he might forget his
aspirations, that he might say to the moment, " Ah, still delay,

you are so fair ! " It is Euphorion who frees him from this danger and reawakens Faust's characteristic discontent. And it was Byron's epochal mission to bring to an end an artistic period (the expression is Heine's), to advance into the life of action, and so to introduce a transformation of the European mind. Of course Goethe's *Faust* had been from the first a call to action, beginning with the words of the Earth-Spirit which Faust failed to understand. The call to action is the keynote of the whole work. Byron was, then, for Goethe, the incarnation of his idea of Faust. So it was really Goethe who was at the bottom of this transformation of the European mind. Byron-Euphorion, who is no longer content to be a poet but who claims to be a man of action, a fighter ! But, with the prophetic vision of old age, Goethe saw, to his sorrow, the course that Europe would take ; and it was not the course along which he had hoped the Second Part of *Faust* would guide it. Faust's final action is not the destructive act of war that Euphorion longed for, and that Napoleon made a reality. Faust's action is a civilising one ; he sets bounds to the sea, wins fertile land from it for a colony of millions of men, and so forms a link between the continents by which they bring their goods for exchange. It is an action of love, bringing prosperity to the nations. And, although happiness must still be constantly won anew, this involves no struggle of nation against nation. Rather is it the war that human civilisation must always wage against the forces of nature which constantly threaten it with destruction. This is the end of Faust's earthly course, which Goethe sought to point out to the Byronic spirit that his own Faust had led astray. And Faust's pathway leads beyond even this last action of love, for his soul is borne up into infinite space towards new spheres of activity. Byron's Manfred, too proud to accept the grace of Heaven or let himself be annihilated by the powers of hell, destroys himself, and even in death remains the Titan, the superman who lets himself neither be carried off by demons nor rescued by angels. But Faust is redeemed by Heavenly love, for, with all his faults, he never ceased to strive for better things. Goethe was not, like Byron, in revolt against Christianity because it humbled man before God. Although its original ancestor was Faust, Goethe had nothing to do with the movement, set in motion by Byron, that was first known in England by the name of Satanism. Goethe, unlike Byron, was not anti-Christian. For him the contrast between Ancient Greece and Christianity was resolved in a higher harmony. They both led towards the same goal, both were streams which flowed into the same sea. For him, ancient Greece was represented not by Prometheus in revolt against the Olympian gods, but by Apollo, the god of noble proportions, of beauty, of æsthetic restraint. It was Ancient Greece, indeed, that helped him to overcome his leanings towards Titanism. And Christianity meant to him a message of moral renunciation, control and resignation, the religion of veneration. Freedom is a curious thing, Goethe once said in connection with Byron. We are made free not by acknowledging nothing above us, but by venerating that which is above us. For in venerating it, we rise to its level. Nietzsche, the heir to Byron's spirit, who from his youth up had felt a close affinity with Byron, once said he had no words, but only a look, for those who dared to mention Goethe's *Faust* before Byron's *Manfred*. One can endorse this statement, in reverse.—But it is not Byron only, it is the whole of European Romanticism that becomes the problem in the Second Part of *Faust*. It is significant, however, that at the moment when everywhere in European literature the figure of the magician appears, it is Faust who renounces magic in order to confront nature simply as a human being.

Up to now we have spoken of the spread of Goethe's influence in the literatures of Europe. It was an influence which, while still active, no longer corresponded to his aims, for it emanated from works which represented a stage in his development beyond which he had already passed. The spread of this influence distressed Goethe in his old age, for it threatened to jeopardise his mission in Europe and even to lead to anarchy and chaos. But the scene changes when we consider the further development of English literature, beyond the range of Byron's influence. At this point we must repeat what has already been said of the characteristic quality of German Classicism ; it was the result of an ethical and idealistic victory over the essential German nature, of struggle and renunciation, whereas French Classicism owes its origin to an innate rationalism, and the Italian Renaissance to an innate sense of proportion and form. It is therefore quite understandable that German Classicism should have asked the help of the Romance literatures, while Romanticism turned to German sources. But the case was different in England, the home of a Germanic nation, where even the national character reveals the same dualism : a natural leaning to Romanticism, and the counterpoise of a strict morality to control and temper it.

This made possible for Goethe a double mission within English literature.   It was in English literature that the European concept of Goethe the Romanticist first underwent a complete transformation ;   and he who had evoked Byronism won a victory over it. If Goethe was at all responsible for Byron's fate, he was able to atone for this by his treatment of another English writer.   In 1824, the year of Byron's death, there appeared Carlyle's translation of *Wilhelm Meister*.   As soon as it appeared, Carlyle's translation aroused the most violent opposition.   Thomas De Quincey, translator of Lessing's *Laocoon* and author of important essays on German literature, utterly condemned both Carlyle's " barbaric " translation, which was an offence to the English mind, and the novel itself, together with its author.   He called Goethe an empty figurehead, and described *Wilhelm Meister* as a book calculated to neutralise the appreciation that Goethe was beginning to gain in England, because it offended English " good sense ".   Other critics called him absurd, childish, vulgar, lacking in taste, inartistic, amoral, obscene.   Yet none of them could prevent the book's having a profound effect on English literature :   that of overcoming Byronism.   When this translation appeared, Goethe was still practically unknown to the English public.   Crabb Robinson would have been the man best qualified (as we can gather from his diaries and letters) to furnish England with an adequate picture of Goethe.   He knew him personally, from visits which, as a young man and also in his prime, he had made to him in Weimar, and from the conversations they had then had. But during Goethe's lifetime Robinson never published anything on Goethe, with the exception of a few translations of poems ; and he spoke Goethe's praises only in private conversations with Charles Lamb, Coleridge and other English writers.   His success was slight, and when he wrote to Goethe in 1829, expressing his admiration and gratitude, he deplored that Goethe was not better known in England.   He blamed this partly on the poor translations which had been published, such as Holcroft's of *Hermann und Dorothea* and Lord Gower's of *Faust*.   Even a good translation like William Taylor's of *Iphigenie* had aroused no interest in England ;   and he could only hope that Des Voeux's translation of *Tasso*, and Carlyle's of *Wilhelm Meister*, would be more successful.

Carlyle as a young man had completely succumbed to Byronism, and it had led him to the brink of the abyss.   The despair that seized him and almost drove him to suicide was not caused, however, by Byronic Titanism, beating itself to death within the prison of man's limitations, but by the destruction of all belief in the meaning of the world and of life, by a universal doubt, by a total negation which was of the devil. Materialistic philosophy made the world for him a lifeless, soulless, all-destroying machinery, a moloch that devours its own creatures. Utilitarianism, while seeking an outlet, left none for him. Eudemonism, in its search for happiness, denied any possibility of it. The world seemed to him dead and void and dark. Carlyle himself states that Goethe's *Werther* was largely responsible for this mood ; and young Carlyle was profoundly moved by Goethe's *Faust* (to which he devoted a long article in 1822) simply because in him he saw a genius's portrayal of his own mood of blank despair. It is significant that Carlyle here quotes from *Faust* such passages as the curse, in which this mood is expressed. And when the crisis reached its height he became acquainted with *Wilhelm Meister*, by the same writer who had created *Werther* and *Faust*, and it was as if a new light had sprung up in the darkness that surrounded and threatened to engulf him. The book did not simply delight him as a work of art, as a novel ; to him it was a revelation of eternal wisdom and a new gospel. Hitherto he had sought only material happiness, and this had brought him misery and discontent ; now he learned that there is a higher gift than happiness, namely spiritual integrity and moral perfection. He had been concerned with aims, and now he learned that true morality has no aim ; it is practised for its own sake, and it fulfils the purpose and object of life. He had lost all sense of purpose, and he found it again in the practical exercise of love which aims at the ennoblement of human society. A slave to materialism, he had despaired of human freedom ; now he learned that the man of moral integrity is the master of his fate and controller of his own life. He had lost God, and now he found Him in the active force that transforms chaos into cosmos, that is alive and creative within man's spirit when he renounces his own happiness, devotes himself to the service of mankind, and guides it towards its high destiny. This reanimating influence of Goethe's meant a true rebirth for Carlyle. Yet this effect was wrought on him not in the first place by the book *Wilhelm Meister* but by the personality of Goethe as revealed in his work—or rather by the change in Goethe which transformed the author of *Werther* and *Faust* into the author of *Wilhelm Meister*. Here he saw a man who like himself had begun in darkness, despair and negation, and who through toil, struggle and renunciation had risen to positive acceptance and to the light. He saw a slave to the passions who had become their ruler, but who found in the service of mankind the purpose of his life and his vocation. This made Goethe an example, a guide and a teacher for Carlyle. Goethe, who won a heroic victory over himself, became an " evangelist " for him, and the sight of a man like this was for him the " gospel of all gospels ", saving him from outward and inward destruction.

Yet Carlyle recognised *Wilhelm Meister's Lehrjahre* as only the first step on Goethe's pathway to the heights ; and he continued to follow with growing admiration the further reaches of this path that led from *Werther*, through *Wilhelm Meister's Lehrjahre*, to the *Wanderjahre*, and from the First to the Second Part of *Faust*. The acceptance of life and the world-service in the *Lehrjahre* still seemed to Carlyle to have something pagan about them ; but in the *Wanderjahre*, which bears the subtitle " Die Entsagenden ", he saw Goethe entering upon the highest stages of religion, the religion of reverence for what is higher than man. Renunciation and reverence, Goethe's two stars, became Carlyle's also. When he read the Second Part of *Faust*, he grasped the magnificent unity and consistency of the whole course of Goethe's life. For, as he looked back from the Second Part, he saw the First in quite a different light. He had had no idea of the way along which Goethe meant to lead his Faust. He had interpreted *Faust* as a work of despair and negation, and this had led him to see in it his own image as in a mirror. But now he saw that even in the First Part the future was foreshadowed, and that the call to creative activity sounded a warning note through it. Now, in *Sartor Resartus*, he quotes from *Faust* no longer the curse but the words of the Earth Spirit : " In Being's floods, in Action's storm. | I walk and work, above, beneath, | Work and weave in endless motion ! | Birth and Death, | An infinite ocean ; | A seizing and giving | The fire of Living : | 'Tis thus at the roaring Loom of Time I ply, | And weave for God the Garment thou seest Him by." Of twenty millions that have read and spouted this thunder-speech of the Erdgeist, adds Carlyle, are there yet twenty units of us that have learned the meaning thereof ? That Nature with its thousandfold production and destruction is but the reflex of our own inward Force, the " phantasy of our Dream ", or the living Garment of God. Carlyle's famous " Philosophy of Clothes " may have been inspired by Goethe's words about the living garment of God. It was only after he had read the Second

Part that Carlyle grasped the meaning of the First. Now he understood also that Wilhelm Meister's development, leading to practical activity in the service of human society, was the natural consequence of this world-religion whose lines Goethe had laid down in *Faust* : that God is the eternal energy immanent in the world ; that the divine part of man is the activity that transforms the chaos of a fortuitous co-existence into the cosmos of human society. Thus Carlyle helped to change the image of the First Part of *Faust* which had hitherto been generally regarded as a supreme monument of Satanic negation, into a message of an eternally positive character. The most important point, however, is that Goethe's central creation was, in Carlyle's view, his *Wilhelm Meister*. The *Lehrjahre* first brought him enlightenment and relief, but the *Wanderjahre* did more by furnishing him with its idea of a world-organisation of work. It is not too much to say that for the first time Carlyle realised that Goethe was not merely the author of *Werther* and the First Part of *Faust* (although this description covered his reputation and his sphere of influence in Europe), but that his supreme significance was to be found in his victory over the Wertherish and the Faustian spirit. What French literature saw only as amazing versatility, Protean disguises of a writer of genius, Carlyle was the first to see as a uniform ascent culminating in a heroic victory over self. And in this he realised the symbolic character of both the ascent and the man. For in Goethe Carlyle saw the true pattern not of superman but of man, the guide and symbol of his age.

But the spectacle of Goethe brought about a change not only in Carlyle's conception of man but also in his conception of the poet. Goethe had indeed effected a change here in the literatures of all Europe. But it was Tasso and the author of *Werther* and *Faust* that completed it. The poet in revolt against society, finding no place for himself within it because its ways and laws are not his, because as a poet he is doomed to loneliness, and confined within an imaginery dream-world to which no reality corresponds.

But the conception of the poet underwent a totally different transformation when Carlyle came to contemplate Goethe. He now saw the poet as the sage, the seer who reveals the divine mystery of creation and thus becomes mankind's teacher and educator, pointing out the way and guiding it into the future. The poet is a hero. It is quite clear that the work upon which Carlyle's world-wide fame rests, his *Heroes* and *Hero-Worship*

(1846), owes its origin to the impact of Goethe upon him.   For
what Carlyle means by a hero—an individual genius who is the
chosen vessel of the eternal divine truth, and who, by revealing
himself to the world through action or speech, leads mankind on
towards its higher destiny—this type of hero Carlyle has taken
from Carlyle's favourite poem, Goethe's " Symbolum ", which
we constantly find quoted in his writings :

> Des Maurers Wandeln
> Es gleich dem Leben,
> Und sein Bestreben
> Es gleich dem Handeln
> Der Menschen auf Erden.
>
> Die Zukunft decket
> Schmerzen und Glücke.
> Schrittweis dem Blicke,
> Doch ungeschrecket
> Dringen wir vorwärts.
>
> Und schwer und schwerer
> Hängt eine Hülle
> Mit Ehrfurcht.   Stille
> Ruhn oben die Sterne
> Und unten die Gräber.
>
> Betracht' sie genauer
> Und siehe, so melden
> Im Busen der Helden
> Sich wandelnde Schauer
> Und ernste Gefühle.
>
> Doch rufen von drüben
> Die Stimmen der· Geister ;
> Die Stimmen der Meister :
> Versäumt nicht zu üben
> Die Kräfte des Guten.
>
> Hier winden sich Kronen
> In ewiger Stille,
> Die sollen mit Fülle
> Die Tätigen lohnen !
> Wir heissen euch hoffen.

That in Carlyle's own day a hero like this should appear, a
completely modern man—*that* was what moved him so deeply and
gave him faith in his own age and in the future.   It was Goethe,
his contemporary, who led him to look into the past, and to find,
in other ages and nations, heroes in whose reverent service mankind could perfect its development.   In Goethe, Carlyle found
the heroic spirit for the first time in visible form.   Now he found

other manifestations of it : the Hero as Divinity : Odin. The Hero as Prophet : Mahomet. The Hero as Poet : Dante, Shakespeare. The Hero as Priest : Luther, John Knox. The Hero as Man of Letters : Johnson, Rousseau, Burns. The Hero as Statesman and King : Cromwell, Napoleon. In Carlyle's book Goethe is not treated as fully as the other heroes ; indeed, he is mentioned only in the chapter " The Hero as Man of Letters ". But this does not indicate any estrangement from Goethe on the part of Carlyle : there is a reason for it. At the time of writing, Carlyle explains, the general level of information about Goethe made it useless for him to try to speak of him there. To the great majority he would still remain problematic and vague. He must be left to future ages. But Carlyle did on that occasion acknowledge his allegiance to Goethe, not as artist and poet but as man of letters in the highest sense of the word, as Fichte had used it : the man of letters as prophet, priest, ·seer, interpreter of the mystery that shows every phenomenon to be but the mantle of the eternal deity. In this sense he calls Goethe a true Prophet in these most unprophetic times, and places him among the heroes of mankind.

So this new conception of Goethe—not as arousing the " mal du siècle " but as overcoming it and bringing health, as the author not of *Werther* and *Faust* but of *Wilhelm Meister*—accomplished Carlyle's inner transformation and recovery. One might be tempted to think that Schiller, the subject of Carlyle's famous book, the first Schiller biography, would have had this meaning for him. For in this work, which appeared in 1825, the chief stress is laid not on young Schiller's Storm and Stress and his poetry of revolt, but on his heroic victory over self, on the idea and the realisation of moral freedom. But Schiller was only a beginning. For this English, or rather Scottish, spirit, Schiller was too visionary and abstract and idealistic. He did not so much dominate life as leave it behind him. Carlyle longed to dominate life without soaring above it. He could not endure an irreconcilable opposition between life and the ideal. He wanted to find and realise the ideal within life itself. And so he came to Goethe, the author of *Wilhelm Meister*, who dominated life. In this aspect Goethe is nearer than Schiller to the English mind, for he is more concrete, and he found the ideal in the activities of practical life. Carlyle was certainly moved by Schiller's heroic spirituality, which allowed matter to impose no conditions, took no thought of happiness but only of obeying the absolute moral law. This led to Carlyle's first stage of enlightenment, and it could not have come from studying either English or Scottish philosophy. But it was Goethe who became his first leader and guide. Through Goethe he overcame the Byronism within himself to which he had fallen a victim. " Close thy Byron ; open thy Goethe," we read in his autobiographical novel, *Sartor Resartus*.

Thus redirected and refreshed, Carlyle set about making Goethe's great qualities known. He wanted his contemporaries to share the same guidance and help that Goethe had given him. One might call this Carlyle's true life-work ; and, if he himself ranks among the " heroes ", he does so because he proclaimed the message of Goethe (which in his view constituted a new gospel) and became Goethe's evangelist. In the *Edinburgh Review*, the *Foreign Quarterly Review* and the *Foreign Review* he worked untiringly for Goethe. He translated some of his poems, the Helen-tragedy from the Second Part of *Faust*, the " Novelle " and " Das Märchen ". His love for Goethe grew into love for German literature as a whole ; and with the four volumes of his *German Romance* (1827) he acted as an intermediary of German Romanticism in England. He gave lectures on German literature, and planned a history of it from its beginnings to the present day. But Goethe remained for him the incarnation of the German spirit. Even his historical and social and political works are full of Goethe's spirit and he sometimes summed them up in Goethe's own words. For instance, he ends *Past and Present* (1843) with lines from Goethe's " Symbolum ", which are a sort of keynote throughout the work. And his famous Rectorial Address in Edinburgh (in which he referred to the principles of education expounded by Goethe in the pedagogical part of the *Wanderjahre*) ended with a quotation from the same great poem. The last words of this poem by Goethe were translated by Carlyle " work and despair not " ; and so we find that Carlyle's most famous and most frequently-quoted words " work and despair not " were really Goethe's. The clearest traces in Carlyle's works were left by *Wilhelm Meister's Wanderjahre*, with their ideas of emigration and world-wide organisation of work ; and Carlyle translated the travel-song from this novel " Keep not standing fix'd and rooted " .

It was primarily the English public to whom Goethe's merits were thus proclaimed, for when Carlyle began to write Goethe was still a stranger to the English. They knew him only as the author of *Werther* and First Part of *Faust,* and they did not care much for Goethe. Their impression of the German people as a whole had been largely taken from Mme de Staël's description of them : " a tumid, dreaming, extravagant, insane race of mortals "—and English practical common-sense could not feel much enthusiasm for such a nation. Carlyle attempted to atone, with his new conception of Goethe, for this wrong which was robbing England of such a valuable educative force ; his first intention, with this in mind, was to guide his fellow-Englishmen beyond utilitarianism and eudemonism, without wishing to deprive them of their capacity for the practical activities of everyday life. And Goethe represented, for Carlyle, the ideal pattern of this kind of activity, albeit in a higher, more spiritual sense, aiming at perfecting the development of man and of society. But Carlyle thought in the first place exclusively of England. He saw Goethe as " the common property of all nations ", the European pattern and guide for the whole age ; for Goethe had in his own case overcome Wertherism, the greatest crime of the age, and recovered from it. Carlyle saw him, then, not only as the greatest man of his age, but as " a man of all—one of the landmarks in the history of men ". In the eleventh of his lectures on the history of philosophy, or the successive periods of European culture from Homer to Goethe (1838), Carlyle depicted his own age, and saw in Wertherism and scepticism its most characteristic feature. But in the last lecture, as in " Past and Present ", he hailed Goethe as the dawn of a new, spiritual world, the creator of new and nobler spheres of action—in fact, the prophet of a new religion.

We have now to consider whether Carlyle's picture of Goethe can be regarded as correct, conclusive and valid—and we find it is obviously one-sided. For it fails to do justice to the essential qualities of Goethe as poet and artist. Carlyle practically omits this side of him. The reason is not necessarily to be found in any lack of artistic sense in Carlyle. It seems that he consciously wished not to draw attention to it, for he considered that what his age needed was not pure art but a higher moral and religious perception. His article on the Helena tragedy in the Second Part of *Faust,* and his translations from Goethe's poems, show that he did not lack appreciation of Goethe as a literary artist. But his one aim was to proclaim Goethe's prophetic, inspired wisdom, his high moral sense, his profoundly religious nature, because these were the qualities that Europe had failed to see and badly

needed.   This was why Carlyle did not do justice to Goethe the
poet, the artist, the creator of form.   There is no doubt that
Carlyle went too far in his attempt to show Goethe in harmony
with the Christian code of Puritanism.   Carlyle was himself a
Puritan.   He envisaged all practical moral activity in the service
of the world as a victory—demanded by God, but joyless and
depending on renunciation—over earthly despair and suffering,
akin to Christ's bearing of His Cross.   He tried to read this into
Goethe, and thereby introduced a somewhat surprising element
into the picture.   At the same time it must be admitted that
Carlyle was the first to realise the essential significance of Goethe's
idea of renunciation, which is far too often overlooked.   But one
ought not to interpret it in such a narrow Puritanical sense as did
Carlyle whose seal bore the word " Entsage " (Renounce) in
German letters.

One thing, however, is certain : this picture of Goethe as the
seer, the sage, and the teacher is true of him in his old age.   In
Wilhelm Meister's Wanderjahre and the Second Part of *Faust,* his
aim was no longer merely the creation of pure art as such, but
the prophetic utterance of ultimate truths and the guiding of
Europe to a higher stage of human culture.   We can be quite
certain that Goethe recognised himself in the picture that Carlyle
had drawn, and that he approved it and took pleasure in the
educative influence he had had on Carlyle.   For this was the
effect which he had hoped to produce and had not found in
the other literatures of Europe.   He saw his influence there only
in the form of Werther's despair and Faust's revolt against moral
codes and law.   He would certainly have taken pleasure in his
educative influence on Gottfried Keller, which was similar to
what Carlyle had experienced.

It must have given him particular satisfaction that it was an
Englishman who was in a position to receive these benefits from
him ; for Goethe had been obliged to watch his Werther-grief
and Faustian Titanism destroying the gifted spirit of Byron.   He
could look upon it, too, as the expression of his gratitude to
England for all that he owed to English literature.   In the past
it had freed him from an intolerable restraint, and now he was
able to give it his support in the interests of law and tradition.
This explains his affection for his spiritual son, Carlyle.   This
affection was neither so ardent nor so strong as that which he
felt for Byron, but neither was it destined to be mingled with
grief and anxiety.   What must Goethe's feelings have been

when (at the age of seventy-eight) he received Caryle's letter (1827) in which he wrote :

> For if I have been delivered from darkness into any measure of light, if I know aught of myself and my duties and destination, it is to the study of your writings more than to any other circumstance that I owe this ; it is you more than any other man that I should always thank and reverence with the feeling of a Disciple to his Master, nay of a Son to his spiritual Father. This is no idle compliment but a heartfelt truth ; and humble as it is I feel that the knowledge of such truths must be more pleasing to you than all other glory.

Carlyle also reported in the same letter that over a thousand copies of his translation of *Wilhelm Meister* (which had only appeared in 1824) were already in the hands of the public. After Goethe's death, he told Eckermann in 1834 that during the past twelve months no fewer than three new translations of *Faust* had appeared, two of them in Edinburgh on one and the same day. But the most important piece of news which he was able to send Goethe (in 1831) was that a " philo-German " Combination had been formed in England, with Goethe as its spiritual centre. A few years earlier, this would have been unthinkable. For his eighty-second birthday this body sent Goethe a present. It was a seal wrought in gold, and on its four sides were engraved the words " To the German Master : From Friends in England : 28 August 1831." The design of the seal itself was that of a star circled by the serpent of eternity, and round it were Goethe's words : " Ohne Hast, aber ohne Rast." This was characteristic of Goethe as seen by England, through the eyes of Carlyle, who had certainly chosen the line. For it gives the shortest definition of the Faust-type of ever-striving individual, and at the same time of wise proportion and restraint. In the congratulatory address which accompanied the gift, we read,

> As it is always the highest duty and pleasure to show reverence to whom reverence is due, and our chief, perhaps our only, benefactor is he who by act and word instructs us in wisdom—so we the undersigned, feeling towards the Poet Goethe as disciples do to their spiritual teacher, wish to express that sentiment openly and unanimously, so that . . . some memorial of the gratitude we owe him (and think the whole world owes him), may not be wanting.

Among the organisers of this presentation, in addition to editors of journals, translators of Goethe's works and diplomats, we find the most illustrious names in English literature : Scott, Taylor,

Wordsworth, Southey, and Carlyle himself. Goethe expressed his thanks in the form of a poem, which he sent " To the Fifteen English Friends ".

> Worte, die der Dichter spricht,
> Treu, in heimischen Bezirken,
> Wirken gleich, doch weiss er nicht,
> Ob sie in die Ferne wirken.
>
> Briten ! habt sie aufgefasst :
> " Tätigen Sinn, das Tun gezügelt ;
> Stetig Streben, ohne Hast."
> Und so wollt Ihr's denn besiegelt.

This poem makes it clear that Goethe felt himself understood by Carlyle and the society he founded ; and it is possible that this present from the fifteen English friends gave him even greater pleasure than did the consignment of works which the French Romantic writers sent him. When, however (in 1831), he received William Taylor's *Historic Survey of German Poetry*, this work could certainly not give him any pleasure, for Taylor, who had studied in Göttingen forty years previously, now suddenly released the precepts and opinions that had annoyed Goethe sixty years before. In a letter to Zelter he writes to this effect. But the cultural influence he had had on Carlyle was the clearest proof he ever got of what world literature could do as a spiritual medium between the nations. Not only had he been of great assistance to Carlyle, but he himself had been stimulated and helped by Carlyle and much encouraged by his interest and co-operation. We can understand, then, why it is that Carlyle was the only foreigner in correspondence with whom Goethe developed his idea of world literature. This gave Carlyle (who translated Goethe's " Weltliteratur " as world literature) a new impetus to work for communication between peoples in things of the mind, and to the further development and more advanced organisation of the human race through peaceful collaboration. It explains too why Goethe's important public pronouncement on his theory of world literature is to be found in his review of Carlyle's *German Romance*, and in his introduction to the German edition of Carlyle's life of Schiller (1830). He dedicated this work to a literary society which hitherto had concerned itself exclusively with its native German literature, but which, under the influence of Goethe's theory of world literature and its expansion throughout the world, turned to foreign literature. This was the " Honourable Society for Foreign Belles Lettres in

Berlin ", which adopted Goethe's suggestion of making Carlyle
an honorary member. In this introduction to Carlyle's book
on Schiller, Goethe did not deal only with Carlyle and his own
connection with him. The introduction is full of the idea of
world literature. Goethe also expressed his gratitude to Carlyle
for his endeavours on behalf of himself and of German literature,
by taking this opportunity of recommending to German readers
Robert Burns, the great poet of Scotland, Carlyle's native land.
The wish he here expressed for a good translation of Burns's
poems was realised fourfold within the same year (by Gerhard,
Heintze, Kaufmann and Freiligrath). And Herwegh's essay on
Burns alluded to Goethe. So it is true to say that through
Carlyle, whose development he had furthered, Goethe's activity
in the cause of world literature found great encouragement.
The connection between Goethe and Carlyle is thus an out-
standing memorial of the benefit that world literature can bestow.

We can certainly attribute to Carlyle's influence the fact
that Goethe's idea of world literature spread over England as
never before. Our proof of this is to be found in German literature. In his " Letters from London " a writer of the " Young
Germany " movement, Theodor Mundt, reports (in *Spaziergänge
und Weltfahrten*, 1838) :

> Throughout my travels, whenever I got into conversation of any
> kind with intelligent people, I have always been nervous of one of
> them beginning to speak of the so-called world literature idea which
> has become fashionable through Goethe, and I am invariably and quite
> obviously anxious to avoid this topic, of which a traveller might so
> easily come to speak. For it affects me strangely, and I am heartily
> sick of all the vague talk about it. The world literature idea pursues
> me everywhere like the Marlborough-tune ; every travelling student
> carries it about in his knapsack nowadays and airs it at every inn ;
> things will get to such a pitch that wandering journeymen will begin
> to beg in its name and plead for charity, no longer now for the love
> of God but for the sake of world literature.

Exaggerated as this picture is, it was based on actual experience.

In a letter to Goethe, Carlyle had reported that appreciation
of German literature, and especially of Goethe's works, was
making rapid progress in cultured circles in England. After
his translation of *Wilhelm Meister*, the readers and admirers of
Goethe had increased tenfold within the last six years. Two
periodicals, the *Foreign Quarterly Review* and the *Foreign Review*,
now contained regular reports on German literature. After
Goethe's death Carlyle reported to Eckermann that his task was

done. English resistance to German idealism was broken. England and Germany were no longer strangers but like members of one family.

Now Carlyle took on a new task, that of making Goethe known in America. It was he who won over Emerson, who at first had been violently opposed to Goethe.

Carlyle's translation of *Wilhelm Meister* led one English author to write an imitation of Goethe's novel, and thus to show that he too found in Goethe a leader and guide. This was Edward Bulwer, whose novel *The Last Days of Pompeii* belongs to world literature. How typical Carlyle's case was, is illustrated by the fact that in his youth Bulwer too had written a work *Falkland* (1827) which had been completely dominated by *Werther*, *Tasso* and *Faust*. *Falkland* is the story of a man of genius who cannot reconcile himself with the world of society, because genius claims its own standard of judgment and has its own code. It was a Byronic work. Ten years later, in 1837, Bulwer's novel *Ernest Maltravers* appeared. Bulwer admits in the preface that it was modelled on *Wilhelm Meister*. This novel of education was the history of an impulsive, weak and irresolute character who through disillusionment and error, but also through honest endeavour, develops into an active member of human society : an apprentice to life who becomes its master. Of course we ought not to overlook what Bulwer himself points out, differences due to the disparity between the nations. In *Wilhelm Meister*, Bulwer explains, the apprenticeship is rather that of theoretical art ; in his own novel, on the other hand, it is that of practical life. He expressly calls his novel the *Wilhelm Meister* of practical life. But the German idea of education, Goethe's idea of training, is quite unmistakably present. The English writer, in seeking to make of his work a " metaphysical novel " in which a deeper, more spiritual significance is seen, reveals Goethe's influence. So Bulwer was justified in dedicating this novel " to the great German people ", " a nation of thinkers and critics, a foreign but familiar audience, profound in judgment, candid in reproof, generous in appreciation ". He could not dedicate the work to Goethe, for he was no longer alive. Otherwise he would certainly have done so.

In this way *Wilhelm Meister*, the novel of education, lived on in English literature. And, after Carlyle's new orientation of Goethe and *Faust*, *Faust* also began to exert a different influence from its former one. The revolutionary, destructive, Storm and

Stress *Faust* gives place to the moral victor. Byron's Faust-like Titanism and cult of the superman led to despair over human limitations, to revolt against them, and thence to defiance of the world and God. After Carlyle, *Faust* was differently interpreted and its influence was different. It is true that in England Darwinism, which so profoundly influenced English literature about the middle of the 19th century, coincided with Goethe's idea of *Faust*. But the application of Darwin's theory of natural evolution to the historical evolution of mankind on its spiritual and cultural side would not have taken place had it not been for the influence of Goethe's works. After the Second Part of *Faust* had appeared, Robert Browning, in 1835, wrote his *Paracelsus*, which is often called the English *Faust*. Paracelsus is a German figure similar to Faust, and like him a learned man who seeks to overstep the limits of human knowledge, and to this end stakes his soul. He is brought by redeeming love to realise that knowledge not used in the service of mankind is sinful egoism. God is realised only in mankind's continued progress. To serve it is to serve Him.

Another work reminding us more vividly of Goethe's *Faust*, whose very title it recalls, was Bayley's *Festus* (1839), which once played an important part in English literature and enjoyed what was probably the greatest success of any work in the Faust-spirit. Its suggestion of Faust's name was deliberate. For its problem is Faust's problem, that of the meaning of sin and guilt in the world which God has created. This solution is found : that God has need of man's guilt in order to unfold his love, His goodness and His grace, and that man must incur guilt in order to free himself from early stain. When the development of the world is completed there will be no more sin and guilt. The created world will then revert to God. Festus, then, corrupted by Lucifer, passes, as Goethe's Faust does, from Heaven through the world to hell, but is redeemed by Christ and led back to God. It is quite obvious that in a work of this kind English Darwinism, the theory of natural evolution, is metamorphosed through the influence of Goethe's *Faust* into the history of intellectual and social evolution. Werther's universal disillusionment, Faust's revolt, the Titanic pessimism that had swayed Byron, had been overcome since Carlyle's day. Goethe had shown English literature the way taken by his Wilhelm Meister and by Faust : his own way.

One thing more remained—to appreciate also the true

significance of Goethe as artist and creator ; and Carlyle did
not accomplish this.   In 1855 Lewes's biography of Goethe was
published.   It was the first complete presentation of Goethe, as
Carlyle's had been the first biography of Schiller.   The first,
that is to say, in conception though not in date of publication.
For Viehoff, the German historian of literature, heard of the
Englishman's intention and sat down and wrote at top speed
his four-volume *Goethes Leben, Geistesentwicklung und Werke*.   The
honour of German literature, he wrote in his preface, would not
suffer an Englishman to be the first biographer of Goethe.
But this event in no way detracts from Lewes's merit.   This
English work showing appreciation of Goethe as a Classical
artist and creator gained immense popularity and helped to
make Goethe better understood even in Germany.   Georg
Brandes, the Danish historian of literature, relates that when it
was translated into Danish, in the early seventies, it taught him
and his whole generation to understand and appreciate Germany ;
and that Goethe thus became for them the ideal figure of
Germany, which had hitherto been seen only through a veil of
national antipathy.

CHAPTER 16

RUSSIA AND POLAND

When we try to visualise the Russia of Goethe's day, we feel lost in contemplation of vast expanses, vast to an extent unfamiliar to the European eye. In this infinity two clusters of domes stand out—St. Petersburg and Moscow. But even they are not enough to bring the picture into focus and to round it off. St. Petersburg and Moscow! The western European capital, and that other which has preserved the eastern spirit of the land : the enigmatic Janus-face of an empire into which Europe looks in vain for its own image. One feels that Napoleon was bound to be lost in these endless distances when he tried to bring them within his European scope. However diverse the lands of Europe may be politically and geographically, yet they have a common background, and are united by the common destiny of Europe. They are variations of the great unity Europe, and the star that stands over them all goes by the name of European civilisation. But, although Russia has considerable geographical links with the continent of Europe, and although since the days of Peter the Great it has also been spiritually orientated in the direction of western Europe, yet it cannot rank simply as a part of the western world. Its western features serve only to make it more of a riddle. Russia and Europe confront each other like East and West, and this difference is merely one of space but an eternally human and spiritual one. *Ex oriente lux.* Out of the East came light. From the East came the message of Christ to the western world. It was an eastern message, for the Oriental feels that the closed and self-sufficing form of human personality represents a culpable departure from the unity of all life. He feels himself to be the brother of all mankind, for all are sons of one father ; and for him to be a brother means putting the love of God into practice throughout human society. The ideal of the East is the holy man who typifies surrender, sacrifice, and extinction of the individual personality.

But when the spirit turned from West to East, it was not a message of love that the West had to take. Alexander's eastward progress was the advance of a worldly conqueror. West and East were united politically, in a West-to-East direction, by the Roman Empire of the East ; and the idea of an Empire embracing both West and East rose as an all-compelling vision in the mind of the Hohenstaufen Frederick II. Later, Napoleon's European bid for power burned away to nothing in the inviolable expenses of the East. From the East comes the Redeemer, from the West the Conqueror ; from the East Love, and from the West Power ; from the East God made man ; from the West man made God : these are the everlasting prototypes in which East and West approach and withdraw again, and from which Orient and Occident spring.

But the same Christianity lies at the roots of Russian and of western European civilisation. Yet European Christianity is built on an older foundation, which Russian Christianity lacks : namely Classical antiquity. For Classical antiquity lives on in European Christianity, which grew on Greek and Roman soil and in its Roman form made a conquest of Europe. In its beauty, its order, its hierarchy as well as in its idea of embodying spiritual power in temporal things, the Roman Church is the true heir of the Roman Empire. But the Russian Church which was born in Byzantium had no Classical antecedents, and the original eastern spirit of Christianity, which had been a revolt from that of Classical antiquity, here retained all its oriental quality. That is why there was no Renaissance in Russia : there was no Classical antiquity to be reborn. And this constitutes what is perhaps the greatest difference between the history of Russian and that of western European thought. Even Luther, with whom Russia could be said to unite in opposition to Rome, was in Russian eyes guilty of spiritual pride. Protestantism and Humanism were thus grouped together from the standpoint of the deification of man ; and they had become closely united in the course of German thought.

It is therefore understandable that Goethe's influence on Russian literature was quite different from that which he had on the literatures of the West, where he overthrew Classicism. In Russian, his influence tended to make thought more humane and European, and thereby started a Renaissance movement which evoked—some centuries late—something that had been lacking in Russian thought. In world literature, the relationships between peoples always show them to be appropriating from foreign civilisations what they themselves do not possess.

It is a striking fact that it was Russian literature that, first of all the literatures of Europe, saw Goethe as " Greek ", at a time when he was everywhere looked upon rather as an " Anti-

Classicist ". True, Werther was translated into Russian as early as 1788 and there it caused the same excitement as we noted in western Europe. But it is remarkable to what an extent the Russian mind resisted it. In this respect Dostoevsky may be taken as its representative, albeit a late one. In his *Journal of an Author*, where Dostoevsky speaks " of the Great and of the Little Bear, of great Goethe's prayer, and of bad habits in general ", he deplores, as he often did, the European sickness, the crippling of the will to live, the craving for suicide, which had also invaded Russia. But he sees a profound difference between the " unreasoned " suicide of the Russian and Werther's reasoned action.

Here, in fact, we have the whole difference between the mind of eastern and that of western Europe. Goethe takes pride in being a man, and Werther does not abandon this pride even at the point of death ; the Russian has only humility. . In Russian literature Goethe's *Werther* was identified with the paganism of Classical antiquity ; and the same is true of Goethe's *Faust*. In the poetry of despair, as Goethe called it, or of Satanism, as Southey described it, the Russian mind saw simply the presumptuous urge towards self-deification. The Faustian striving, which Goethe's western European mind saw as an effort to reach God, seemed to the Russian mind the exact opposite. It saw in the Faustian spirit the determination to win spiritual power, in the same way as Napoleon embodied the determination to win temporal power. In his novel *The Possessed* Dostoevsky counts this spirit among the demonic forces which penetrated Russia from the West and destroyed the Russian character. And when this despotic, self-deifying, western human type culminated in Friedrich Nietzsche's idea of the superman, it became obvious that Dostoevsky's prophetic words had anticipated the whole of Nietzsche. They indicated the final consequences of the European method which were not realised until the end of the 19th century ; it became clear that he had opposed something which did not then exist but which was bound to come. It was the inevitable climax of that European deification of man begun by the Greeks, continued in European Humanism, intensified in Faust, Napoleon and Byron, and culminating in the idea of the superman. Already, before Napoleon's day, Dostoevsky was Napoleon's great antagonist, and they were to one another as Christ and Antichrist. Dostoevsky's aim was to dominate the mind of Europe in the 19th century in the opposite direction from that chosen by Nietzsche. He wished to lead it towards Christ, the God made man, not to the man made God, to the man who seeks not to exalt but to humble, not to rule but to serve, not to assert himself but to be broken ; who seeks to be not the master but the loving brother of all men.

It was impossible for Dostoevsky, who in this matter repre-sents the Russian mind, to ignore the European problem of Werther's universal disillusionment and of Faust's revolt ; for in these lay the greatest danger to the Russian spirit, so differently constituted and prepared for so different a message. And Dostoevsky did in fact treat the problem of Werther not only in the *Journal of an Author* but also in his famous *Confession of a Suicide,* where he tried to provide a cure for this European sick-ness that had now infected Russia. In this confession; a suicide justifies his action by stating that nature has no right to create man capable of knowledge, for knowledge with its human limitations is misery. Man has therefore the right to rid himself of this affliction and to erase himself from life. But Dostoevsky goes on to reveal the tragic sophistry in this logical European argument, which can be valid only if one presupposes that the soul is not immortal. Without belief in the immortality of the soul, life has indeed neither meaning nor purpose. But with it, the believer is associated more closely and more intimately with this world. The eastern Christian idea here checks the advance of the European sickness. It is in his essay on Byronism that Dostoevsky treats the problem of Faust's deification of man. For Byron was the medium through which the Faustian spirit conquered Russia. In this essay, Dostoevsky does indeed call Byronism a holy sickness, for it was the product of the disillusionment following on the French Revolution and the moral bankruptcy of the revolutionary ideal. It therefore meant that European civilisation, that godless error of western rationalism, was being consumed in its own fire. But that does not mean that Byronism is the spirit that will lead humanity out of Europe's error and confusion, and the development of the 19th century shows it to be mistaken.

There is one occasion on which Dostoevsky deals directly with Goethe's *Faust.* This is in his novel *A Raw Youth,* where he makes a composer draw up the plan of an opera whose subject is taken from *Faust* ; and this is one of the most significant links between Goethe and Dostoevsky. For it is no mere chance that makes this composer lay a Scene in the Cathedral. Faust himself, and the problem of Faust, are left untouched. It is Gretchen, seduced, innocently guilty, threatened with ever-lasting damnation, in whom alone his musical visions are centred. Faust, ceaselessly striving and thus growing worthy of redemption, remained foreign to the Russian mind which saw no possibility of redemption for such a character. Faust's Titanism is swallowed up in Gretchen's loving, though sinning, humanity. Grace alone can redeem. The scene here conceived with com-pelling power follows that of Goethe fairly closely. But two important differences stand out. The " prolonged, persistent " aria of Mephistopheles—for he takes the place of the evil spirit— is filled with tears and despair, because he has nothing but dam-nation to pronounce on Gretchen. This shows a highly char-acteristic divergence from Goethe's Mephistopheles. And at the end, when the swooning Gretchen has been borne away, there surges a mighty chorus ending in a shout of triumph, Hosannah. But the most important point is that it was the Scene in the Cathedral that inspired the composer's music, and that Faust was so completely eclipsed by Gretchen. For Dostoevsky, *Werther* and *Faust* were simply proofs of the wrong way the West had taken.

It was, then, simply the logical outcome of Goethe's influence, begun with *Werther* and *Faust*, that led Russian literature to look to Goethe as the great Classicist, and that guided the eastern mind towards the West.

When the famous Russian writer Karamzin (who drew the attention of Russian readers to the West, and whose story *Poor Liza* shows traces of *Werther*'s influence) came to Weimar, in 1789, he failed in his efforts to visit Goethe, who was at court or in Jena. But when Karamzin once saw him at a window, he stood still and looked at him for some minutes. " A truly Greek face ", he summed up his impression in his *Letters of a Russian Traveller*. Herder and Goethe, he wrote, who are familiar with the spirit of the ancient Greeks, have also modelled their language on that of the Greeks, and this has made it the richest and best at the disposal of the poet. That is why neither the French nor the English have such magnificent translations from the Greek as the Germans possess. With them Homer is really Homer. Goethe may have heard this opinion of Karamzin's from Herder, who talked to Karamzin about Goethe and read him Goethe's " Meine Göttin ", that " truly Grecian " poem.

Goethe's first direct contact with the Russian mind has quite

an opposite effect to this. We shall see how Goethe gave a
Classical—one might almost call it a western—trend to Russian
literature ; and how he in turn was guided by Russia towards
the East, towards Asia. The marriage in Weimar of the Heredi-
tary Prince with a Russian Grand Duchess established a connection between Weimar and Russia which Goethe celebrated
with a *Masque of Russian Nations.* Soon after this (in 1811) a
young Russian, Uvarov—who was later to become the notoriously
reactionary statesman—sent Goethe a memorandum containing
suggestions for an Asiatic Society which would further a knowledge of the language and literatures of the East, both ancient
and modern. Goethe replied expressing his admiration and
pleasure, and the wish that Uvarov at the head of an Asiatic
Institute might soon diffuse new light over the two continents,
Europe and Asia, to both of which the Russian Empire belonged.
He mentioned further in his letter of thanks that his own love of
the Indian Vedas had been constantly enhanced by the reports
and zealous efforts of the English ; that some of the Indian
legends ("God and the Bayadère", "The Pariah") had moved
him to adapt them and he had at one time contemplated writing
a poetic version of the Vedas. But now the Oriental Society
would create a whole new world in which he could wander amid
richer profusion, and employ our talents in fresh activities.[30] In
1814, when Goethe received some of Uvarov's writings (among
them an essay on *Wilhelm Meister*), he mentioned in his letter of
thanks that in the meantime he had begun a study of the East
(the *West-Eastern Divan*) but that his ignorance of the languages
had been a great handicap. On this occasion, however, he had
once more considered Uvarov's suggestions for an Oriental
Society, and had derived from them much that was of use for
his purpose. And Goethe sent Uvarov the *West-Eastern Divan* to
show that he had ventured with some skill and good fortune into
a realm in which Uvarov was completely at home. It is clear that
this was Russia's message to Goethe, even before he wrote his
West-Eastern Divan. It drew his attention to the East, and
showed him that in this empire belonging to both Europe and
Asia it was possible to combine East and West in one higher
unity. It was not without reason that Goethe liked to wear side
by side the two high decorations which Napoleon and the Czar of
Russia had bestowed on him. They symbolised for him the West-
Eastern spirit which it was his own aim to realise in his *Divan.*

Russia, then, gave Goethe new stimulus by turning his

attention to the East.   And Goethe learned from Uvarov how he directed the attention of the Russian mind towards the West, and had a share in originating a Russian type of humanism.   In 1817 Uvarov publicly dedicated to Goethe his essay (written in German), on the writer of antiquity, Nonnos.   For Goethe this acted as another stimulus to further endeavour in the sphere of world literature.   This public sign of respect from Russia gave him great happiness for, as he wrote to Uvarov, now for the first time, after so many setbacks, the influence of the work that he had done was becoming obvious, and he could see how his contemporaries were helping the realisation of his hopes, and beginning to feel themselves part of one great entity.[31]   It was not only this, but rather the " precious " example of Uvarov that Goethe held up to the German people, so that instead of being shut in by their own limitations they should gladly accept the conditions of the outside world in order to exert an influence over it.   For Uvarov, in his preface addressed to Goethe, explained that he had used the German language in which to write his work on a writer of antiquity, because the renaissance of Antiquity was due to the Germans.   Other nations might have contributed important preliminary studies, but if the higher philology was to develop into a complete whole, this palingenesis would take place nowhere but in Germany.   For this reason it was hardly possible to express certain new opinions in any language but the German. The writer hoped that the mistaken idea of the political superiority of this or that language on scientific matters had been abandoned.   It was high time that each should choose the language best suited to the range of the ideas he was about to cover, no matter what that language was.   Goethe published this preface in *Kunst und Altertum* and contrasted it with the " miserable restrictions of a chilling linguistic patriotism " then prevalent in Germany.   All cultured Germans would do well to note with gratitude these instructive remarks, and young men of promise should feel encouraged by them to make themselves masters of several languages which would be of lifelong service to them.[32]

   In 1828, Goethe received from Nikolaus Borchardt, a member of the Institute for Enlightenment and Public Instruction in Moscow, the manuscript of an essay : " Appreciation of Goethe in Russia.   For the better appreciation of Russia."   It was the German version of a Russian article on Goethe's *Helena*, together with the Russian translation of a portion of it which the poet

Shevirev had published in 1827 in the *Moscow Messenger*. The number had appeared with a portrait of Goethe. Borchardt himself had prefaced his translation of this article with an explanatory note. But in the letter which accompanied the essay we read : To the sublime master from among all the models to be found in German literature, he ventures to offer his mite before the altar of Europe's esteem. Indeed, the sole worth of this homage is to be found in the news that a fuller appreciation of Goethe was now developing in Russia also, and that he was now exerting over the chorus of Ruthenia's Muses an influence which added the final blossom to the garland of immortality belonging to the German prince of poets. Borchardt calls him " our " honoured Goethe, for in his spiritual citizenship of the world he belongs also to Ruthenia. In Borchardt's introduction to Shevirev's article he mentions how Russia, which had hitherto been under French domination in things of the mind, was now turning to England and Germany. The *Moscow Telegraph* and the *Moscow Messenger* had since 1825 and 1827 respectively been promoting this development. No periodical, no journal (not to mention more important works) had failed to mention the greatest bard of Germania with enthusiasm and the deepest respect. Translations were continually appearing of single poems or portions of his works. Knowledge of the German language was constantly spreading, and not only were most of Germany's best modern writers being translated, but also German philosophy and science were being introduced by means of periodicals. The works of Goethe, Schiller, and Klopstock were regarded with religious awe. Byron's wish, to be able to understand the sublime prince of poets in his own language—had become Russia's law. But Russia's intelligentsia wanted not merely to read and understand ; to possess him completely was their desire and intention. As a proof of this, there followed the translation of a version of *Helena* by Shevirev. And a circle had been formed in Russia, the " Friends of Wisdom ", to which Shevirev belonged, and which aimed, mainly through the literary medium of the *Moscow Messenger*, at making German thought known in Russia, and in this way at instilling fresh life and youth into it.

In answer to Borchardt's communication Goethe sent him the following letter :

When one has seriously devoted many years of one's life to cultivating one's own personality and preserving in one's writings the stages in one's own mental processes in order that those who come after may be prepared for what they will encounter, it is extremely pleasant now in one's old age to realise that a goal once distant has been reached, a daring wish has been fulfilled. . . . We in the West have been made familiar with the merits of your poets in various ways, especially by Mr. Bowring, and been able to deduce the existence of a high level of æsthetic culture in the great area over which the Russian language is spoken. Yet, in my own case, I was unprepared to find such deep and sensitive feelings developing in the remote East, feelings which one could not find more charmingly and gracefully expressed in the western lands which have centuries of development behind them. I was astonished to find the tangle of problems presented by my *Helena* solved with such penetration and natural spirituality, although I have grown accustomed to finding that the advances made in recent times must not be measured by the standard of earlier centuries. And a very refreshing contact with Mr. Zhukovsky assured me of the most sympathetic reception and active interest. In your case, Sir, one has every reason to congratulate you on your helpful and stabilising influence on the education of a great nation. . . . The ancient Imperial city which we recently thought lay in ruins has miraculously risen from its ashes, and as you and your worthy friends are to meet at such a remarkable place and at such an epoch-making time, be sure to make the most of your intellectual opportunities. Thus you will, by sincerity and integrity, solve many difficulties and promote much happiness. . . . Give my regards to your honoured friends, continue to exert your influence so that man may learn to know himself, to feel his own worth and dignity, but at the same time to become conscious of the place assigned to him in the world and particularly in his own personal circle.[33]

Borchardt published this letter of Goethe's in the *Moscow Messenger* (1828) both in the original and in a Russian translation, and it aroused a veritable wave of enthusiasm among Russian authors. Pushkin wrote in a letter to the publisher, Pagodin : " The journal surely must justify the expectations of true friends of literature, and the recognition paid to it by the great Goethe. Honour and fame to our noble Shevirev ! You have acted well in reproducing the letter from our German patriarch."

Goethe's *Helena* thus became an epoch-making event for Russian literature. But it was Goethe's last display of activity in the cause of world literature. Almost at the same time as Shevirev's essay, both Ampère in the *Globe* (1827) and Carlyle in the *Foreign Review* (1828) wrote articles on *Helena*. Goethe seized this opportunity to institute a comparison in the spirit of world literature. He did so in letters to Carlyle and Zelter, in conversations with Eckermann, and publicly in *Kunst und Altertum*

(1828) : " Helena in Edinburgh, Paris and Moscow." It is an extremely condensed comparison of immense content :

> The Scot tries to pervade the work, the Frenchman to understand it, the Russian to assimilate it. In so doing Messrs. Carlyle, Ampère and Shevirev have unwittingly exemplified all possible categories of interest in any product of art or nature. At the same time it is obvious that these three types cannot be strictly separated, for each is constantly being used to help out the other. German readers might perhaps combine all three.

Goethe was unwilling to commit himself further. He asked Eckermann to state his views on their conversations in greater detail. This Eckermann no doubt intended to do, but did not achieve.

Now *Helena* is without doubt a " Classical-Romantic Phantasmagoria ", as Goethe himself called it when it was first published, before the posthumous appearance of the Second Part of *Faust*. It represents the realisation of Goethe's aim : the reconciling of the two tendencies in Europe, and naturally this was noted in the Russian essay. Shevirev saw their union particularly in the fact that feminine beauty was here represented as the Middle Ages had worshipped it, endowed with a spirit and a soul ; and that Euphorion who represents Christian poetic art is, except for his lyre and his clothing, a celestial being. *Helena* solves the problem of the birth of Romanticism for, with the transformation of beauty, there was bound to come a change in the art of literature too. In the essay we read that the first half of *Helena* is entirely after the Greek manner, whose secrets the immortal Goethe more than any other writer had made his own. This fact is exemplified by *Iphigenie, Hermann und Dorothea* and other works, and it is plain that the characteristic individuality of Goethe's nature is seen in his Classicism.

In 1829, Shevirev, then aged twenty-three, visited the eighty-year-old Goethe and mounted the staircase of the Goethe-House. It was decorated with casts of Classical statuary and an inscription of the stranger's greeting " Salve ". Goethe came towards him with the " regular features of his Greek profile " and his " Classical, statuesque head ", and, seating himself in his armchair, adopted " the attitude of a Jupiter enthroned ". It seemed to the Russian youth at that moment that the conception of Goethe in terms of Classicism which he had gained from *Helena* was here confirmed by what his eyes were witnessing. (The letter in which Shevirev describes his visit to Goethe is printed in the *Vierteljahresschrift der Goethegesellschaft* for 1937.)

But it was Zhukovsky, the real pioneer of Russian Romanticism, considered in Russia to be a sympathetic translator of Goethe's poéms, who wrote the following poem. It appeared below the picture of Goethe, in the number of the *Moscow Messenger* which contained the *Helena* essay : " Under freedom's boundless sway he hovers, an all-pervading thought, over the Universe—and everything in this world grew clear to him, and ever he remained invincible." [34]

The dedication, in Russian and French, with which Zhukovsky sent a picture by Carus to Goethe, contains an obvious allusion to *Helena* : " Thou, from whose lute a world of wonders flowed, who didst raise the mysterious veil of Creation, animating the past and foretelling the future." (*Vierteljahresschrift der Goethegesellschaft*, 1937.)

Goethe said of the picture that it expressed " the whole of Romanticism " ; and the same might be said of those poems by Zhukovsky, though they refer to *Helena*.

We see, then, that Goethe was instrumental in calling to life a Romantic movement in Russia also, and he had ample evidence of this. The letters of two " Friends of Wisdom " who visited him in Weimar in 1825 show his great interest in Russian literature : these friends were Shevirev, who wrote the *Helena* essay, and Rozhalin who translated *Werther* : " Goethe ", we read in Rozhalin's letter, " is interested in everything that concerns Russia, has read all the available French, German, English and Italian translations of our works, and asked me what had been translated from English and German into Russian . . ." In 1821, the Englishman Bowring published a Russian anthology in English, " through which ", Goethe wrote, " we are brought closer to those distant eastern talents which are separated from us by a language less widely known ". Now Goethe was able to read Zhukovsky's poem, in which he felt a particular interest because the young writer during his first visit to Weimar in 1821 had made a deep impression upon him. A cordial friendship was then formed between Zhukovsky and Goethe. When he left, he presented Goethe with the following poem :

To the Great and Good Man

Author of mighty revelations, I shall guard in my heart the magic of these moments, which fled so happily in your presence. Your magnificently glowing evening sun hints at no decline ! You are a youth upon God's earth and your spirit is still creative as was His.

My heart still hopes to meet you once again here ! Your genius will not soon lay aside the garment familiar to us on earth. In the far North your Muse has made the earth beautiful for me ! And my genius Goethe gave life to my life ! Oh why was it not my fate to meet with you in my youth ? Had I done so, my soul would have kindled its torch at yours ! And a totally different world of marvels would have taken shape around me ; and it may be that posterity would have learned this of me too : he was a poet.

But although he regarded it as prophetic, oriental and profound, Goethe received this valedictory poem somewhat coldly, and he levelled the same criticism against Zhukovsky as he did against the whole Romantic movement in Europe ; namely, that of Romantic subjectivity, and indeed Zhukovsky might have been urged to be more objective.[35] So in this case also we find Goethe experiencing again what he had already experienced with regard to his influence in Europe : he was seen through too Romantic eyes, and had too Romantic an effect.

But it is important to note that the Russian Romantic movement was awakened to a much greater extent by the German Romantic movement itself than by Goethe ; and this was by no means the case in the literatures of Europe. With its achievements in the sphere of religious and national poetry, the German Romantic movement guided Russian literature to its own sources, in this case the Christianity of the Eastern Church. Along with Herder is sponsored the movement in Russia which was prolonged far into the 19th century and was known as Slavophil.

But Goethe's descendants are to be found among the so-called Westerners. In him they saw what they wanted to give to Russian literature : more clarity, roundness, order, form, control. For Tolstoy, Goethe was only the frigid Olympian who cultivated art for its own sake, the example of what literature ought not to be. For Dostoevsky, he was the prophet of the deification of man. But he was seen in quite a different light by a young Russian writer, Alexander Pushkin, who, on account of his good looks, is sometimes called the Russian Goethe and who, in fact, gave Russian literature a Classical bent. He did not begin by doing this, for at first he was completely under the spell of Byron, and the work which is erroneously called the Russian *Faust*, *Eugene Onegin*, is largely imbued with the spirit of Byron. But the change in Pushkin has not been fully understood. It was a change which seemed to have something in common with Carlyle's, for the significance of Pushkin (like that of the English writer) is to be found not so much in his Byronism as in the fact that he overcame Byronism. We cannot claim that Goethe contributed as much to this achievement as he did in Carlyle's case. But in his diary notes Pushkin writes : " Goethe exerted a great influence over Byron. Faust troubled the imagination of *Childe Harold's* creator. Byron attempted more than once to wrestle with this giant of Romantic poetry—and each time, like Jacob, he was lamed." Pushkin rejected all comparison of Byron's Faustian drama *Manfred*, and of *The Deformed Transformed*, with Goethe's *Faust*. He criticised Byron's subjectivity and his extravagant individualism ; but he considered *Faust* to be the greatest creation of the poetic spirit, and it seemed to him to be as representative of modern poetry as the *Iliad* is of Classical antiquity.[36] Pushkin himself wrote a tail-piece to Goethe's *Faust*, a scene between Faust and Mephistopheles in which the latter derides Faust for his longing for Gretchen, when even in the supreme moment of passion he experienced a feeling of weariness. It is not quite clear what special aim underlay this Faust-scene. It recalls so vividly one of the scenes in Goethe's *Faust* that one might be tempted to think of it as a translation or version of it. It does not fill any gap in *Faust*, or supply any needful addition. It may only belong to a project for a complete translation or version of *Faust*, and be a study for something of the sort. The feeling which pervades Pushkin's *Faust*, that everything is superfluous and wearisome, no longer corresponded to his own mood or philosophy, or to his conception of Goethe's *Faust*. He notes in one place in his diaries that in his poem " The Demon " he sought to represent the spirit of denial or doubt which the great Goethe was right in calling the enemy of mankind ; he wanted to show its unhappy influence on the age, and to overcome it. The poem runs as follows :

In those days, when all was new, all life's impressions, the glances of maidens and the murmur of the woods, and in the night the song of the nightingale ; when noble feelings, freedom, fame and love, and the inspired arts made the pulse beat faster—in those days a genius of ill-will began to haunt me in secret, suddenly darkening the hours of hopes and happiness. Our meetings were full of sadness. His smile, his mysterious look, his keenly caustic speech poured cold poison into my soul. He tempted Providence, called all beauty a dream, despised inspiration, cast doubt on love and freedom, looked on life with scorn ; and there was nothing in the whole of nature that he blessed.[37]

All these facts tend to make one doubt that Pushkin intended to limit himself to this one scene between Faust and Mephistopheles. He was too near to Goethe for that.

Towards European Romanticism Pushkin adopted an attitude rather like Goethe's own, and it is quite possible that in fact Goethe trained and guided his development towards the style of Classicism, the beauty and harmony, the proportion and simplicity—to those qualities, in fact, on account of which he is often called the Russian Goethe ; and it may be that in this was Goethe helped to overcome Byronism in Russian literature as in others.

In the same year that Pushkin's *Faust* appeared, Goethe made him a present of his pen, with these lines :

> Was ich mich auch sonst erkühnt,
> Jeder würde froh mich lieben,
> Hätt' ich treu und frei geschrieben
> All das Lob, das du verdient.

We cannot say whether Goethe knew of Pushkin's *Faust*. It may be that he heard of it from Zhukovsky, from whom in any case he gained an idea of Pushkin's works. Zhukovsky may have translated some of Pushkin's poems for him. Goethe's present reached Pushkin through Zhukovsky, and in this way a personal relationship was established between the greatest writers of Russia and Germany ; but it must remain a matter for Russian research to give a final answer to the question whether any cultural, educative influence was exerted by Goethe on Pushkin.

How high Goethe's reputation and influence now stood in Russia can be measured by two poems on his death [38] : these poems are the work of two important Russian writers and tell us much of Goethe as seen through Russian eyes ; there is not a single word in them about the youth of Goethe during which he exerted the most vital influence on all other literatures— except on the writings of Carlyle. These two men honour the mature, wise, fully developed Goethe : one of them is Baratynsky, whom Pushkin describes as the greatest of Russian elegiac poets, a profound, prophetic thinker. He promises the dead poet everlasting fame because in his lifetime he had already attained to unity with the All, and had endowed his temporal shape with an immortal content. As a serene spirit, then, no longer troubled by any remnant of mortality, he can soar towards the endless light. We cannot but be reminded by all this of the Second Part of *Faust*, although the Writer could not have known it at that time.

The second poem is by Tyutchev, one of Russia's greatest

lyric poets who, fired by the fundamental idea of Goethe's philosophy of nature, creates this magnificent image : like the leaf, the Urphänomen of the plant, as a single man, as a leaf from the tree of mankind, as the Urphänomen of man, Goethe falls ripe and unwithered from the tree of universal human life.

Within the whole scope of the European conception of Goethe, there is nothing that comes so near Goethe's essential nature as do these poems.

It was Uvarov who delivered the memorial address on Goethe at the general meeting of the Saint Petersburg Imperial Academy of Sciences.[39]

* * *

Goethe's influence on Polish literature naturally differed from his effect on Russia. Poland lies entirely within the civilisation of western Europe, so here, as in the other literatures of Europe, Goethe was not honoured as the reviver of antiquity, the Greek poet, but was counted among the most important stimulating influences upon Polish Romanticism. His influence went hand in hand with that of Byron. It was in the first place *Werther* and *Faust* that fathered the Polish Romantic movement, which so far did not differ from the Romantic movement of any other European people. But it was natural that in Polish literature the seeds Goethe sowed should develop in a different way and according to the specific national character. German Romanticism, to which—outside Germany—Goethe was also reckoned as belonging, led every literature in Europe back to its own national sources. In this lay its real significance—although it did not fully correspond with Goethe's ideas—for those whose cosmopolitan outlook led them to realise that Romantic nationalism was threatening to divide the peoples of Europe. Polish Romanticism bore a different aspect, because Poland's situation at the time was different from that of other nations. Poland was under Russian domination, and all its aspirations were directed towards liberation from this national martyrdom. This was bound to give a special character to Polish Romanticism, and to distinguish it from the Romanticism of other nations. German Romanticism too, of course, is connected with Napoleon's foreign domination. But the German Romanticists took refuge from the sufferings of real life in dreams and tales of the past. And, although they quickened the legends and songs of their people with a view to rousing the national consciousness of the Germans and of promoting German unity and preparing for the liberation, they did so with a constant backward look. Italian Romanticism cannot be understood without reference to Austrian oppression. But that filled it with a topical modern spirit. It was different in Poland. What gave Polish Romanticism its individual character was this : that in the minds of the Polish people Poland's martyrdom was merged in Christ's martyrdom, that the national liberation was identified with the liberation of mankind, that the vision of a happy future for Poland was also their vision of a happier world. In short, Polish Romanticism bears a Messianic character.

Goethe had played an important part in this movement. He learned from a Polish officer who visited him in 1813 that almost all his works were known both to the speaker and throughout Poland, and that many had been or were being translated. His guest says that when he heard this, Goethe sent for some " French, cosmopolitan champagne " and drank with him the health of the writers and literatures of the two nations, German and Polish. In his important manifesto on Classicism and Romanticism and the spirit of Polish poetry (1818), one of the first works of Polish Romanticism, Casimir Brodzinsky, the translator of *Werther*, pays tribute to Goethe as the representative of Romantic poetry. In his view this is characterised by national, popular and fantastic qualities. Polish literature was subsequently dominated by the struggle which broke out all over Europe between Classicism and Romanticism.

Victory came for Romantic poetry with Adam Mickiewicz's *Ballads and Romances* which appeared in 1822. In the preface to the work, *On Romantic Poetry*, Mickiewicz renounced Classicism ; at the same time Goethe was put forward as the representative of Romanticism. The same collection contains a poem " Romanticism " : a girl imagines that she has been in the arms of her lover, who is dead, and the people believe in the reality of her experience. An older man declares it is trickery and superstition, but the poet defends the truth of what the people believe. He considers that feeling and belief are truer than reason and scientific knowledge. Mickiewicz had formerly been completely under the influence of Voltaire and of French Classicism. In him therefore we see the typical transformation which is noticeable all over Europe. It is notable also that Goethe and Byron were the two writers who exerted the strongest influence on the Polish writer, and that Goethe's *Werther* and *Faust* made the deepest impression on him. (Thousands of copies of the Polish translation (1820) of *Werther* were sold in the space of a few days.) In the second and fourth parts of his chief work, the *Requiem*, which appeared in 1823 before the other parts, the influence is unmistakable. Indeed, the fourth part is often known as the Polish *Werther*. A man whose love led to his suicide appears to the people in the form of a ghost, and pours forth in bitter lamentations the remembrance of the happiness, once tasted and now lost, of his love. This work sprang from the writer's personal experience. But what gives this shadow of *Werther* its Romantic and national individuality is that it is connected with the ancient Polish popular tradition of ancestral rites. It thereby becomes a strange mixture of popular custom and modern sentimentality. In 1827 there appeared Mickiewicz's essay " Goethe and Byron " in which he deals with the two most important precursors of his own work. In addition he translated some of Goethe's poems, among them " The Wanderer " and " Mignon ".

When at last in 1829 the writer, who had been banished to Russia, was able to travel abroad—he was never to see his native land again—he visited Goethe in Weimar. They had already made contact. Mickiewicz already possessed a present from Goethe : a pen which he had used for the first time and which he sent him in 1828 with the following lines :

> Dem Dichter widm' ich mich, der sich erprobt
> Und unsre Freundin heiter gründlich lobt.

Mickiewicz was the son-in-law of the Polish pianist Szymanowska, whose inspired playing dispelled in the form of tears Goethe's suffering caused by his love for the young Ulrike von Leventzow. The last part of his *Trilogy of Passion* has immortalised this experience in poetic form. It was Szymanowska who first told Goethe of Mickiewicz and led him to read the German translation of his novel *Conrad Wallenrod*. With this introduction and recommendation Mickiewicz was thus no stranger when he first came to Goethe's house. Goethe at once told him he knew he (Mickiewicz) was one of the pioneers in the new direction which every literature in Europe was now in process of taking. Goethe knew, too, from experience, how hard it was to swim against the stream. Mickiewicz replied that Goethe himself illustrated how men of great genius had the power to draw the current towards them. And on his part he, Mickiewicz, who owed him so much, was able to help Goethe by tracing for him at his request the whole course of Polish

literature, of which Goethe knew very little, for he knew no
Slavonic language. But, as he said, " l'homme a tant à faire
dans cette vie ". Of Polish literature, then very little translated,
he knew only the novel by Mickiewicz already mentioned, and
an Almanach which Odyniec (who had come with Mickiewicz
to Weimar) had edited, and which contained extracts from
contemporary Polish writers, Goethe appeared to be specially
interested in what Mickiewicz was able to tell him about Polish
folk-songs.

Their conversation, however, reveals a difference which is also
seen in their works. Goethe held the view that poetry, and
indeed all literature, in striving with ever-increasing urgency
towards general truth, must necessarily acquire an increasingly
general character. Mickiewicz, however, stressed the need for
retaining the national character of the works. And the Polish
writer was present when David, the French sculptor, refei ed
to the question of national sympathies and antipathies,
Goethe gave his views on the subject. He pointed out how
the inherent differences in conceptions and feelings, or rather
in ways of conceiving and of feeling, which characterise whole
races as well as individuals and are the result of prejudices or
pride or mistaken opinions or consummate ignorance, are apt
gradually to form impassable barriers which divide mankind,
as mountain ranges or seas isolate geographical regions. This,
Goethe said, imposes on men of more advanced culture the
duty of working in a spirit of moderation and understanding
to establish possibilities of contact between peoples, such as
facilitating navigation or opening up roads through the mountains.
Free trade in ideas and feelings would enrich and increase the
general welfare of mankind as much as an exchange of com-
modities. The only reason why this has not so far been the case
is that in intercourse between nations there are none of the
established moral laws and principles that safeguard personal
contacts in private life, and harmonise them. It is not known
whether Mickiewicz made any reply to these ideas ; but it is
certain that he could not share them. And on the question of
Faust, which he saw in the Weimar theatre, he said nothing to
his friend and met Goethe's question with a curious and marked
silence. Was his mind already occupied with the idea of a work
suggested by *Faust*, and was he already conscious that this Polish
Faust was bound to have a totally different character from
Goethe's ?

There are many signs of the Polish writer's readiness to be fired by Goethe's *Faust*. Does the reason for this lie in the fact that Poland was then torn between national pride and utter impotence? Or in the feelings of homelessness and grief for a fatherland in servitude? At any rate it is sufficiently remarkable that the first Faust-music is the work of the Polish Prince Radziwill. Written in 1810, this music was played when *Faust* was produced in 1819 at the court in Berlin, and it has remained the traditional theatre-accompaniment to *Faust*. But the most representative example is of course Mickiewicz. In 1831, when the Polish revolt collapsed and his Catholic faith was thereby subject to a severe test, he wrote the third part of his *Requiem*. This appeared in 1833 after Goethe's death, and has often been called the Polish *Faust*, the fourth part being known as the Polish *Werther*. But this work, which does indeed recall *Faust*, reminds one also of Byron ; and, in her essay on the " drame fantastique ", George Sand compares Goethe's *Faust* with Byron's *Manfred* and with Mickiewicz's *Conrad*. Their subject, she says, is man's struggle with God, in Goethe's case for Truth, in Byron's for the Power to Forget and in Mickiewicz's for Freedom. And here she does indeed light upon the Polish character of this work written in the Faust-spirit. For longing for the liberation of the fatherland is the keynote of the modern literature of Poland. And so we have Conrad, a poet, whose aim like Byron's is to use art to promote the freedom and happiness of his own land and of all mankind, revolting against God and calling him to account in the matter of Poland's fate. But God does not grant freedom to His people. Just as the poet is about to curse the deity, he collapses. But the devout, humble, Monk Peter sees in a dream Poland's future freedom and happiness. And at the Last Judgment Conrad is rescued by angels, for it was through love of his people that he sinned. Here we see the influence of the Second Part of *Faust*, and Mickiewicz took the opportunity of inserting a direct expression of homage to Goethe. But still there remains a highly characteristic difference. This consists not only in the topicality (though this is veiled in mysticism), the time-content, the smouldering rage against Russia to be found in the Polish *Faust*, but in its out-and-out political spirit. Here we are concerned, not as in *Faust* with the development of human personality, but with the fate of a nation. Faust's universally human content is replaced by the idea of nationality, Faust's longing for limitless freedom of the spirit by the longing for political freedom. True, in Mickiewicz's work it is the poet himself who is the hero, as in *Faust* ; and his Titanism, his revolt against God, constitutes as in *Faust* the drama of a soul's development. But it is the soul of the Polish nation, its martyrdom, its longing for freedom, and the hero is merely its representative. Even Mickiewicz's modern epic *Taddäus* (1838) which the writer himself declares was stimulated by *Hermann und Dorothea*—and the affinity is unmistakable—reveals the same difference. Not only does this idyllic picture of rural life in Old Poland differ, in its setting among the nobility, from Goethe's middle-class epic, not only does it recreate a lost world while Goethe's work deals with his own day. Much more important is the fact that this epic, which begins in such an idyllic strain, outgrows the idyll and develops into a national epic in which we are concerned no longer with a love-story but with the antagonism between Poland and Russia. And Goethe, although he gives his idyll a background of world-history, that of the French Revolution, keeps it simply as a background against which stand his human figures, true of any age.

It is reported that in 1832 Mickiewicz translated the " Prologue in Heaven " and the whole of the First Part of *Faust*. Even if this is true, the translation is now unknown. But Mickiewicz makes Tuardovsky, a Polish Faust-figure of the 16th century, into the hero of a work. His is the story of a man who sells himself to the Devil for the sake of the pleasures of this world, who manages to save himself by singing a hymn, but is forced to hover between Heaven and earth until the Day of Judgment. It is perhaps justifiable to assume that Mickiewicz intended to modify this story by making his hero claim the Devil's help for some higher national cause.

The Faustian spirit which Mickiewicz roused in Polish literature was especially active in the thirties ; the most obvious example of its activity is Krazinsky's *Undivine Comedy* (1834). It must be admitted that in this Faust-inspired work there is no question of Poland's national problem. In it we feel the spirit of " young Europe ", and of the outbreak of revolutions all over Europe, for here it is a question of a common fate, of the future of the European community. It is noticeable too, in French and in English literature, that Goethe's *Faust* undergoes this metamorphosis in the works which were inspired by the original. Faust's purely human problem becomes the problem of a society stirred to its depths by the Revolution ; mankind's path into the future is pointed out ; all who tread it are beset by agony and trials. The Faustian question has become the social question. But the Polish writer gives a different answer to this question from that of the rest of Europe. His infernal vision is this : that the social warfare between aristocracy and the masses is leading Europe into an abyss, into a complete void, over which at the end Christ's Cross is to rise. It is the lovelessness of the European world that Krazinsky sees on both sides. The aristocrat lives in a Romantic dream, in delusion and imagination, and this leads him to think not of mankind but only of himself ; while the people forget love in their determination to gain equality. So the Faust-inspired work by this Polish writer differs from the works produced in England and France and animated by the idea of progress. But, although Krazinsky at least approaches the outlook of western Europe in making of his Faust-problem the social problem of the 19th century, he returns in his *Irydion* (1836) to the essential theme of Polish Romanticists. The hero of this work (a son of Greece and of Germany, and in this respect an irresistible reminder of Euphorion the son of Faust and Helen), makes use of Christianity to aid his revenge on Rome for its subjugation of Hellas. Tempted by Satan, who in the figure of Masinissa acts as his adviser, he performs dreadful and criminal actions in the name of God. But the writer's last vision shows us Irydion's rescue on the Day of Judgment. God decrees that he shall himself work out his own salvation by taking on a new life in which he will free Poland and become the Messiah of his people. Here Krazinsky has once more sounded the keynote of Polish literature. Euphorion, the spirit of heavenly poetry, who seeks to acquire instead the martial spirit, as Byron did in joining the war for the liberation of Greece, is doomed to destruction. But Irydion will lead the fight for the liberation of Poland. It is obvious that in this Polish work Goethe's *Faust* has undergone a complete transformation ; and yet its stimulus remains unmistakable. *Faust*, indeed, reveals its inexhaustible depths of symbolism in its capacity for constant fresh interpretations ; and its form which, passing on from age to age and people to people, each time animated by a different conrent and a different spirit, everywhere inspires new poetic activity. *The Tragedy of Man* by the Hungarian writer Madách (1861) belongs also to this tradition.

In 1830, when Goethe, proposed by Brodzinsky, became an honorary member of the " Societas Regia Philomatica

Varsaviensis ", he expressed his thanks in these words : he had already happily attained his aim of being of some use to his own nation and of deserving its notice ; but it was an unexpected joy to him to find the influence of his activities extended to the peoples of other lands which differed from his in race and language.[40]   Slovacki, Poland's great poet, declared that this almost unanimous election of Goethe completed the victory of Romanticism.

CHAPTER 17

WORLD POETRY

Goethe's efforts in the cause of world poetry are the common ground on which the influences he experienced and those he exerted mingle. World poetry acted as a stimulus on him, and he contributed more than anyone else to its effectiveness as a means of intercourse between the nations.

The difference between world literature and world poetry in Goethe's use of the words was dealt with in the first part of this book. And world poetry and folk-poetry are not identical. The poetic gift is independent of rank or education and therefore, as Goethe once said, it belongs to the king and the knight as much as to the people. But the nearer it is to a simple and natural life, the more genuine it is. That is why folk-poetry is the purest form in which world poetry finds expression. It is also the most striking proof of the existence of world poetry, because here it flourishes as a natural poetic form without assistance from education. Although world literature and world poetry ought not to be confused with each other, yet they are inextricably bound together. World poetry is one of the most vital phenomena of world literature ; that is to say, the mediating activity between the nations must first be seen in the form of world poetry, the folk-poetry of the people. For in it the character of every people stands out most clearly, and through it the peoples can learn to know one another. On the other hand it can bind the peoples together by bringing them to realise that the gift of poetry is common to them all. Goethe's conception of folk-poetry was that it gives expression to the characteristics of individual nations, and that is why he often speaks of " characteristic folk-poems " or " national songs ". At the same time this characteristic quality is only the national expression of human nature. So folk-poetry is at the same time the poetry of a nation and the poetry of mankind, and there is only one poetry : genuine poetry. Its outward forms differ according to circumstances among the various peoples and ages. This makes world poetry of great importance to world literature, which aims at making world poetry known to the different peoples.

We know from *Dichtung und Wahrheit* that Goethe owed to Herder his first realisation of poetry as the universal endorsement of every nation ; and the importance of this conception cannot be estimated. At the least, it upset every canon of art, every code of rules, and it formed the basis of Goethe's humanism. In collecting German folk-songs at Herder's suggestion, young Goethe was as yet far from any mediation in the cause of world literature ; his aim was limited to bringing his own people to know themselves. But it was the beginning of his activity in this direction, and was to develop later in new directions. A people must know itself before it can know other peoples, and this in turn adds to self-knowledge by making comparison possible. In 1806, Goethe warmly praised *Des Knaben Wunderhorn*, the collection of folk-songs made by Arnim and Brentano which was dedicated to him. He then asked the publishers to find out without delay what other nations (the English in the greatest degree, the French less, the Spaniards in a different sense and the Italians scarcely at all) possessed in the way of similar songs, and to publish them in the original and in translations. We must remember that Herder's first collection of folk-songs contained only Germanic—that is to say German, English and Scandinavian—songs, but his second collection included the whole of Europe. The collection which appeared after his death and became widely known under the title *Stimmen der Völker in Liedern* (a title not supplied by Herder) embraces the entire world.

In all parts of Europe affected by Romanticism, the national folk-songs were being collected and the peoples made known to each other in this way ; and apart from Herder's work this can be attributed mainly to Goethe's instigation. He liked and studied characteristic folk-poetry and tried to foster it in every way.[41] His own example and constant encouragement assisted the collecting of folk-songs among the nations of Europe. This was proved to him by the numerous examples and collections that were sent to him in manuscript before they had appeared in print. He welcomed and made use of them all. All this helped to develop his idea of world literature, and it is to be noted that the expression " world poetry " precedes " world literature ". We find it first in the essay, written in 1826, on " Serbian Poems ". It is not mere chance that it occurs here. For it was Serbian folk-songs that first confirmed his conviction (partly due to Herder) that there is no one universal world poetry which takes differing forms according to circumstances. " Neither content nor form need necessarily be handed down : wherever the sun shines, it is bound to develop." Among the folk-songs sent to him from every quarter of the globe, Goethe regarded with special interest those which came from the East. Songs reached him " from Olympus to the Baltic and ever inland towards the North-East ". It was particularly the Slav people whose folk-poetry helped him to realise the existence and nature of world poetry ; and the diffusion of this he considered one of his most important services to the cause of world literature.

We can of course trace back to Herder in the first place the rise of these songs of the Slav peoples. His remarks on the Slav peoples in his *Ideas towards a Philosophy of the History of Mankind* made a profound impression, and indeed mark an era in their history by encouraging a Slavonic revival. Herder writes as follows : These nations inhabit what could be the most fruitful zone of Europe if it were fully cultivated and opened up for trade. Therefore it can be presumed that legislation and politics will help to replace the warlike spirit by regular industry and peaceful trade among the nations. You too, then, long suppressed but once industrious and happy peoples, roused at last from your long sleep of indolence, freed from your chains of servitude, will take action. You will develop your prosperous lands from the Adriatic to the Carpathian Mountains, from the Don to the Mulde, where you will be able to hold your ancient festivals of peaceful industry and trade. We have from several quarters received articles of use and beauty made by this people ; it is therefore to be hoped that others will supply what these lack, will collect the gradually vanishing remnant of their customs, songs and legends, and that finally a history of this race as a whole will be supplied, helping to complete the picture of mankind.

Herder's call was echoed throughout the Slavonic literatures. But, in addition to the efforts of the Heidelberg Romanticists, Goethe too played an important part in the rise of the Slav folk-songs. His influence is particularly obvious in the revival of the Serbian songs, and in their turn these songs had a great influence on Goethe's idea of world poetry and his efforts to foster it. In his youth he had given a wonderful rendering of a Serbian " Morlakian " folk-song—not, indeed, from the original but from a French translation. This was the " Lament of the Noble Wife of Asan Aga ", which appeared in 1778 among Herder's folk-songs and may be considered an event of European import-ance. Goethe admits that he never mastered any of the Serbian dialects, and was thus cut off from the original literature of these

great nations.   But he never lost sight of the value of those works
which reached him.   And his intuitive genius made it possible
for him when translating the " Lament " to render it with " a
feeling for the rhythm and a consideration for the phrasing of
the original ".   Once, some young Serbs in Vienna were invited
to give some idea of their own national songs, but they turned
down the proposal.   They could not imagine that anyone could
really admire their artless songs which were despised by men of
education in their own country.   They feared, moreover, that
the intention was to sneer at the Serbs, to humiliate them by
contrasting their simple rural poems with the correct poetry of
Germany, which was composed according to the rules of art,
and in this way to hold up to ridicule the uncultured state of
their nation.   To persuade them, however, that their type of
poetry really was appreciated, they were shown this " Lament "
of Goethe's.   This greatly pleased them, and led them to supply
that song, among others, in the original.   " Thus do goodwill
and good sense bring about happy results."   Goethe himself
never tired of making the acquaintance of new Serbian poems in
translations with which Hungarian friends supplied him at his
own request.   But these were only isolated songs, and could
not give him any complete picture of this type of poetry.   Even
in 1814, when Wuk Stephanovich Karadjich sent him a collection
of a hundred Serbian folk-songs along with a manuscript translation, he could form no complete estimate.   In the West, affairs
were becoming more and more confused.   He took refuge in
the Far East, for the *West-Eastern Divan* was beginning to occupy
his thoughts, and for a while he lived in blissful seclusion remote
from West and North alike.   But Slavonic interests prevailed
again.   In 1814 Wuk followed up his first collection of songs with
a Serbian Grammar, and in 1818 with a Serbian-German-Latin
dictionary as well as a new edition of the Grammar.   In 1823 he
began to publish his great collection of Serbian folk-songs in the
original.   This collection grew during Goethe's lifetime to three
volumes, and after his death a fourth was added.   In October
1823 Wuk visited Goethe in Weimar, and in November he sent
him a number of prose translations of Serbian songs.   Of these
translations by Wuk, " The Death of Kralewitsch Marko "
appeared in 1824 in *Kunst und Altertum*.   And now Jakob Grimm
learned the Serbian language, translated Wuk's Grammar in
1824, and added a preface to it.   This preface provided the
material for Goethe's article " Serbian Songs " (1825), although

the review of Wuk's collection of lyrics in the Göttingen *Gelehrte Anzeigen* in 1823 is probably not, as was long supposed, the work of Jakob Grimm. But it was Grimm who made translations from the collection in the trochaic measure of the originals, and sent one of these rhythmic translations to Goethe, who published it in 1823 in *Kunst und Altertum* (" The Division of the Inheritance "). Towards the end of 1823 Goethe set about writing his first article for *Kunst und Altertum* on " Serbian Literature ". It consisted chiefly of an extract from the review which had appeared in the Göttingen *Gelehrte Anzeigen*, and Goethe withheld it from publication. But in 1824, when he read in manuscript the series of metric translations of Serbian folk-songs by Therese Albertine Luise von Jakob, known as Talvy, he decided to write the conclusive article " Serbian Songs " which appeared in 1825 in *Kunst und Altertum* and drew attention of all Europe to these lyrics. Talvy's translations, which appeared in 1825–26, included the following dedicatory poem written in gratitude for Goethe's help and co-operation as shown in his letters to her : " A hint from you called them into being. Perhaps their puzzling words may say nothing to many ; their voice will speak and not be understood ; but your approval suffices and is surety enough that they have both poetic beauty and human truth."

The facts are these : in 1824 when Talvy sent some translations from Wuk's collection in manuscript to Goethe as " an offering of the most heartfelt admiration ", he encouraged her to amplify and publish the series. And he advised her about the choice, translation and arrangement of the poems. Goethe's article, after a general consideration of " individual folk-poetry " and an account of Serbian lyrics, concludes with an announcement of Talvy's translations which had not yet appeared, and with remarks that clearly show Goethe's motive for occupying himself with world poetry ; it was his interest in world literature. He stresses the particular fitness of the German language for purposes of translation, which enables it to keep close to the original. Goethe admired the exquisite themes of these Serbian lyrics, especially the theme of love. He obviously was more in sympathy with the love poems than with the heroic poems which must often have appeared to him too wild and uncouth. Among the love poems he found some " which can be classed with the Song of Solomon—and that is saying a good deal ". In connection with this article, a conversation took place with Riemer and Eckermann about the themes of Serbian poems ; Riemer

remarked that Germans had already used these themes before
meeting them in Serbian lyrics, whereupon Goethe replied :
" The world is always constant, and conditions are repeated ;
one people lives, loves and feels like another, so why should not one
poet write like another ?   The situations of real life are the same,
so why should the situations in poems not be the same ? "   In
1826 Goethe announced the appearance of the second part of
Talvy's work, together with Rhesa's *Lettish Songs* and Amelie
von Helvig's translation of Tegnèr's *Frithiof Saga*.   In an essay
on " Serbian Poems " Goethe said that the translations by Grimm
and Talvy, through which we could already look upon these
lyrics as our own German property, had now been joined by a
third, an excellent translation by Wilhelm Gerhard.   He also
announced a coming new collection under the title *Wila*.   Translations by Gerhard were printed in *Kunst und Altertum*.   *The
Social Songs of the Serbs*, which Gerhard translated, convinced
Goethe anew, by their resemblance to the lyrics of France and in
particular to those of Béranger, that there was one universal
world poetry.   And this is where the expression first occurs.
The essay on " The most Recent Serbian Literature " deals with
the poem " Serbianca " (written in the style of the ancient
heroic songs) by Simeon Milutinovich, who had supplied Goethe
with exhaustive details of the content of his work.   In this essay
Goethe urges Gerhard to translate, and expresses the hope that
Grimm, Talvy and Gerhard may continue the work of interpret-
ing Serbian literature.   In 1825 Goethe had the pleasure of
reporting that the German effort in the matter of the Serbian
lyrics was being emulated in the other literatures of Europe.
He announced their translation into English : *Serbian Popular
Poetry, translated by John Bowring*, London, 1827.   As early as
1821 Bowring had published a Russian anthology, and Goethe
now recommended these two collections to all who were looking
to the East and studying Slavonic poetic art.   In the same year,
Goethe announced the versions of Serbian lyrics which had
appeared in France in 1827 under the title *La Guzla, poésies
illyriques* and were said to be genuine ancient lyrics, but were
written by Mérimée.   " It is not long ", writes Goethe, " since
the French began to show eager interest in foreign methods of
writing, and granted them certain æsthetic values.   And it is
only a short time since they also began to show any inclination
to make use of these foreign forms in their own productions.
But what is new and strange is that they appear behind the mask

of foreign nations." It is unlikely that Goethe had heard of the Czech translation of Serbian lyrics by Hanka (1817). Here we see the seed, which young Goethe had once sown with his translation of the Lament, now flowering abundantly. These " extraordinary productions of our South-Eastern neighbours, which we have watched gradually burgeoning, and yielding fruit " had become the property of Germany and then of Europe. " The dam is broken that separated us from Serbian literature ; it flows in on us in a full tide. " Serbian poetry, Goethe stated in his essay " National Poetry ", has so spread among the literatures of the West, that it needs no further recommendation.

Hand in hand with Goethe's influence in furthering Serbian folk-poetry there went his preoccupation with other national lyrics, eastern though not Slavonic, particularly those of modern Greece. These were near to them and in relationship and, according to Goethe's view, were inferior in poetic value, but they did much to confirm his conviction of the existence of a world poetry. He at once realised (we learn from a conversation he had with the mythologists Creuzer and Daub) that the spirit of these lyrics is a combination of that of the Scandinavian and Scottish races with that of the South and of ancient mythology. Goethe first read them in 1815, in manuscript, in a collection of modern Greek lyrics in the original, with translations by Natzmer and Haxthausen. In the same year, when Haxthausen read some of them in Wiesbaden, Goethe strongly urged him to publish them and promised his support. The Greek struggle for freedom from the Turkish yoke, which roused the enthusiasm of Europe, naturally increased the interest in modern Greek poetry. But it was from France that Goethe got the impetus that decided him to make his own translations. For in 1822 Buchon sent him " as head of the modern school of poetry and as the only man beside Thomas Moore qualified to translate the poems of modern Greece " the most remarkable of all these lyrics, which he had had translated into French by a Greek. Of these Goethe actually translated six which he published in *Kunst und Altertum* (1823) " Heroic Songs of Modern Greece and the Epirus ". He added to these a seventh from another source, " Charon ", which seemed to him from the point of view of poetry to rank highest of all the modern Greek lyrics, and which he also recommended to sculptors as a subject. (Later there appeared " Modern Greek Love Scholia ".) The French had indeed forestalled the Germans who " for years had been groping about at it " ; for in 1824 Fauriel's *Chants populaires de la Grèce moderne* appeared. This was a collection of originals with a French translation and critical notes. But Goethe, though doubtless glad to benefit by Fauriel's explanations, declared that the gain was not in other respects a great one, for the finest and most important poems were in his own already published translation.[42] In 1828 Goethe had several opportunities of studying modern Greek literature and of giving his views on it. He wrote on Rizo Néroulos's lectures in Geneva : *Cours de Littérature grecque moderne* (1827), which were translated by Christian Müller ; on Iken's *Leukothea* (which appeared in 1825), a collection of letters (by a man of Greek birth) on the political structure, literature and poetic art of modern Greece ; also on the *Eunomia* (1827), examples of modern Greek poetry and prose in the original, and in translations taken from English and French works or dictated by native Greeks ; and finally on *Modern Greek Folk Songs* in the original and in a German translation by K. Th. Kind, which formed the third volume of the *Eunomia* (1827). " This is a most welcome and useful little book, another step in our progress towards an appreciation of the merits of modern Greek national poetry." The eastern national poems, we read in the notes to this critical survey, " stretching from South to North, are very distinctive ; and ought to be regarded as precious stones of different kinds, each having its own form, texture and colour ".

In former years Goethe had done much to help the rebirth of Greek antiquity, and his *Iphigenie* had been translated in 1818 by the Greek Johannes Papadopoulos, who also visited him in Weimar. Now we see how in his old age Goethe also helped the rebirth of modern Greece, and how he endowed its poetry, so different from that of antiquity, with the mission of establishing intercourse between the peoples in the cause of world literature.

To the Serbian and modern Greek were added the Bohemian folk-songs. Since his journey to take the waters in Bohemia, Goethe's interest in this country had been vivid. He was pleased to note how its wealth of scientific and æsthetic education was beginning to spread, and what lively interest was felt there, as elsewhere in Europe, in the nation's past. Of particular importance in Goethe's case was the publication by Hanka in 1818 of the *Königinhof Manuscript*, which soon appeared also in a German translation by Svoboda. Goethe, like others, failed to see at the time that these so-called " Old Bohemian " poems were a forgery.

Like others he regarded them as priceless relics of an early age ; and he revised one of the songs " with boldness both as poet and critic, by restoring the correct order of the verses ". The resulting poem, " Das Sträusschen. Old Bohemian ", appeared in 1823 in *Kunst und Altertum.* The monthly journal which the " Society of the Bohemian National Museum " had published since 1827 in German and in Czech, aimed at furthering an exchange and interaction between German and Bohemian poetry by means of translations from both languages ; and Goethe saw in this a gateway " through which they can come out to us and we pass in to them ". In this journal Goethe was able to read many genuine lyrics belonging to Slavonic, namely Bohemian, Moravian and Slovakian folk-poetry. He now drew the attention of the German public also to the " Bohemian poetry " and " Old-Bohemian poems " to be found in the *Königinhof Manuscript* and in this monthly journal. He also earnestly begged the Society to continue its publication of the ancient and modern poems of Bohemia, for this was the surest means by which it could keep in touch with the greater public of Germany. Goethe was also helpful in his criticisms of Karl Egon Ebert's modernisations of Old-Bohemian poems, of the sonnets of the Slovenian poet Kollár, who in 1817 visited him in Weimar and whom he urged to collect and translate Slovenian folk-songs, as he had heard much of their variety and beauty. He also encouraged Gerhard, the translator of Serbian poems, to devote all his energies to the Slavonic languages, and to translate Bohemian poems. (The long essay : " Monthly Journal of the Society of the Bohemian National Museum " which appeared in the 1830 annals of scientific criticism is not the work of Goethe himself ; it was completed and executed under his headings by Varnhagen.)

Goethe received many tributes from Bohemia, expressing gratitude for his stimulating and helpful activity. He was at once elected an Honorary Member of the Society. The journal contains a poem by Ludwig Zeitteles entitled " Goethe's Recovery " (1823). In the *Annals of the Bohemian Museum,* which from 1830 replaced the monthly journal, " Goethe's utterances on Bohemian literature " were referred to with pride and gratitude. But it was in young Joseph Stanislaus Zauper, later to become Bohemia's most important pedagogue, that Goethe found a disciple and prophet who gave him fresh youth ; and, if he got from Bohemia a new understanding of folk-poetry, he in his turn awoke in his young friend appreciation of the ideals of Greek antiquity. In 1832 Goethe received Machácek's Bohemian translation of his *Iphigenie*.

Lithuanian folk-songs, too, played their part in the formation of Goethe's theory of world poetry and contributed to it in the spirit of world literature. As early as 1782 he had incorporated some of Herder's translations of Lettish folk-songs in his short drama *Die Fischerin*, and he had gradually amassed a considerable collection of these thoroughly Germanised poems which, like much else, he allowed to lie fallow, hoping for what now actually took place. In 1825 he received the collection *Dainos* (published by Rhesa) of Lithuanian folk-songs. This realised one more of his wishes and he reviewed the collection in *Kunst und Altertum* (1829). A lengthy draft of this notice also contained the following general reflection on world poetry :

> I am often surprised when I see folk-songs being regarded with so much astonishment and admiration. There is only one kind of poetry : everything else is an approximation or a pretence. Poetic talent is granted to the peasant as much as to the knight ; with each it is a matter of his realising his condition and dealing with it worthily. In doing this, simplicity of circumstances is rather an advantage. That is why the more highly educated classes, when they turn to poetry, seek out nature in her simplest mood. But we must admit that it was a king who wrote the Song of Solomon.

This, then, is the world poetry of eastern Europe, to which we must add Goethe's translation of a Finnish song. But both North and South are of far less importance than the East. In 1811 Goethe received Wilhelm Grimm's translation of the Danish heroic ballads, and in his letter of thanks he stated that he had long had a high opinion of these relics of Nordic poetry and had often delighted in individual examples. Now, however, they had been collected, and would have a much greater effect. One ballad puts us into a receptive mood for another, and these distant voices are better heard when they sound together. It is very pleasant, Goethe goes on to say, to see how certain things find favour in different countries, each of which treats them after its own fashion.[43]

In 1821, Goethe had great pleasure in receiving a Spanish anthology, and enjoyed it, though he was handicapped by his limited knowledge of the language. This " Spanish pleasure garden " (*Floresta de Rimas antiguas Castellanas ordinada per Don Juan Nicolas Pöhl de Faber*, Hamburg, 1821) stirred him to fresh study of this magnificent language and literature. In 1822 the

Spanish Romances, translated by Beauregard Pandin, elicited from him some general observations on world poetry (though the word was not yet used) and on the difference between folk-songs and songs of the people ; that is, between folk-songs which are the product of the uneducated—and songs of the people, which are typical of every people without exception. These may express if not their whole character at least some of its salient features. The songs of Spain have a tendency to embody the Idea directly in every-day existence, even in life at its most commonplace. But the Idea as imposed directly upon life appears fantastic and ridiculous. That is why Spanish humorous ballads are written in the same spirit of *Don Quixote*.

In his *Italian Journey* Goethe refers to the Italian folk-songs. The review of the *Egeria*, a collection of Italian folk-songs by W. Müller and O. L. B. Wolff in *Kunst und Altertum* is not the work of Goethe.

In this way world poetry opened up in all directions for Goethe. In 1826 the Philhellene Iken sent him a notice, with extracts, of a collection *Asprospitia* which he had planned with Kosegarten. In his letter of thanks Goethe assigned the work to its place in the great harmony of the " poetic echoes from all ages " which sounded in particular from the East, in Serbian, modern Greek, Lithuanian and Bohemian folk-songs. Even the little that Iken sent him seemed to Goethe noteworthy, for " every contribution to this great poetic festival of all is valuable. Man will come in time to see that poetry belongs to the whole of mankind, that it is active everywhere and in all of us, in varying degrees. The general public does not appear to me to be hostile to this view ; indeed it is gaining acceptance, and even among our neighbours the French is being stressed to a gratifying extent." [44] In Goethe's endeavours on behalf of world poetry, he always retained the point of view of world citizenship, of hoping to unite the whole of mankind. The spirit of Romanticism, on the contrary, with its rebirth of national literature, divided rather than united the peoples.

Towards the end of his life, however, his liking for this type of poetry decreased. In 1828 he said to Eckermann

The gloomy Old German era has as little to give us as the Serbian lyrics and barbaric poetry of that sort. We read it and for a time find it interesting ; then put it aside and leave it behind us. Man suffers enough from his passions and the blows of fate without needing to add to them the obscurities of a barbaric past. He wants clarity and encouragement. He needs to turn to those periods of art and literature in which great men reached a perfection of culture which brought them contentment, and the ability to share with others the serenity it had given to them.

In 1830, speaking to Chancellor von Müller, he said it had been a happy time when the translation of Serbian poems first appeared, and we were transported so naturally and vividly into those unfamiliar conditions. But he added : " All that is now remote from me, I do not want to hear any more of it." In his last years his work for world literature was no longer concerned with world poetry in the sense of folk-poetry, but with highly cultured literature and outstanding personalities. His mission of civilising a Europe which had succumbed to Romanticism made this inevitable. And he had become increasingly sceptical about the artistic spirit of his nation. A conversation with Eckermann in 1827 shows that when he compared it with that of the Ancient Greeks or indeed of the modern English, French and Italians, he had to admit how much easier it was for talent to develop in those nations, for they had a higher and more advanced national culture. The old songs lived in the mouths of the people, who had heard them in their cradles, so that they formed an integral part of their lives. Their songs were on the lips of their people ; they were heard in the fields sung by mowers and harvesters and by merry fellows in the inns. But what does a German poet hear sung by his own people ? Which of his own songs do they know by heart ? In the people, as such, there is only silence. What must Goethe have felt when he remembered the time when fishermen sang fragments of Tasso to him ? " We Germans are of yesterday. For perhaps a hundred years we have worked hard in the name of culture, but it will be hundreds of years yet before our fellow-countrymen as a whole are cultured enough to honour beauty as the Greeks did, to take delight in a beautiful song, and to have it said of them that it is long since they left barbarism behind them." The painful experience that was implicit in these words convinced Goethe at the last that that condition could not be improved through primitive folk-poetry but only through literature on the highest level of culture.

CHAPTER 18

PROSPECT

We can perhaps form some idea of the range of Goethe's interests connected with world literature, during the last years of his life, by reading the following remarks contained in one of his letters, together with an account of the visits of many English men and women to Weimar. Their visitors were kindly received by his daughter-in-law, Ottilie von Pogwisch, and talked with Goethe, who was particularly interested at that time (1827) in Dupin's description of a journey to England. In Goethe's letter we read :

The prairies of Cooper transported us to the West of America. The French works *Les jours des barricades* and *Les états de Blois* (by Vitet) recalled periods of the greatest confusion. But I was stimulated by reading a collection of Scottish Romances, to set about translating some of them. And I must not forget to mention the Swedish history, most praiseworthy work, by a Captain von Ekendahl, who is now here on a visit.[45]

We must not allow ourselves to be confused by certain strange manifestations of world literature in Weimar. Goethe's theory of it, his activity on its behalf, the visits of so many guests from abroad (especially from England, Scotland and Ireland), all led, at Ottilie's instigation, to the appearance of a weekly journal, printed in manuscript form, and bearing the not inappropriate title of *Chaos*. At first its only contributors were members of Weimar society. But, to use Karl von Holtei's expression in his reminiscences, its columns were soon opened to the tongues of all nations, though the English remained predominant ; and in fact the Romantic translator Gries sent from Jena the following lines for *Chaos*, in which they were printed :

Britisch, Gallisch und Italisch,
Daran scheint es nicht zu fehlen,
Wüsst' ich etwas Kamtschadalisch,
Möcht' ich wirksam mich empfehlen.

Ach, ich freute mich zu Tode,
Könnt' ich Türkisch radebrechen !
Aber Deutsch ist aus der Mode,
Und ich weiss nur Deutsch zu sprechen.

Geduld, verlass Dich auf mein Wort,
Gar Vieles ändert sich auf Erden ;

Und geht's nur so ein Weilchen fort,
Wird bald das Deutsche hier am Ort
Als fremde Sprache Mode werden.

Manches lässt die Zeit uns seh'n,
Was uns einst gedeucht als Fabel.
Sonst hiess Weimar Deutsch-Athen,
Jetzo ist's das Deutsche Babel.

Chaos contained contributions in German, French, English, Italian, Spanish and Greek, and indeed things were somewhat chaotic in Weimar. But in Goethe's mind the literatures and civilisations of the world were resolved into a cosmos, and the light that he shed in the world seemed like the colours of one single beam refracted in the Romantic movements of the different literatures.

In the meantime, even during his life, there were signs of a change, particularly in Carlyle's case and in Russia, in the conception of Goethe. For although elsewhere Goethe with his *Götz* and *Werther* and the First Part of *Faust* gave a Romantic turn to the literatures of Europe, in the cases of Carlyle and of Russia it was no longer young Goethe but the Goethe of the present, that is of his old age, who became a cultural and guiding force for young authors.

This is in fact what characterises the change in the conception of Goethe, and in the influence that Goethe exerted in the world after his death. Formerly, young Goethe had paved the way for a Romantic revival in the literatures of Europe by helping to dethrone Classicism. But now an age whose aim was precisely to overcome Romanticism had to determine its own attitude to him. The nearness of the dates (1830) of the outbreak of the Revolutions (1830) and of Goethe's death (1832) is of vital significance. Goethe was unmoved by these revolutions ; the scientific dispute between Cuvier and Saint-Hilaire which broke out at that time in the Academy in Paris was much more important in his eyes. This symbolises the fact that the " Kunst-periode " (an expression coined by Heine) closed with the end of Goethe's life. Modern times, modern literature, began and were characterised not only by realism but also by a vigorous spirit of social and political revolution. It is the literature of " young Europe " to which the French Romantic writers (Victor Hugo, George Sand), the English (Byron, Shelley), and also the Italian (Manzoni) already belong. Indeed we can hardly apply the word Romantic in the German sense to this progressive literature of agitation and emancipation. Thus had the conception of Goethe altered in these more recent times. People hardly remembered that with his *Werther* and *Faust* and *Prometheus* he himself had been a revolutionising force in the history of Europe. They failed too to see that with his *Wanderjahre* and the Second Part of his *Faust* he was as " modern " as anyone, that he spanned the ages as he did the nations.

At any rate after his death Goethe ceased to be a spiritual bond within Europe, for opinions of him in Europe began to be divided. At this point a movement arose in opposition to the tendency to make literature a medium for politics, to subordinate it to ends that had nothing to do with art. This movement sought to exalt art to the rank of a goddess, a ruler over life. It is the movement to which Gautier gave the name " l'art pour l'art " and which spread across Europe. It cited the authority of Goethe—not, of course, the Goethe of *Götz*, *Werther*, and the First Part of *Faust*, but of the Second Part and especially of the Helena-tragedy, that is to say Goethe in his old age, Goethe " the Olympian ". The other movement which aimed at enrolling literature in the service of political and social progress, was particularly irritated by Goethe's Olympian qualities. The same phenomenon was thus seen with different eyes and measured by different standards.

What, then, is this Olympian quality on which the whole conflict turned ? We are not including in this connection the conception which " Young Germany " had formed of Goethe through Börne and Heine, although this may not have been without influence on foreign literatures. One of the first in French literature to see and criticise. Goethe as an Olympian was Sainte-Beuve, and we shall depict Goethe as he saw him. In one of Sainte-Beuve's essays, Goethe and Bettina were dealt with in a way that reminds us that Börne also stated his notorious conception of Goethe in a discussion of the correspondence between Goethe and Bettina. It was not that this great connoisseur and critic of poetic art lacked respect for Goethe. One can gather from what he says of Mme de Staël's book, *De l'Allemagne*, how the Golden Age of German genius came into being with Goethe, and how with his death there followed the degeneration and decline of German literature. He gave this age the name : " le siècle de Goethe ". But how did he see Goethe in his old age ? As the Olympian, enthroned on a chill summit high above men with their joys and sorrows : receiving their homage and their sacrifice, himself without love or hatred, without sympathy as without passion, comprehending everything with complete objectivity, viewing everything, giving it scientific arrangements and artistic form. Everything served as material for his art, without distinction and without preference. Art and science came to contain for him the meaning of life. In his demand for beauty he turned away from the ugliness, poverty, misery, and dark aspects of life, unless these could serve him as effective artistic contrasts. He sounded harmonies and closed his ears to every discord. For him nothing really existed outside his own personality. He worshipped himself alone, his own ego, and contemplated the drama of the created world in order that as an artist he might re-create it.

That the real Goethe was never like this need hardly be stated. We know that as the author of *Werther* and *Faust* he not only took account of the world but actually changed some aspects of it. In his old age Goethe as a person probably did make this Olympian kind of impression. But we have only to look behind this mask of divinity and we shall recognise—among many other very un-Olympian traits—that, although he did exalt art and science over life, yet he designed them for the service of life to which they were called to impart a higher and more humane form. Sainte-Beuve declared, however, that this Olympian did not belong to Homer's Olympus, because Homer's gods came down from Olympus ; they participated in the Trojan War, they took sides, and helped their favourites.

What seems most remarkable is that Sainte-Beuve conceived Goethe's Olympian quality to belong to a specifically German poetic type, which he contrasted with Voltaire, the representative of the French cast of mind. Voltaire knew nothing of this Olympian attitude. He fought with words in the service of enlightenment, progress, humanity. The very word German meant, to the French writer of that time, Romantic. And this is the curious point, that Goethe's Olympian quality was regarded as the extreme consequence, the last climax, of Romanticism ; so between the Goethe who in his lifetime was taken to be a Romantic writer (and as such helped to rouse Romanticism in Europe) and this " Greek " conception of Goethe there was no difference in kind, but only one of degree. Fundamentally, then, the conception of the German spirit remained the same, that is to say Romantic. This Olympian quality ranked as Romanticism, because it represented a life within a dream, within the unreality of art, because it detached the poet from the life of the community and withdrew him into a state of solitude, because it was the climax of individualism, of the isolation of the completely self-absorbed ego, and because it thus robbed art of its social function in real life. This reproach was repeatedly levelled at German literature and not only by French writers. It was made with particular violence when, after the war of 1870–71, Barbey d'Aurevilly blamed Goethe for being the model for the "impassibilité" of the Parnassian poets, who had merely shifted their ground from Olympus to Mount Parnassus. This reproach—for as such it was intended—was repeated again in the interesting book *La Crise de notre Littérature* by Louis Reynauld. He sought to lay the blame on the German Olympian attitude, the art for art's sake, the æstheticism which had come to France from Germany particularly with the Second Part of *Faust*. A strange transformation, indeed! Up to now the characteristic quality of German poetry had been seen—and was to be seen again—in its lack of form and shape; but now the cult of pure form was said to have come from German literature. There is doubtless some truth underlying this idea, and it would be worth while to follow it up more closely. We might see whether in German idealism, in the Kantian idea (taken up by the Classicists) of the purposelessness of art and the disinterestedness of beauty, in Schiller's play-theory of art, one could find the sources of what Théophile Gautier christened "l'art pour l'art", Parnassian poetry and æsthetics. This, at any rate, was the accusation : that art was being robbed of its mission for human society, being separated from life and relegated to the clouds, whereas in his essay " De la prétendue décadence de la Littérature on Europe " Lamartine cited Goethe, with his inexhaustible richness, as the most important witness against this supposed decadence. One could not speak of decadence when a poet, like the gods of Olympus, was not subject to the weaknesses of old age, was so deified that his grave was sought in the stars rather than in Weimar. It certainly is an exaggeration to say that the Parnassian poets, Leconte de Lisle, Sully Prudhomme, their spiritual father Théophile Gautier, and also Flaubert were disciples of Goethe. But there are the connecting paths between Olympus and Mount Parnassus, between Goethe and these poets who sought to overcome subjective Romanticism, and created a new Classicism with their objective artistic creations entirely remote from their own personality. The confession that Gautier puts into the mouth of one of his characters might have been written by Goethe : he says he is a pagan of the age of Greece. For him the earth is as beautiful as Heaven, and he holds perfection of form to be true virtue. A statue pleases him better than a ghost, and the bright light of day better than the twilight. He never sees before him mist or fog or anything vague or drifting. His sky is cloudless, or if there are clouds they are as solid as though chiselled.

In his youth, Goethe had been one of the most important awakening forces of French Romanticism. Now the Olympian Goethe, who had himself received the blessing of Italy and of French Classicism, with its perfection of form, its dignified attitude and its clarity, helps French poetry to overcome the Romanticism which is essentially foreign to its nature, and to introduce a new Classicism. Gautier took as his model the " Olympien de Weimar ", " le poète marmoréen ", " le grand plastique ". Gautier as an old man wished to give his native land a picture of a poet's serene, productive old age, already an image of the higher life and seeming to anticipate immortality, as Goethe had done for Germany. A very pronounced taste then developed for the works of Goethe's later years, whereas up to that time the Goethe of his earlier days had occupied a higher place in the estimation of Europe. (In his book on El Greco Barrès too has expressed his liking for those strange works of great artists in their old age, such as the Second Part of *Faust*.) Gautier at least can truly be reckoned as a disciple of the artist Goethe in his old age, enthroned above the storms of time. He places the following sonnet at the beginning of his best-known collection of poems, *Émaux et Camées*. The very title suggests the Parnassian poets' emulation of the plastic arts, and the poem was intended as a French pendant to the *West-Eastern Divan* with which Goethe had withdrawn from the storms of Europe :

> Pendant les guerres de l'Empire,
> Goethe, au bruit du canon brutal,
> Fit *Le Divan occidental*,
> Fraîche oasis où l'art respire.

> Pour Nisami quittant Shakespeare,
> Il se parfuma de çantal,
> Et sur un mètre oriental
> Nota le chant qu'Hudhud soupire.

> Comme Goethe sur son divan
> A Weimar s'isolait des choses
> Et d'Hafis effeuillant les roses,

Sans prendre garde à l'ouragan,
Qui fouettait mes vitres fermées,
Moi, j'ai fait *Émaux et Camées*.

It was Gautier, too, who noted with astonishment how Leconte de Lisle as a young man already had an air of Goethe in his old age.

But although the Parnassians with their forms borrowed from Classical Greece invoked the memory of Goethe and in particular of Helena (who is also made the heroine of a drama by Leconte de Lisle), yet we must admit that Goethe did not thereby exert an influence productive of any real change in French poetry. For in its whole tradition it was already founded upon a basis of Classical antiquity. He had only awakened in this art an awareness of its own national tradition. It had no need of the everlasting German longing for the Classical land of Italy, or of acquiring Classical form there. For it bore within itself the inheritance of Classical antiquity. There is a poem by Gautier, " La Chanson de Mignon ", which is highly typical. A girl, stirred by Mignon's song of yearning " Kennst du das Land ", wishes to leave the man she loves and go South. But he detains her : does France not contain art just as beautiful as any to be found in Italy ? Is nature not just as beautiful with its flowers, fruits and rivers ? And is the sky too not just as beautiful ?—Here we have the whole difference between Goethe and Gautier, between German Classicism, which always yearns for something unattainable, and French Classicism, which is the natural fruit of the soil and the race.

Goethe's real significance for French Parnassian poetry lies in the fact that under this temple of Apollo he built a dark crypt which gave it new depth. Although it was his *Helena* that was specially dear to the Parnassian poets, the Faustian spirit that is wedded to this Helena did not fail to leave its mark on them. Sully Prudhomme wrote a lyrical, dramatic poem " Le Bonheur " with Faust as its hero, and beside Leconte de Lisle's *Poèmes antiques* there stand also his *Poèmes barbares*. Goethe seems here to go hand in hand with Schopenhauer who was then becoming known in France. The Parnassian " impassibilité ", perhaps better translated as absence of suffering, even of will-power, than as an absence of passion, is evolved as a way of deliverance from the depths of a profound pessimism. There are various different sources of Classical art. It may come, as in Italy, from the southern serenity of nature, its clear air, and the natural feeling for form that is inherent in men of the South. It may, as in German Classicism, be the fulfilment of an ethical demand made by the human type we recognise in Faust. It may develop, as in French Classicism, out of the sense of order, symmetry, unity, clearness and discipline. But Schopenhauer pointed out a new way, by proclaiming art as a deliverance from the ever-restless, ever-feverish will to live, this primary factor in the world and source of all suffering. The deliverance lay, he said, in the fact that art transforms the will into tranquil contemplation, beyond desire and beyond volition, by freeing things from their endless interconnections, lifting them above the hurrying stream of life, and isolating them within itself. The work of art is at peace within itself. Something of this, and something too of the Indian idea of sanctity which Schopenhauer extolled as the final deliverance even beyond art itself, is contained in the Parnassian "impassibilité". But it contains also Goethe's victory over the Faustian spirit by the serenity of his old age and the harmonious representation of dark mysteries, which is apparent in the Second Part of *Faust*. Behind and beneath Parnassian poetry, there are mysteries till then absent from French Classicism. With their insight into the tragic depths in Greek antiquity, to which the Second Part of *Faust* had opened their eyes, the Parnassian poets have actually anticipated Nietzsche.

> Heureux les mort ! L'echo lointain des chœurs sacrés
> Flottait à l'horizon de l'antique sagesse ;
> La suprême lueur des soleils de la Grèce
> Luttait avec la nuit sur des fronts inspirés.

This is taken from *Poèmes antiques*, in which gloomy visions from Ossian and the Edda also rise and reveal Northern influence ; further, in both *Poèmes barbares* and *Poèmes antiques* there are Indian poems which extol Nirvana.

Flaubert also, though not a Parnassian, had close affinities with the movement whose art strove for the utmost objectivity. He once said of himself " au fond je suis allemand " ; and it was only with the greatest toil and effort that he was able to free himself from his northern fog and cloud. He honoured Goethe so highly, and quoted him and his works with such frequency, that one is justified in taking for granted Goethe's influence in his case. But did Goethe bring him fog or light ? Flaubert too experienced the dangers of Romanticism, its illusions, dreams and longings. His Madame Bovary perishes as a result of this kind of Romanticism which snatches her from her narrow middle-class world. The hero of his novel of education, the *Éducation Sentimentale*, is on the other hand an ambitious young man of lofty aspirations whose spirit loses its power of flight, and who sinks in the sluggish stream of commonplace, middle-class existence. It is quite clear that the conflict between dream and reality, this motive which constantly recurs in the works of European Romanticism after Goethe's *Werther* and is also the basis of Flaubert's works, concerned that writer deeply. It may afford an explanation for that remarkable utterance, " and at heart he was a German ". It may have been the hazy dreams and longings of German Romanticism that brought him into this state of conflict. But Goethe, whose sublime, unromantic objectivity he—like the Parnassians—so greatly admired, pointed the way for him out of this conflict. It was the way of the purest, most impersonal artistic creation, totally detached from the artist's own ego. After he had been completely shattered in his youth by the First Part of *Faust*, its place was finally taken by the Second Part, and his late work *La Tentation de St. Antoine*, which he began to write shortly after he had re-read *Faust*, reveals the influence of the older Goethe. Like Faust, St. Antony at the beginning of the work lives in seclusion and solitude. Then temptation visits him in the form of alluring visions in which the hidden longings of his soul are revealed. Not the Christian Heaven, but the Olympus of the gods, rises before him and promises him a fuller life. The Greek gods beckon, and in a flight through the air Satan unfolds before his eyes, as in Byron's *Cain*, all the glory of the world. The difference between this work and *Faust* is admittedly great : St. Antony does not yield to temptation. It is only in the form of visions that the longings of his soul rises to the light. The end is like the beginning : St. Antony remains a saint, and Christ's grace shines out for him as before. Prayer remains, at the beginning as at the close. Faust, on the other hand, following his obscure impulses, experiences the life of temptation and only after he has strayed and sinned finds deliverance. Here we have the æsthetic solution of the problem of Faust. In this figure Flaubert has obviously depicted himself. Was he a conqueror of life, living in saintly seclusion ? In a certain sense he was. For he was the type of the artist who renounces life in order to be able to create, who, through art, satisfies his desire to live, who lives a higher, finer existence of his own choosing which he is unable, like Goethe's

Faust, to create in reality. What a contrast there is between Goethe and Flaubert : Yet it is quite conceivable that Goethe helped him to find the way out of his Romantic dreams and the conflict between dream and reality, by giving him training in strict Classical form. Thus he might find in art the sphere which otherwise he could enter only in dreams, although this meant renouncing reality.

But Parnassian poetry was not the only kind which could claim Goethe as its ancestor. Symbolism too, which superseded it and moved from Mount Parnassus to Montsalvat, owned allegiance to Goethe, and this is a fresh proof that Goethe's influence must not be construed in one sense only. He created at the same time both form and music, for he conjured up figures from the world of Classical antiquity and also sang the most musical songs that have ever been heard. The aim of symbolism was to transform poetry not into plastic form, as did the Parnassians, but into music. " De la musique avant toute chose " are the opening words of Verlaine's " Art Poétique ". " De la musique encore et toujours " comes later in the same poem : But this was what links Goethe with Richard Wagner, the object of the Symbolists' especial admiration. With Wagner's music the German " lied " became once more influential, particularly in France. Among the poems of Verlaine there are some which have closer affinities with Goethe's lyrics than any other French poems. On the other hand it speaks well for the constant tradition of Classical antiquity in French poetry that Verlaine, the Wagner-enthusiast, the musician whose instrument was language, was inspired by Goethe's " Classical Walpurgisnight " from the Second Part of *Faust*, and not by the " Romantic Walpurgisnight " of the First Part. The poem which he wrote on that occasion is called " Nuit de Walpurgis Classique " and it begins : " C'est plutôt le sabbat du second *Faust* que l'autre. Un rhythmique sabbat, rhythmique, extrèmement rhythmique." Into Goethe's " Classical Walpurgisnight " Verlaine introduces the notes of the hunting song from Wagner's *Tannhäuser* ; and this corresponds with the aim of the Second Part of *Faust*, namely to remove the barriers between Classical and Romantic, between Classical antiquity and the Middle Ages, to unite *Helena* with *Faust*.

If we look at the Europe of that day, we see that everywhere the light falls far more on the Second than on the First Part of *Faust*.

Even in the North, where because of his Grecian leanings, Goethe met with considerable opposition, we find a writer belonging to world literature. Hans Christian Andersen surprisingly giving the title " Goethe's Faust and Esther " to a chapter of his novel *To Be or Not to Be* (1857). In this chapter he is concerned with the Second Part, which the girl reads aloud to the man she loves, following upon a conversation on immortality. In the short story by Turgenev, " Faust ", which had already appeared, we have the opposite : the man reads *Faust* aloud to the women he loves. In Turgenev's work, *Faust* brings to light something in the woman that would better have been left unrevealed, and so motivates the catastrophe. But in Andersen's case the reading would not have had this effect, because it was the Second Part that was read. Andersen felt that Goethe belonged to the Classical world of beauty, and seemed an Olympian figure lit up by the sun of Christianity. When the hero of the novel, who had understood the First Part of *Faust*, was unable to follow the drift of the Second Part Esther explained, with a depth of insight remarkable for that period, the organic unity of the work in which each part has its necessary function. This hour became an important event in the history of his life, bringing him a clear perception of his own nature.

When Andersen came to Germany for the first time, Goethe was still alive. But he had heard of the latter's attitude of proud aloofness. Besides, none of Andersen's work had yet been translated, and he had no introduction to Goethe. He did not want to visit Goethe until his name was known in Germany. But this did not come about till after Goethe's death. In spite of this Andersen did visit Weimar, the centre from which so much light had radiated into the world and illumined his own life as a writer. He wrote to this effect in the *Story of my Life*. So Goethe the Olympian did after all succeed in gaining the entry into the North which Grundtvig sought to deny him as the enemy of the Nordic spirit, and Kierkegaard as the enemy of Christianity. The beauty of the Second Part of *Faust*, of which one writer had shown himself so deeply sensible, had brought this about.

In Russia, however, reaction soon set in to the " l'art pour l'art " movement and to the whole Olympian conception of poetry. Here both the Slavophils and the Westerners, usually antagonistic, were at one for their own reasons. For Kireevsky, a critic turned Slavophil, it meant a betrayal of the one truth of Christianity that the mind of Western Europe should seek to find

the highest truth in the beauty of art, which after all is but a dream
and an illusion. In this connection the end of the Second Part
of *Faust* was hotly repudiated. The reclamation of marshland
and the cutting of canals (actions with a purely civilising aim)
afforded no solution of the European problem and no opportunity
for the redemption of the soul.

The Westerners, on the other hand, had a different reason
for repudiating the Olympian conception of poetic art. Their
aim was to enlist literature in the service of a European civilising
process of enlightenment, humanity, justice and the dignity of
man. Life should not serve merely as a content for the forms of
art ; art has a social function to fulfil in the life of the human
community. Goethe was regarded by the Westerners as the
prototype of the Olympian artist, and as such was charged with
æstheticism, detachment from the community, and egotism. But
Classical perfection such as his was of immeasurable importance
for the progress of civilisation in Russia, so an attempt was made
to enlist his influence in this connection. Belinsky, the most
influential among the Westerners, rigorously opposed all art for
art's sake, and all forms of virtuosity, as unsuited to modern times.
Even the greatest artistry cannot dazzle for long if it confines
itself to bird-song, and imagines that the earth is not worthy of it,
that its place is in the clouds, that human suffering and human
hopes ought not to disturb its somnambulistic state and its poetic
intuitions. In his article " On Criticism " (1842) Belinsky
excluded Goethe from this condemnation. It must be admitted,
he wrote, that with his typically German character and philosophical resignation Goethe might be said to conform to the ideal
of the poet who sings as the bird sings, for himself alone, asking no
one else to listen. But even Goethe could not but pay his tribute
to the spirit of his day. His *Werther* is the shrill cry of the age.
His *Faust* raises all the ethical questions that could arise in the
heart of modern man. His *Prometheus* breathes the prevailing
spirit of the day, and many of his lyric poems express philosophical ideas.[46] Belinsky on one occasion also defended Goethe
against his German assailant Wolfgang Menzel ; and during
Goethe's lifetime a Frenchman had already done the same thing.
On that occasion Goethe took it as a sign of world literature then
developing.

In his great work *Realists* (1864) Pisarev saw Goethe in an
even more Olympian light than did Belinsky. He differentiated
him sharply from writers like Béranger, Leopardi, Giusti and

Shelley, who were not only writers but also men who loved and
sought to help their fellow-men by means of their works. Goethe,
he said, had never loved anyone but himself, and had never used
his art in the service of the human community. In spite of this
it was quite right to call him a " useful " writer, for after all he
had been and would continue to be of great use to the human
community to which he was so indifferent. Great creative
minds help even where they go astray. Goethe would never
become the favourite of the masses and for that reason would
never affect their spiritual life. That could be achieved only by
one who loved the masses. But the guides and leaders of the
masses often themselves stand in need of spiritual help. For
such men are indeed thoughtful and enlightened workers, but
are by no means men of genius. They are capable of understanding Goethe, but could never have produced what his genius
has produced. For them his works are a powerful galvanic
battery which supplies them with fresh energy. They read Goethe,
and what they receive from him streams on into that living sea
that is called the masses, and into which all our thoughts and
endeavours end by flowing. Thus the formal Privy Councillor
and patrician Goethe exerted an influence by means of the ideas
and feelings that his works have evoked in the restricted circle of
his chosen and highly cultured readers, to the benefit of his humble
and simple fellow-men.[47]

This spirited attempt to reconcile Goethe with the modern
mass-movement, indeed even to make him serve its ends, while
still retaining his aristocratic personality and exclusive gifts, seems
thoroughly typical of Russian mentality. On the other hand
Turgenev, a great admirer of Goethe, proves himself more of a
Western artist in that Goethe guided him to artistic forms along
Classical lines. In an article on Russia's first complete translation of *Faust* (by Vronshenko), Turgenev records his own
thoughts on Goethe and *Faust* (1845). From these it is obvious
to what a great extent Goethe was seen as an artist who resolved
every contradiction in his Classically tranquil soul, and who, as a
poet, concentrated on harmony. Faust seemed to have affected
only the enthusiasm of his youth. If we take literally what he
writes in his short story " Faust ", we find that there was a time
when he knew the First Part of *Faust* by heart, word for word, and
felt he could not read it often enough. And in 1844 he translated
the dungeon-scene ; in Paris he gave readings of *Prometheus* and
Satyros in translation. On the other hand we gather from the

short story "Faust" (1855), in which Goethe's work produces such a fatal effect, that it was no longer the Faust-spirit by which Turgenev in later years was affected. It was rather Goethe's Classical epic artistry that became a pattern for Turgenev.

In this lay the great contrast to Tolstoy who denounced Goethe as an Olympian writer, a representative of "art for art's sake" and of the Capitalist world, together with everything that was not religious, social or popular literature. We must bear in mind that when Tolstoy was younger, and conscious of his artistic powers, and particularly when he was writing his great work *War and Peace*, he read Goethe as well as Homer, and had noted : "Goethe : *Hermann und Dorothea* . . . very great influence." At that period he saw in *Faust* a product of thought, a work capable of expressing what no other art could. But, on account of its Homeric-epic character, *Hermann und Dorothea* was the work from which he could derive most benefit in the development of his own epic art. In 1861, he visited Weimar and the Goethe-House. But later, when he underwent a radical change, Goethe and all his other gods fell from favour and became victims of his new convictions about the nature of art.

In this case it was Goethe's epic and Classical work that influenced a Russian writer so profoundly. But *Faust* also gave proof of the inexhaustible power of its symbolism in Russian literature of the 19th century and indeed beyond it. In Odoev-sky's *Russian Nights* one of the main characters, to whom the young Russians go whenever they want to discuss intellectual problems, bears the name Faust. But this has very little to do with Goethe's *Faust*, and only exemplifies the Russian tendency to intellectual discussion which would naturally flow freely in conversation with a mind at once so philosophical and of such ambiguous brilliance.

On the other hand the modern revolutionary spirit of Russia has contrived to establish a direct link with the end of the Second Part of *Faust*, and to work out to its last conclusions the social undertaking which Faust attempts at the final stage of his life on earth, that of reclaiming land from the sea for millions of people to settle upon. We have the drama *Faust and the City*, by Luna-charsky, which was projected in 1906 and received its final form in 1916. What seemed to the Russian writer so problematic about the end of *Faust* that he was stimulated to write a sequel was the relation of a social work to its creator, a man of genius who rules in an absolutist although enlightened fashion over his creation. This is where Lunacharsky takes up the story. His Faust built a town on land which he had reclaimed from the sea, and ruled as Duke over that flourishing community. But his own son, urged on by Mephistopheles, attempted to depose him and to mount the throne himself. The people seized the reins of power. Faust voluntarily renounced his rule and took his place in the community as one of the people. His gift to them was a vast machine constructed by himself, an iron Robot capable of performing all the menial tasks, so that from then on man could devote himself wholeheartedly to the progress of science and the enjoyment of life.

In this way a link was formed between even revolutionary Russia and Goethe. The social creation which in Goethe's *Faust* was achieved by the active genius of a great personality was, in the Russian Faust, detached from its creator and developed as a free community.

In the minds of the earlier Slavophil writers, this work would not have been represented a solution of the problem. But the gulf between the Slavophil tendency in Russia and the ways of thinking of the Classical Goethe train of thought is not so hard to bridge as might be expected. On one occasion Dostoevsky affirmed that the most essential quality of the German people was its consistent Protestantism. Germany, he said, stood for an unceasing protest against Rome and the Roman way of thinking, against the paganism of old as well as against Catholicism, against the desire of Rome to rule man all over the world. The Roman people in the battle of the Teutoburger Wald protested against the idea of the Roman Empire and the conception of a European type of man. In Luther's Reformation it protested against the new ideal of a universal conception of Christianity as the world-wide empire of the Roman Church. In fact, throughout its whole history, Germany had constantly protested. It had not yet made its own new, positive contribution to the world ; it had only lived by contradicting its enemies. So it was possible that in the future, when Germany had destroyed everything against which it had been protesting for nineteen centuries and its enemies were vanquished, its own spiritual life might suddenly be extinguished simply because it would have no further reason for living ; there would be nothing left against which it could protest. In the meantime a third universal conception had taken on an imposing shape in the East, the Slavonic conception of the future, the third possibility of a decision on the fate of Europe and of mankind. But this Slavonic conception was as much despised by the German people as was the Roman or the Catholic.

Dostoevsky's definition of the German spirit as a ceaseless protest is not a bad one, for it really does protest in every direction, to the East and to the West. It was only that Dostoevsky failed to realise that in Goethe the German spirit had already made its own new positive contribution, which is indeed comprehended in this protest. It is the plea for a mean between eastern emotion and western reason, between the Faustian urge of the North and the beauty of southern form. The German spirit, embodied in Goethe, protests against the West as against the East, because its contribution which comes from the heart of Europe is the conception of a universal humanity. But the Russian contribution which Dostoevsky proclaims as the third, the future universal, conception, was distinctly formulated by him in his famous speech on Pushkin. It is true, we read, that European literature can produce examples of men of colossal genius—Goethe is not named among them—but can anyone name a single one possessing the capacity to reproduce the essence of foreign nationalities as our Pushkin can ? It is just this gift, the greatest gift we have, that Pushkin shares with our whole nation, and that makes him our national poet. No other man of genius in Europe could ever embody in himself so skilfully as Pushkin did the spirit and nature of a foreign people—not even that of a neighbouring people of the same race. On the contrary, the European men of genius, when they turn to other peoples, transform the foreign nationality of that people into their own, and interpret it according to their own nation's way of thought. Of all the poets in the world Pushkin alone possesses the power of transporting himself into the mind of a foreign nation. This is just what gives his work its wide appeal and makes it a factor in the nationalism which we hope for but have not yet achieved, and of which Pushkin has been the first prophet. Where does the power of Russian nationality lie, if not in its urge towards universality and comprehensive humanity ? The destiny of the Russian is indeed a universal one. To become Russian in the complete sense is to become a brother to all men, a universal man, one may say. The division of Russia into Slavophils and Westerners is one great misunderstanding, for, to a true Russian, Europe is as dear as Russia itself, simply because our destiny is the realisation of universal human unity. To be a true Russian is to endeavour finally to reconcile within oneself the

European contradictions, to point out in the universal all-uniting soul of the Russian, the way of escape from the European state of dissatisfaction, to receive all men in brotherly love, and so perhaps to make the final contribution to the universal harmony and brotherhood of all peoples in accordance with Christ's teaching. But this universal unity will not be achieved by the sword, and will not take the form of any political unity such as Cæsar or Napoleon aimed at ; neither will it come through the temporal power of the Roman Church. It will grow only out of brotherly love and on a basis of service for all. It will be the spiritual unity of the peoples in Christ.

This, then, is the Slavonic conception which Dostoevsky proclaimed and which his prophetic eye saw in Pushkin. It is an arresting thought. Does this not—to say the least of it—sound the note of Goethe's idea ? Is Goethe not the comprehensive poet, the universal man ? And his idea of a world literature, in which the peoples speak to each other, hear and understand one another, learn to tolerate and respect one another, has no other aim but that of a spiritual reconciliation among the peoples ? It must be owned that Goethe's idea has a different origin from that of Dostoevsky. In the man of the East it is the Christian emotion of love and brotherly feeling which determines him to sacrifice himself and sink his own personality, to transport himself into the mind of the foreign peoples. This helps us perhaps to understand why in Russian literature (so at least it is said in Russia) there are as good translations from foreign literatures as there are in German literature. (In the Russian view, for instance, Zhukovsky's translations from Goethe's poems and Lermontov's version of the " Wanderers Nachtlied " are unsurpassed masterpieces.) With Goethe it is his urge towards the perfection of humanity in his own personality that fits and determines him to unite in his own self everything that is human. In the East it is the conception of every people, of all men, as being the children of God. In the West it is the conception of an Urphänomen of man, a constant human type traceable through all the variation of peoples and individuals. With the Russians it is the will to serve all men. With Goethe it is the will to gain all. But whether it is Goethe's urge to comprehend the whole, or Christian brotherly love, the aim is the same. And in either case it is poetry that seeks to attain it. Goethe's ideal was of course Ancient Greece. But in him this ideal does not conflict with Christianity.

However great the differences may be, the aim remains :
harmony, peace and unity. Even where Goethe's Faustian
urge was expressed in Europe's deification of man and led to
Napoleon, Byron and Nietzsche, not all the links with the East
were broken. For, after all, everything arises out of the urge
to overcome the materialism and rationalism of the 19th century.
A nobler vital energy flames forth in the East as in the West,
whether according to Apollo or to Christ, and whether the aim
is man made god or God made man : in either case we have
a new longing in man for the divine. For even the most widely
different streams flow towards the same ocean. But world literature, as Goethe thought of it, has precisely this mission : to
reconcile antagonistic principles, to build arches and bridges. We
are often told that we must make an absolute choice between
Goethe and Dostoevsky. But this is not the case. They can
and do exist side by side. How many minds, indeed, have been
formed and guided by both !

Once, after the First World War, when intellectual representatives of the different peoples met in Pontigny in the attempt to
reach an intellectual reconciliation, they discussed the question
whether agreement could be reached as to which minds had
most strongly influenced the youth of Europe. They agreed on
the following : Whitman, Nietzsche and Dostoevsky, and when
André Gide suggested the addition of Goethe's name, this was
accepted. Admittedly, unanimous resolutions decide nothing in
cases of this kind. But unanimity such as this is to be valued as
a symbol, and in this connection we once again recall Goethe's
poem for the *Divan*. He found a higher unity above both Greece
and Christianity, the third empire in which each is reconciled
with the other, and whose name is Humanity. Who can say
whether Iphigenie is a Greek or a Christian ? In her purely
human nature which can diffuse blessing, turn barbarity into
culture, redeem from a curse and clear from guilt, any distinction
of this kind has lost all significance. In short, Goethe represents
the sacred mean between East and West.

Dostoevsky, then, stretched the arch of peace from East to
West, and Goethe from West to East. It is true that when Goethe
turned from Europe to the East he steeped himself not in the
Eastern Christianity of Russia but in the poems and religions of
the Far East. Even in his West-Eastern period he retained his
European nature. On his spiritual journey into the Orient he
wished to expand his own too rigidly controlled personality, and

did so after the fashion of his favourite poet Háfiz, in the blissful prodigality of his love for Suleika. He felt bound to hold his own against Napoleon's will to power, and he did so as Háfiz had done against Timur the Conqueror : as a writer and a man of creative genius. If he felt the longing for death and destruction by fire, it was that devout longing which renews itself in flame and seeks each time to rise again to new life. His religion preached renunciation and aimed not at abasing oneself before God but at taking one's place within the divine order.

> Gottes ist der Orient !
> Gottes ist der Okzident !
> Nord- und südliches Gelände
> Ruht im Frieden seiner Hände.

Goethe himself succeeded in stretching the arch of peace towards distant parts of the world. He was able to establish intellectual connection between the Old World, Europe, and the New World, America. After some of his American visitors had given their impressions in American journals, [48] and Longfellow had delivered at Harvard University the first lectures ever given on *Faust* (1838) and had published translations from Goethe's poems, including the notable translation of " Wanderers Nacht- lied ", Emerson formulated the conception of Goethe which remained for long the accepted one in America. One might perhaps expect that Goethe who, when contemplating the New World with a feeling of liberation from the burdens of European civilisation, would have transmitted that civilisation to the New World which had still so much to learn. But Emerson's concep- tion of Goethe is a far more modern one. In the first place it was a question of overcoming the resistance that American Puritanism offered to Goethe's entry into the world of American thought, and which was strong in Emerson himself. But the correspondence between Carlyle and Emerson shows how Carlyle succeeded in opening up the way for Goethe even in the mind of Emerson, whose Puritanism had given him these very reasons for violently resisting Goethe's influence. In the end, Emerson was able to write in his *Representative Men* (1850) the chapter on Goethe that Carlyle had not written in his *Heroes and Hero-Worship*. It is called " Goethe ; or the Writer ", and he is ranked with Plato the Philosopher, Swedenborg the mystic, Montaigne the sceptic and Shakespeare the poet. The traces of Puritanism are still obvious here, for Emerson declares that Goethe did not ascend to the highest levels from which man's genius has spoken ; he was incapable of a self-surrender to the moral sentiment, and there were nobler strains in poetry than his. There were writers poorer in talent whose tone was purer and touched the heart more deeply. Goethe could never be dear to men : even when he devoted himself to truth, he did not serve even truth itself for its own sake but used it as a means of culture and in particular of self-culture. For he valued everything in proportion as he himself could learn from it. It was religion and morality of which Emerson felt the absence in his work and in the man himself. He even considered this lover of all arts and sciences as " artistic " and thought him a lawgiver of art, but not an artist. But there were other sides to Goethe for which thoughtful Americans admired him and which had a lasting influence upon them. For Emerson, Goethe represents not the poet but the writer, that is to say the type of mind that is not essentially creative, but is capable of perceiving and describing the connection between things. This is quite a different conception of the writer from that of Carlyle, who understood by it the manifestation in modern times of the seer, the prophet, the promulgator of divine wisdom. For Emerson too, as for the whole of Europe at that period, it was the Second Part of *Faust*, in addition to *Wilhelm Meister*—no longer the First Part or *Werther*—that represented the climax of Goethe's lifework. He saw in it a philosophy of life cast in poetic form, the work of a man who was a master of history, mythology, philosophy, science and national literatures, a vast encyclopædia. In this work Goethe had recorded the results of eighty years of observation, and this reflective and critical wisdom made the work the most perfect flower of its age and gave it its great significance. According to Emerson there was no doubt that Goethe was a poet in the true sense of the word and that he suffered from his microscopic sight—for he seemed to see out of every pore of his skin. But the wonder of such poetry lies in its superior intellectual scope. Goethe's mind covered such a vast expanse that he was able to comprehend, classify and unite all the detached units making up the vast material of modern research. He clothed our modern existence with poetry, and embraced the age in all its variety. *Wilhelm Meister* is crammed with wisdom, with knowledge of the world and of the laws of existence. What particularly distinguishes Goethe in the eyes of French and English readers is a quality which he shares with his whole nation—a reverence for essential truth. In England and America there is a respect for talent ; in France a delight in intellectual brilliance. The

German intellect lacks the vivacity of the French, the fine practical understanding of the English, and the American's spirit of adventure. But Goethe has a certain probity which never rests content with a superficial performance. The German public asks for this type of predominant sincerity. For them talent alone cannot make a writer. There must be a man behind the book, a personality whose inner urge it is to bear the burden of truth. Emerson sees in Goethe at once the head and body of the German nation, not because he has great talent but because truth shines through his words. The old Eternal Genius who constructed the world has confided himself more to this man than to any other. Goethe's autobiography *Dichtung und Wahrheit* introduces into the world a thought now familiar to it but a novelty to England when that book appeared : that culture is the reason for man's existence : that he exists, not for what he can accomplish but for what can be accomplished in him. Goethe was born into an over-civilised age and country, when original talent was bound down under the load of books and mechanical aids, and the distracting variety of claims. It was he who taught men how to dispose of the mountainous miscellany, and even to make it serve their ends. In this he can be ranked with Napoleon. Both are representatives of the impatience and reaction of nature in the face of the power of conventions—two realists, each of whom has set the axe to the root of cant and show, for their own age and for all time. Goethe teaches us courage and shows us that our own age is not after all inferior to all the others. The disadvantages of any epoch exist only for the faint-hearted. The world is ever young.

This, then, is the conception of Goethe which has become orthodox in America. It is different from the European conception, and bears unmistakable signs of its American origin. What strikes us forcibly is that young Goethe, who helped to release the Romantic movement in Europe, is here left completely out of account, but that after his death Goethe is by no means regarded —as he was in Europe—as the Olympian and the representative of " art for art's sake ". This was unsuited to the American way of thinking and would only have made Goethe's entry into the New World more difficult. As in Europe, so in this young world, the idea men had of Goethe was determined by Goethe in his old age. That was not Goethe the writer and artist, but the wise and experienced Goethe, the man who examined, collected and classified. By combining the mass of material which an ancient

civilisation had accumulated in Europe, by uniting an " atom-
istic chaos " in one organic unity, he showed how it could be
coped with, and in so doing opened up the way towards a free
future. Thus it was essentially the young pioneering spirit of
America that formed the conception and made Goethe its guide
and helper. Here we have the older Goethe, the creator of the
Second Part of *Faust*, as a representative of humanity assuring
them of constant reinvigoration, and imparting to them courage
to conquer the past and step out unburdened towards the future.

This, then, distinguishes the Anglo-Saxon conception of Goethe
from the one which crystallised in France after Goethe's death,
and which is less that of a prophet and seer (as with Carlyle) or
that of a pioneering investigator working for the future (as with
Emerson) and more that of a Classic Olympian artist. But, all
the same, a certain unity is noticeable. For a civilising mission is
soon attributed to his Classic art, and it thereby loses its Parnassian character of " art for art's sake ". It is now *Iphigenie* that
attracts attention. At this point Goethe is regarded no longer as
a Romantic, indeed, but also no longer as an Olympian enthroned
in isolation. What he has in common with France and the Latin
world is the beautiful and sublime form, the clarity of mind,
humanism—all qualities now recognised as an essential part of
his nature. He was the first German writer to be received into
the circle of Latin civilisation as a worthy member of equal rank.
This meant that he lost something of his power to influence the
world, for now he simply gave back, as it were, to France the
Classical education he had received from her. He ceased to be
what the Romantics in Europe had looked up to, a renewing
force, liberating, breaking fetters, freeing forms. Instead, he
takes his place among the greatest cultural forces in the world.
In Paul de Saint-Victor's book, *Les Femmes de Goethe*, it is no longer
Gretchen and Klärchen but Iphigenie who stands out most
clearly. And in his essay " Sainte Odile et Iphegénie " Hippo-
lyte Taine tells us how, when he visited the convent of St. Odile,
mythical visions of the Greek gods rose in his mind and reminded
him how closely all the divine powers are bound together in one
single human spirit. In order to get the interpretation of this
feeling which only a poet can give, he opened Goethe's *Iphigenie*.
He there saw her as the purest image of ancient Greece, the purest
masterpiece of modern art, a Greek who is at the same time a
Christian saint, only without the mystic and frenzied attributes
of mediæval saints. The unity of antiquity and Christianity, of

soul and body, of the religions of this world and the next, of all
that had been disunited in the course of the centuries, is restored
in her. And Goethe is the only poet since the great artists of the
Renaissance who succeeded in creating such an image of human
unity ; and even he succeeded only once.

This conjuration of Iphigenie on the part of Taine is recalled
in the case of Maurice Barrès. In his journey to Sparta he visits
a convent on the site of a former temple of Artemis ; there rises
before him the image of Goethe's Iphigenie, and he acknowledges
his love for this " Germanised Greece ". He tells, further, how
in Italy he followed in Goethe's steps the development of his
Iphigenie. He calls it " une pièce civilisatrice ", and this in the
mouth of a French writer is doubtless the highest praise that can
be bestowed on any work of literature.

Continuing the list of those who were anxious for the preservation of the Latin quality in French literature, and who were at the
same time its chief representatives, those who admitted Goethe to
a citizen's full rights within their circle of Classical culture, we
must at this point make mention of two great names : Anatole
France and André Gide.

In 1876 Anatole France wrote a version of Goethe's ballad
" Die Braut von Corinth ", in the form of a dramatic work " Les
Noces Corinthiennes ". He added that he had kept closely to
Goethe, whose genius had lit up the obscurity of all these marvels
of antiquity in which he had found the material for his ballast.
In this work Goethe shows the two lovers—separated by their
parents and united again by a mysterious power—as victims of
the strife of the Gods which had convulsed the world from the
days of Nero to those of Constantine. The bride of Corinth is his
creation. It is characteristic of Anatole France's Latin turn of
mind that it was precisely this poem of Goethe's that he rewrote
as a drama. In this poem the decline of the gods of old, as a
result of Christianity, is shown in the tragic destiny of a pair of
lovers. But it is still more characteristic of him that he banished
from Goethe's ballad the last touch of gloom that recalled
Romanticism. He achieved this by not making the bride a
nocturnal spectre and deadly vampire, but by setting everything
in the broad daylight of ordinary life. Anatole France said of
the Second Part of *Faust* that it suffered cruelly from the fact that
Helena was shut up in a Germanic castle. For Faust was a
barbarian. But Helena belonged to the Latin races, to the
French. German literature could subsist without Greece, but

French civilisation on the other hand is inevitably Latin ; it is not Germany but France that is naturally destined to completeness, order and harmony. He therefore could not grant Helena to the Faustian spirit. But he did admit in the case of Goethe— though only in his case which was a stroke of good fortune in the intellectual life of Germany—that he really had made Helena his own.

And finally, André Gide gave this answer to an inquiry into the influence of German thought in France : Nietzsche, he considered, had left traces but it was hard to say whether one could call him a good influence. The harm he had done must be weighed against the good ; and the scale dipped perilously on the side of the harm. But with Goethe, quite the opposite. Gide here regrets that he did not achieve greater influence ; for in the whole of world literature there was not his equal. His was the only literary personality whose great wisdom we could set against certain excesses in the intellectual life. His was indeed a completely rational influence, and this in no way detracted from his poetic quality. The only individual whom France had to compare with Goethe was Montaigne, the famous humanist and greatest ethical thinker that France has produced—and yet how immeasurably more important Goethe is. True, Goethe's influence on France was limited almost entirely to the moral sphere ; in the realm of art it was practically non-existent, or, rather, the artistic influence of the great German Classicist merged in the stream of Græco-Latin culture, forming with it one perfect unity, whose significance for France admittedly was and is quite incalculable.[49]

These, then, were the French writers who included Goethe in their own Græco-Latin range of culture. To them we must add Moréas, for whom Goethe was Germany's greatest artist, and who said that in his old age Goethe was sorely grieved at having helped to destroy the Greek temple, and had tried to re-build it.

Of course there were also in France some who declared Goethe's Hellenism to be fundamentally insincere. It is like a counterstroke on the part of France in return for Lessing and Schlegel having misrepresented French Classicism as a mere outward imitation of antiquity. Schlegel had compared Racine's Phedra with that of Euripides, and now Souvestre in his *Causeries* compares the Prometheus of Goethe with that of Æschylus, and finds that Goethe has only donned a Greek mask behind which is hidden Faust. His knowledge of antiquity is merely a semblance ; he has simply grasped the outward form of Classical poetry without seeing beyond or behind it. After the war of 1870-71, when the intellectual relationship between Germany and France was extremely strained, Barbey d'Aurevilly expressed the same doubts about Goethe's Hellenism. He denied that Goethe possessed any creative power, and called him simply a " traducteur " and an " imitateur ". Remembering the convulsion of national sentiment at that time, this view is understandable. But when Paul Claudel (who considered Goethe, Luther and Kant the three evil spirits of the German people) declared it odd that Goethe, the writer of Faust, " this work of a hideous imagination, redolent of disaster and despair, of the air of the graveyard if not of the madhouse, where one is surrounded by ghosts and dreadful phantoms —that this same Goethe is praised as a representative of Classic beauty and light ", and when Claudel goes on to declare of *Iphigenie*, which Barrès admired so greatly, that it resembled Greek works only as a copy resembles the original[50]—this judgment must surely be traced back to his Catholicism, which came between him and Goethe just as it did between Goethe and Calderon. For the movement of the Latin Renaissance in France aimed not only at the restoration in French literature of the Latinism which belonged to its origin, heritage and nature. It wanted also the restoration of French Catholicism ; and the bond that united these two forces, Latinism and Catholicism, was to be found in their common love of unity, order, clarity, soundness of construction, and beauty of form.

Goethe could maintain his high position wherever this bond was loosened, wherever emphasis was laid on the rebirth of the Latin—that is to say of the national—spirit. In 1927, the Jubilee year of French Romanticism, the victory of Victor Hugo's *Cromwell* was celebrated and led to the outbreak of violent conflict about whether Romanticism had proved a blessing or a curse to French literature. Voices were heard accusing it of ruining the Latin spirit of France, of threatening French civilisation. Others asked what had been the actual effects of German Romanticism, and of German influence from *Werther* and *Faust* up to Wagner, Schopenhauer and Nietzsche. One answer to this question was that it had brought chaos for order, vague metaphysics for clarity and reason, historical relativism for absolute values, universal disillusionment and the cult of death for a confident and serene attitude to life, dreams and delusions for reality, individualism and national egotism for the majesty of the humanitarian ideal, reaction for progress, dissolution into anarchy for a well-defined

beauty of form, and barbarism for civilisation.   Yet, even at such
a critical moment as this, Goethe, who after all was one of the
most important stimulating forces of French Romanticism, and
whose *Werther* and *Faust* were naturally also included in this
condemnation, held his ground at every point—thanks to the
humanism of his outlook and the beauty of his literary forms.

The second moment of danger for Goethe's world reputation
came with the First World War, which altered national judgments
everywhere.   Wars are always of capital importance for intellectual relationships between peoples, and in such crises intellectual
representatives entrusted with the preservation of eternal values
outside politics and disregarding national prejudices, are too
often found wanting.   But it is obviously easier for a victorious
people to do justice to the intellectual achievements of a defeated
one, than vice versa.   After the war of 1870-71, it was possible
to publish the book by Barbey d'Aurevilly, who was after all a
writer of some importance, although it distorted the image of
Goethe to the point of absurdity.   After the First World War,
the attitude of France to Goethe was entirely different.   When
the storms of passion had subsided, he towered like some sunlit
peak from out of the dull dead-level of national hatred, and was
once more able to shed his light on all sides.   At that time the
intellectual community in France was particularly ready and
anxious to make use of the common European spirit to reconcile
the nations which had been riven apart.   The great conception
of Europe as an entity had seldom occupied poets and writers
to such a degree, and now it was realised that this conception was
one with Goethe's profoundest aim, and that there could be no
better guide towards this kind of European unity.   For where
could one find a mind more clearly representative of Europe as
a whole than that of Goethe who, in the marriage of Faust and
Helena, the Germanic spirit with the spirit of antiquity, had not
only created a poetic symbol but had given it embodiment in
his own person and in his poetry.

At the celebrations in 1932 of the centenary of Goethe's
death, it was no less distinguished a man than Paul Valéry who
gave the festival speech at the Sorbonne, " En l'honneur de
Goethe ".   This great French writer and thinker honoured
Goethe as the hope of a world that longed for a European civilisation based on the Greek ideals of beauty and understanding,
which it had seen realised in an ideal of personality.   For, thanks
to the sublime freedom of his spirit, Goethe had been able to rise

above the contrasts of fact and inspiration, observation and intuition, botanical science and lyricism, Classicism and Romanticism, criticism and demonic impulse, Apollo and Dionysus, Heaven and hell, thought and action, and to achieve their synthesis. At that time, in 1932, some important works of Goethe were appearing in France, in which he was praised as the spiritual bond uniting Europe, the bridge linking the European nations together, the leader and guide towards spiritual unity in Europe. In his book *Goethe le grand Européen* Andée Suarès declared that for Europe there was no salvation but in the spirit of Goethe, for he himself was the spirit of Europe. Léon Daudet's work *Goethe et la synthèse* also appeared, in which he was proclaimed as the synthesis of Germanic, Latin and Classical Greek elements, and by virtue of the synthesis a universal spirit.

But in this same Goethe-year, 1932, it became obvious that this union of the Germanic and Classical elements, which France stressed so strongly, did not do justice to the spirit of Goethe that had spanned the whole world. For every people, even the Slavonic races, in the voices of their poets, writers and men of learning, bore witness on this occasion. And even revolutionary Europe found, thanks to the vast span of this spirit's range, that it was possible to honour its ancestor, the Goethe who had hitherto been regarded as a conservative. Its mouthpiece was the great representative of European letters, Romain Rolland. In a special number of the review *Europe*, marking the centenary of Goethe's death, there appeared an article to which he gave the title " Meurs et Deviens ! "

Previous to this, in the preface to the last volume of *Jean Christophe*, Rolland had cried to the younger generation, " Be greater and happier than we were ! I myself say Farewell to my past soul, I throw it behind me like an empty slough. Life is a succession of deaths and resurrections. Let us die, Christophe, that we may be borne again." But, after he had come under the influence of the revolution in the East, Romain recognised in Goethe something that had not been seen in him before : the personification of the revolutionary cast of mind. Rolland even declared that it was to this Goethe that he owed a great debt of gratitude for his own development. It seemed to him childish to speak of Goethe's Olympian calm. The harmonies he sounded were not completed, but were about to be. His way led through discords towards their resolution, perhaps unattainable and situate in infinity. He could never be grasped, for he was involved in a ceaseless process of transformation. No standard could be applied to him. For the secret of this genius lay in his utterance " Stirb und Werde ". Each man, Rolland went on to say, selected from Goethe's immense range of thought whatever was akin to his own nature. Rolland had chosen this utterance ; and this continually dying and becoming, forever-changing, Goethe was his. But this " Stirb und Werde " was not merely to be taken as the law that governs the life of the individual. It was also the law of human society. Gods and states must perish, earthquakes must shake the consciences of individuals and of society, if the moral and social world were to survive the inevitable metamorphoses. Faust strides ever onwards, and his banner is that of ceaseless transformation.

In this way, then, and in this Goethe-year, not only all the nations, but both the Old and the New World met in Goethe.

In the concert of the nations' voices there was one discordant note, and it came from Spain. It was the article by Ortega y Gasset " In Search of a Goethe from Within ", published to mark the centenary of Goethe's death. In the European crisis, we read, which is a world-wide crisis, it becomes clear that the inheritance of the Classical writers cannot help us. Indeed it is obvious that the crisis itself is developing into a crisis of Classicism, which is as useless for the present as for the future. Goethe is found wanting when tried before the tribunal of man whose hopes are wrecked, before the court of justice of human misery. More than this ; he is the most questionable of all artists, because he is a Classical writer of second rank who has lived on the inheritance of the Classical writers. What had hitherto been written about Goethe had represented him as if he had been part of a monumental work on optics. Goethe had been viewed from without, like a statue. Now the time has come to see him quite objectively from within, to discover his vocation, and to ask if he had remained faithful to it, and whether he had realised his entelechy. The truth is that he was repeatedly unfaithful to it. He sought his own inner destiny as Wilhelm Meister and Faust did, and he never discovered it. His life was one continual desertion. He fled to Weimar, and this was the greatest error in the whole history of German literature. His vocation was to be a herald of the dawn, his mission was to be a poet, to use German poetic art to rouse poetry throughout the world. If he had not gone to Weimar, if he had lived a life of uncertainty and distress, what blessings he would have brought to mankind !

He would have created that German literature that only he could
have brought into being, a literature which would have united
passion and proportion, the storm of feeling and the imagination
that the other literatures of Europe lack, the proportion that
France and Italy possess in excess.   In Weimar Goethe acquired
" Iphigenism ", but why did he stay there ?   He petrified ; the
sense of proportion overwhelmed him, and Weimar alienated
him from the world and from himself.   He neither took his
destiny into his own hands nor did he resolve to follow his own
vocation.   He made no profession of faith, and simply kept
himself in a constant state of preparedness.

       This conception of Goethe is not really a new one.   We must
remember Kierkegaard, and also the fact that the state of crisis
in Europe did not suddenly come into being with the World War.
The whole complexity and distraction of the modern mind had
already found expression in literature.   We can understand how a
writer like Strindberg once acknowledged that he knew it was not
given to him to wander over the regions of harmony as Goethe
had done.   But had a poet, who was chosen to take up the cross
for millions of his fellow-men, the right to evade his vocation ?
He, Strindberg, lived in another age from Goethe's, and mankind
asked other questions to which there were other answers.   Goethe
had been a poet of quiet observation and a man of great prudence. [51]

       Of course this ought to be taken simply as the personal state-
ment of a man whose mind was inharmonious, as Strindberg's
was.   There are no doubt others among that generation, racked
with problems, who failed to find the way to Goethe.   But
Ortega's strange conception of Goethe, seen from within, seems
highly questionable.   The man who abjures the Classical mind,
especially at this critical time when some orientation in the
intellectual firmament seems more than ever necessary, is like
one who, in the midst of a storm, throws the compass overboard
in order to steady the tossing boat, or who, in the darkness, would
like to put out the stars.

       Was it not precisely this Goethe, the herald of the dawn, who
roused the world and woke Romanticism in Europe ?   Was that
not a storm ?   But he knew the danger of the storm, and the
blessings of right proportion, and for this reason he quelled the
storm within himself and achieved proportion.   If Goethe's
mission was not fulfilled, it was not his going to Weimar that was
responsible for this : the fault lay with the world which did not
follow along the same road to Weimar.   It was not he who evaded

his vocation but mankind that did so.   The search should be for a vision of mankind from within.

It did seem once as if the world would yet find the way to Weimar.   And that was in 1932, when all the nations sent their representatives to the great Goethe-festival there, to pay their tribute and to express their gratitude for what they had received from him.   One felt the breath of the spirit that sprang from Goethe's ideas of world literature, and its realisation seemed to be at hand.   But anyone who was present at that festival and took part in it, must even then have noticed signs which awoke gloomy forebodings.   It was soon obvious that these were in reality funeral celebrations, doing honour to a Goethe that was dead.   Shortly afterwards catastrophe broke upon the world, because one people had betrayed its greatest mind, because Faust, succumbing to the temptation of his satanic leader, had descended into hell.

And yet we must not lose faith in Goethe's spirit and in his idea of world literature.   More than ever before, it is the duty of the poets and writers of every nation to act in accordance with that spirit.   Along political lines and by means of world-wide organisations alone, it will never be possible to assure a peace in which human civilisation will be able gradually to grow towards perfection.   Without the spirit, Goethe's spirit, this aim will remain for ever unattainable.

In *Wilhelm Meister* Goethe calls the leader of the world-wide confederacy " the link ".   May the spirit of Goethe act as a leader for a world now struggling out of chaos towards the light.

APPENDIX

The twenty-one passages from Goethe's works, diaries, letters and conversations, in which he makes use of the expression " World literature ".

1. Diary, 15th January 1827 : " Dictated to Schuchardt on the subject of French literature and world literature."

2. *Über Kunst und Altertum*, Vol. 6, part I, 1827 (Le Tasse, drame par Duval) : " The extracts from French periodicals that I give are not merely intended to remind readers of myself and my writings : I have a higher aim of which I shall give a preliminary outline. We hear and read everywhere of the progress of the human race, of the wider prospects in world relationships between men. How far this is the case it is not within my province to examine or to determine : for my part I seek only to point out to my friends my conviction that a universal world literature is in process of formation in which we Germans are called to play an honourable part. The nations all look to us, they praise, blame, adopt and reject, imitate and distort, understand or misunderstand us, open or close their hearts towards us : We must accept all this with equanimity because the result is of great value to us."

3. Letter to Streckfuss, 27th January 1827 : " I am convinced that a world literature is in process of formation, that the nations are in favour of it and for this reason make friendly overtures. The German can and should be most active in this respect ; he has a fine part to play in this great mutual approach."

4. Conversation with Eckermann, 31st January 1827 : " National literature has not much meaning nowadays : the epoch of world literature is at hand, and each must work to hasten its coming."

5. Conversation with Eckermann, 15th July 1827 : " It really is a very good thing that with this close intercourse between Frenchmen, Englishmen and Germans we have a chance of correcting each other's errors. This is the great advantage that world literature affords, one which will in time become more and more obvious. Carlyle has written the life of Schiller and has estimated him throughout as it would have been difficult for a German to do. On the other hand we can judge Shakespeare and Byron, and know how to evaluate their merits perhaps better than the English themselves."

6. Letter to Boisserée, 12th October 1827 : " In this connection it might be added that what I call world literature develops in the first place when the differences that prevail within one nation are resolved through the understanding and judgment of the rest."

7. Letter to Carlyle, 1st January 1828 : " Now I should like to have your opinion on how far this *Tasso* can be considered *English*. You will greatly oblige me by informing me on this point ; for it is just this connection between the original and the translation that expresses most clearly the relationship of nation to nation and that one

must above all know if one wishes to encourage a common world literature transcending national limits."

8. *Über Kunst und Altertum*, Vol. 6, part 2, 1828 (External relations): " My confident statement that in these truly stirring times, and with the consequent greater ease of communication, there is hope of a world literature in the immediate future, has met with the approval of our western neighbours, who to be sure could do great things in this matter, and they have expressed their views on it as follows."

9. Letter to Zelter, 21st May 1828 : " Please note that the world literature I have called for is deluging and threatening to drown me like the sorcerer's apprentice : Scotland and France pour forth almost daily, and in Milan they are publishing a most important daily paper called *l'Eco*."

10. Letter to the Editor of the journal *L'Eco*, 31st May 1828 : " The first forty-seven numbers of the journal which you are launching in Milan have been a most pleasant surprise to me ; with their content, and the attractive form you have given them, they will make the most pleasing contribution to the universal world literature which is spreading with increasing energy, and I sincerely assure you of my interest."

11. *Über Kunst und Altertum*, Vol. 6, part 2, 1828 (*Edinburgh Reviews*) : " These journals, as they gradually reach a wider public, will contribute most effectively to the universal world literature we hope for ; we repeat however that there can be no question of the nations thinking alike, the aim is simply that they shall grow aware of one another, understand each other, and, even where they may not be able to love, may at least tolerate one another."

12. The Congress of Natural Scientists in Berlin, 1828 : " In venturing to announce a European, in fact a universal, world literature, we did not mean merely to say that the different nations should get to know each other and each other's productions ; for in this sense it has long since been in existence, is propagating itself, and is constantly being added to. No, indeed ! The matter is rather this— that the living, striving men of letters should learn to know each other, and through their own inclination and similarity of tastes, find the motive for corporate action."

13. From Makarie's *Archives* (probably 1829) : " Now, in the first stages of world literature, if we look closely we can see that the German stands to lose most ; he would do well to ponder this warning."

14. Letter to Zelter, 4th May 1829 : " The exaggerations forced upon the theatres of Paris, that great wide-spread city, do harm to us who are still far from finding them necessary ourselves. Yet these are the consequences of advancing world literature, and we can find comfort only in the fact that though the common cause comes off badly yet individuals are helped and benefited ; from time to time I receive very gratifying proofs of this."

15. Letter to C. F. v. Reinhard, 18th June 1829 : " The various branches of world literature react sharply and strangely on one another ; if I am not mistaken, taking a broad and general view, the French gain most by it ; they have, too, a kind of premonition that

their literature will have, in the highest sense, the same influence on Europe that it gained in the first half of the eighteenth century."

16. Scheme for *Kunst und Altertum*, Vol. 6, part 3, 1829 : First Version : "World literature". Second Version : "European, in other words, World Literature".

17. Conversation with Willibald Alexis, 12th August 1829 : "In this conversation also there appeared references to a common European or World literature, one of the favourite themes of the winter of his life which is still haunted by spirits of his imagination."

18. Introduction to Thomas Carlyle's *Life of Schiller*, 1830 : "There has for some time been talk of a Universal World Literature, and indeed not without reason : for all the nations that had been flung together by frightful wars and had then settled down again became aware of having imbibed much that was foreign, and conscious of spiritual needs hitherto unknown. Hence arose a sense of their relationship as neighbours, and, instead of shutting themselves up as heretofore, the desire gradually awoke within them to become associated in a more or less free commerce." [Translation by C. E. Norton, *Correspondence between Goethe and Carlyle*, London, 1837.]

19. Draft of the above Introduction (see 18) : "But if this kind of world literature—as is inevitable from the ever-quickening speed of intercourse—should shortly come into being, we must expect from it nothing more and nothing else than what it can and does perform."

20. Draft of the above Introduction (see 18), 5th April 1830 : "Not merely what such men write to us must be of first importance to us ; we have also to consider their other relationships, how they stand with reference to the French and the Italians. For that after all is the only way towards a general world literature—for all nations to learn their relationships each to the other ; and each is bound to find in the other something attractive and something repellent, something worthy of emulation and something to be avoided."

21. Letter to Boisserée, 24th April 1831 : "In the case of the translation of my latest botanical studies I have had the same experience as you. Some passages of capital importance, which my friend Soret could not understand in my German, I translated into my kind of French ; he rewrote them in his own, and I am quite convinced that in that language they will be more generally understood than perhaps in German. A certain French lady appears to have thought of using this system already ; she has the German translated to her simply and literally, and then proceeds to endow it with a grace peculiar to her language and her sex. These are the immediate consequences of a general world literature ; the nations will be quicker in benefiting by each other's advantages. I shall say no more on this subject, for it is one which calls for a good deal of elaboration."

NOTES

(Quotations from Goethe's works are from the Weimar Edition.   W. indicates the section Works ;   Sc., Scientific writings ;   D., Diaries ;   L., Letters)

PART I

1. W., Vol. 41^2, p.   307.
2. L., Vol. 43, p.   222.
3. W., Vol. 42^2, p.   505.
4. L., Vol. 15, p.   149.
5. Sc., Vol. 13, p.   449.
6. W., Vol. 41^2, p.   348.
7. W., Vol. 41^2, pp. 305 ff.
8. W., Vol. 41^2, p.   339.
9. W., Vol. 41^2, pp. 69 ff.
10. W., Vol. 41^2, p.   308.
11. W., Vol. 41^2, pp. 217 f.
12. Sc., Vol. 13, p.   449.
13. W., Vol. 42^2, p.   500.
14. Conversation with Eckermann, 15th July 1827.
15. Ibid.
16. Sc., Vol. 6,   p.   221.
17. W., Vol. 41^2, p.   345.
18. W., Vol. 41^2, p.   311.
19. Letter to Carlyle, 15th June 1828 ; cf. W., Vol. 41^2, pp. 346 f.
20. W., Vol. 41^2, pp. 304 f.
21. Sc., Vol. 7,   pp. 165 ff.
22. W., Vol. 42^2, pp. 502 f.
23. L., Vol. 45, p.   187.
24. W., Vol. 42^2, p.   202 ; cf. L., Vol. 45, p. 295.
25. W., Vol. 42^2, p.   201.
26. W., Vol. 41^2, pp. 179 f.
27. W., Vol. 42^2, p.   500.
28. W., Vol. 41^1, p.   179.
29. W., Vol. 42^1, pp. 186 ff.
30. W., Vol. 41^2, pp. 179 f.
31. L., Vol. 15, p.   234.
32. W., Vol. 42^2, pp. 491 f.
33. W., Vol. 42^2, p.   497.
34. W., Vol. 42^2, p.   500.
35. W., Vol. 42^2, pp. 501 f.
36. W., Vol. 41^2, p.   348 ; cf. L., Vol. 44, p. 108.
37. W., Vol. 42^2, pp. 91 f.

PART II

1. Sc., Vol. 12, p.   56.
2. L., Vol. 35, p.   281.
3. L., Vol. 35, p.   279 ; Vol. 36, p. 386.
4. L., Vol. 35, p.   193.
5. W., Vol. 41^1, pp. 73 ff.
6. W., Vol. 31, p.   83.
7. W., Vol. 32, p.   337.

8. W., Vol. 33, p. 188.
9. W., Vol. 36, p. 41.
10. W., Vol. 45, p. 240.
11. L., Vol. 23, p. 115.
12. W., Vol. 45, pp. 176 f.
13. W., Vol. 41¹, pp. 352 ff.
14. L., Vol. 25, p. 284.
15. L., Vol. 20, p. 16.
16. W., Vol. 40, p. 186.
17. L., Vol. 27, p. 33.
18. L., Vol. 32, p. 234.
19. W., Vol. 42², p. 50.
20. Sc., Vol. 13, p. 314.
21. L., Vol. 29, pp. 383 f.

PART III

1. From Schelling's *Life*, Vol. 1, pp. 307 ff.
2. W., Vol. 28, pp. 142 ff.
3. W., Vol. 35, p. 247.
4. L., Vol. 20, p. 170.
5. *Goethe-Jahrbuch*, Vol. 8, p. 13 ; 11.
6. Correspondence with the brothers von Humboldt, p. 51, Humboldt also notes here that Chénier actually turned *Werther* into a tragedy, not yet printed.
7. *Goethe-Jahrbuch*, Vol. 20, p. 115.
8. Correspondence with the brothers von Humboldt, pp. 160 f.
9. L., Vol. 23, p. 409.
10. L., Vol. 24, pp. 160 f. ; cf. pp. 185 f. ; p. 191 ; p. 280.
11. W., Vol. 35, pp. 173 f.
12. W., Vol. 41², pp. 233 f. ; cf. p. 340.
13. L., Vol. 20, pp. 227 f.
14. W., Vol. 41², p. 340.
15. L., Vol. 44, p. 166 ; cf. W., Vol. 42², p. 187.
16. W., Vol. 42², pp. 493 f. ; p. 514.
17. L., Vol. 21, p. 364.
18. Sc., Vol. 11, pp. 52 f.
19. Sc., Vol. 13, pp. 116 f. ; Vol. 7, p. 181 ; p. 214.
20. Sc., Vol. 5¹, pp. 421 ff. ; cf. L., Vol. 45, p. 312.
21. Sc., Vol. 7, pp. 169 f.
22. Sc., Vol. 7, p. 188.
23. L., Vol. 49, pp. 44 f.
24. L., Vol. 43, p. 19.
25. L., Vol. 44, p. 101.
26. W., Vol. 42², pp. 87 ff.
27. L., Vol. 36, p. 61.
28. D., Vol. 10, p. 219.
29. W., Vol. 42², pp. 38 f.
30. L., Vol. 22, pp. 40 f. ; p. 43 f.
31. L., Vol. 28, pp. 40 f.
32. W., Vol. 41¹, pp. 126 f.
33. L., Vol. 44, pp. 78 f.
34. *Goethe-Jahrbuch*, 1916, p. 180 : another translation, Otto Harnack, *Essays und Studien zur Literaturgeschichte*, p. 236.
35. Conversation with Chancellor von Müller, 7th September 1827.
36. Pushkin, *Articles and Diaries*, translated by Fega Frisch, p. 49.

37. Translation by Fega Frisch. Lermontov's later poem " The Demon ", 1838, will also recall Goethe's *Faust*. Gogol, on the other hand, was most strongly influenced in his youth by Goethe's Classical epic *Hermann und Dorothea* (and also by Voss's *Luise*), and his first work *Hans Küchelgarten*, 1829, ends with a veritable panegyric on Goethe (cf. *Euphorion*, 1922, p. 629).

38. Vyacheslav Ivanov, " Russian Poems on the Death of Goethe ", *Corona*, Year IV, No. 6.

39. Address on Goethe, read at the general meeting of the Imperial Academy of Sciences, St. Petersburg, 1833.

40. L., Vol. 47, p. 35.

41. W., Vol. 41², p. 136.

42. L., Vol. 38, p. 194.

43. L., Vol. 22, pp. 147 f.

44. L., Vol. 40, pp. 302 f.

45. L., Vol. 43, pp. 107 f. Young Thackeray, who came to Weimar in 1830, was one of the many Englishmen who visited Goethe during his last years. Thackeray's account of the visit was first published by Lewes in his work *Life and Works of Goethe*, Bk. 7, ch. 7.

46. *Russian Critics*, translated by Fega Frisch, Munich, 1921, pp. 43 f.

47. Ibid, pp. 298 ff.

48. Everett in 1817, Bancroft in 1824, Ticknor in 1830. Goethe's most successful ambassadress in America was Margaret Fuller, who translated *Tasso* (1835) and the *Conversations with Eckermann* (1828). She had been converted to Goethe by Emerson and Carlyle. She was the first to overcome the opposition to Goethe which existed in America and which was based on Puritanical and moral grounds. Her mission for America was like Carlyle's for England. Goethe's *Faust* also made its way into Spanish Latin-America and resulted in the so-called Gaucho-Poetry. For in 1866 was published *Fausto*, a story in verse by Estanislao del Campo : in the Pampas one gaucho tells another in popular primitive language the story of Goethe's *Faust* which he has seen in the theatre in Buenos Aires. The first edition of this work ran to two thousand copies.

49. *Die Literarische Welt*, 1st February 1929.

50. Paul Claudel, *Figures et Paraboles*.

51. Hermann Kesser, *Vom Chaos zur Gestaltung*, p. 145.

PREVIOUS WRITINGS BY THE SAME AUTHOR AND RELATING TO THE PRESENT WORK

1. DIE ROMANTIK ALS EUROPÄISCHE BEWEGUNG. (*Festschrift Heinrich Wölfflin*, 1924.)
2. EUROPA UND DIE DEUTSCHE KLASSIK UND ROMANTIK. (In : *Deutsche Klassik und Romantik*, 3. Aufl. 1928.)
3. GOETHES IDEE EINER WELTLITERATUR. (In : *Dichtung und Zivilisation*, 1928.)
4. GOETHE DER WEST-ÖSTLICHE. (Ibid.)
5. GOETHE DER EUROPÄER : Goethe und Napoleon—Goethe und Byron—Goethe und Dostoyevsky. (*Die Horen*, 1928–29.)
6. GOETHES EUROPÄISCHE SENDUNG. (Berner Antrittsvorlesung, *Der Bund*, 1929.)
7. WELTLITERATUR UND VERGLEICHENDE LITERATUR-GESCHICHTE, (*Philosophie der Literaturwissenschaft, herausgegeben von Ermatinger*, 1930.)
8. GOETHE UND DIE WELTLITERATUR. (*Jahrbuch der Goethe-gesellschaft*, Bd. XVIII; 1932.)

INDEX